Shadworth H Hodgson

Time and space

a metaphysical essay

Shadworth H Hodgson

Time and space
a metaphysical essay

ISBN/EAN: 9783741161384

Manufactured in Europe, USA, Canada, Australia, Japa

Cover: Foto ©Thomas Meinert / pixelio.de

Manufactured and distributed by brebook publishing software (www.brebook.com)

Shadworth H Hodgson

Time and space

TIME AND SPACE

A

𝔐𝔢𝔱𝔞𝔭𝔥𝔶𝔰𝔦𝔠𝔞𝔩 𝔈𝔰𝔰𝔞𝔶

BY

SHADWORTH H. HODGSON.

ΤΩΝ ΑΜΟΘΕΝ ΓΕ ΘΕΑ ΘΥΓΑΤΕΡ ΔΙΟΣ ΕΙΠΕ ΚΑΙ ΗΜΙΝ.

LONDON:
LONGMAN, GREEN, LONGMAN, ROBERTS, AND GREEN.
1865.

CONTENTS.

PART I.

INTRODUCTION.

	PAGE
1. Appeals to consciousness	3

CHAPTER I.

THE SCOPE OF METAPHYSIC.

2. Subject and Object	6
3. Necessity and Universality	9
4. The term a priori	11
5. Metaphysic is philosophy	13
6. Metaphysic and religion	16
7. Cogito ergo sum	19
8. Metaphysic and psychology	30
9. Metaphysic and ontology	30

CHAPTER II.

THE NATURE OF THE COGNITIONS OF TIME AND SPACE.

10. First and second intentions	33
11. Elements and aspects of phenomena	45
12. The formal element in consciousness	61
13. The unity of phenomena in space	87
14. The unity of phenomena in time	108
15. Time and space as pure objects	115
16. The exhaustive divisibility of time and space	125
17. The infinity of time and space	102

CONTENTS.

CHAPTER III. PSYCHOLOGICAL.

THE ORIGIN OF THE COGNITIONS OF TIME AND SPACE.

	PAGE
18. The object of Psychology	144
19. Three classes of theories	149
20. Theory of a Soul	153
21. Theory of an Ego	164
The phenomenon of Reflection	173
22. The physiological theory	192
23. Origin of the formal element	210

CHAPTER IV.

PRESENTATION AND REPRESENTATION.

24. The empirical ego	219
25. Representation	227
26. The immediate and remote object	237
27. Remote objects in connection	251

CHAPTER V.

SPONTANEOUS REDINTEGRATION.

28. Redintegration	256
29. Analysis of redintegration	264
30. Results of the analysis	273
31. Volition	283
32. Division of functions in consciousness	286

CHAPTER VI.

VOLUNTARY REDINTEGRATION.

33. Abstract and general notions	295
34. Their nature	301
35. The law of Parcimony	305
36. Critical and acquisitive reasoning	311
37. The principle of acquisitive reasoning	316
38. Induction and Deduction	318
39. Relation of critical and acquisitive reasoning	332
40. The three orders, Essendi, Existendi, Cognoscendi	333

PART II.

CHAPTER VII. METALOGICAL.

DIVISION 1.
THE POSTULATES AND THE CONCEPT-FORM.

§		PAGE
41. Existence and Non-existence	. .	345
42. Consciousness and thought	. .	350
43. Origin of the laws of thought	. .	355
44. The Concept-form	. .	360
45. Some remarks on Hegel's Logic	. .	364

DIVISION 2.
THE CONCEPT.

46. The nature of concepts	. .	409
47. Some cases examined		413
48. The logical object and the logical unit		419
49. Categories or forms of thought	.	425
50. The combination of concepts	.	428
51. The import of propositions	.	432
52. Categorical propositions	.	436
53. Hypothetical propositions	.	448
54. Disjunctive propositions	.	451
55. Hypothetico-disjunctive propositions	.	453
56. Syllogisms	. . . . .	455
1st. Categorical. 2d. Hypothetical. 3d. Disjunctive. 4th. Hypothetico-disjunctive.		
57. Empirical and formal reasoning	.	469
58. Review of the analysis of the laws of Logic	.	477

DIVISION 3.
RATIO SUFFICIENS.

59. Cause and Reason	.	487
60. The formal cause	.	493
61. Intuition and thought	.	494
62. Nihil Absoluti	.	503

CHAPTER VIII

REASON.

	PAGE
63. Intuitive reflection	509
64. Reasoning reflection	513
65. Retrospect of metaphysical philosophy	520
Plato. Aristotle. Post-Aristotelian philosophy. Giordano Bruno. Descartes and his successors.	
66. Other domains of the reason	539
Relation between ethic and physic. Ethic. Connection of ethic and law. Poetry.	
67. Progress of science generally	552

CHAPTER IX.

IDEAS.

68. Classification of ideas	563
69. Three instances examined	568
70. Faith	573
71. The logical idea of God	576

EPILOGUE . 588

TIME AND SPACE.

PART I.

INTRODUCTION.

§ 1. THE writer of the following pages submits them, not without a sense of their imperfection, to the judgment of his contemporaries. The questions treated of labour under one kind of difficulty peculiarly their own. It is not every reader who will be prepared to admit, that, in one part of metaphysical enquiries, the proof to be required differs in its nature from the proof to be required in the purely objective sciences. But that it is so follows from the nature of the matter, at once subjective and objective. In the purely objective sciences a writer need have no doubt about his facts; he can protect himself by definitions and by distinctions, and can always make clear what the precise object is, about which he reasons. For instance, in Political Economy, he can obviate ambiguities in his object-matter by defining Wealth to mean "every commodity which has an exchangeable value;" and, consequent on this definition, he can define Productive Labour to mean labour which produces such commodities; for every one is agreed that there are such commodities and such labour. But where this has not been done, but is still in process of doing, there every man must be judge for himself, whether his own internal experience bears out the assertions of the writer. For the facts of metaphysic, like those of every purely objec-

§ 1.
Appeals to consciousness.

tive science, are facts of consciousness, and their obscurity and the difficulty of observing them make their interpretation, or their analysis, doubtful. The very questions at issue are, What are the facts? What is their analysis?—and Is there any phenomenon answering to a given definition?—of which there is no judge but consciousness itself. Such questions, for instance, are the analysis of the cognitions of time and space, the analysis of consciousness in its simplest concrete shape, the question whether we are immediately conscious of the Will, and so on. If the meaning of the term red was not sufficiently agreed upon, we should have to appeal to the consciousness of individuals to decide what colour should be distinguished by this name; and those who were colour-blind would be heard before the decision was arrived at, but not afterwards.

A great part of metaphysic, not by any means the whole of it, and a continually though slowly decreasing part, is in this unfixed and undetermined state; and it is natural that this should be the case with this the most complicated and dependent of all branches of knowledge, though it is one which, from the universal and obvious presence of some of its elements, was cultivated among the earliest. In this unfixed part of metaphysic the appeal to consciousness must still be permitted; there the proofs must not only be examined but performed by every one for himself, with a view to the establishment of a sufficient consensus of judgments; and the aim of the metaphysical writer in this part of his task must be, not to give convincing inferential proofs of his positions, but to state and describe the phenomena so as to lead and assist the reader in finding the proofs for himself, or in other words, to aid him in going through the trains of reasoning in such an original and independent way, as can alone procure, I do not say the conclusions here reached, but any real conclusion at all.

By the term consciousness, in this Essay, is always meant consciousness as existing in an individual conscious being; and proofs drawn from such a consciousness can have no validity for other conscious individuals, unless they themselves recognise their truth as descriptions applicable to the procedure and phenomena of their own consciousness. Doctrines, if true, will ultimately be recognised as such by all individuals whose consciousness is formed on the same type, that is, by all human beings.

11. Appeals to consciousness.

CHAPTER I.

THE SCOPE OF METAPHYSIC.

Ἀναγκαιότεραι μὲν οὖν πᾶσαι αὐτῆς, ἀμείνων δὲ οὐδεμία.
Aristotle.

PART I.
CH. I.
———
§ 2.
Subject and Object.

§ 2. THE true opposite of the term metaphysic is empiric, whether empiric is employed in dealing with states of consciousness or with external phenomena. States of consciousness and external phenomena, whether abstract or concrete, whether considered as particular and unclassified or as general and classified, are known to us by experience either direct or indirect, by perception or by inference; that is to say, they are the data of empirical knowledge or science; while metaphysic is employed in tracing the conditions of such data. Thus Kant says in the Prolegomena, § 1, that metaphysical cognition is a cognition which lies on the far side of, or beyond, experience,—jenseit der Erfahrung liegende Erkenntniss.

Metaphysic takes its stand at the point of junction between the mind which knows and the world which is known, and deals with the relations which obtain between them, so far as these relations are necessary and universal. Metaphysic may therefore be approached both from the side of psychology, or the laws of consciousness and the organ of consciousness, and from that of physical science, or the laws of external phenomena. In saying this I am not forgetting that external phenomena are presented to us only in consciousness, nor on the other hand that states of consciousness, when reflected on, are as objective as external phenomena. It is enough that this difference of aspect, this distinction κατὰ μέρη, has given rise to a division of existences κατὰ μέλη, a division of them into mind and matter, and their appropriated sciences, psychology and the physical sciences. Following the route of either of these groups of sciences, we come to ground which is common to it with the other group, the common ground of phenomena with a double aspect, subjective and objective. This common ground of psychology and physic, phenomena in their most abstract shape, is the proper field of metaphysic. It considers phenomena as they possess an objective and a subjective aspect, and not as they are dependent on a series of events in the kingdom of mind, or on a series of events in the kingdom of matter. It is an analysis of phenomena, as such. Standing thus at the meeting point of the two groups of cognitions, psychological and physical, metaphysic contains, as its proper object-matter, those cognitions only which are common to all objects of knowledge and to all modes or states of consciousness. In other words, it is only certain universal modes or forms of consciousness and of objects external to consciousness which are the object-matter of metaphysic. The reason of this is, that all the others fall properly into their places in the other sciences to which they belong, while those which are universal, both in consciousness and in its objects, are distinguished broadly by this characteristic from the rest, and, besides the place which they hold in any of the other sciences, have another place in that science, or mode of contemplation, which brings into one view both object and subject as the two only constituents of the whole imaginable or conceivable universe. The importance and also, considering the constitution of our minds, the necessity of this latter science, called metaphysic, rests on the fact that this distinction of subject and object is the most general and ultimate distinction at which we can arrive in all knowledge. If the human mind is compelled to push its enquiries to the furthest point attainable by it, it is to this distinction that it will come the last, from whatever point of view it may start, and whatever road or science it may take. It is the ultimate distinction in the analysis of the universe from the human point of view, and therefore it is the starting point of metaphysic, which is the applied logic of the universe, the method of stating the problem in its lowest terms.

Some may suppose that there is a point of view from which this distinction of subject and object, or, what is the same thing, of consciousness and the objects of consciousness, is not the ultimate and highest distinction possible, but some other distinction between existences, as for instance that of Inner and Outer, or that of Form and Matter. From such a point of view, states of consciousness themselves would still be classed as, what in fact they are, special modes of existence, and perhaps, under the first distinction, as outward manifestations of an inward spirit, or, under the second distinction, as forms into which the matter of the external world is cast and moulded. Now what is there to show that a method of regarding the universe founded upon such distinctions as these is not more complete and legitimate than a method founded on the distinction of subject and object? This only consideration, so far as can be at present evident, namely, that it adopts a single term or category, that of existence, into which to introduce its distinctions, a category unexplained, unconnected, meaningless; that it leaves vague and undetermined, because out of relation to any thing else, the totality of the phenomena which it proposes to classify, and thus in fact starts with assuming an Absolute. Of such a single, non-relative, existence it must be admitted, that it has no meaning and no predicates, that it is in short pure nonentity and merum nihil. If however it should be replied, that by existence is meant relative existence, such existence as is relative to us and our capacities, this is only to admit in other words the greater validity of the distinction between subject and object. For by a relative existence is meant an objective existence, an existence the correlate of consciousness, the only existence which in fact we can conceive or imagine. Let this objective existence be divided or distinguished as it may, it will still be one aspect only of the ultimate distinction into subject and object, or rather it will itself involve its opposite, the subjective aspect; and the further distinctions introduced into it will be distinctions of the object of consciousness only, and not of an absolute existence apart from consciousness.

§ 3. Now with reference to the doctrine that the cognitions, which are the object-matter of metaphysic, are necessary as well as universal, it must be remarked that the term necessary is but the correlate of the term universal; what the latter is in the world of objects that the former is in the world of consciousness. Whatever is necessary in thought exists also always without exception in the object of thought; and whatever exists always without exception in the object of thought is necessary in thought. It is not said, that whatever exists always in "things-in-themselves" is necessary in thought, for of things-in-themselves we have no experience; but, so far as any thing is an object for us, whatever is universal in the object is necessary in the subject. Necessity is a term which has meaning only in reference to our cognition; it is subjective in its reference; while the term universality is objective, not referring however to existence per se, but to objective existence for us. We shall have to consider in the course of these pages whether any causal relation obtains between these two correlates, necessity and universality. For the present it is enough to explain, that no necessity can be admitted to exist in the objective world; that what we call a necessary sequence is necessary solely in reference to our understanding, because we refer the consequent to a special antecedent, and bring it thus under some law which we think of as fixed, at least so far as the particular case under consideration is concerned; and that the only thing which corresponds to our notion of necessity in nature is the phenomenon of universality. Universality means, that the thing in question, whatever it is, never is otherwise; necessity means, that we cannot conceive it otherwise. In the former case there is no impossibility introduced; in the latter case there is an impossibility, but it is one of thought not of fact, subjective not objective. Like the terms subject and object themselves, the terms necessity and universality are but two aspects, inseparable from each other, of the same phenomenon.

§ 4. It remains to be noticed in what sense the cognitions of time and space, and any others which may prove entitled to rank with them, can be said to lie beyond experience and to be a priori. All abstract cognitions, such as those of time and space, can be arrived at by generalising from experience; and this property is common to all abstractions, of whatever kind they are. No one can be surprised that this property is possessed by those most general and abstract of all cognitions which are the object-matter of metaphysic. But it is equally clear that it is not this property which entitles them to be placed beyond experience, jenseit der Erfahrung, or to be called non-empirical, or a priori. What so entitles them is the addition of this character to their other character of universality or necessity, so that they are previously existing elements of every possible cognition or object of cognition. Now there are two distinct senses of the term a priori, which I do not remember ever to have seen clearly distinguished. Sometimes, since every condition is previous in order of time to its consequent, the knowledge of the consequent derived from a knowledge of its conditions is said to be a knowledge a priori; and again, those existing conditions which are causes of a given effect, those conditions without which the effect could not be what it is, are said to be a priori conditions, since, when we know what the effect is, we conclude that such and such conditions must have preceded it in order of time. These two modes rest upon priority in order of time, and constitute one sense of the term a priori. The other sense of this term has nothing to do with priority in order of time, but solely with priority in order of logic. For instance, the figure of a triangle drawn on paper exists only when three lines meet each other at three angles; the three lines and the three angles are the a priori elements of the triangle; but they are not previous to it in point of time, but exactly simultaneous, for the length and position of each line, and the size of each angle, are determined respectively by the length and position of the other lines and the size of the other angles, that is, by the other elements of the triangle. Before the triangle was formed, there were neither the lines of such and such a length and position, nor the angles of such and such a size. The triangle is the brief synthetical expression for these lines and these angles, and the lines and the angles are the analysis of the triangle. Now any of these elements of the triangle, which being given the rest are deducible, or all these elements taken together, may be called the a priori elements of the triangle; but in neither case are they prior to the triangle in order of time, but only in order of logic. And if the term a priori is applied to any of the metaphysical elements of objects, it must be in this second sense of the term, and not in a sense implying priority in order of time.

Applying these remarks to time and space, the results of any analysis may be considered prior in logic to the whole analysed, and therefore a priori to that particular object; but time and space are a priori κατ' ἐξοχήν, inasmuch as they are a priori to all objects of cognition, to cognition and existence itself. Themselves cognitions generalised from experience, and in that point of view later than experience in order of time, they are discovered to have been also elements of those very cognitions of experience from which they are generalised, present in them as constituent elements undistinguished before analysis. As to their becoming known to us as separate cognitions, they are later than many other cognitions; but as to their own existence in knowledge unseparated, they are simultaneous with all and every other cognition. The question of the origin of these cognitions will be discussed in Chapter III.; but with reference to the mind of man as he now exists, and to all his other cognitions, these two cognitions of time and space at least are a priori, in the sense just explained; that is, are elements of any and every particular experience, entering into every one of them as its necessary form.

§ 5. So far as to the leading features and distinctions of metaphysic, as a separate phenomenon. It remains to regard it as a whole, and in relation and contrast with other branches of knowledge. Metaphysic is, properly speaking, not a science but a philosophy; that is, it is a science whose end is in itself, in the gratification and education of the minds which carry it on, not in any external purpose, such as the founding of any art conducive to the welfare of life. This is the distinction between science and philosophy, that science does not include its own end, but is pure knowledge whose end is something external to itself, while philosophy is carried on for the sake of the learning and knowing alone which it involves. Nor is this the popular distinction between intellectual pursuits which lead to something, and those which only, as it is called, sharpen the mind. Intellectual pursuits which are employed to sharpen the mind are already pursued for an end external to themselves, and cannot deserve the name of philosophy. Philosophy is pleasurable and noble emotion no less than knowledge; the two elements are inseparable, are logically and not empirically discerned. In other words, its end is in itself. The need to philosophise is rooted in our nature, as deeply as any other of our needs. "Tutti gli uomini naturalmente desiderano di sapere," says Dante, a true philosopher, in the opening passage of his Convito, translating Aristotle's words at the beginning of his Metaphysic, Πάντες ἄνθρωποι τοῦ εἰδέναι ὀρέγονται φύσει. And Plato says in the Sophistes, Ἀλλὰ μὴν ψυχήν γε ἴσμεν ἀκουσαν πᾶσαν τὰν ἀγνοοῦσαν. And the attempt to satisfy this need has at all times produced philosophies, which have been founded on the special sciences as they from time to time existed, and which have taken from the growth and development of these latter their own form and colour. For the great problems which in all ages have proposed themselves to man, such as these, Whence he and the world came; Whither they go; What is the meaning of the whole scene of existence, as it unfolds itself before him, and of which he himself is a part; Is it truer to explain it by the analogy of this, or of that, familiar phenomenon, as of a dream, a tragic or a comic drama, of a battle or a war, or a lawsuit, or a journey;—these questions and such as these must for ever, whether answerable or unanswerable, whether conceived as questions or only as meditations, possess for him the profoundest interest; and to attempt their solution must be one of his most attractive labours. Now the very condition of prosecuting the enquiry is metaphysic, that is, the analysis of the phenomena whose history and import is to be studied. Before the laws of the succession of phenomena, and therefore also before the laws or law of their tendency and final end, the nature of the phenomena must be analysed. This analysis or statical study of the nature of phenomena is metaphysic. Modern philosophy has attained at least to this, that it can not only state the problem to be solved, but also lay down the conditions of its solution with certainty and precision. This we owe chiefly, perhaps, to Descartes and Kant. But each age, as it advances to a greater distance from these fathers of modern philosophy, must perforce alter something in the systems which they moulded, and re-state the old questions in terms allied to the advancing discoveries of the sciences on which metaphysical philosophy is founded.

It is idle to object against metaphysical philosophy that it is not a special science; and yet it is into such an objection that most of the complaints commonly made against it are resolvable. For in fact all men who reflect are metaphysicians, and all sciences have a metaphysical side; a system of metaphysic is merely a gathering up into one connected whole the scattered notions which each reflecting man entertains respecting the ultimate nature and scope of his own pursuit. The difficulty is to carry the metaphysical method far enough. Men soon become tired of distinguishing logically; they demand that the objects of reasoning should be exhibited empirically or as concrete wholes, and ask what the external end or good is in such enquiries. As men are most familiar with the special sciences, which are all empirical or employed with whole objects, abstract like the figures of geometry, or concrete like those of the sun and stars, they are apt to demand that all science shall be reduced to the same shape, that is, that metaphysic shall cease to be metaphysic by giving up its distinguishing charac-

PART I.
CH. I.
§ 5.
Metaphysic in philosophy.

teristic. This demand, when it is made without previous examination of the nature and claims of metaphysic itself, appears to me to be one of Bacon's Idols of the Theatre. Even Auguste Comte thought that in establishing his Philosophie Première, in the Politique Positive, vol. iv. page 173, which corresponds to the Prima Philosophia of Bacon, and is a system of the few most general laws of all the sciences philosophically arranged, an analysis not of phenomena as such but of the universe of phenomena as a whole, he was carrying the metaphysical method far enough. He went somewhat farther, indeed, in his latest work, the Synthèse Subjective, but even there he did not go beyond the notion of a system of general laws of empirical phenomena, and of thought occupied with empirical phenomena, as such. In my view, however, this is but a small part of true metaphysic. It goes beyond this, and refers even such general laws as these to their conditions and elements, without resting satisfied with having it shown that they are the result of a complete induction. If we are to have a philosophy, or a science which is its own end or reward, it must advance to the ultimate possible limit, and not stop short at the point of arranging inductive principles in a philosophical manner; for this may aim only at the external reward of aiding the special sciences.

§ 6. Lord Bolingbroke, in his first Letter to Pope, Works, vol. v. page 83-4, edit. 1809, distinguishes his First Philosophy from what he calls metaphysical pneumatics and from ontology, on the one hand, and on the other from the Prima Philosophia of Bacon. Proceeding to describe what his First Philosophy is, he defines it by its objects, "natural theology or theism, and natural religion or ethics." I have already distinguished metaphysic from such philosophy as the Prima Philosophia of Bacon, and shall later on distinguish it also from ontology; but I cannot admit that ethic or religion or theology are the objects of metaphysic. Metaphysic has to take account indeed of every class of phenomena, but its special business is with the elements universal and necessary of all phenomena alike, as such. It must explain all without exception, and deny none on pain of being untrue. But it approaches phenomena from the cognitive side, and treats them as cognitions, not as feelings or emotions. Since the implication of matter with form in phenomena is universal, and the implication of different kinds of matter with each other is almost universal, the distinction expressed by the Aristotelic ᾗ, or the Spinozistic quâtenus, is of almost universal application; and is, besides, the only method of obviating the illogical vagueness of such expressions as "this rather than that," "this more than that," expressions which have their ground in the same almost universal implication just spoken of. Feelings and emotions are the object-matter of ethic, religion, and theology, rather than of metaphysic. What is the reason and extent of this "rather than"? It is this, that, since feelings and emotions are also at the same time cognitions, metaphysic treats them so far as they are cognitions, and ethic so far as they are feelings and emotions. Cognitions are the object-matter of ethic; not however in their character of cognitions, but only so far as they are feelings or emotions. This is the first step in the limitation of ethic; the next step is, that not all feelings and emotions, as such, are the object-matter of ethic, but only those feelings and emotions which contain, or with which is combined, a feeling or emotion of a pleasureable or painful kind. Ethic thus becomes the general science of practice, as distinguished from pure speculation. Ethic is a systematic cognition of feelings, metaphysic of cognitions.

Religion is a term for a particular and important class of ethical emotions, namely, those which are of a spiritual kind, or which satisfy the sense of delighting in what is right as distinguished from what is wrong, that is, which satisfy the conscience. Religion consists of emotions. "Thou shalt love the Lord thy God with all thy heart, and with all thy soul, and with all thy mind; and thy neighbour as thyself;—on these two commandments hang all the Law and the Prophets." Matth. xxii. 37. But now, looking away from the particular emotions which constitute any particular religion, the Christian for instance, religion itself in the abstract has never been investigated, or its nature analysed, with sufficient accuracy. It will however be found, I apprehend, that it consists in the union of two characteristics, 1st, that it is an emotion of some particular kind, as love, or hope; 2d, that the moral goodness of this emotion is self-evident, that is, the emotion is felt as an ultimate end in itself, as being its own warrant, needing and admitting no proof of its moral goodness beyond its actual presence in consciousness. All those emotions, and only those, which contain this second characteristic are religious emotions. Religion is spiritual emotion.

Theology is the embodiment of religion in doctrines, that is, in cognitions, which give it a shape cognisable by the intellect, and relate either to the great object of religion, God, or to the conditions of its existence in man, or to the duties and actions which are its consequences. Theology therefore is of the same nature, and is to be broadly distinguished from metaphysic on the same ground, as ethic. While metaphysic can overlook no phenomenon and no truth, of whatever kind it may be, or in whatever part of the mind it may come forward, theology and ethic, which are cognitive systems or sciences also, and as such have the investigation of truth for their ultimate purpose, may be carried on in harmony with metaphysic, and may even derive advantage from the results therein obtained. No truth, wherever found, whether in theology, ethic, or metaphysic, can possibly be antagonistic to religion; the only danger is, that error should be mistaken for, and maintained in place of, truth; and against this danger, sober and searching enquiry, neglecting no facts and denying none, is the surest preservative. Further light will probably be thrown on these preliminary remarks in the course of the Essay.

§ 7. It was the above-mentioned dualism of subject and object which was in Descartes' mind when he said to himself, Cogito ergo sum; which sentence is the fountain-head of all modern metaphysic. It was the result of reflection, and the shortest and simplest way in which the act of reflection could be expressed. It contains the first distinction of reflection on phenomena, the distinction into object and subject, into consciousness generally, abstracting from all particular objects of consciousness, which is here established as being beyond the possibility of doubt, and the particular objects of consciousness which may be doubted. The reflective act and one of its objects, one of the two things distinguished by it, namely, consciousness, are together the fact which Descartes here asserts to be beyond the possibility of doubt. The first reflection is the first certainty, the first certainty as distinguished from undoubting acquiescence. And thus reflection is the starting point of philosophy; the object asserted by it as certain, consciousness, is the thing which is the object of philosophy, of which reflection is one mode. There are then two senses in which the Cogito or the Cogitatur of Descartes is to be taken, one in which it stands for the act of reflection, the other in which it stands for one of the two objects of reflection, consciousness generally. He begins by seeing what things he is not certain of beyond the possibility of doubt. Nearly every thing is in this category; at last he puts the question about Sense; Meditatio II.: "Sentire? nempe etiam hoc non fit sine corpore, et permulta sentire visus sum in somniis quæ deinde animadverti me non sensisse:" Here sense is not distinguished from the objects of sense; it therefore shares their uncertainty. He proceeds: "Cogitare? hic invenio, cogitatio est, hæc sola a me divelli nequit, ego sum, ego existo, certum est." Here at last he can distinguish consciousness from its objects, the operation from the results. In the next page he follows up his enquiry: "Sed quid igitur sum? res cogitans; quid est hoc? nempe dubitans, intelligens, affirmans, negans, volens, nolens, imaginans quoque, et sentiens." Et sentiens, — here sense is distinguished from its objects, and is become part of the indubitable operation of reflection itself, of the Cogito or the Cogitatur. Here is the first answer to the question, What is it to exist, or What is existence? Existence is consciousness generally, in some or all of its modes; or in other words, that exists which is revealed by consciousness.

Now the current theory, I believe, is this, that existence or Being far exceeds consciousness; that many things exist of which we actually have not, and many other things of which we cannot have, the least knowledge; that consciousness may and does make progress in penetrating into the former field, that of actually unknown existence, and in making many things actually known to us which before were actually unknown, but existing beyond our knowledge; while it is debarred from all progress whatever in the latter field, that of unknowable existence, which nevertheless is actually existing beyond our possibility of knowledge. If we so conceive, consciousness may be likened to a candle shining in a vast circle of darkness which it tends to illuminate more and more, while beyond this circle is a space of neither light nor darkness, which cannot, by its nature, be ever illuminated by the candle's rays, however powerful they may become. There is thus formed a notion of an existence, real and actual, but out of all relation to consciousness, not only unknown at present, but unknowable for ever; an objective existence which can never become subjective, an existence absolute, per se, a world of things-in-themselves.

But to this existence I prefer to give the name non-objective existence, for I think it will become clear as we advance, that consciousness is limited only by existence, no less than existence is limited only by consciousness; that the two things are coextensive; that each is the opposite aspect of the other, the gold and silver side of the same shield.

From whichever side we approach, that side seems to us the smaller of the two, appears as a limit imposed on the other. If we approach from the subjective side, asking what we can know, what can become an object of our consciousness, then we represent to ourselves possible existence as far exceeding consciousness, and consciousness as conquering certain limits of existence, "won from the void and formless infinite." If on the other hand we approach from the objective side, and ask what exists or is capable of existing, then existence seems a small part of what we can imagine or conceive to exist, to be as it were an oasis of firm actual ground in the middle of the desert of the great Might-be, or Might-have-been. In the first case there appears to be a great field of non-objective existence, in the second case, of non-existing imagination or conception. The truth appears to be, that existence and consciousness are coextensive, one as wide as, and not wider than, the other. Non-objective existence, and non-real consciousness in conceiving or imagining, are terms without meaning. Whatever can be present in consciousness has some degree of reality, the only question is, how much, or of what sort, how permanent, how arrived at. There may be names which are names only, whether the things supposed to be signified by them are supposed to lie in non-objective existence or in non-real consciousness. And if we attempt to describe the subordinate position supposed to be occupied either by consciousness to non-objective existence, or by existence to non-real consciousness, this very description is, and can only be, by means of expressions which in regard to this case are figurative, being drawn from cases of real consciousness and real existence. The language borrowed from experience within time and space is here made use of to express our relation to things supposed for the moment to exist beyond time and space, beyond consciousness. How else can absolute impossibility of knowledge be characterised, except by figurative language? For whatever man can name, that he thinks he can in some way know, and that by naming the unknowable he brings it within the grasp of his knowledge; and, whether he in fact is so or not, he necessarily makes himself in the proceedings of his consciousness πάντων μέτρον. On the one hand, then, the attempt to characterise existence beyond the possibility of our knowledge requires the use of figurative expressions drawn from existence within our knowledge; and on the other hand, there is a natural and spontaneous assumption that every thing that exists stands in some nameable relation to our consciousness. All the meaning of the names applied to existence beyond consciousness is drawn from existence within consciousness; and there is a spontaneous assumption that we are warranted in applying those names. In other words, the terms applied to non-objective existence, such as absolute, per se, beyond experience, transcendent, and so on, have a connotation, but no object denoted by them. Yet the very making use of them implies the assumption that there is something denoted by them. If, then, there is something denoted by them, this something has predicates drawn from actual experience, and is of the same nature as objects of actual experience. Either the term non-objective existence is a name without meaning, or the object to which it is applied is an object within the range of our knowledge. In the latter case it is synonymous with objective existence, or existence simply. Again, with regard to the term existence. Either the term existence has a meaning, or it has none; if it has none, it would be better to cease employing it; but if it has a meaning, then it must be, to the extent of that meaning, an intelligible object of consciousness. So that we can name nothing, with a meaning in the name, but what has objective existence or existence for consciousness. To sum up all in a few words, it is impossible to know that any thing exists, without at the same time knowing something of what it is, or of what we imagine it to be.

It is the assumption of the subordinate position of consciousness to existence, of this primary relation of limiting and limited, of revealer and revealed, which is the ultimate ground of the distinction between phenomena and things-in-themselves, the Kantian Dinge-an-sich. If a limit, which would not otherwise have existed, is imposed by the Subject, that is, by the fact that all existence has to be made known to us if at all, through consciousness, then we must assume the possibility of there existing, both in the things we are conscious of and also beyond them, that is, both as to quality and as to quantity, both as to intension and as to protension, something which we do not and cannot know; not only which we cannot know perfectly, but which we cannot know even imperfectly, that is, at all. The primary dualism of subject and object, when conceived as the subordination of consciousness to existence, the limitation of existence by consciousness, the revelation of existence, within certain limits subjective in their nature, by consciousness, if unbalanced by the counter conception of the subordination of existence to consciousness, gives an intended meaning to the expression things-in-themselves, and at the same time banishes them from our consideration; admits the possibility of their existing, but condemns them to a non-objective existence; and if the term existence has a meaning, this conception is self-contradictory. But the same primary dualism, when conceived as a dualism of two equal and coextensive factors or members, mutually limiting each other, is the ground of the expressions, All knowledge is relative, and All existence is relative existence. And one consequence of disregarding metaphysic, and busying the mind exclusively with objective existence, is, that objects themselves, the phenomena of experience, come to be considered as things-in-themselves; and thus the popular view of them is practically, and as by a kind of forgetfulness, adopted by men of science, who would be the last willingly to accept it.

Let us adopt for a moment this hypothesis of a thing-in-itself, a Ding-an-sich. Now what is this Ding-an-sich which we reject from knowledge and from objective existence, or rather what is it not? Consciousness, we will suppose for the moment, carves out from existence the objective world; the Ding-an-sich is that which cannot be reached or affected by consciousness; and thus, wherever we find an universal law or mode of consciousness, there we assume that we may be in contact with the Ding-an-sich. If things which exist in time and space are, to that extent, knowable by us, then the Ding-an-sich, which is by hypothesis unknowable, must be independent of those forms; and if things which can impress or affect our sensibility are so far knowable, then the Ding-an-sich cannot be capable of impressing our sensibility, for otherwise it would be knowable. Thus we are guided in our notions of what it is not, and ipso facto unable to conjecture what it is. It will be seen in the course of the Essay whether there are any positive grounds for supposing that relative existence is infinite in any sense; that is, for holding that there can be no existence beyond some at least of our capacities for knowledge. For it may well be that our consciousness may be limited in some respects and unlimited in others; if now in any respect it is unlimited, in that respect it will include all existence; objective and relative existence itself will be unlimited in that respect; and the Ding-an-sich will in that respect vanish. If the necessary and universal forms of consciousness are themselves infinite, then the Ding-an-sich, if it exists at all, must be included in them, and in that respect, or to that extent, cease to be a Ding-an-sich.

On the non-existence of the Ding-an-sich, see Schelling's Vom Ich, oder über das Unbedingte, Vol. i. of collected Works, p. 210. And on the complete mutuality of the subjective and objective kingdoms, see his masterly Einleitung, in the Ideen zu einer Philosophie der Natur, Vol. ii. of collected Works. It is the lasting service of the post-Kantian philosophers, Fichte, Schelling, and Hegel, each in his degree, to have established the doctrine of the perfect coextensiveness and mutuality of existence and consciousness. But it is not necessary, it is even forbidden by the method in which alone this doctrine can be proved, to follow them in characterising this coextensiveness and mutuality as identity, or as the Absolute. The union of the infinite and the finite, and the supposed union of the absolute and the relative, or of the Ding-an-sich and its phenomena, is to be sought in the individual consciousness and within its limits, by an analysis of its objects and its procedure; it is not to be placed in an absolute, or an infinite, or a Ding-an-sich, out of, prior to, or the source of, consciousness or its objects. What the absolute, the infinite, the Ding-an-sich are, that is, how they are conceived or imagined in the individual consciousness, how they come to be so conceived or imagined, and how far they are words without meaning, will have to be exhibited in the course of this Essay. They will be found to depend on the union of two functions of consciousness, volition and intuition. Schelling, in his Fernere Darstellungen, vol. iv. p. 356, quotes from Fichte the sentence, "dass nämlich der endliche Geist nothwendig etwas Absolutes ausser sich setzen muss (ein Ding-an-sich), und dennoch von der andern Seite anerkennen muss, dass dasselbe nur für ihn da sey (ein nothwendiges Noumen sey)." Schelling explains the contradiction by including the finite mind and its Ding-an-sich both together in the Absolute; but here it will be attempted to analyse the contradiction itself as a phenomenon, and to assign its causes and its elements. The absolute, the infinite, the Ding-an-sich, like all other objects, can exist only in consciousness; the only questions are, what is their nature and analysis, and what is their origin. Schelling says, in the Fernere Darstellungen, p. 378, "Sich vom Reflex, worin das an sich Erste immer als Drittes erscheint, mithin überhaupt vom Bedingten und der Synthesis zum An-sich, zum Kategorischen und durch sich selbst Evidenten zu erheben, ist überhaupt etwas, das sehr

PART I.
CH. L.
§ 7.
Cogito argumm.

vielen versagt scheint. Daher die Unfähigkeit, sich
die reine Subjekt-Objektivität der absoluten Form als
absolute Einheit zu denken." But I ask, by what
right can that "which constantly appears as third"
be transformed into "that which is in itself first"?
It can only be done by abstracting from the form of
time in one moment, in order to exhibit the object
in its essence or value, an essence simultaneous with
the object itself, and then the next moment re-introducing the form of time, in order to exhibit the object
in its essence as prior to the object as a phenomenon.
Taking, for instance, any series of phenomena in order
of history, the last phenomenon, or the result, of the
series is analysed into its elements in order of logic;
and then that element which is most important in
order of logic, where abstraction is made of time,
being necessary to the existence of the whole phenomenon analysed, is considered to have been present
as a cause from the first, in the earliest phenomenon
of the series in order of history. It is true that what
is first in order of history is often last in order of
cognition; but where the cognition is a logical cognition, considering its object statically, and classing its
elements in order of logical importance, there it does
not follow that what is last in order of cognition, or
first in order of logic, is first also in order of history.

Thus, founded on the dualism of subject and object, conceived as two equal and coextensive members
or factors, there arises before us the conception of the
world distinguished, not divided, into two kingdoms,
the kingdom of knowing, and the kingdom of being,
a principium cognoscendi and a principium existendi.
As in a court of justice guilt does not exist till it is
proved, so here existence is nothing until known.

But we require, if possible, some more special knowledge of this dualism; we wish to see the modus operandi of consciousness, its method, and its nature; to see whether, besides witnessing to the fact, and to some particular modes, of existence, it witnesses also to any necessary or universal modes of it. It was such questions as these which received an answer in the doctrines of Kant as to time and space, which doctrines will be reconsidered in these pages. The doctrines of Kant form a system which not only is more complete than any that preceded it, but also contains principles which are the firmest foundation for the labours of succeeding philosophers. The marvellous system of Hegel reposes on a Kantian basis; but reasons will be given later on for the conclusion, that this was not the true edifice which should have arisen on that foundation. The fundamental principles still remain; and the following pages are an attempt, first, to analyse and interpret them, and then to raise on them the true superstructure of philosophy. Much will be found in this Essay which has been said, and in many instances far better said, by other post-Kantian writers, Schelling, Hegel, Coleridge, Schopenhauer, Sir W. Hamilton, Mr. Mansel, Professor Ferrier, Mr. J. S. Mill, Mr. H. Spencer, for instance; resemblances to whose doctrines, and differences from them, and at the same time also some of my many obligations to their writings, will disclose themselves to the reader as he proceeds. What is distinctive and new in it will, I think, be found to arise chiefly from its keeping more exclusively to a purely metaphysical, as distinguished from either a psychological or an ontological, point of view.

§ 8. What is the difference between psychology and metaphysic? A difference in their object-matter. The object-matter of psychology is the mind, or consciousness in relation to the bodily organs which are its seat; that of metaphysic is consciousness in relation to its objects. Psychology is thus a special part of physiology, that part which links physiology to metaphysic; it is a special science or a portion of special science, and may be called the natural history of consciousness. To put the distinction between metaphysic and psychology in another shape, it may be said that psychology regards the mind and its states of consciousness as members of the kingdom of Being alone; while for metaphysic they, in common with all other kinds of objects, are considered as members of both the kingdoms of Being and Knowing. Thus psychology is occupied not only with the organs of consciousness, its material conditions, and its conditions of existence, but also with its results considered as objects, that is, with the laws of the association of ideas, and filiation of opinions and systems of philosophy, as concrete phenomena of consciousness; while metaphysic is busied with these objects only so far as they are objects of consciousness; in order, first, to distinguish in them their subjective from their objective aspect, and secondly, to analyse them into their component parts, and classify the elements which compose them.

§ 9. Metaphysic has been characterised, in § 1, as the applied logic of the universe. As such it is an entirely statical and not a dynamical theory. In other words, it is no theory of the causæ existendi of the world or of consciousness; it does not give the origin or the genesis of existence; this, so far as it is possible, is the task of the special empirical sciences, whether physical or psychical. But it is the causa essendi, or nature, of the world of existence which metaphysic undertakes to examine; to analyse the structure of objects, as objects of consciousness, and to resolve them into their elements. It does not pretend to determine whether the ultimate elements, which it reaches in its analysis, existed separately prior to the wholes or empirical objects which are their synthesis, nor to show how this is possible. Such a problem would be of a dynamical nature. There is no reason given in metaphysic for supposing that historically, in the order of nature, the simple existed before the compound, still less that the a priori elements existed separately before the empirical objects which yield them to our analysis. What is first in analysis is last in synthesis, and vice versâ; but both analysis and synthesis, whether employed upon particular objects of perception or upon general notions or universals, are modes of statical enquiry, and warrant no conclusion as to what is first and what last in dynamical enquiry, or in the order of history. How consciousness is produced, how motion arises in objects, how feelings come to be combined with cognitions, how the world itself came into existence,—these are questions with which metaphysic has nothing to do; metaphysic has but to accept the facts as they are, and to analyse them into their simplest elements. What and where are the elephant, the tortoise, and the stone,—these are dynamical not statical, empirical not metaphysical, questions; they relate to the history of empirical events, not to the analysis of facts.

To mistake the ultimate elements in analysis for

Part I.
Ch. I.

§ 9.
Metaphysic
and
Ontology.

the first empirical existences in historical order of time, and from this to suppose that metaphysic can or ought to assign a cause or causes of existence to the universe, is to transform metaphysic into ontology. Not indeed by the route of the Ding-an-sich, or by that of an imagined substance or substratum of objects, but by a route not less certain. If in metaphysic we can go so far back in analysis, as to name elements of objects which are themselves a priori or logically previous to all experience and non-empirical, it is directly contrary to our own procedure and principles to make these into causæ existendi of empirical objects; for to do so we must first transform them into empirical objects themselves.

Ontology rests on the transformation of abstractions into complete objects or complete existences. But all ontological systems do not adopt the same kind of abstractions to transform into complete existences. One route to ontology has just been pointed out, that which adopts abstract elements of objects or of cognitions for this purpose. There is another which adopts abstract aspects of phenomena, that is, either their objective or their subjective aspect. An instance of the first is Spinoza's system, instances of the second are Schelling's and Hegel's. Spinoza regards the Absolute as Substance, Schelling as Reason, Hegel as Mind. All such transformation is foreign to metaphysic, whose last word is—analysis.

CHAPTER II.

THE NATURE OF THE COGNITIONS OF TIME AND SPACE.

> Infinitum illinc idemque per omnia finis,
> Atque heic finitum proprio sine fine videtur.
>
> *Giordano Bruno.*

§ 10. HUME has the merit of being one of those philosophers who have kept closest to phenomena themselves, without mixing up with the analysis of them considerations of their possible origin or causes; phenomena are with him the beginning, middle, and end of his investigations. But in doing this he produced a picture of the universe as if it were unconnected, the work of chance, incoherent; especially was this the case with his theory of causation, which led Kant to undertake a still more searching investigation of phenomena, resulting in a discovery in phenomena themselves of the principle of their connection and consistence. He did this by directing his attention to an old distinction which had its origin with the philosophers of Greece and was always considered one of the cardinal distinctions of philosophy,—the distinction of Matter and Form. This distinction, taken together with that between analytic and synthetic judgments, is the corner-stone, the guiding thread, in Kant's work, the Kritik der Reinen Vernunft; and on that point philosophy is still standing. The application which Kant made of this distinction, the particular shape which his system built upon it assumed, has been often, and in many points successfully, attacked; yet the distinction remains an essential and an ultimate one, and especially so in that matter to which he first applied it, the theory of perception; the distinction itself, apart from the theory which Kant built upon it, is sound. And this distinction will be built upon throughout the course of this Essay, with what success remains to be proved by the event.

But there is another distinction, only less important and general than that between matter and form, which, owing its origin equally to Grecian antiquity, is also equally applicable and essential now to metaphysical questions; and on this distinction, in addition to that between matter and form, and in conjunction with it, I hope to establish the theory of this Essay. Aristotle drew the distinction between πρώτη and δευτέρα οὐσία in the Categories; the Schoolmen, or rather I believe the Nominalists among the Schoolmen, transformed this distinction into one between prima and secunda intentio animi. See William of Ockham, Summa totius Logicæ, Pars I. cap. xii. xiv. Now without entering into the question as to the exact meaning attached by Aristotle or the Schoolmen to these phrases, I will give what I think is the true modern shape of the distinction, as available for philosophical discussions at the present day, retaining the nomenclature of the Nominalists, and distinguishing first from second intentions.

It is a current theory at the present day, that all perception includes comparison; not only that a process takes place in the nerves or brain which is equivalent to or results in comparison, but that when we perceive any object we perceive it as a distinct object only by referring it quickly but consciously to a class of objects to which it bears some relation or some resemblance; that for instance when I see light I classify it at once as similar to light objects seen before; or if I have not seen light objects before, I classify it with other sensations, or with objects of existence as existing. If this were so, what would become of the first object, or could there ever be a first object perceived? It seems that there could not, for the first object could not by hypothesis be perceived until another object was perceived to classify or compare it with. This leads us to the conclusion that, although all subsequent perception includes comparison, the first and simplest object perceived contains in itself parts or elements which may be combined, but cannot properly be said to be compared, with each other when the object is perceived; that the first and simplest objects are the results of a synthesis or synthetic movement of consciousness, while all subsequent and more complex objects than these are the results of a comparison. It remains still to be seen whether the first and simplest objects of perception are complex and synthetic in this sense; but supposing them to be so, it follows in the next place, that not only these simplest and those more complex objects of perception are complex and synthetic, but also that the acts of perception must be complex and synthetic also; that is, they must include a perception of two objects in the one case, and of two parts or elements of objects in the other case, and a perception of a relation between them, which perception of relation is in the one case a comparison, in the other is merely synthesis. Perception of the first and simplest objects is a synthetic act, perception of all other objects is an act of comparison. The first and simplest objects of perception are complex, all other objects of perception are compounds of these.

But now are the first and simplest objects of perception complex? The reply can only be, Name any object that is not so, abstract or concrete, a thought or a thing. There will be found to be none; and for this assertion to be proved true, I trust rather to the course of this Essay as a whole than to any remarks which I could make here at once. The object perceived and the act of perceiving it are then each of them complex, even in the case of the least possible object or moment of consciousness.

But to call the act and the object complex is to call it distinguishable into parts or elements in itself; for otherwise it would be simple. Here then we reach the distinction mentioned in the preceding chapter between empirical and metaphysical objects; empirical objects are complex, complete, objects; metaphysical objects are incomplete, elementary, objects, only in combination forming complex, complete or empirical objects. See the distinction between metaphysical and physical analysis stated and applied to the distinction between matter and form, in Giordano Bruno's Dialogue De la Causa, Principio et Uno. III. vol. i. p. 252, Wagner's edit. The same holds of acts; empirical acts are complex and complete; metaphysical acts are the elements or moments of these. And both metaphysical acts and metaphysical objects differ from empirical acts and objects by having an existence only in logic, λόγῳ μόνον ἐνεργείᾳ δ' οὔ.

Now the case of the metaphysical objects or elements in perception I leave for the present, content

with having here shown their nature and position.
But I follow up the case of the metaphysical acts,
elements, or moments of the empirical act of perception, since this will lead most readily to the distinction between first and second intentions. The simplest empirical act of perception includes, it has been
seen, three elementary acts: 1st the perception of
element A, 2d the perception of element B, 3d the
perception of their relation; these three taken together constitute the empirical perception of the
object A, or of the element A as an object. But
how is it known that these are the elementary acts
and these the elementary objects included in the empirical perception, when by hypothesis the three elementary acts and objects cannot be known separately?
Solely by analogy from cases where an empirical object is compared with other empirical objects and
perceived in consequence as what it is; where for
instance an object is perceived as a marble statue
from being classed with former or other instances of
marble statues. From the analysis of the doubly
concrete case names are given to the elements in the
analysis of the simply concrete case, where the members of the analysis are not concrete perceptions but
elements of perception. We name the metaphysical
elements of analysis as if they were empirical objects
of perception; but this cannot alter their nature and
give them independent existence. Let us now examine the doubly concrete case farther. What is the
character of the three acts of perception which constitute it? They are not all exactly alike. If I had
never seen marble statues before, should I be unable
to see this one if it were presented to me? I should
not be unable. If I had had no sight before, should

I be unable to see this marble statue if it were presented to me? I should still see it. If I had had no sensations at all before the statue was presented to me, should I be unable to see it on its being presented? I should still see it. I should have the sensation of whiteness and of a certain extension of whiteness, but I should not know what that sensation or that extension was. If now I had seen other objects, I should know something more of this sensation by comparison with them; if I had seen other marble statues, I should know that this was of the same sort, though I should not know the meaning of its being of the same sort, or of the term sameness. Here we have the three concrete acts contained in the doubly concrete act of perception. The first is that which presents or in which is presented the object in question, as it would be presented to a man who had had no other perceptions. The second is that in which certain other objects, marble statues in this case, are presented or represented, as the case may be; and the third is that in which the object of the first act is classed with or excluded from the objects of the second act. Here are three concrete acts of perception so closely connected together and performed so quickly, that they can only be distinguished by close mental inspection; but yet each act a complete empirical act, not only existing logically or as a metaphysical act, and with a separate character of its own. The first of these three acts of perception I call a perception of an object in its first intention; when we perceive an object as a man would perceive it who saw in it an object for the first time, or when we voluntarily abstract from a perceived object all that is imported into it by our perceptions of other relations and objects, in both of these cases I call it having before us an object in its first intention. The first case arises in perception and without volition, the second arises in reasoning and in consequence of volition; the first case is intuitional, the second logical; the first a percept, the second a concept. The second of the three acts composing the doubly concrete perception may or may not give an object in its first intention; if a man had seen but one marble statue before, the representation of that would be a first intention; but usually the class to which an object is referred in perception is perceived as an object or collection of objects in the second intention. The third of the three constitutive acts gives already an object in its second intention, for we cannot suppose that the relation, which is its object, is thought of or perceived in such an abstract way as would make it fall under the second or logical class of first intentions. Finally the whole doubly concrete perception itself, the perception of the object as a marble statue, is a perception of the object in its second intention; and this is the perception which is properly opposed to the first of the three constitutive perceptions, namely, that of the object in its first intention. First intentions may accordingly be defined as objects in relation to consciousness alone; second intentions, as objects in relation to other objects in consciousness.

The distinction between first and second intentions though arising in perception can only be employed by logic; it is discovered in perception by analytical reasoning; it is a fact in all domains of consciousness, but it is an instrument only in reasoning. The neglect of this distinction I believe to vitiate more arguments than the neglect of any other logical distinction, perhaps with the sole exception of that between the causæ existendi, essendi, and cognoscendi. On this distinction between first and second intentions hangs that between definition and description; for the doctrine that all perception includes comparison, taken without the limits here assigned to it, has naturally led to the confusion between the two kinds of acts. It was thought that all perception not only included but could be analysed into acts of comparison, and, as description was the result of comparison, therefore, it was concluded, definition must be a result of comparison also, and therefore only a more accurate kind of description. The fact however is, that it is as necessary to keep description and definition separate, as it is to keep separate first and second intentions. Definition is the expression of a first intention, description of a second intention; definition ought to give those qualities of an object which belong to it by itself, without reference to other objects, or to whether these qualities belong to other objects also; description ought to give those qualities which show the fitness of an object for such and such a purpose, its similarity to, its rank and importance among, other objects; definition gives the analysis of an object, description characterises it. Definition and description supply a corrective for the unavoidable ambiguity involved in the shortness of single names. The name of an object may be meant to be taken, or may be actually taken, to mean either the first or second intention of the object it is applied to, or ambiguously to cover both. Expand the name however into a sentence or a phrase, and it is more easily seen whether it results in a definition or a description, whether the sentence presents an object intended to be kept strictly and solely before the mind in the traits mentioned, or whether its equality or inequality, its similarity or dissimilarity, to other objects, its relative position and importance, is the thing present to the mind of the speaker. It may be asked, How can a definition express a first intention, since a definition consists of two objects, at the very least, connected together, since it expresses the analysis of the object or name to be defined? The answer is, that any object, however complex, may be made a first intention by keeping it alone before the mind and separating it from other objects; it may include any number of relations within it, but must not be compared with objects without it. It is then an object in relation to consciousness alone, as distinguished from an object in relation to other objects in consciousness; an object taken in relation to other objects in consciousness is a different object from itself out of that relation; the two sets of objects together become a new object in the first intention. The distinction of objects of first and second intention is discovered to exist in very simple cases of empirical perception, but this distinction, found in nature and independent of our volition, is capable of being applied voluntarily to other cases in reasoning; the process of nature in perception can be repeated voluntarily in reasoning. The discovery of it in perception shows that it is a natural and legitimate process, it does not restrict the process to the spontaneous proceedings of consciousness. The names of simple feelings or the feelings themselves cannot be defined, for instance the sensation White. If a definition is attempted it must be by a reference to something else, for instance by its causes, as the meeting of a particular ray of light with the retina, or by its effects, as the absorption of rays of heat, or by its relations, as the opposite of black; and in these cases there arises a description of White, and we have before us a new object composed of the original object, White, and some of its relations to other objects, and the description of White is a definition not of the original object but of this together with some of its relations to other objects; and of this object there is perhaps no single name, but the definition serves for one, and this object is an object of the first intention. The same phrase may be a definition of an object and a description of part of it, a definition of it in its first intention and a description of that part of it in its second intention. There may be names of complex objects as well as of simple objects, there may be descriptions of complex objects as well as simple; but there can be definitions only of complex objects. There may be names of simple objects of the first intention as well as of complex objects of the first intention; but there can be definitions only of complex objects of the first intention; which is equivalent to saying that definitions belong to reasoning, a voluntary process of consciousness, while names belong both to spontaneous and to voluntary processes of consciousness, both to perception and to reasoning. From this it also follows that definitions are not necessarily definitions of names, there may be definitions of objects of which there are not names, and there may be names of objects of which there are not definitions. Both names and definitions are marks for others, or expressions for ourselves, of objects of consciousness; marks which have their distinctive properties and uses. The following is a distinction of objects which was current

among the Schoolmen, and derived from Aristotle; I take it from St. Augustine's Categoriæ decem ex Arist. decerptæ, cap. 3.
  I. Res omnes quas natura peperit—sunt.
  II. Ea quorum imagines animo videndo formamus et recolimus—percipiuntur.
  III. Illa quibus ea quæ sunt animo impressa efferuntur—dicuntur.

Names, definitions, and descriptions fall alike under the third head; all alike are expressions of the objects contained under the second head, or if not so, yet at any rate of those contained under the first head; so that definitions are only so far expressions of names as they are both together expressions of objects belonging to the first or second head. What the relations obtaining between the first and second heads themselves are, it is one main purpose of this Essay to investigate. A definition is a name of the first intention in an expanded form; a description is a name of the second intention in an expanded form. A definition is the expression of an object as it exists for consciousness alone, that is, of the object as it is, or in its essence; a description is an expression of an object in its relation to some one or more objects besides itself in consciousness, that is, of its comparative value to consciousness. In definition it is indifferent what other objects may be; whether they are like or unlike the object defined, that is beyond the question for the present; in description it is essential that the circumstance or circumstances mentioned should be known as common or not common to the object described with other objects. For instance when I say, Demosthenes is a patriot, I describe him in comparison with other men, some of whom are and some of whom are not patriots, and I indicate his comparative value among men by the description. But if in saying these words I fix my thoughts on what Demosthenes is, irrespective of what other men are, and place him as an object before me, as a man who feels and acts from the feeling of love to his country, I have before me an entirely different object, an object composed of Demosthenes and his country and his feelings and acts towards his country; and this is an object in the first intention, and the words which convey or express this object are a definition and not a description; they may not be a perfect definition, the perfect definition of an object so complex as a human being would fill a book, but they are part of a definition and not part of a description. The use of names and phrases in the first intention implies neither praise nor blame, but states simply facts of analysis; but their use in the second intention, involving comparison with others, nearly always implies either praise or blame; and thus the confusion between the two intentions is not only the fruitful source of errors in reasoning but of quarrels in practice, when words spoken in the first intention, without arrière pensée, are understood in the second intention as implying blame. Definitions and descriptions have no marks in grammatical form or structure by which they can be distinguished from each other; if they had, the subject would have been cleared up long ago; but the objects which they express, the things signified by them, are essentially different. It is of the utmost importance in reasoning to distinguish which kind of object or significatum it is which is expressed, or concealed, by a word or set of words;

whether that object is a first or a second intention, and the act of words a definition or a description. True as it is that the subtilty of nature far surpasses the subtilty of thought, it is no less true that the subtilty of thought far surpasses the subtilty of language. It may be hoped that, some day or other, language will develop forms corresponding to the above distinguished forms of consciousness.

§ 11. I return now to the point passed over shortly before, the consideration of the analysis of objects into their metaphysical elements, and make an application of the distinction now established between first and second intentions. An analysis of any object confined strictly to that object itself, without drawing its relations to other objects into the analysis, is an analysis of the object in its first intention. Such an analysis will include neither the cause nor the mode of origin of the object analysed, nor its importance or meaning compared with other objects; it will classify, not the object as a whole, but its parts as parts of the object; it will not classify its parts as similar or dissimilar to corresponding parts in other objects, but solely with respect to their functions in the object itself to which they belong. The result will be to give the elements of the object analysed, and not its aspects or any of its aspects. Take now any empirical phenomenon, from the simplest to the most complex, isolate it from others, treat it as an object of the first intention, and analyse it as such, without asking how it came to be what it is, or whence it derived its characteristics, or what other things it is like. It will be found that all its characteristics fall into two classes; some are material, or particular feelings, others are formal, or particular forms in which these feelings appear.

Every feeling must exist for a certain length of time, and some feelings must exist also in a certain position in space, and some also in a certain extent of space. The time and the space in which feelings exist is called the formal element of the phenomenon; the feeling, whatever may be its kind, is called the material element of the phenomenon. Whether space is always included in every phenomenon, whether it is always a part of the formal element in phenomena, may be left for the present undecided; it is clear that time always is so, for if we had not a feeling in some duration, however short, we should have it not at all empirically. So that, leaving out of view the question whether the formal element always includes space as well as time, it is still quite certain that a formal and a material element is included in every empirical phenomenon. These two elements are entirely different in kind from each other; and there is nothing in any phenomenon whatever which does not fall under one or other of these two heads. I do not know what it is or how to name it, if there is any such; but if there is, then, as Hume says, "I desire that it may be produced." Here then we have the two ultimate, heterogeneous, inseparable, elements of all phenomena in their first intention, namely Feeling and Time, or as it may turn out afterwards Time and Space; and these names, Feeling, Time, and Space, are names of the elements in their first intention; names of them in the second intention are Matter and Form, or material and formal elements of phenomena. Every phenomenon as such contains these two elements, time, or time and space, on the one side, and feeling on the other. This is empirically and experimentally certain; on this as a verifiable fact I take my stand, and shall appeal to the experience of every one whether it is not so, whether he knows any phenomenon which does not contain these two elements, and further whether he knows any phenomenon which contains more than these two elements; for I shall attempt to show that no phenomenon or variety of phenomena, as such, however rare or complex, contains any thing which cannot be reduced to or analysed into these. This is the analysis of phenomena in their first intention.

It is generally supposed that two other things are elements of phenomena, either besides or instead of those which have been mentioned. These two elements, which are supposed to be elements of all and every phenomenon without exception, are the Subject and the Object. "Along with whatever any intelligence knows," says Prof. Ferrier, "it must, as the ground or condition of its knowledge, have some cognisance of itself." Institutes of Metaphysic, Sect. I. Prop. I. Every phenomenon according to this, whatever other elements it may contain, must contain as elements an object and a subject; one of its elements must be the object, another must be the subject. The meaning of this I apprehend to be, that feeling itself, the material element of perception, is capable of being considered by itself, as an object of the first intention, or at least by way of abstraction and without prejudging the question whether it is or is not separable from the formal element; that feeling itself considered in its first intention is capable of further analysis, and that so analysed it consists of or at any rate contains as elements a Self and a Not-self. Feeling, according to this view, is not an ultimate object, or element made objective, but is capable of analysis. Phenomena, so far as they contain feeling and so far only, abstracting from their formal element, are not indecomposable, but two inseparable elements are present in them which combined constitute feeling, that is, constitute every determinate particular feeling, no matter which. These elements are Self and Not-self. It seems to me that to state this theory is to disprove it; to bring it clearly before the mind's eye is to show its incorrectness. For what are these elements? What is Self, what impression does it make, what is it in its first intention? What is Not-self, its impression in the first intention? Is it not clear that we have no distinct notion of either of these elements, as we have of the feeling of light or sound, of the time a sound lasts, or of the space a light occupies? Is it not clear also that we must ask these questions about them, and so must refer them to one or other of the before-mentioned elements of phenomena, the formal or the material; that if they were known to us, distinguishable by us as elements of phenomena, it would be as modes, or a mode, or particular kind of feeling? Whatever then Self and Not-self may be, they are not elements of phenomena generally.

If however they are not elements of phenomena generally, they must fall under the second mode of looking at phenomena, they must belong to phenomena considered not in their first intention, but in some of their second intentions; they must arise in phenomena in consequence of a later-introduced distinction, from a comparison of some phenomena with others, from the relations of a phenomenon to others and not from its elements within itself. This they do; and the distinction in question between Self and Not-self, being fundamentally the same as that between Subject and Object, is one which applies to all phenomena without exception; it is the fundamental distinction in philosophy, although it is not a distinction at all in direct analysis of phenomena; the reason of which is evident, for all philosophy is reflection; and these notions, Subject and Object, arise first, and are the first to arise, in reflection, and are in fact that object which distinguishes reflection from direct consciousness. This distinction is the object which, as the object of a particular mode of consciousness, distinguishes that mode from others; consciousness drawing this distinction, or having this distinction as its object, is called reflection. It would no doubt simplify matters very much, and would therefore be very desirable, if circumstances would permit, to suppose that consciousness is in its ultimate and simplest empirical perceptions reflective as well as perceptive. The richer the germ, the easier it is to imagine the growth of the entire tree from it. But on the other hand, the fewer the elements in the germ, the more complete is the explanation, if it succeeds, which deduces from it the tree.

Usually this question is treated without distinction of first and second intentions. Phenomena are no sooner mentioned than it is considered how they arise, or what they relate to, instead of what they are. Phenomena are divided into subjects and objects, and then straightway are asserted to arise from the meeting of subjects and objects. Or if subject and object are held not to be phenomena, then phenomena are said to arise from a conjunction of an Unknown which underlies consciousness with an Unknown which underlies objects. But, known or unknown, subject and object are straightway assigned as the condition of the existence of phenomena, and phenomena explained by a reference to their mode of origin, or by a distinction between them and what is called absolute existence. The phenomenon becomes thus a tertium quid, arising from the meeting of two factors, known or unknown, called the subject and the object; and each of the two factors is besides often supposed to contribute something from its own fund towards constituting the phenomenon; either the subject contributes the matter, and the object the form; or vice versâ; or else the object contributes both and the subject contains the contributions; or the subject contributes both and creates the object as their receptacle. But what is the fact? Do either of the two elements, material and formal, bear marks of a subjective or an objective origin, of being contributed by the subject or by the object? Is either of them subjective and not objective, or objective and not subjective? I am entirely at a loss to determine which of the two elements should most properly have either character exclusively attributed to it. They both appear to me to be equally and alike subjective, equally and alike objective, and to bear both characters at once. I can indeed attend to the subjective character of either of them, and I can attend to the objective character of either of them; but this is by a voluntary act, and an act of abstraction. I cannot avoid seeing them in both characters alternately. Both characters of each of the two elements are entirely independent of my will; when once I have made the distinction of subject and object, every thing appears to me as bearing both characters; this only depends on my will, which character at any particular time I will attend to.

Besides, it is impossible that the elements, matter and form, should bear originally the character of objectivity or subjectivity, if what has been already said is true; for this would be to import subject and object into phenomena as elements; Time, Space, and Feeling would have some other properties, as subjective or objective, besides those recalled or denoted by their names.

The distinction between Subject and Object in phenomena arises first in reflection, and the phenomenon of reflection will be analysed in the following chapter. So much however is already plain, that reflection will discover subject and object in phenomena not as elements but as aspects, not from the analysis of phenomena in their first intention, but from the comparison of them with each other or in some one of their second intentions. Every phenomenon will then as a whole appear to have an objective aspect and a subjective aspect, will be capable of being considered as an existence and also as an object of consciousness, or, what comes to the same thing, as an object among objects, and also as a mode or state of consciousness. And what is true of any phenomenon taken singly is true also of any number, or of the totality of phenomena, taken together; one or all alike can be considered in two ways, first analysed into elements, secondly regarded as a whole or as wholes, the aspects of which from without are different, but each of which aspects contains the same two elements, heterogeneous but inseparable, formal and material. The aspects of each and all phenomena are two, like their elements; the aspects depend upon how we approach the phenomenon in reflection, whether as a mode of consciousness or as an object among objects; but in either way, whether viewed from the objective or subjective point of view, each aspect contains the same two elements, formal and material. The annexed diagram may help to make my meaning clearer.

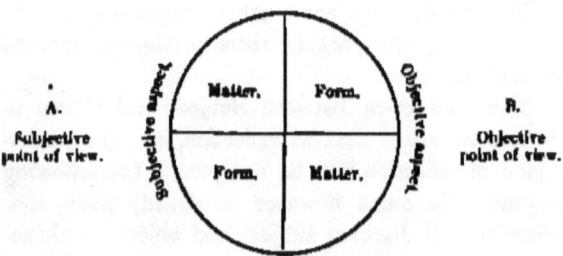

The two elements, matter and form, in the phenomenon, are distinguished by direct attention in perception; the two aspects, subjective and objective, are distinguished by attention in reflection; but the analysis of the process of reflection, the origin and nature of the two aspects, subjective and objective, the introduction of the cognitions, Subject and Object, into phenomena, or the transformation of phenomena into modes of consciousness and modes of existence, is reserved for the next chapter, where it will be introduced in a different connection. Keeping however this further examination in reserve, it will be useful to dwell on the distinction between the two modes of examination a little more at length. Phenomena in their first intention are objects of consciousness consisting of two elements, form and matter; phenomena in their second intentions are existences which, in addition to this character of being objects of consciousness, are related objectively to each other. These two characters are possessed by all phenomena without exception, and must be possessed also by those, if any such should disclose themselves, which appear to be the conditions or contributing causes of the rest. Mind and matter, subjects and objects, if they assume a distinct place among phenomena as causes or conditions of other phenomena, must be themselves also phenomena, and present the characteristics of phenomena; that is, must consist of elements in their first intention, and possess a subjective and objective aspect in their second intention. So that in accordance with this view we shall have nothing before us but phenomena, instead of having before us phenomena resulting from the concurrence of two unknown substances, mind on the one side, and existence or matter on the other, or composed of the contributions of two kinds of existences, mental or absolute on the one side, and material or absolute on the other. What is called mind, and what are called existences, and that which Kant calls der transcendentale Gegenstand, will have melted into phenomena, out of which indeed they originally grew. We shall no longer be able to say with the Nominalists 'such and such a conception is not a real existence, it is a mere fiction or intention of the mind;' nor with the Realists 'such and such an object has no true existence, it is merely empirical;' for all phenomena are at once both objective and subjective, and if they are the one must of necessity be the other. In the next place it will be seen that theories of perception are a part not of metaphysic but of psychology, of the science which examines the laws of the conditions and causes of consciousness as objects, not of that which analyses the phenomena of consciousness themselves; of a science in short which treats of objects in some of their second intentions. And it follows that what are called, on the theory of a representative perception, impressions, images, and ideas of objects, are the objects themselves, and not merely evidence of the objects; that in fact there are no objects but these so called evidences of objects. From the subjective side, or in their subjective aspect, these so called evidences of objects are not merely evidences to the mind, but they are the mind itself. Thus, with whichever of the two we begin, the mind perceiving or the object perceived, we find one thing only before us, namely, the phenomenon, which was before thought to be only the intermediary between the mind and the object. And be it observed that this old division into three, mind, object, and intermediary, exists equally on a theory of immediate, presentative, as on a theory of mediate, representative, perception. The difference between them is solely this, that on the former theory the intermediary phenomena are the result of the contact of mind with the object, are that which springs from the concurrence or out of the contributions of two things or substances, more or less unknown and mysterious, called mind and object; while on the latter theory the intermediary phenomena are the medium and condition of that concurrence. But in the view here brought forward, both mind and the object, whether conceived as entirely unknown or more or less known, are wrapped up in, and developed out of, the phenomena analysed; how much known, and how wrapped up in and developed out of phenomena, must remain undetermined till the process of reflection is examined in the following chapter. Phenomena alone remain in the world, and mind and the object are no longer separate empirical things, or separate unknown things, or separate absolute things, but two inseparable aspects of phenomena. From one side the world is all mind, from the other all existence. It is impossible that any thing should exist unless possibly present to consciousness; it is impossible that any thing should be present to consciousness unless possibly existing. And since consciousness and existence are completely correlative and coextensive, therefore it is impossible that any thing absolute should exist. Neither on the side of the unknown mind, nor on that of the unknown existence, is it possible that an absolute can exist or be; for every thing, whatever exists, call it what we will, is relative to consciousness, or has a subjective side. If it is argued that we may imagine or conceive an existence transcending our faculties and beyond the range of our knowledge, I reply that the very doing so brings it within them, for we are furnishing an instance of the very thing which is here observed, namely, conceiving or imagining an existence and supplying it with a subjective side; such existence would be, while imagined or conceived to exist, present as a possible existence in consciousness; its essence, quâ existence, would exist, for it would be already present in consciousness as possible, as analogous in point of existence to all actual existences, in being so present. Analogous—there lies the point. Unknown existence, so far as it is existence, must be analogous to known existence; either the word existence has a meaning or it has not; if it has, it is the same in both cases, and if it has not, then it has no meaning in the phrase 'known existence.' I find all philosophers with two exceptions, with exception of the metaphysical ontologists, such as Schelling and Hegel, who deduce every thing from mind, and of the empirical ontologists, who deduce every thing from matter (in their sense of the term)—with these two exceptions, I find all philosophers conceiving the world as produced by two independent factors, variously conceived both in their nature and in their connection with each other; for instance, mind sometimes as the coefficient, sometimes as the mirror of matter, but still two separate independent factors, mind and matter; and this, whether they find these two factors both immediately present to consciousness in every instance of external perception, with Prof. Ferrier, or only inferred to be present from those perceptions and their objects, which is the more usual way. I on the contrary conceive the world not as produced by two factors, these or any others, but as presenting two characters or aspects, in one of which it is entirely mind, in the other entirely matter, (to adopt terms in their current meaning, though more suitable to the current theories than to mine). Mind and matter become transformed, in my theory, from factors into aspects of the world, each of which is an aspect of the other, and the world indifferently one or the other, according as it is regarded. My theory therefore is not a theory of causation, but of analysis of the world—an applied Logic of the world, as I have already said.

If these conclusions, so far as they respect the complete correlation of existence and consciousness, are accepted by any one with difficulty, the cause will not be far to seek. The cause will be the habit of regarding the existence or non-existence of particular objects as entirely independent of our minds, and of our imaginations concerning them. From this habit we reason to the world of existences in general, and conceive that this also is independent, as to its existence or non-existence, of our minds and imaginations. When we speak of the existence of a particular object in a particular time and place, we mean that it could be seen, touched, or otherwise perceived, if we were present at that time and place; so also of the world of existences in general, we mean by its existence now and here that it is present to consciousness now and here. The parallel is exact, and we argue thus: as the presence of the particular thing there and then was independent of our consciousness, so the presence of the world of existences here and now is independent of our consciousness, and so also the presence of other, absolute or unknown, existences is independent of our consciousness. True, the parallel is exact; but both cases include the same fallacy. The absence of the particular thing was not its absence from consciousness, but from presentative consciousness, it could not be seen or touched or perceived presentatively. If it were absent from consciousness altogether, we could not bring it before the mind and say of it that it was absent. To go back to the old phrase,—when we speak of the existence of a particular thing in a particular place and time, we mean—what?—that it could be seen, touched, or otherwise perceived if we were present at that place and time. Is this being independent of consciousness? It is, on the contrary, explaining existence to mean capability of being perceived; it is making actual existence equivalent to being actually perceived, and actual existence at a particular place and time equivalent to being actually perceived at that place and time. And so also in the case of existences generally; by the absence of the whole world of existences is meant its absence from presentative consciousness; if it were absent from consciousness altogether, its absence could not be brought before the mind at all. Such an absence would be equivalent to the ceasing of consciousness. The fallacy in both cases is the same; existence is not the equivalent of presentative consciousness, but is independent of presentative consciousness; and that whether we are thinking of the existence of an object of daily experience or of worlds unknown. From this it is argued that existence is independent of consciousness altogether, which is equally false both in the case of particular familiar objects and of imagined worlds. Such is the nature of the fallacy; but what is its history, and how come we to be deceived by it? Through neglecting the distinction between objects in their relation to consciousness alone and objects in their relations to other objects in consciousness, between objects in themselves and objects in their origin and causes, that is, the distinction between first and second intentions. When we say that particular objects existing in a particular place and time are independent of our consciousness, we mean that the causes of their existence there and then as objects are not to be found in us, but in other objects; we mean that we did not produce them, but that something else independent of us was the condition of their existence. Independence in this sense, in which it is truly asserted of objects, is then fallaciously applied to objects considered in themselves or in relation to consciousness only; and the assertion, that objects are independent of the mind, is understood as if it meant that objects, or some objects, have no subjective side, and are independent of consciousness not only in their origin but in their nature.

Accordingly, when in this Essay presence in and absence from consciousness generally is spoken of, it will not be meant to indicate presence in and absence from presentative consciousness only; but the term consciousness, employed simply without limitation, will be used in its widest sense as including all its possible modes; in which sense it is the exact equivalent of the term existence, including likewise all modes of possible existence, verified or unverified, actual or potential. It will be seen in proceeding, how a single moment of consciousness is or may be the equivalent of the whole universe as its object, namely, by its modes of time and space which are common to both. Existence, what is it? We are so familiar with it, that we think we understand it. But there is no understanding without explanation, definition, analysis. The answer, given by philosophers to their own enquiries as to what existence is, has usually been in substance the same, namely, that it is a mode of the Absolute; that is, of some real existence which is the cause, or the essence, or both, of the apparent existence about which the question was originally put. Answers of this kind are ontological, and become the basis of systems of ontology. They labour under the fallacy of obscurum per obscurius. They do not explain the phenomenon of existence, but add to it another imagined phenomenon to be explained; παραπλήσιον ὥσπερ ἂν εἴ τις ἀριθμῆσαι βουλόμενος ἐλαττόνων μὲν ὄντων οἴοιτο μὴ δυνήσεσθαι, πλείω δὲ ποιήσας ἀριθμοίη,—which sentence is part of Aristotle's criticism on Plato's theory of the εἶδη, Metaph. B. xii. cap. 4, § 5, and which, as I remember with pleasure, was first pointed out to me by Prof. J. M. Wilson of C.C.C. Oxford. Existence is obscure enough as it is, without inventing a second existence beyond it. The true answer to the question, What is existence? is not ontological but metaphysical. It is impossible to refer existence, the most general class or name of all, to a higher or more comprehensive class or genus. To use Aristotle's phraseology, it is impossible to make it a species by differentiating the genus to which it belongs, for it is itself the highest genus. But it may be possible to point out its characteristics, its propria, some quality or qualities which are coextensive with it, belong to it in all its instances, and belong to all instances of it so far as they are existences. There is one such characteristic, namely, that of being present in consciousness, taking consciousness in its widest sense and including therefore both possible and actual presence in consciousness. This is an analytical, and therefore a metaphysical not an ontological answer to the question, What is existence? Analytical, not indeed from the point of view of direct perception, but of reflection, as has been explained already. Whatever therefore can be perceived, conceived, or imagined, exists; exists either potentially or actually, in the past or present or future. It is necessary to classify existences, and not to confound one kind with another, or value all alike. For metaphysical purposes the classification should be instituted by asking how objects are present in consciousness. First, presentative must be distinguished from representative perceptions; in the former the object is, as a rule, more vivid than in the latter.

Representative perceptions again are divisible into those which are capable and those which are incapable of verification by presentation, or by testimony founded on the presentations of others. And representative perceptions which are capable of verification may again be divided into those which are capable of verification at present, and those which are conceived as capable of verification at some distant time. In short, some scale of truth must be introduced into the conception of existences, by which they may be distinguished from each other.

§ 12. I come now to the special subject of this chapter, the consideration of the formal element of consciousness in its first intention. Of the two points of view already distinguished, the objective and the subjective, the subjective is the only one which is necessarily universal; in adopting the objective point of view, abstraction is made of the subjective, but in adopting the subjective it is impossible to abstract from the objective. The subjective contains both aspects at once, the objective only one. The subjective point of view therefore is the one proper to this chapter, to the consideration of all objects in their first intention.

Feeling is the material element in consciousness, the element which in some modification or other constitutes all consciousness. The question is, What is the formal element combined with feeling in all cases, whether it is time, or time and space, or time and motion, or motion alone, or space alone, or space and motion, or whether there are any other formal elements, in addition to or in exclusion of these; and again, What are the connections of these with feeling and with each other, whether one is derived from another, and which are the original and which the derived elements; such in general are the questions to be answered.

Feelings may be roughly classified as follows: 1st, the feelings of the five special senses which have defined organs, sight, touch, hearing, taste, and smell; 2d, feelings which have as yet no specially defined organs, such as hunger, the sensus communis in all its branches, feelings of heat and cold, of muscular tension, and others,—these two classes are commonly called sensations; 3d, feelings which arise only in redintegration of the feelings of the two first classes, such as desire, aversion, love, hate, anger, fear, joy, grief, admiration, feeling of right and wrong, of honour and dishonour, of justice and injustice, of effort and resolution, and many others, all of which are called emotions, and which are also sometimes distinguished, either by differences in kind or by differences only in degree, into two classes, emotions and passions. These three classes comprehend all feelings. Now every feeling, whether sensation or emotion, must occupy some duration of time however short; it could not be a feeling if it did not; and this I think is immediately and empirically certain to every one. But only two of these feelings must in and by themselves occupy extension in space as well as time; these two feelings are the sensations of sight and touch; and, of these, sensations of sight cannot be assumed to occupy by themselves more than two dimensions of space, namely, length and breadth, or superficial extension; sensations of touch also appear primarily, or in the first instance, that is, in one single touch uncompared with others, to occupy only superficial extension or two dimensions of space. The questions accordingly have been raised, first, whether space in its three dimensions is not capable of analysis into its two dimensions occupied by sensations of sight and by single sensations of touch, and secondly, whether these two dimensions of space are not themselves capable of analysis into sensations occupying time successively. If the latter were the case, the entire range of our feelings would be capable of analysis into two elements only, time and feeling.

Another series of questions has been opened up by the current distinction of feelings into internal and external. Taking its origin from the apparent place of the object perceived, from the distinction between the body of the observer and objects external to his body, the distinction between the internal and external sense was originally a distinction between feelings which arose within the body and those which arose from objects outside the body. But when this distinction between body and external objects gave place, in consequence of physiological and psychological investigation, to a more subtil one between a mind or soul, dwelling somewhere and somehow in the body, and things external to the mind or soul, among which the body itself was included, then the distinction between the internal and external sense had to support itself on other considerations; and the two senses were then distinguished from each other by their respective forms, the internal sense was that which had time, the external sense was that which had space, for its form. Time and Space became the distinguishing characteristics of the two senses, the internal and the external. Since however the mind was conceived as a single mind, as the unity of these two senses, internal and external, and not as consisting of two isolated senses, the perceptions of the one sense were necessarily conceived as passing over into perceptions of the other sense. Accordingly, what the external sense was to outward objects, that the internal sense became to the external sense, and translated the space relations of the external sense into time relations of the internal sense; the internal sense became, in fact, the mind, and the external sense became its organ for supplying it with intelligence of every thing outside itself, including the body which it inhabited. All feelings which existed only in relations of time, that is, in succession, and not also in relations of space, and these feelings only, constituted the mind properly so called; and these feelings existed, as Hume observed, literally *nowhere;* "the greatest part of beings," he says, "do and must exist after this manner." Treatise of Human Nature, Part iv. Sect. 5. The distinction of internal and external objects thus became a distinction between the mind and objects; in other words, the distinction between Subject and Object coincided with that between objects in time and objects in space. Those things alone were objective which occupied space, those were subjective which occupied only time. What was internal was mental, what was external was material. Yet the mind itself was conceived as existing in the body, an external object, and consequently as having position in space; and the mind was the object of psychology. Hence, from the explanation of the terms mental and internal to mean existing in time only, arose the insoluble contradictions of a mind existing only in time and yet having a position in space, and having a position in space and yet not occupying space; besides the difficulty of seeing how a mind, conceived as an object not occupying space, could be brought into connection with space-occupying objects. Kant, though adopting the distinction of internal and external sense, does not fall into the error of making this distinction coincide with the mind, as the object of psychology, and the world of material objects; for he replaces the mind by his Unity of Apperception, the Ich denke, a subjective act which binds together all states of consciousness and all phenomena, and of which the internal and external senses are modes of operation; the Ich denke can never be an object by itself. Yet since the distinction of the internal and external sense may be retained together with the notion of an objective mind to which they belong, it will be useful to devote a few words to its consideration; and, as it was shown before that the distinction of the material and formal elements in consciousness did not coincide with that between object and subject, so now I will attempt to show the same in the distinction between the formal element in the internal and external senses.

I will attempt to show four things; 1st, That phenomena which are perceived in two dimensions of space, phenomena of the senses of touch and sight, although also occupying time, do not owe their occupation of superficial extension to their occupation of time, but that their space-relations are not capable of analysis into relations of time; which is the answer to the second of the two questions proposed above; 2d, That phenomena occupying time do not owe their objectivity to their being referred to phenomena occupying space; 3d, That phenomena occupying space

F

PART I.
CH. II.

§ 12.
The formal
element in
cognitions.

do not owe their subjectivity to their being perceived in time; 4th, That phenomena of both kinds, in time and in space, owe both their objectivity and their subjectivity to reflection, irrespective of their being represented in reflection as occupying space or time.

1st. If we had not the senses of sight and touch we should be without any cognition of space. Feelings which coexisted in our bodies would appear as a succession either of simple and definite, or complex and indefinite, feelings. Analysis of coexistent feelings would be nothing else than resolving the complex into a succession of simple feelings. Phenomena would be nothing but a series or succession of feelings, now simple, now complex. With sight however the case is different. The eye opened to the light sees a whole surface, one small portion of it distinctly, the rest indistinctly; it sees part bright, part dark, part clear, the rest obscure; this is the phenomenon of seeing; and I cannot conceive how any one can suppose that the space-relations of this surface of light are reducible to relations of time. It is enough to contrast the two things, in their simplest forms, with each other, to see the difference in kind between the two; the form of sight is as different from the form of hearing, as the sensation of sight from the sensation of hearing. The interpretation of the phenomenon of seeing is another thing; the comparative magnitude of the parts of the surface, their comparative shape and distance, may need other senses to bring them into notice, the sensation of muscular tension and of the degree of effort involved in it, in the machinery of the eye, for instance. But the extended surface is seen at once, and is seen as something different from feelings which are not extended.

Or if it is urged that we see points of light first and
then compose the surface out of these, still the point
itself, be it the minimum visibile, is extended or it
could not be seen. Similar is the case with touch.
The whole surface of the body is endowed with the
organs of touch. Here, if the body is touched in two
or three different places at once, it is true that this
will not produce the perception of its being a single
extended surface; different positions of the sensation
will be all that is perceived, and perhaps not this at
first; for though each point touched is extended, yet
there is no continuity of these points as in the surface
seen by the eye. This kind of continuity is introduced into phenomena of touch either by a tolerably
large surface of the body being touched at once, or
by a comparison of the places touched with the order
of succession of the touches in time. But in both
cases the space-relation is not perceived, but only interpreted, by a reference to the time-relation. Something is added, in these two senses, to the two elements of time and feeling, something which, though
always appearing in time and connected with time,
is yet not capable of analysis into time, nor yet into
time and feeling taken together. For it may be
asked, If time and feeling taken together constitute
space-relations in the case of the two senses of sight
and touch, why do they not constitute them also in
other senses? It is again impossible to conceive the
space-relations of superficial extension to be merely a
mode of expressing to consciousness briefly the successive relations of feelings, or as a shorthand way
of writing time-relations, since the question recurs,
whence we get this very different mode of expressing
the time-relations; and besides, the space-relations

§ 12.
The formal element in consciousness.

are, if more brief and compendious, yet more explicit and distinct than the time-relations which they are supposed to express, and what they lose in point of time they acquire in another direction, in space. I conclude, then, that time-relations and space-relations of superficial extension are different in kind, and cannot be resolved one into the other.

2d. Suppose a man not to have the senses of sight and touch, but only those senses which present feelings in succession; would those feelings which he has in succession be unreal, or less real than before? Every one will answer that they would be equally real. They will be phenomena, just as much as if they were accompanied with other feelings which occupy dimensions of space. Their connection with those other feelings can alter nothing in their reality, as first intentions, though it supplies them with new relations, and in this way with new significance. But this reality is the ground of their afterwards appearing, as will be seen in the answer to the 4th point, objective; that is, their reality is the ground of their objectivity.

3d. Phenomena occupying space do indeed all of them also occupy time, but this is not the cause of their having reality. The reality of these phenomena, as of those which occupy only time, consists in the feeling which they contain, not in the form in which that feeling appears. In both cases the reality of the phenomenon is in its being felt, not in the mode of its being felt. And its reality is the ground of its subjectivity.

4th. Both kinds of phenomena are equally real, for both contain feeling; but as yet they are phenomena only, they are present in consciousness, but not present as either subjective or objective. The reality of either kind does not depend upon the reality of the other; one kind is more complex than the other, but the additional character which that kind possesses is not a modification of the time-relations common to both kinds, but an addition of a new and different nature. The reality of each is independent of the other, and depends upon the feeling which each possesses equally. The reality is the ground of the distinction of subjective and objective, not the difference in the form of the two realities. It is within the reality of the phenomena, or within the phenomena so far as they are real or contain feeling, that the distinction into objective and subjective arises, and not within them so far as they contain a different kind of form. If the distinction of objective and subjective arose from the different kind of form in phenomena, then this distinction would be already there as soon as the two kinds of phenomena had arisen; and would not be remaining still to arise in them. But it has not already arisen in them, but they are as yet mere phenomena, mere feelings possessing equal reality or unreality. It must be from something in the phenomena, still to be differentiated, that the distinction of objective and subjective arises, and not from what is already differentiated, namely, the formal element into time and space. Every development of a new character in phenomena, in the present case of the new character of subjectivity and objectivity, is a sinking back into the nature of the phenomenon in which it is developed; Hegel's word for it is Vertiefen; it is a bringing out of something latent in the phenomena, and each new character or forward movement of development is also a back-

Part I. Ch. II.

§ 12.
The formal element in consciousness.

ward movement, or the stirring up deeper and deeper depths, and the bringing to light of some cause,—a cause of the kind known as potentiality or δύναμις,—from below or behind the phenomenon which develops itself, and both effect and cause, energy and potentiality, begin to exist at the same moment. Now it is a commonplace of philosophical criticism, that we must not mistake the occasions of our coming to the knowledge of anything for the coming into existence of the thing itself; for instance, we must not mistake the increase in the returns of crime, owing to the more perfect means of statistical information, for an increase in the amount of crimes committed; and in application of this rule it may be supposed that our coming to the knowledge of the newly developed characters in phenomena, namely, their subjectivity and objectivity, is not coincident with the first existing of these characters in phenomena, but that they existed previously as subjectivity and objectivity, and we afterwards find it out. But how is this possible? How is it possible that they should exist previously in phenomena as subjectivity and objectivity, without being perceived as such? It is impossible, for it is a contradiction in the terms. Their previous existence was a potential one, δυνάμει ἐνεργείᾳ δ' οὔ. And their potentiality is an inference, arising, as will be seen more clearly from the Chapter on the Ratio Sufficiens, from the form of time; an inference from their actuality, that is, from the actual development of the new character in consciousness. Nothing new can arise without bringing with it the inference of its potentiality previous to its arising. But this potentiality is not actuality, has not the character which is its ἐνέργεια. Subjectivity and objectivity exist first when they exist actually. They do not exist actually in the phenomena of direct perception. Time and space do exist actually in the phenomena of direct perception; we are actually conscious of them though we do not reflect that we are conscious of them, and though we have not distinguished them from their content. But objectivity and subjectivity we are not conscious of at all until we reflect on direct perceptions. They then first exist actually, and their previous potentiality is then first inferred. Time and space have no potentiality, for they are always, and in every thing, actual. I conclude therefore that, since the distinction of objectivity and subjectivity has still to arise in phenomena, it does not arise from the distinction of the two kinds of form in phenomena, time and space.

It is difficult to see what use there would be for the terms objective and subjective, supposing them to depend on the difference of form in phenomena, unless they were intended to express a different degree of reality in the phenomena differing as to form. And this is the meaning which is usually attached to those terms; the term objective signifies, as usually employed, something more real than subjective; and the term subjective usually signifies something comparatively unreal. So that if the two kinds of phenomena are equally real, and yet the terms objective and subjective coincide respectively with these two kinds of phenomena, either the terms objective and subjective must cease to signify difference in point of reality, or the characters which they signify must depend on something else besides the difference in form of the two kinds of phenomena, that is, they must depend on some distinction in the feeling they contain. If however the terms objective and subjective do not coincide respectively with these two kinds of phenomena, then they may depend on the feeling or material element in phenomena, in virtue of which phenomena are real, without signifying a difference in degree of reality between the classes of phenomena which they are employed to designate. The distinction into objective and subjective is one which arises within the reality of phenomena, and distinguishes that reality into two kinds, not different in point of degree of reality but in point of the character of that reality. When many phenomena have occurred in consciousness, that is, at a certain advanced point in the history of every individual man, a distinction is drawn between what is common to all phenomena and what is peculiar to single phenomena or sets of phenomena. They are recognised as being all alike in being feelings, and different in being particular determinate feelings; as the first they are all one, as the second they are all different. The first perception that phenomena are all alike in being feelings is the first dawn of reflection; it is the first generalisation in matter of consciousness; phenomena have already been compared with one another in their differences of feeling and form, and already formed into groups which we call usually 'objects;' nurse and mother, table and food, &c. &c. have been already distinguished; but that these groups have any connection of kind with each other has not yet been perceived; the first perception that they are all alike in being feelings is the first perception that they are subjective, and at the same instant also that they are objective, that is are still as different as before from each other in their determinate particular qualities. They were before perceived as different, they are now perceived as the same; which gives new meaning to the previously perceived difference. They were phenomena, they are now objective and subjective; each and all phenomena are both at once, and bear both characters at once. Connected as feelings, and in this common character, they altogether form a group, like the groups of 'objects' already formed; but it is a group of a different character and expressed by a different word; 'Baby' has become 'I;' not that any thing is proved by the word, but that my meaning is rendered clear by it. The perception of self, or self-consciousness, the perception that feelings are *mine*, is in fact the same thing as that which is expressed by saying that feelings are all alike feeling. Whatever things are alike in one point are one in that point; when these things are feelings they are subjectively one, for feeling is a word which we all understand by experience as well as by any explanation; there is no understanding it, and we must content ourselves with familiarity; it is already a subjective word, and if we would have an explanation we must explain the word subjective by feeling, and not feeling by subjective.

This operation of reflection refers equally to phenomena in space and to phenomena in time; for both are equally feelings, and both are equally real. Phenomena of both classes have acquired a double character, a reference to each other and a reference to consciousness, or as it has been previously expressed a subjective and an objective aspect, each of which aspects contains both elements of the phenomenon, the formal and the material.

PART I.
CH. II.

§ 12.
The formal
element in
consciousness.

The consideration of this fourth point has caused me to make a spring in the regular development of the subject, to pass over the formal element directly present to consciousness, and take up the thread at the point of reflection; the reason being that the distinction of objective and subjective is as yet usually considered to be involved in that of time- and space-relations, if not as a necessary element, yet at least as a condition of all phenomena. The purpose of metaphysic is to arrive at the lowest empirical phenomena of consciousness, then at their elements, whether one, two, or more; to trace as it were the stream of consciousness and of existence to its source or sources, and to decide the relation of these sources to each other. The sources of all phenomena must be discovered; whether there are any sources which belong to all phenomena without exception; whether all the sources do so; and, if any do not, whether these are deducible from the others or have an independent existence. It must be remembered that in isolating any phenomenon whatever, even an element of consciousness, we treat it as if it were an empirical or complete object, and as if there might have been a time previous to its coming into existence. This method, which is common to all reasoning, does not however make the elements of consciousness into empirical objects, but leaves them at the conclusion of the process just what they were at the beginning, unless reasons should have been discovered in the course of it for considering them to be different. To reason about an element of consciousness is to assume, for the purposes of reasoning, that it is a complete object; and, the reasoning ended, the assumption is dropped.

Time is involved in every moment and in every object of consciousness; and this is a fact which is incapable of proof by inference, because the inference itself supposes its truth. It is however immediately certain to every one; some time is occupied by every instant of consciousness however short. But it is not so with space, and this therefore requires examination. If the senses of sight and touch were denied us, and we had only the other senses and the emotions, we should not have the cognition of space immediately; perhaps it would be going too far to say that we could never attain to it at all. It is perhaps impossible to imagine the precise shape which our consciousness would assume under these conditions. But as it is, the space-senses sight and touch, and the sense of effort or muscular tension involved in both of them, are brought into play simultaneously with the other senses, and in connection with them. The inner and outer senses are at work together, and both connected, as we know afterwards, by belonging to one organised body. One of the first groups of phenomena which forms itself in consciousness is the phenomenon called the body; touch, sight, and sense of muscular tension together produce this combination; a space is marked out within which all our other feelings are found to fall, though they have not all definite places assigned them in it. It does not derogate from the necessity or validity of the space-relations that they are only given by two senses directly; it would be sufficient if they were only given by one sense; if only that sense was always operative in connection with the others. The cognition of space-relations arising at all, in connection with phenomena of the other senses, binds together those relations with phenomena of the other senses, and gives these phenomena relations to the rest in space. A distinct portion of space is marked out by the senses of touch and sight combined with the sense of muscular tension, all three of which senses involve time-relations; this space is called the body, and within it sensations of hearing, taste, smell, hunger, heat, cold, and others, together with the emotions, are perceived as arising and existing, all perceived as in themselves occupying time, and from this connection perceived as also occupying, though not perhaps filling, a definite portion of space. That portion of space, in three dimensions, called the body, gives unity in point of space to all its feelings whether internal or external, that is, to all its world of phenomena. But inasmuch as it is a portion of space in three dimensions, the portions of space from which it is marked out must have three dimensions also, for they are perceived as enclosing it on all sides; and in fact the three space-dimensions occupied by other phenomena are perceived pari passu with the same three dimensions in the body itself; the body is perceived by being separated from other phenomena of sight and touch.

We started however with only two perceived dimensions of space, and have ended with the perception of three, which are involved in the perception of our own bodies as solid objects surrounded on all sides by other objects at various distances. This perception has been produced by the combination of three senses, sight, touch, and muscular tension, none of which alone could give it. If any single sense alone could give the perception of the third dimension of space, as Mr. Abbott in his Sight and Touch argues that sight can, the work of the metaphysician in this point would be much simplified. But I cannot admit that sight alone can give this perception. When, for instance, we see an object passing, as we know afterwards, behind another and concealed by it, what is really seen is the concealment or becoming invisible of one at the moment of its contact with the other; and it is referring this phenomenon to a supposed cause, and not analysing the phenomenon itself, to say that one of the objects must be behind the other. What is depth, or distance in depth, in its first intention? It has no explanation, no analysis, but itself,—the third dimension of space. But how does it differ from the other two dimensions of space? In requiring the two former to be given in order to its being understood. A superficies must be taken, and then objects out of that superficies are in depth; that is, a point of departure must be taken to contrast it with, directions from which it is excluded. Now in empirical perception, this point of departure is given only by sensations of touch. Imagine a man fixing his eye on a point in the horizon, turning round and thus combining sensations of muscular tension with sight, and coming again to the same observed point in the horizon; this will not give him a perception of the circular figure of the horizon; he will see the same superficies repeated, as often as he turns completely round, but he will not know that he is in the centre of it; he will have no fixed point wherewith to contrast the coloured superficies. Imagine him now to see his own body in addition, and this will be a fixed part of the same superficies; but still a part of a superficies only, not the central part of a circular superficies, but only a fixed part of it while the other parts are changing. Suppose him however now to be endowed with touch, and to touch as well as see his own body; then the fixed part of the visual landscape, or coloured superficies, always seen when any other parts of the landscape are seen, becomes in addition the only object of touch, the only object which he perceives by both the senses of sight and touch. He gains, by the addition of the sense of touch, a point of departure from which to measure the superficies, which he saw previously as only superficially extended; and the third dimension of space means for him now distance from something actually tangible. The meaning of the third dimension of space is originally, then, the distance from one tangible point to another in objects of sight. Whatever may be the proportions in which these two senses, or that of muscular tension, contribute afterwards to the interpretation or measurement of comparative distances or magnitudes, of linear or superficial extension, or of depth, the sense of touch is indispensable as a constituent of the perceptions in which depth first becomes an object of consciousness.

Equally inadequate is the sense of touch, either alone or combined with muscular tension, but without sight, to supply perceptions in which the third dimension of space is perceived. Sensations of touch alone, or combined with those of muscular tension, can give a succession of feelings of superficial extension, but cannot bind these sensations into a solid whole without the combination of visual sensations. I can touch a surface, but I do not solely from that know in what direction the series of touches go, nor distinguish a direction of a surface from a direction vertical to it. The only kind of cases where a combination of a whole series of touch-sensations into a solid whole is apparently possible is in grasping a small object, where the fingers meet each other as well as touch the surface all round. Here we have an entire series of touches on the outside of an object, just as in the above case of vision we had an entire series of visual images seen from the inside of the object, the horizon; we receive the impression of resistance at all points, but we get no perception of the solid space between those points. Nor, if we did receive this perception, could we extend the experience to other cases where the series of touches could not be complete, that is, to space generally, for there is nothing to connect the two kinds of cases; without sight we cannot perceive our own bodies as solid, and consequently not space generally in three dimensions. Sight therefore is an essential constituent of the perception of depth. But again the same remark must be made here, namely, that this fact does not show in what relative proportion touch and sight are necessary to the measurement or interpretation of magnitudes. The sense of muscular tension alone is obviously less competent than touch to give the perception of depth or distance, for it does not even give that of superficial extension.

If we could assume space in its three dimensions, and objects occupying it, as already existing in and by itself, and needing only to be perceived by us, then perhaps sight alone, or touch alone, would suffice to this perception; for the question then would be one of mere interpretation. But to assume this is in fact to assume that we possess the perception of space, as a form of consciousness, previous to its becoming filled by sensible impressions. These two apparently opposite assumptions are fundamentally the same; in both of them space is conceived as lying before us, as an absolute, to be perceived and interpreted. But if the very existence of space is its being perceived, and if consequently, in reasoning about it, it must be conceived as first coming into existence when it is first perceived, then we have to account not only for its interpretation but for its original perception; and the senses have to produce its perception and its existence. And for this purpose the senses have to be examined separately, in order to see what each sense by itself involves, and how much it can separately contribute to the complete perception of space in three dimensions. Sight contributes, at the least, perception of superficial extension; so also touch; the combination of the two produces, at the least, perceptions of the three dimensions, for part of the visual superficies is pushed to a distance from the fixed part, the body, when we touch the body and not the rest of the superficies, and yet the part of the superficies so pushed remains a superficies still. This is the origin, the creation, of the third dimension of space, when reasoned of as if it were an empirical object. Sight and touch however come into operation together, and consequently the perception of the third dimension of space begins simultaneously with that of its superficial extension. The object and the state of consciousness called perception of things in space of three dimensions is a highly complex state and object, but not necessarily later in time than any of the simpler states or objects of which it is composed; it is we who import the notion of growth in time into it, by our analysing it into its elements and then composing it afresh by their combination. In other words, the senses of sight and touch contain the logical elements, but not the historical causes, of the perception of objects in three dimensions.

Logical language and the language of reflection, together with the modes of thought this language expresses, being that necessarily used by us in analysing the phenomena of perception, we naturally, but not therefore correctly, imagine that perception advanced by the same stages as those which we have discovered in the analysis of its objects, and that it not only reached that result which we analyse, but that it reached it by the same route, and gained successively the same stages, as our two processes, analytical and synthetical, successively traversed and reached. For instance, we have analysed space into three dimensions, and therefore imagine that perception saw first one of these and then the others; or we distinguish the first and second from the third, and then imagine that perception saw the first and second together as distinguished from the third. But there is nothing to show that this was the case. Visual perception sees a superficies, but it does not see a superficies as distinguished from a solid; if it did so, it must have previously seen the solid. It sees what we afterwards, in order to distinguish it from a solid, call a superficies. It has never conceived the question whether there is any thing behind the superficies or not; it sees colours which may be either superficies or solid, and which turn out to be solid. A superficies without a solid, and a line or a point without a superficies, are objects of abstraction, provisional images only; and when it is said on one side and admitted on the other, that sight sees only a coloured superficies, it is meant that this is the least.

τὸ ἀναγκαῖον, which in our reflective and logical language can be expressed to be seen; that sight sees this at the least, without asking how far it may go towards the next logical mark or division, trinal extension, which would include too much, and without entering in any way into the question what potentialities may be involved in this perception of superficies; for the phenomenon of sight, the coloured surface, has not been yet analysed by the perceptive consciousness. The addition of touch to sight, combined in time, does not add a new distinct direction to an old distinct one, does not add depth as distinguished from surface to surface as distinguished from depth; but it changes the previously potential superficies into an actual solid; it makes us see into the superficies, and perceive it as, or transform it into, solidity. Space in three dimensions, therefore, does not become such by a composition of distinct, separate, parts or directions, but by a combination of sensations into one indivisible whole, a whole which, although complex, is not separable except logically and provisionally.

Since space in three dimensions is an indivisible though complex whole, it does not arise in consequence of comparison or reasoning, which are processes concerned with complete empirical objects, or with abstractions treated as such objects. But in perceiving space in three dimensions no such empirical or complete object has been arrived at, until space itself has been perceived; and the three dimensions of space are not capable of being treated as such empirical objects, until they have been abstracted from space itself as a whole. In the perception of space there is synthesis, but not comparison.

Such is the nature of the formal element of all external sensations, known as space, and such is the combination of the sensations which gives rise to it, or which first presents consciousness with phenomena in three dimensions. It now becomes possible to answer the question proposed at first, whether motion is or is not a formal constituent in perception. What do we mean by motion? For different feelings existing in order of time there is another name, Succession. For different feelings existing in space and time together the most appropriate term is Motion. According to this, sensations of muscular tension alone constitute no cognition of motion, but only of succession; but changes in a coloured surface, changes in touch, or changes in sight and touch together, constitute the cognition of motion. Motion accordingly in its lowest and simplest terms is succession in the objects of sight or of touch. When such succession is perceived, motion is perceived; that is to say, motion is the name of this particular combination, not the analysis and not the explanation of it. Not the analysis of it, because on the contrary succession of feelings of sight or of touch is the analysis of motion; not the explanation of it, because it cannot be perceived or conceived without itself involving the very succession it would explain; unless indeed it is considered as an occult and absolute cause, and this is no explanation. Neither again is motion a constituent of objects in three dimensions of space; for, though successions of feelings of touch and sight together constitute such objects, they do not require to be first gathered up into perceptions of motion, before they combine to constitute them; it is because successions of feelings of touch and of sight combine

PART I.
CH. II.

§ 12.
The formal
element in
consciousness.

together, and not because each succession is a motion, that objects in three dimensions arise.

It may now be objected that there is more than these elements,—there is their combination; and that this combination is motion. The answer is,—this their combination is time. Feelings succeeding one another in time are combined already; if those feelings are also in space, they are still combined as before in time; that is, their succession is their combination; and are besides combined in space by their space-relations. Their combination has already been accounted for, that is, referred to its proper element in the analysis. Accounted for in this sense it has been fully; but accounted for in another sense it has not been, and the mixing up these two senses in which phenomena can be accounted for is a common source of error. Was it meant by asking after the combination of feelings in motion to ask how they came to be combined, or what was the cause of their being combined, instead of asking what was the analysis of the phenomenon of their being combined? Was it meant to ask how feelings come to be combined with time and space relations,—the material with the formal element of cognition; and how phenomena come to contain these two elements at all? These are questions which are not answered here, and which never have been answered; they involve an attempt to spring beyond the last elements of consciousness, and they move only by employing the cognitions the cause of which they ask for; they are intelligible only because they contain the cognitions which they seek to render intelligible.

Motion is sometimes conceived as the combination of feelings in time with feelings in space, or of the time-relations with the space-relations in feelings, or as a succession of feelings in space-relations,—in which sense it has been already analysed; and sometimes it is conceived as the cause or the fact, the objective fact as it is called, or the occult cause or fact as it is sometimes called, underlying that combination. Here comes out the result of dividing the world into two sets of objects, subjects or minds on one side, and objects known or knowable by these subjects on the other. On this supposition there must be occult facts or occult causes, which are known only by their effects or manifestations, which are phenomena; there must be occult facts or occult causes on the side of the subjects, which are known only by their effects or manifestations, the cognitions or states of consciousness. Everywhere are Things-in-themselves, unknowable but imagined as existing; imagined as the double of phenomenal existence in order to account for it; there must be a cause of every thing, it is said, even of the elements of phenomena; multiply then these elements by 2, and call the result their cause. And that this is really the origin of the conception of Things-in-themselves or occult facts or causes, is shown in this instance by the exact similarity in nature and position between the real combination of feelings, namely time, and the imagined one, motion as an occult cause. Motion contains nothing but the formal element in cognition; it is simply that element made into an object by itself alone without a material element, and supposed to be the object perceived in its manifestations, in perceiving phenomena.

One of the questions which was proposed at the beginning of this section has now been answered, namely, whether motion was one of the formal elements in consciousness. It has been shown that it is not, but is an empirical fact or phenomenon, capable of analysis into feeling, time, and superficial extension of space. And if motion is thus put aside, I do not know what other claimant there can be for such a rank. For force, about which so much is said in physical science, is but motion considered as determined to a particular direction or mode, and sometimes to a particular degree or measure of intensity. But the claim of space, in its three dimensions, to that rank, may yet be contested. In fact it has been shown that this cognition, space in three dimensions, does not spring up full formed with the first or simplest exercise of consciousness, but that its growth can be traced through combination of the data of the two senses of touch and sight; besides which, its being original only with two of the senses, and with those two only in combination, while the majority of the senses are originally without it, seems to show that it is not universal in phenomena or necessary in consciousness. Now, if its necessity in consciousness required the support of a theory of its being an innate or connate form of an objective mind, then these considerations would be fatal to its claim; for they would show that the connection between that psychological object and this its form of consciousness was not universal and without interruption, but that the mind might and originally did operate without operating under this form. But the necessity and consequent universality of space, in three dimensions, is not dependent on any objective psychological theory. Space is necessary, not because it is a native form of the operation of the mind, but because, being irreducible to any thing else, it is all-embracing and exhaustive in its nature, and occupies the whole field of being. True, the particular phenomena in which it arises may be pointed out, namely, the two senses of sight and touch in combination; these are its sources, or the phenomena in which it is involved. But, in the first place, these cases never arise alone, but always in conjunction with some of the other phenomena of which the entire consciousness is composed; and then, this being so, the nature of the cognition of space, so combined with the rest, determines its necessity, for its nature is such that no feeling can escape it; it combines with the rest as their frame and dwelling-place, from which they can afterwards only be released provisionally and during a process of abstraction. True, space is composite; but it is composed only of itself; true, it is not like time present in every moment of every feeling, but, except by an effort of volition, every moment of every feeling is present in it. Space is the necessary formal element of the senses of sight and touch taken together; but it is the necessary formal element of the other feelings only on the supposition that these two senses are an inseparable part of the consciousness which is the complex of those other feelings; in other words, it is only for an individual human consciousness, as we find it actually existing, that objects in space are inseparable from objects in time; but this is enough for the purposes of analysis of an individual human consciousness.

§ 13. With the arising of phenomena in three dimensions arises also the distinction of the pheno-

PART I.
CH. II.
—
§ 13.
The unity of phenomena in space.

mena into those within and those without the body. For the perception of the third dimension of space takes place only in distinguishing the body as a solid and tangible object from the space surrounding it, which must be therefore perceived as solid or in three dimensions. The phenomena are thus conceived as capable of being separated from each other in the third dimension of space. Another conception is connected with this, that of matter as impenetrable; in which sense, so far from being taken to mean, as in this Essay, only the material element in consciousness, it means masses or molecules of some impenetrable stuff, which is in some way or other the opposite of feeling or consciousness. Putting these two conceptions together, there arises the conception of a world which is a congeries of material objects, surrounding the body on all sides, and endowed with qualities which operate upon each other, and upon the body, and produce changes in it which modify the states of the consciousness seated within it.

It is easy to imagine how these two conceptions were combined, so as to produce the conception of a world of material objects. The quality of impenetrability is nothing else than the sensation of touch including or combined with the sense of muscular tension. I do not speak of the causes or antecedent conditions of this quality, but of what it is for consciousness alone; and if we are told of or imagine objects which are impenetrable, but in so slight a degree that we cannot perceive them to be such actually, but can only infer the quality by proof of its effects, as, for instance, in the case of the air on a still day, yet it is plain that the inferred resistance or impenetrability of the air is only understood or imagined by referring it to cases of actually perceived resistance. In the great majority of instances of actually experienced tangibility, this sensation is accompanied by sensations of sight, and by sensations of sight in which a continuity or contact of surface with the body is seen. Break the visible continuity and the sensation of touch ceases, renew one and the other is renewed. Again, other sensations, such as odour and sound, become stronger in proportion as the tangible object is brought nearer to the body, and weaker as it is removed. When we actually have sensations of touch, we actually have also, in most cases, a variety of other sensations; but this is the case with no other of the sensations, to any thing like the same degree. No other brings with it the other sensations; we may hear, see, smell, in some cases even taste, without touching or feeling any muscular tension; but if we touch, we can also do some one or more of the rest. Touch then, with the sense of muscular tension, is a sense with which all or any of the rest can be combined; at the same time it is impossible to be closer to any object than in touching it; the object supposed to be touched is in visible continuity with the body; and the quality of impenetrability is not capable of being expressed or conceived ultimately in any other way than as a sensation of touch combined with muscular tension.

Suppose now the very frequent case of objects, which have been touched, removed to a distance but still visible; they will be represented as tangible, we shall remember that we touched them; yet the surface still actually visible is no longer actually tangible. The two senses are no longer in combination, but we know by experience that a tangible surface must be

PART 1.
CH. II.
—
§ 13.
The unity of phenomena in space.

also visible, though a visible one need not be tangible; we remember that, the more distinctly visible any thing is, the easier it becomes to touch it, and that the same holds good of the other senses. Tangibility is thus conceived as the condition of the other senses; and since we represent the once touched and still visible object as tangible, we now make it the seat of visibility, and consider the object as tangible to be the object proper, and the other sensations, visibility, odour, sound, and taste, as inherent in or dependent on it. The cognition of space in its three dimensions having been already gained, this object is then referred to some part of space distant from the body, and space thus becomes filled with tangible objects, that is, with different masses of matter in which the other sensations inhere.

The removal however of the seat of these sensations to a distance, while they are felt all the time in the body, compels a change in our way of regarding them; they must be regarded as caused in us by a property of the tangible object; in other words, we cease to look at the sensations as objects for consciousness alone, and to ask what is their range as sensations, and we begin to enquire how they are produced in the tangible objects and transmitted from them to our bodies. Phenomena which are visible but not actually touched become thus removed by the imagination to a distance, because, consciousness argues with itself, if they were at the surface of the body they could be touched; since they are not touched, they are not at the surface of the body. Where are they then? Somewhere in that third dimension of space which has been already discovered. They must exist in the two first dimensions of space, for they are visible; yet they are not tangible, that is, not close to the body; but since they are represented as tangible, it follows that they are in such a place where they could be touched if the body were near enough, that is, they are separated from the body by the third dimension of space.

To examine now the validity of this conception. It may well be that tangible matter and motion, in masses or in molecules, are the causes or conditions of our sensations of qualities of every kind; but this does not alter the case as to the nature of those sensations, or those qualities, as objects for consciousness alone. The sensations themselves cannot be analysed into tangible matter and motion, though their causes may. Different modes of motion, mechanical, chemical, or vital, may pervade all matter which is either capable of being actually perceived by touch or imagined as being so capable if our senses were more acute; and this tangible matter may pervade all space, and be the cause or condition of the different qualities which we perceive by the senses in space; but it cannot be the analysis of those qualities themselves, as they are known immediately to consciousness. As immediate objects of consciousness, the qualities which are known by the other senses are in precisely the same case as those which are known by the sense of touch, including muscular tension; that is, are nothing else than the sensations of those senses themselves. And they resemble the sensation of touch also in another respect, namely, that they too are in immediate contact or continuity with the bodily organ which perceives them, and extend from it into space in three dimensions at least so far as the tangible object from which they appear to proceed; light occupies the space between us and the sun; a sound or an odour occupies the space between us and the tangible object perceived by these senses. Suppose consciousness to be placed at any intermediate spot, with the requisite media, the atmosphere for instance, and it would have the same sensation. The sensation is there if its conditions are; and by 'being there' is meant, that if consciousness were there it would have the sensation, just as in the case of other objects. This is the view which I wish to establish in place of the conception, above described, of what I may call the duplicity of phenomena, as cause there and effect here, as quality in the tangible object and feeling, caused by the quality, in the body of the observer. Feelings and qualities are convertible, or at least equivalent, terms, one the subjective aspect of the other; where one is, there is the other; and the same causes are the causes of both.

The question is one concerning the distribution of the contents of space. The erroneous conception is, that the extension represented as tangible is the extension actually seen; the true conception is, that the extension actually seen is continuous with, but not the same as, the extension represented as tangible; that the visibility of the extension is combined with its tangibility, but not confined to the limits to which its tangibility is confined. If I take the object to mean its tangibility combined with its visibility, then the object occupies all the space as far as it is visible, while its tangibility occupies a small portion, at the centre, of that space. The sun, for instance, is not the object seen when we see light, but is the tangible centre of the object, light; a tree or house or any other such object, in the same way, is the tangible object at the centre of the coloured rays which are the visible object. Perhaps the object is audible, odorous, gustable, as well as tangible and visible; if so, it occupies the whole of the space occupied by the widest of these properties. Suppose now the object to be presented to consciousness; part of it only as just described is presented, the rest is represented; the parts not actually touched, the rays of light or colour, of sound, of taste, not falling on the senses of the body, are represented. So that, whether we take the object in the widest sweep of its qualities, or limit it to the sweep of its tangible quality only, we must have a large portion of it an object of representation. The common opinion limits the object, not to the sweep of its presented tangible quality, but to that of its tangible quality presented and represented. It can derive no support from the coincidence of its limit with the distinction between presentation and representation; for both views equally overstep this line. The rest of the qualities of the object in their wide sweep it calls effects of the object in those tangible limits, effects of the motion of its particles. Here are two opinions, both describing the same object, but in different ways; one describes the phenomena as consisting of an object and its effects, the other as consisting of a combination of objects.

The test to which I bring these two conceptions is the distinction between first and second intentions. Are not effects of an object themselves objects? Have they not a nature, a kind, of their own, previous to being known as the effects of another object? Is not the term effect applied to them in their second and not in their first intention? They may be effects of some other object, or of some constitution or cause in that other object; but the present question is, what they are for consciousness alone, and not what their relation is to other objects in consciousness, or what they are in that relation. Now for consciousness alone every quality is a sensation, and the single name, of colour, sound, and so on, expresses the two things, first the sensation, then the sensation as extended in space, or as quality. All these qualities, except tangibility, may certainly be considered also as effects of the motion of tangible particles, if it is remembered at the same time that they are something else for consciousness alone, namely, sensations of sight, sound, and so on. But if they are conceived as inherent in the tangible objects, and yet as direct objects for consciousness, they become reduced all to one quality, tangibility, as the sensation of motion in tangible particles; and then we must consider tangibility as the only sensation, which is absurd. The sensations other than touch cannot be analysed, in their first intention, into sensations of touch, though their antecedent conditions may perhaps be so analysed, that is, though they may be found to depend upon different kinds of motion in tangible objects. Conceive them as qualities inherent in the tangible object only, and they become themselves modes of tangibility; but conceive them in their own shape as sensations, and they occupy space in three dimensions, precisely as tangibility itself does.

One of these theories has been called true, the other erroneous; but are not both true, and each of them compatible with the other? They are incompatible only if both are regarded as metaphysical conceptions, or conceptions of ultimate analysis; but true and compatible with each other, if one is regarded as a conception of metaphysical or ultimate analysis of phenomena, and the other as a conception of physic, or of psychology; of the account of the conditions and history of phenomena. This is their true relation to each other. The distinction of objects within and objects without the body is a distinction of physic, and at the same time a distinction of psychology; the objects in both parts of space are of the same nature, tangible, visible, audible, and so on, and different only in the place which they occupy in space; the distinction is a division. But the distinction between the formal and material elements of these objects, and also that between their subjective and objective aspects, are distinctions which relate to the objects of both of these divisions alike; with the objects of whichever division you begin, you find the same distinction of form and matter, of objective and subjective aspect, forced upon your notice; and these are distinctions and not divisions. They are more general than the divisions of place alone, and must be examined first, in order that the examination of consciousness, considered as seated in the body, and of its objects, considered as seated outside the body, may be subordinated to their requirements. The metaphysical distinction of the subjective and objective aspect of phenomena, which I may call the empirical ego and the world of qualities, will be found to harmonise completely with the physical and psychological distinction between consciousness seated in the body and its objects in space outside the body; for the whole of space is occupied by qualities, and the whole of space is occupied by feelings, and the body itself is but that complex of qualities which is constantly present, as a complex of feelings, in consciousness. When the action and reaction of feelings on each other in space is in question, those feelings become to us qualities, since we abstract from their relation to the mind; when we ask what they are to ourselves, they remain feelings. And this is the case wherever we may imagine ourselves to be; a feeling does not cease to be a feeling and begin to be a quality at a hairsbreadth distance from the body or nervous matter; light which is a feeling extends from the sun in all directions, and is felt by the sense of sight everywhere; in all space it is a quality, and in all space it is a feeling.

The world of qualities, as different from the world of feelings, arises only in consequence of an abstraction supposed to be complete from the consciousness which perceives them; and this supposed complete abstraction is thought to be possible and natural only in consequence of dividing consciousness in space from its feelings, and making both into objects. But this complete abstraction is a delusion and impossible, because, even while the separation is being made, both the things separated are objects and feelings of the same consciousness; the qualities themselves are feelings when present to consciousness for the purpose of being divided from the mind, and the mind is in the same case. Psychological division in space of the mind from its feelings makes both members of the division into an absolute, into objects each of which is supposed to exist even if the other should not exist. But metaphysical distinction makes these qualities again into feelings, notwithstanding that they may occupy the whole of space. Feelings and qualities are the two aspects of the same world; but

OF TIME AND SPACE.

for metaphysic the world is a world of feelings, since the conception of feeling includes that of something felt, that is, quality; but the conception of quality does not include that of feeling.

Very early the distinction was drawn between objects which touched one another and objects one of which had, besides this, the sensation of being touched by the other. All objects could be felt only by means of touch in the former sense; if the object felt did not itself touch the body which felt it, it must put in motion something which did; and the question was, what this medium, τὸ μεταξύ, was; whether it belonged to the feeling body, as in the case of the senses of touch and taste, or was something foreign to it, as in sight and hearing. Arist. De Animâ, iii. 6, et seqq. Touch in the first sense, which may be called contact, was evidently an interpretation of touch in the second sense, that is, of touch as a sensation; the closeness between objects in contact was an inference from the sensation of closeness in the sensation of touching visible objects. Aristotle showed that even objects of touch were not strictly close to the part of the body which felt them, but were felt through a medium just as the objects of the other senses were, though this medium was part of the body itself. De Animâ, iii. 11. But the imagination had already firmly established the notion of objects being separate independent existences, led thereto by the sense of touch wrongly interpreted, and all enquiry had to be conducted on that basis. The consequence was the distinction between objects and their qualities, by which the objects were known as audible, visible, tangible, and so on. Take for instance a visible and tangible object as the object of

PART I.
CH. II.
___
§ 13
The unity of
phenomena
in space.

enquiry, e. g. a table; it has the tangible quality
hardness, the visible quality brownness. Both these
qualities are known, if either is, by an effect they
produce in the medium between the object and the
sensitive part in our bodies. As an object the table
requires this medium as much in the sense of touch,
in order to produce the sensation of hardness, as in
the sense of sight to produce that of brownness.
The object is not immediately touched; there is the
skin covering the nerve-extremities, and the nerve-
substance itself, or as Aristotle called it the σάρξ,
intervening. The original opinion was that the object touched was immediately present to the sensitive
part in touch; to show that there was a medium was
virtually to show that the object so conceived was a
fiction of the imagination, and that the object touched
was the quality of tangibility, not a supposed object
of which this was a quality inherent; for in that case
a quality in the medium would be what was immediately present to the sensitive part of the body.
And thus we may read a profound meaning into
Aristotle's words, De Animâ, iii. 12. Καθόλου δὲ
περὶ πάσης αἰσθήσεως δεῖ λαβεῖν ὅτι ἡ μὲν αἴσθησις ἐστι τὸ
δεκτικὸν τῶν αἰσθητῶν εἰδῶν ἄνευ τῆς ὕλης. The ὕλη was
the object itself, the substance of which the qualities
were properties or accidents, or, in modern German,
the Ding-an-sich. Yet though Aristotle established
clearly that in touch we perceive a quality and not
the thing itself, he saw neither that after this there
was no ground remaining to believe in the existence
of the ὕλη, nor that the confusion between the ὕλη
and tangibility was the cause of the distinction drawn
between an object in itself and its qualities; and he
continued to argue on the same basis of an unknown

ὕλη and known qualities of ὕλη. But now instead of ὕλη there remains only the space occupied by sensible qualities, with complete obliteration of the divisions between sensitive body, medium, and object with inherent qualities.

But may it not be objected, that, in showing that the sensation of touch is not in immediate contact with the object supposed to be touched, but that there is a covering of skin between the nerve-extremity and the object touched, we rather prove a duplicity in the sense of touch itself than remove duplicity from the other senses? If this objection is made, I reply: the feeling is in the nerve-extremity, but where is the quality of tangibility? In the nerve-extremity also. But how come we to transfer it or extend it to the skin, the glove, or the table? In consequence of the simultaneous and inseparable accompaniment of a sensation of sight; the sensation of tangibility is always accompanied by the sight of a continuous surface, or continuity between my finger and the table. The tangibility of the table is in the nerve-extremity as we feel by touch, it is continuous with the table as we feel by the simultaneous sight of the finger and the table. The object then which is in truth touched is an object continuous with the nerve-extremity, and consisting of the medium and the visible object supposed to be touched. There is therefore no duplicity introduced into the object of touch, but this object is continuous and solid in exactly the same sense as the object of sight is.

Now all the special senses depend on touch in the first of the two meanings distinguished above, namely, contact. The objects of all the senses are immediately present to the nerve-extremities, and the

Part I.
Ch. II.

§ 13.
The unity of phenomena in space.

feelings consequently are in the body in the same way as those of the sense of touch are. All the senses are in this way a kind of touch in the sense of contact, but each with a peculiarity of its own which procures it its name. All feelings, of all the senses, are continuous, indivisible into an objective part and a subjective part, and solid; but one kind alone is the feeling of touch; from the three dimensions of which latter kind of feeling, when combined with sight, all the other feelings derive not tangibility but solidity. The formal element is transferred from touch and sight to other feelings; its own material element remains peculiar to touch. But it may be objected here, that, if we are not justified in transferring the material element of tangibility to objects of sight and sound by association, neither are we justified in transferring the formal element of solidity to the other senses besides touch and sight. Transfer, it may be said, both or neither. But solidity and tangibility, I reply, are quite different things and stand on quite different grounds. The sensation of touch is the last of a series of conditions on the completion of which the perception of solidity arises; the perception of a body as solid arises from the combination of feelings of sight and touch in superficial extension with their time-relations. The perception of our own body as solid arises in this way; and the perception of our own body as solid gives solidity to every thing about it; for if the space which it occupies is solid, the space which surrounds it must be solid also; for the body is perceived as solid only by being distinguished from objects on all sides of it. The perception of solidity therefore is not due to association, as the transference of tangibility to objects of sight is. Solidity is always perceived when it has been perceived once, but tangibility may be erroneously inferred.

Phenomena, whether of one or more or all the senses, exist accordingly both in time and in three dimensions of space. No 'here' and 'there' in phenomena is possible; there is only one continuous phenomenon, in which and of which are all its differences, parts, and kinds. There is one consciousness and one universe; each fact is the counterpart but not the cause or the effect of the other. Consciousness with all its modes of feeling and its two modes of form is one and indivisible; the universe with all its qualities and its two modes of form, the same two modes as in consciousness, is one and indivisible also. Sight reveals continuity of superficial extension, touch and sight together reveal continuity of superficial and solid extension. Suppose now that in these modes of extension an empty place were found, that in the surface revealed by sight a portion was dark and invisible, that in the surface revealed by touch a portion was intangible and did not affect the nerve of touch, cases which are frequent; then the dark portion and the intangible portion, being contrasted with the light and the tangible portions, become portions of space, have position and figure. Space suffers no rupture, but its material co-element only. What is the cause of this phenomenon? Has it not been shown that the material element is equally essential to consciousness with the formal? If then the material element vanishes anywhere, ought not there the formal element to vanish also? The solution is, that the place left empty of the material element is filled with the representation of that element; there is no

**Part I.
Ch. II.**

**§ 13.
The unity of phenomena in space.**

material element in presentative perception at that place, but the gap is bridged over either by a material element supplied by representation, from whatever source this may be drawn, or by a representation of the gap becoming filled without designating by what kind of material element. The dark portion of the visible surface is only itself present to consciousness by being contrasted with the light portions; the intangible portion of the tangible surface is only present to consciousness by being contrasted with the tangible portions. In other words, the formal element is always actually and presentatively present in all consciousness, the material element may be present in representation only and provisionally. Hence the power which we have of forming an image of space and of time without any particular material element; in this image the material element is only provisionally present. But the material element can never be present in consciousness without the actual presence of the formal element. Some time, or some time and space together, every feeling must occupy. I do not say, some definite time, some definite figure; these may be provisionally present. But while we can banish matter from time and space, and keep it only provisionally there, that is, without specifying what kind of matter it is to be, we cannot so banish time and space from matter. Sensations of sight and of touch must always be in time and space; sensations of the other senses must always be in time. The cause of this is probably to be sought in the infinite number of modifications of the material element, while the formal element has but two modifications, time and space. Time and space may be presented as empty, without any particular material content; in that case their particular duration and figure is their matter, the lines which circumscribe the space and the points which limit the time, which they owe to matter, become the material element in the phenomena. When time and space are so presented, they are said to be pure, by abstraction of their material element. Matter, which cannot be so abstracted from form, can never be a pure object; it would cease to be an object at all at the moment that the abstraction was completed. This is the great distinction between the material and formal elements in consciousness, namely, that the formal element must be always actually present, while the material element may be only provisionally present in it. Matter changes, vanishes, leaves empty spaces and empty times in consciousness; time and space alone never change, never vanish, never leave spaces which are not space, nor times which are not time; are always continuous, always the same. They cease only when consciousness itself ceases. And this I think is a true description of the facts of consciousness, however it may be sought to account for them.

§ 14. So far as to the unity of phenomena in space. But the same question arises also with reference to phenomena in time; phenomena appear in time also as involving a duplicity, a now and a then, an existence now in the mind, and then in the past course of history or in its anticipated future. It may for instance be objected: You say there are two forms of feeling; some feelings present themselves in time alone, others in time and space together, and you speak as if the time-element in both classes of feelings was the same, only that in the one case it has a space-element in addition. But the fact is,—and this shows that the old division into an internal subjective and an external objective sense is correct,— the fact is that there are two separate kinds and two separate portions of time contained in those feelings which occupy space as well as time; there is one time-element which is subjective and of the same kind as that occupied by feelings which occupy time alone, and there is another which is objective and is occupied by the feelings in exactly the same objective way in which they occupy space. Tangible and visible objects are present in consciousness for a certain time subjectively, they occupy space objectively and for that time; but not only for that time, but also for as long as they occupy space; they have a place and a duration in time in the world of objects, as well as a place in space. When I see an oak, it exists for a minute in my mind, but it exists five hundred years objectively, and in the same objective sense as that in which it is said to exist as part of the visible and tangible landscape. There is, therefore, an objective and a subjective time, though you have only mentioned one, the subjective.

If I should not succeed in answering this objection, I hope that the plainness with which I have exhibited it will shield me from the imputation of wishing to leave any difficulties dark. My answer to this objection is, that the oak considered as occupying this second portion of time, this objective portion of time, does not exist as part of the object or phenomenon of presentative perception, with the analysis of which we are more directly concerned. The oak existing in that second, objective, portion of time, the five hundred years, is an object of representation only, believed on evidence interpreted by my experience of time in presentative perceptions. The universe in its entire duration prior to this actually present moment, nay even this actually present moment itself, if it be true that

Le moment où je parle est déjà loin de moi,

is in the same case. There remains therefore no other time in presentative phenomena than the time which I spoke of as the only one, the same in kind with the time involved in feelings which exist in time only; and this time is both objective and subjective, equally the one, equally the other, as is discovered by reflection; that is, it is mine and the tree's both at once. Similarly with space; the visible and tangible landscape of which the oak was a portion is the only extended object present in presentative perception. Beyond an extent which Mr. Bain describes as "a range of about a third of a circle, right and left, up and down," all other visible and tangible objects are present to consciousness only in representation. The object which I have before me in presentation is this portion of space and the first portion of time, the minute, filled together by certain feelings. If I mix up with them, or add to them in the following minute, representative perceptions, I may in that next minute have before me the five hundred years of the oak's life, and ages before that also, and also the whole depth of sky above and beneath the earth, Europe, England, the field "of many one," with the oak there standing, the events that have passed around it and that may pass before it is gone, and in times when it shall have gone and been forgotten. The so-called objective portion of time, then, turns out to be time as the form of an object of representation not of presentation. But nothing in representation is or can be more real than things perceived in presentation. So that if this portion of time is called objective to distinguish it from the minute in which it is perceived, it cannot be in the sense that what is subjective is less real than what is objective.

Will however any one maintain that the distinction between subjective and objective coincides with that between representation and presentation, that every thing which is merely represented is merely subjective, every thing which is really presented is really objective? In that case, every thing not contained in the actual object of the present moment is merely subjective; the course of the world up to the present moment, the space of sky seen at the Antipodes, our own ancestors, are merely subjective; nor will it avail to reply, that they are now indeed subjective, but have been actually presented to consciousness once, that our ancestors have lived in a world of people to whom they were objects of presentation; for the people themselves, the consciousnesses to whom they were objects of presentation, are themselves merely subjective too, all alike are objects of our representation. The addition of a further characteristic to those objects cannot make them more real, if the added characteristic is itself also merely subjective. The objects, then, of representation not only are now subjective, but, where they do not belong to the actual experience of the person representing them, i.e. where they are imagined as well as represented, they have never been any thing else; while as objects of former presentation they are inferences from objects of present or actual presentation. This conclusion is inevitable on the supposition that the distinction between subjective and objective coincides with that between representation and presentation, and that what is subjective is unreal.

It is in representation that the time and space occupied by the object come to be thought different from the time and space occupied by it in presentation. In representation the time and the space occupied by presented objects are taken up and included in a new or rather newly-recalled object which occupies, may be, an immense extent of space and duration of time; and this is the case, whether the originally presented object is still presented or itself also represented; which latter would happen if we suppose the eyes to be shut after seeing the oak, and the scene to be recalled in memory. Between presentation and representation there is a great difference, as important a difference as any in philosophy; but the distinction between the time and the space, which are contained in the object of representation, and the time and the space (called by the objector subjective) contained in the moment of representation in the mind, does not arise solely from this difference. That distinction arises in consequence of reflection upon the phenomenon of representation; but yet not solely from this; it arises from that reflection taking a particular course, and distinguishing not subject from object, but the mind and its body taken together from other objects, according to the explanation offered in the following chapter. The mind, together with the body which it inhabits, is in this course of reflection made into an object similar to other objects, and an object of such a kind as to be a partial mirror, as it were, of the rest of the objective world. The world is divided into two classes of objects, this mind, "the wind-borne mirroring soul," on the one hand, and the objects and events which it mirrors on the other. These classes of objects have their separate and appropriate times and spaces in which they exist and in which they are perceived to exist; but both are objective and subjective in the same sense, that is, both are what are commonly called objects, and neither is a subject. The distinction between the two kinds of time and space, occupied respectively by the object, as an object of this mind, and by this mind itself, as containing their image in its consciousness, is accordingly a distinction which arises in a particular kind of reflection on the phenomenon of representation, and not in this phenomenon of representation by itself, that is, as it first arises in consciousness, or as it is interpreted by reflection alone in its proper sense.

But in order here to decide the question of the unity of phenomena generally, whether presentative or representative, in time, the nature of representative phenomena must be examined. What then is the phenomenon of representation as distinguished by reflection proper from the phenomenon of presentation? The object of representation is distinguished from that of presentation solely by an inferior degree of vividness, distinctness, and completeness in its material element. The events and objects of yesterday from noon to midnight were presented to me yesterday and occupied twelve hours. To-day they are represented to me and occupy five minutes. They are equally objects in both cases, and equally subjective. In both cases their presence in the mind and the time they occupy in that can be distinguished, in the kind of reflection above described, from the time the events themselves occupy as objects. In both cases the times occupied are equal, are really the same. In the presentation the time is twelve hours; in the representation the time is five minutes. "No, you object; the objective time in the representation is twelve hours, the subjective is five minutes. Hence the difference." Times which contain the same events and objects are the same length of time; but do the five minutes and the twelve hours in representation contain the same events; that is, are they filled with the same material element? Certainly they are. Just as the small circle of the retina contains the same colours and forms which are spread out over the whole surface of the object seen, so the five minutes contain the same objects and events which are spread out over the twelve hours in the representation. As the object in the former case was one object in superficial extension of space, so here in the representation of the events and objects of a day there is one object in one time, which may be called five minutes or twelve hours according as we consider it as part of the mind or as part of the other objects mirrored by the mind. Distinguished however into two objects by reflection proper, that is, distinguished into two objects of five minutes and twelve hours respectively, but without being placed in different portions of space,—that is, in the mind and without it; distinguished therefore into two aspects of the same object,—what is the difference between them? The difference between them in this case is solely the difference in the distribution of the material element. In the five minutes that element is gathered together, in the twelve hours it is separated by spaces of time provisionally not actually present. The twelve hours contain just so much material element as can be contained by five minutes; and this difference in length is rectified by the recollection that there are gaps containing other matter which is omitted. In other words, the five minutes or twelve hours, objects of representation, are a repetition of part only, and that a less vividly present part, of the same twelve hours as an object of presentation. This omission of the matter enables the twelve hours to be the equivalent of the five minutes; since, if all the matter was contained in them which was contained in presentation, they would require an equal length of time in re-presentation; it would require from noon to midnight to-day to represent the events and objects contained in the time from noon to midnight which were presented yesterday. The same remarks apply to the case of the five hundred years of the oak-tree; only that in this case these years are not remembered but imagined. If events sufficient to fill every minute of five hundred years were imagined one by one, not one minute but five hundred years would be required for the purpose. In all cases of representation there is a decrease either in vividness, or in amount, or in distinctness of the order of occurrence of the material element, or in all at once, in the object represented, compared to the object as it was presented. Something is omitted, either from the material element itself, or from its arrangement, or from both, in the object of presentation; and the object with these omissions is the object of representation. In order to signalise that there are such omissions, and that the object of representation is a faithful transcript or repetition of the object of presentation only so far as allowance is made for such omissions, the object of representation may properly be called a provisional image. For all kinds of knowledge are referred to presentative knowledge, as the most vivid and the most distinct and the most complete which is possible; representative knowledge is but the substitute for, and means of attaining, presentative knowledge, or as it is properly called actual experience.

I do not maintain that five minutes is the same length of time as twelve hours; but that the difference between them is due solely to a difference in their material content. No distinct portion of time is, strictly speaking, pure time; the material element gives both its divisions and its determined length to every portion of time; so that, if you could abstract entirely from the material element, the portion of time called five minutes would in no respect differ from the portion of time called twelve hours, for all division and limitation of time would in that case be taken away. Now this cannot be done; consciousness requires both elements, formal and material. But the material element may be abstracted from so far as to leave only the divisions which it has impressed upon the formal element; and then there remains what is called time as a pure object, or time of determined lengths, e. g. five minutes, or twelve hours, which are of course different in point of length. When twelve hours are represented in five minutes or in a second, they differ from the second or the five minutes only in respect of their divisions and lengths enclosed by the divisions, that is, in respect of what they derive from their material element. The divisions and lengths of the twelve hours are objects of representation, the time itself is common both to the twelve hours represented and to the second in which they are represented. The twelve hours and the second are one object in one time, just as the visible landscape and the impression on the retina are one object in one space.

If representation differs from presentation only in the vividness, distinctness, and arrangement of its material element, then the formal element in presentation and in representation is the same; there is no difference between presentation and representation in so far as their formal element is concerned. In an object presented and in the same object represented the time and the space occupied is the same; the two objects differ only καιρῷ, i. e. in point of position in their times of being present to consciousness (which as will be seen farther on is the characteristic signalised by the term Sameness), and in certain changes in their material element. There is no corresponding change in their formal element. Just as it was shown above, that in presentative perception a space empty of feeling was still space, the matter of which was supplied by representation from other parts of space, so also in the objects of representation the omitted material element is what is supplied by representation, the formal element remains the same as before. It makes no difference whether the object present in consciousness is one of presentation or representation, the formal element in it is equally vivid in both cases. I do not say that it is equally distinct or the arrangement of its parts the same, because distinctness and arrangement of parts depend upon the material element contained in the object as well as upon its formal element; in other words, upon the division of the formal element by the material, as will be seen farther on. The presence, not of particular lengths, figures, or arrangement of parts, in the formal element, but of the formal element itself in the object, is equally certain and equally vivid in representation and in presentation. The same might be said of the material element itself, taken generally and in the abstract, that is, of feeling, if the word feeling could be understood as meaning not this or that particular feeling, but merely as signifying that representation involves feeling of some kind or other equally with presentation. Of feeling, however, the modes are innumerable, of the formal element the modes are only two, time and space; so that we can speak of time and space in their first intention with a definite precision incompetible to the object, feeling, in its first intention, for feeling has innumerable modes, while time and space have only divisions. Or to put the case in another way, it may be said that feeling is one object divided by time and space and co-extensive with them; but the feeling here and the feeling there, and there, and there, differ from each other in kind, as well as in position and quantity in time and space, and that innumerably and infinitely, while the parts of time and space so divided, though equally innumerable and infinite, differ not from each other in kind. And this I believe is what is meant by those who maintain, that, while feeling is a general and abstract term, time and space are not general and abstract, but particular, terms indicating objects or forms of thought of a particular nature. There is a time and a space distinct from every particular portion of either of them; the relation between those portions and time and space generally is that of parts to a whole. But there is no such thing as feeling distinct from every particular feeling; the

PART I.
CH. II.

§ 14.
The unity of phenomena in time.

relation between these is that between a logical abstract and general term and a logical concrete and particular term; feeling in the abstract can never be anything but a provisional image, but time and space are always also an actual image; feeling generally and time and space generally are wholes of very different kinds, and in two very different senses.

If then there is only one time and only one space, and if these are equally vivid in representation and in presentation, we may truly say that time and space are always presented, even in representation. The difference between presentation and representation lies solely in the material element. When I look straight before me I see a surface occupying "about a third of a circle, right and left, up and down;" this is the object of presentation. When I recall the fact that I can turn round and see a similar surface on all sides of me, the material element contained in those represented surfaces is less vivid than in the presented surface, and they are said to be represented on that ground; but the space contained in them is as vividly present as in the presented surface, and is presented to me in them, while the material element is represented only. When I interpret these surfaces by experiences drawn from the sense of touch, the surfaces become solid, and I find myself in a space of three dimensions presented to consciousness just as before. One and the same space in three dimensions is presented to me, disclosed indeed partially by one sense, partially by another, but completely by all together. There is one consciousness, and correspondingly there is one space, whatever may be the cause of there being but one of each. But what is meant by there being but one consciousness? This:

OF TIME AND SPACE.

that the feeling is continuous in point of time. Continuity of time and continuity of space interpret each other, for both are continuity of feeling in time. So also when I imagine a series of events, and objects in and about which they take place in the past or the future, the time in which they occurred or are yet to occur is presented to me; the past and the future are less vivid than the present only because the material element contained in them is less vivid. This leads to one of the fundamental differences between the formal and material elements. It is this, that the formal element, time and space, is not the object of sense, that is, of any particular sense whatever, but is the accompaniment of all and every of the senses in a more or less complete degree. By the term material element is meant the feeling contributed or perceived by some sense or some kind of sensibility. By the term formal element is meant something which accompanies the material element inseparably, but without being capable of being ascribed to, but which must be distinguished from, that sensibility and its proper object in every instance. If this is a true account of the difference between the formal and material elements, it makes it easy to understand how the formal element is presented even in representation; for it is involved in all consciousness, without depending on the degree of vividness of the sensations.

§ 15. The two elements of all consciousness and of all objects of consciousness are, according to what has been said, a priori and jenseit der Erfahrung, not as the occult causes of experience but as its metaphysically distinguishable elements. They are also necessary elements of consciousness and of all objects of consciousness; for by necessary I mean, as was said in the preceding chapter, the subjective aspect of universality. It is impossible to be conscious and not be conscious of a feeling in time and space. The proof of their necessity is direct, practical, empirical, inevitable. Since however we never have feeling in the abstract but always some determinate feeling, and determinate feelings are innumerable, while time and space, modes of the formal element, are two only; in other words, since feeling in its first intention is informal, unlimited, and we can only know about it that it is in consciousness, not what it is, while time and space we can know, in their first intention, not only that they are in consciousness, but also what they are (a distinction which has already been pointed out as one of the greatest importance between the equally necessary, formal and material, elements in consciousness), I shall cease noticing, except incidentally, the necessity of the material element, and speak only of that of the formal element, time and space. It may be said that we can have feelings not in space. I admit that the majority of our feelings, all except those of the senses of sight and touch, can be represented in consciousness with abstraction made of other feelings occupying space and of space-relations; I admit that in representation the abstraction of time from space is possible, so as to represent feelings in time alone without space, though it is impossible to represent feelings in space without time. But I assert that feelings so abstractedly represented as occupying time alone are provisional objects only, and never are represented without the proviso tacitly made that they exist in space as well as in time. I do not admit Hume's postulate, that whatever we can imagine to exist separately can possibly really exist separately. Whatever we imagine to exist separately does actually exist separately in the way in which we imagine it; now we imagine time to be provisionally separate from space; it is therefore provisionally separate from space; I do not grant that because we can provisionally separate them, they can exist actually separate. This postulate rests on the theory of two substances, of the object and its evidence in the mind, which I renounce. My imagining two things separate is taken for evidence of their being possibly separate in a world of absolute existences. No. My imagining two things separate is their being separate, so far as I can and do imagine them to be so. And this I admit to be the case with time and space, namely, that I can represent time to myself in a provisional image independent of space, space in a provisional image independent of time except the time occupied in representing it, and feeling in a provisional image independent of either or both, except the time occupied in representing it; consequently, that the provisional image of space includes, as its provisionally present elements, time and feeling; but that time may be represented in a provisional image of which feeling is a provisional element, but space only a provisional accompaniment. Feelings in time are never presented or represented separate from the provisional accompaniment of space; though this may be owing to their constant association by the simultaneous exercise of the different senses, or to some laws of nature which are the objective aspect of that association. Consciousness has two formal modes, time and space, different but inseparable and simultaneous; the two senses which reveal space, sight and touch, exist simultaneously with those which reveal time by itself; hence their inseparability in any way except provisionally; and hence the difference in the modes of connection between them, namely, that in all time there is involved space as its accompaniment, in all space there is involved time as its element.

Now as to the necessity of time and space, it is not said that they are necessary per se, or objectively, but that they are necessary to our consciousness, or subjectively. Universality, or presence in all objects without exception, is necessity subjectively, or in consciousness; they are two sides or aspects of the same phenomenon. Necessity, if used in an objective sense, can only be a conditioned necessity; for instance, if it rains, the earth will be wet; the earth will not necessarily be wet unless on the supposition that it rains. So in time and space objectively, if I say, all existence is necessarily existence in time and space, you directly ask me why? that is, under what condition I assert that it is so. Now universality cannot have an objective condition, for then it would not be universality. There is then no objective condition of this universal fact; and its necessity consists only in the knowledge of the fact, that is, it is its subjective aspect.

It is sometimes held that time and space are merely generalisations from experience. All abstract and general cognitions may be generalised from experience, and as those of time and space are general and abstract in the highest degree, they also may be generalised in the same way. But this property, which they possess in common with other general and abstract cognitions, does not prove that they do not possess other properties which are peculiar to themselves, and which distinguish them from others. And in point of fact they do possess such a property, namely, that they alone of all abstract and general cognitions cannot be annihilated in or banished from thought. It may be said that, after all, this is only apparently impossible because it never is so; and that the fact of its never being so, however strict that never may be, however much we may try to banish them and fail, is after all only an empirical impossibility; that it rests on a fact in the constitution of the universe which might be otherwise; that in short in order to show necessity we must do more than show empirical, contingent, universality; we must show the cause of that universality. But this is to take necessity in an objective sense, whereas I am arguing for it in a subjective sense, that is, as consisting not in being the cause of universality, but in being the subjective aspect of universality itself. A cause of universality is a contradictory notion, for universality, ex vi termini, must include its cause, which is absurd. But universality may be perceived, or imagined, or assumed, and in any of these ways it is subjective, and as such called necessity.

That the ultimate standard of any truth is the inconceivability of its negative has been conclusively shown, in my opinion, by Mr. Herbert Spencer, in his Principles of Psychology, Part I. § 6, 7. Objects are only given to us in consciousness, and what we cannot avoid being conscious of we call necessary. Whatever this world of existence may be or include besides, we have a starting-point for our knowledge of it, namely, the cognitions of time and space as the formal element in which all feeling exists; we know it only as the object of our consciousness, and we are unable to present or represent any object or any feeling to our consciousness except under these forms. In other words, time and space are necessary not because we know the causes which produce them, not because they depend on an innate or supersensual constitution of the mind or soul, but solely because their negation is inconceivable. It is the moment of consciousness which is decisive for itself and while it lasts. The effort to escape from these forms of consciousness is convincing to any man of their necessity to him at that moment at any rate. Every such effort only rivets them faster, for it supplies an instance of doing against your will the very thing which you labour not to do. You are trying to miss a mark which you are under an absolute compulsion to hit. So long as this is the case, so long must the marksman regard his mark as necessary. The view here taken rests on no theory of the objective constitution of the mind. Every theory which regards the mind and its forms of thought as objective existences, cannot attribute necessity, in the present sense, to either of them as such. The argument for the necessity of time and space can receive no support from any such theory; and on the other hand it cannot be weakened by any such theory, by any explanation relating to their origin or conditions of existence, such as will be found in the following chapter. What time and space as cognitions, or as forms of feeling, are, is a question to be kept entirely distinct from the question as to how we, or minds involved in bodies, come by them. Their nature, value, and importance to consciousness alone, are distinct from their history.

It is quite true that this subjective necessity is an

empirical fact, and it may appear to some that all cognitions which come from experience, that is, all empirical facts, are matters of fact only, and never contain in themselves necessity or a cognition that they must be as they are, as well as that they are so; and that therefore this subjective necessity is one in appearance only. But the appearance is in this case the reality. It is not an inference from the phenomenon, but an inseparable aspect of the phenomenon itself. It is to the empirical evidence of the necessity of time and space that appeal is made, to the fact in every one's experience that time and space are irremovable from consciousness, either in imagination or actual inspection of objects. Let any one try to think at all, and all his thoughts will presuppose them; or starting intentionally from within them he will find himself unable to transcend or go beyond them. The negation of every other object is conceivable, only not of these; for what is negation itself but the removing an object in imagination out of time and space? Consciousness is feeling in the forms of time and space.

Taking now time and space as separate objects, in which the material element is provisionally present, the following definitions of them, or analyses of them in their first intention, arise; part of which definitions has been proved by what has already been said, and part remains still to be proved in what follows. Time and Space as such objects are called the pure object.

TIME. Time has one dimension—length. It is infinitely divisible in thought; it is infinitely extensible in thought. It admits of no minimum in division, and of no maximum in extension. For these reasons it contains every thing; nothing is short enough to slip through it, nothing long enough to outrun it. It is one in nature, for all its parts are still time. It is incompressible, for no single part can be annihilated.

SPACE. Space has three dimensions,—length, breadth, and depth. It is infinitely divisible in thought; it is infinitely extensible in thought. It admits of no minimum in division, and of no maximum in extension. For these reasons it contains every thing; nothing is small enough to slip through it, nothing is great enough to outstand it. It is one in nature, for all its parts are still space. It is incompressible, for no single part can be annihilated.

We thus obtain such a datum as is required by Mr. Spencer in his Principles of Psychology, Part 1. chap. 1, 2. as the beginning of all philosophy; a datum within the limits of consciousness, a belief or a cognition. The characteristic, or second intention, of such a datum, namely, that it must be an immediate ineradicable belief, does not give the datum itself in its first intention, does not tell us what the datum is. Belief is no datum, but the characteristic of certain classes of data. Feeling, the material element in consciousness, though a necessary and universal element, and ineradicably certain, offers no criterion for distinguishing one phenomenon from another, for it is the same in all phenomena alike; it is impossible to say *what* it is in its first intention. Time and space alone unite the properties of being immediately and ineradicably certain, of being universally present in all phenomena, of being knowable in their first intention and defined as what they are. and of being in nature the same, in all objects however different. They thus become the common basis or bond of union between all other cognitions, and as such the starting-point and corner-stone of philosophy.

The importance to philosophy of having some necessary truth as its corner-stone,—whether innate or connate is indifferent, so long as it is necessary,—consists in this, but without such a truth there would be no criterion of reasoning, phenomena of presentative perception would alone be true, and no inference from them would be valid; all reasoning would be hypothetical and tentative, and entered on, as the Sceptics said, ἀδοξάστως, that is, without entertaining an opinion as to its truth, but only as to its utility or its convenience. Scepticism would in that case be the only philosophy possible; and the only solution of problems the unphilosophical one of Solvitur ambulando. If now there were no such necessary truth discoverable, the only philosophical course, however much against the grain, would clearly be to admit the fact, and to live and reason under protest, ἀδοξάστως, as the Sceptics said. It would be impossible in that case to reject the argument of the Sceptics as to our ignorance of any criterion of truth; for, according to that well-known argument, a criterion is requisite before we can prove anything, and proof is requisite before we can admit a criterion. Sextus Emp. Pyrrh. Hyp. lib. II. cap. 3, 4. It is clear that reasoning goes on equally under both suppositions, the Sceptics reason equally with those who hold the doctrine of necessary truth; but the nature and therefore the value of this process of reasoning is the point in question. Only if reasoning contains a necessary element can it be distinguished from other processes of which we are conscious, for only then can it contain truth.

Without such an element, the process of reasoning contains no more truth than the process of walking or of eating. With such an element, it is the process of acquiring true and systematic knowledge. All men reason; the question is, what is the nature of that process which all alike perform, and of the results which all alike reach. It will be my endeavour to show, and to show by analysis, that this process and its results, whatever they may be, do as a fact contain a necessary element, and the same necessary element which is contained in the process of presentative perception and in the simplest instances of consciousness. No one, not even the Sceptic, doubts the reality of a phenomenon, while it is a phenomenon. The Sceptic doubts not its reality but its truth; he doubts that its nature can be discovered, because he doubts that its nature is perceived. But its nature is perceived; in every phenomenon is perceived its formal and its material element; and the same formal element is perceived in every phenomenon, namely, its time and its space. The criterion and its proof, instead of moving in a vicious circle, coincide; instead of presupposing each other as a condition, they are given at once in one cognition; both characters are borne at once both by time and by space. Neither the formal nor the material element need any demonstration, for they together constitute the phenomenon. But the formal element, as being the same in all phenomena, is the source of their truth, the starting-point of all demonstration. The criterion therefore, which the Sceptics require to be proved, is as certain as the phenomena to which it is to be applied, and about which the Sceptics do not doubt. See Sextus Emp. Pyrrh. Hyp. lib. II. cap. 9. τί ἐστί τι φύσει ἀληθές.

§ 16. The most important feature in time and space is their divisibility without residuum, or their exhaustive divisibility. It will be seen in the second Part that on this property depends the whole of logic and the postulates. Divisions are introduced into pure continuous time and space by the material element in cognition; where one sensation ends, another begins; where one colour for instance ends, or where one sound ends, another begins; and in emotions, when we cease to be affected by one feeling, we begin to be affected by another. There is nothing intermediate between the two sensations or feelings. Wherever we are conscious of a difference in feeling, whether it is between colours on a surface, or between feeling resistance to touch and ceasing to feel it, or between the presence and absence of any feeling, there time and space are divided. Now between two such states of consciousness we are accustomed to speak as if a line of division existed, or as if a point of time intervened, which lines or points were themselves portions of space or of time. By using this language we render ourselves liable to one of two opposite errors, and lay ourselves open to one of two opposite objections. Either this line in space and this point in time are conceived as occupying space and time, and then they become themselves subject to be divided again, in conformity to Aristotle's principle, Nat. Ausc. lib. VI. cap. 1. § 3. τῶν συνεχῶν διαιρετῶν εἰς ἀεὶ διαιρετά, and then we have only added to the portions of time and space which need to be divided, and have not really divided them at all; or the line is conceived as length without breadth, and the point is conceived as containing no quantity of time, and both thus become unreal, inasmuch as they are inconceivable as separate objects of consciousness. If we choose to adopt the terms point, line, surface, as divisions of space, and the term point, or present moment, as a division of time, we must bear in mind, while we do so, that these terms are names not of objects but of operations, of events, the result of which they express; that they have no separate existence, but are modes of representing the fact of a division in consciousness; the instantaneous change in the current of our consciousness, and of which we are conscious, is rendered plain to us under the figure of a visual line or point of demarcation,—a line or point which cannot be an object of consciousness, except the two objects which it divides are present in consciousness, when it exists as a modification, part, or element, of that whole divided object.

Space, metaphysically considered, has nothing to do with the geometrical abstractions of points, lines, and surfaces. As these terms are used in geometry they are abstractions, or qualities on which the attention is fixed to the exclusion of other qualities which are equally essential to the nature of the object common to both. 'A point has no parts and no magnitude,' that is, we attend to its position alone. 'A line is length without breadth,' that is, we attend to its length alone. 'A surface has length and breadth alone,' that is, we abstract from its depth. These are concepts, or, as I prefer to call them at present, provisional images, of objects of perception, formed by abstraction for certain scientific purposes. If now we speak of space being divided by points, lines, and surfaces, meaning such abstractions as just described, we lay ourselves open to misunderstanding, either as if we asserted space to be divided by objects which, as having no separate objective existence, but being abstractions formed for the convenience of geometers, are unreal; or as if we took actual empirically known portions of space, which are themselves liable to division, such as actually visible points, lines, and surfaces with some depth, as the means of dividing space without a residuum. But metaphysical divisions are real objects; nevertheless not separable from the objects, or the two parts of the object, which they divide, but are as inseparable in consciousness from the divided object as the material and formal elements themselves are. Mathematically points, lines, and surfaces are treated by themselves as provisional images; but metaphysically no division exists, even in thought, apart from the objects or object divided by it. How then comes mathematic to be able to treat the divisions apart? It is because it starts, not from the metaphysical divisions, but from visual or tangible lines or divisions; or supposing it to start from the metaphysical divisions, it begins by imagining these, the points, lines, and surfaces, to be separate empirical objects, and then abstracts from them respectively length, breadth, and depth, still treating them as separate but provisional objects; for this is the special purpose which mathematic has in view, namely, to ascertain the possible modes of dividing pure space and time, and the relations and laws of relation of their parts or quanta. Not only in its method, which is abstraction from assumed empirical objects, but also in its purpose or scope, mathematic is a special and conditioned science, in the same sense, though not in the same degree, as other special sciences are, as political economy for instance. Metaphysic points out what this condition is, namely, that the divisions, points, lines, and surfaces, are hypostasised by mathematic, that is, made into or treated as if they were empirical objects, from which abstraction of length, breadth, and depth could be made. The divisions in mathematic and metaphysic are the same ultimately; that is, are inseparable from the objects which they divide; but the difference is, that, while in metaphysic they bear this character all along, from beginning to end of its procedure (for the scope of metaphysic is to examine what they really are), in mathematic they reach it only by abstraction of properties which have been attributed to them by mathematic itself for its own purposes; mathematic first imagines that its divisions have a separate, empirical existence, and then abstracts from them portions or elements of this existence; it first makes them concrete, and then makes them abstract, in order to investigate how space and time may be divided, and the relations which its divided parts bear to each other.

Space metaphysically considered is not divided by points, lines, and surfaces at all, understand the terms as we will, either as geometrical abstractions, or as empirical visible or tangible objects. When two sensations limit each other in consciousness, when we are conscious of a change in sensation, space is already divided; and if a line of demarcation is perceived, it is as the result of the process and not as the condition of it; that is, the objects on both sides of the demarcation are perceived before the demarcation itself. The same is the case with sensations in time. The change from one sensation to another is instantaneous, and the moment in which it takes

place is empirically indivisible. Even when there is
a series of changes, each so slight that we cannot
name, can hardly even perceive it, even then the
moment when we do perceive each change in the
series is indivisible. There is no time occupied in
the passage, for we are conscious all the time, and
are conscious of none. Hence the division is exhaustive, without residuum. Time is bisected in a
moment, no time elapsing between the two segments.
The indivisibility of the moment of division, change,
or transition, in consciousness, is the fact which constitutes or necessitates the indivisibility of the point
or line of demarcation in objects, considered as such,
both in time and space. We have nothing to do
with the points, lines, and surfaces of geometry, and
are clear of all such controversies as whether these
are portions of space or not; whether solids consist
of, or are divisible into, or are formed by the motion
of surfaces; whether surfaces hold similar relations
to lines, and lines to points; and whether points,
lines, and surfaces exist really as they are geometrically conceived to exist; and clear also of the corresponding questions about time, such as whether
time is composed of present moments, τὰ νῦν, and
how long such a present moment is to be conceived
to last. It is enough for the metaphysician, that
experience shows that, by means of the material element in consciousness, divisions are introduced into
time and space, divisions which occupy no portion of
time and space, except as belonging to the portions
which they divide, and which therefore cannot be
again divided. These divisions are not objects by
themselves, either empirical or provisional; they are
not portions of time and space; they cannot be pre-

PART I.
CH. II.

§ 16.
The exhaustive
divisibility of
time and space.

PART I.
CH. II.

§ 16.
The substantive divisibility of time and space.

sented to consciousness alone, apart from the sensations of which they are divisions; but they inhere in sensations; they are dividings not divisions, modes of sensation, acts of consciousness, which do not become independent objects because we afterwards express them by empirical extended signs, as lines and points. Did these acts occupy an empirical moment of time, we should be conscious of them during the transition; but this is not the case; we are conscious only of the change when it has happened, and when the terminus a quo and the terminus ad quem are visible at once. Empirically speaking and with reference to the minima of consciousness in time and space, it is true to say βιβάδικιν οὐ βαδίζον· for as an empirical moment of time the moment of transit is indivisible.

The moment that we fix our attention on the division itself, that moment we erect it into an object, and must conceive or imagine it as occupying time and space, and not merely as dividing them; but this need not, and cannot, be as occupying time and space by itself, but together with the feelings on each side of it, between which it is the limit. This is a second step; we have the division completed before we need to take this step, and we need to take the step at all only in the interest of the geometer or mathematician or logician, not in that of the metaphysician until he becomes a logician. The consideration of divisions as instrumenta divisionis of time and space, as objects expressed by points, lines, and surfaces, belongs to the mathematician; that of time and space themselves and their division in consciousness, apart from the mode in which that division is expressed, is the business of the metaphysician.

When Aristotle says, Every continuous quantity, whether of time, space, or motion, is divisible into portions which are again divisible into other portions, and so on for ever, he assumes the fact of divisibility without a residuum in the sense in which it is here intended; by the division of a continuous quantity he means its division into two or more portions which are exhaustive of the whole, without waste, so to speak, in the section. This divisibility arises from the changes in sensation, in the objects of perception, time and space being united with a material element in cognition; and its being done without waste or residuum is due to no other cause than this, that the change of which we are conscious from one sensation to another occupies not two moments of consciousness, but one, a moment, as we call it, empirically indivisible, no moment intervening between the two sensations which is occupied by neither of them. It is true that there may appear to intervene a mixture of two sensations; but this is in cases where we see less instead of more clearly. And then the mixed sensation is to be itself again distinguished from its two simple sensations, so that there will be two moments of change and transition instead of one, and three objects divided from each other instead of two. If blue and yellow run into each other on a coloured surface, the green which appears between them may occupy space, but there will be three portions of space to be distinguished instead of two; we gain nothing by removing the question a step farther. The point to be observed is, that there is no intermediate space, which is neither blue nor yellow nor green. This fact in consciousness I name the divisibility of time and space exhaustively, or without a residuum.

§ 17. It remains to consider the infinity of time and space. Infinity no less than necessity when predicated of time and space is a relative term, that is, applicable to consciousness only, or to objects in relation to a Subject. Those two objects, in or under which we perceive all other objects, are themselves objects of consciousness and have no absolute character. As such objects they are infinite, that is, they cannot be transcended by consciousness, but must always be before the mind when it is conscious. Consequently they cannot be seen or thought of as complete wholes. It is this character of time and space which is marked by the word Infinite.

Aristotle, who seems to have tried to eliminate the infinite, τὸ ἄπειρον, from philosophy as far as he could, is yet constrained to admit that it leads to contradictions to deny the infinite in all senses of the term. In the Nat. Ausc. book III. ch. 6, he says: "Ὅτι δ' εἰ μή ἐστιν ἄπειρον ἁπλῶς πολλὰ ἀδύνατα συμβαίνει, δῆλον· τοῦ τε γὰρ χρόνου ἔσται τις ἀρχὴ καὶ τελευτή, καὶ τὰ μεγέθη οὐ διαιρετὰ εἰς μεγέθη, καὶ ἀριθμὸς οὐκ ἔσται ἄπειρος. "Ὅταν δὲ διωρισμένων οὕτως μηδετέρως φαίνηται ἐνδέχεσθαι, διαιτητοῦ δεῖ, καὶ δῆλον ὅτι πῶς μὲν ἔστι, πῶς δ' οὔ. The umpire which he needs he finds in his ruling distinction of δύναμις and ἐντελέχεια. But this is vague to modern minds, and requires interpretation; and moreover Aristotle does not follow it to the full extent of its guiding power, for he will not allow an ἄπειρον κατὰ πρόσθεσιν in space to exist even δυνάμει. But it is a weighty support to the view taken in this Essay, that the infinity of time and that of space, μεγέθη, in some sense, is placed by Aristotle among the facts to be explained by any true theory of these matters.

But even against the relative infinity which is here maintained as appertaining to time and space there are arguments brought forward, apparently conclusive, arguments which bring us back to the position of Aristotle in search of an umpire, for they seem to show that the conception of an infinite in any sense is an impossible one, that is, that it involves contradictions; and consequently that we can think neither of time nor of space nor of any other nameable object whatever as infinite.

The relative infinity here maintained has two modes in space and two in time; that is, time is infinite in extension, κατὰ πρόσθεσιν, and in division, κατὰ διαίρεσιν, and space the same; in other words, time and space cannot be divided so far that they are not divisible farther, nor extended so far that they are not extensible farther; and must be so represented in thought. Now it is these assertions which are on the other side alleged to contain, implicitly, contradictions; and since it is asserted at the same time that the opposite view to this, the view namely that time and space are finite, that is, that in division and extension a point can be reached beyond which we can neither divide nor extend farther, is also one which involves contradictions; and that, since by the logical laws of contradiction and excluded middle one of these views must be false, and the other, its contradictory, must be true, while both as involving contradictions can be shown, as is alleged, to be false, the mind in its consciousness is thrown into contradictions with itself from which there is apparently no escape. But it is the business of philosophy to reconcile apparent contradictions, not to acquiesce in them. Contradictions unsolved are the stronghold of scepticism, and that class of contradictions now under discussion was the stronghold of the philosophical sect of Sceptics in Greece, contradictions which were not solved but overridden by Neo-Platonism. Kant attempted their solution in the Antinomies of Pure Reason; and Hegel took them up and incorporated them in his logical system, which renders his system the most profound and complete system of Ontology which has ever been proposed; but it is unsatisfactory, not because it incorporates and therefore solves these contradictions, but because it does so only by recourse to Ontology. He maintains that Contradiction is the ultimate essence and the ultimate law of all things, of the universe and all its parts from the greatest to the least, thus bringing all things indeed to the same level, but not by bringing the contradictory up to the level of the non-contradictory, but by bringing the non-contradictory down to the level of the contradictory; and this is only possible by transforming logical and relative notions into absolute entities, that is, by making the assumption that metaphysic is a science of the Absolute, that is, an Ontology. Ontology is like an attempt to leap off from one's own shadow; it attempts to predicate a second intention of the Sum of things as such; as if the Sum of things could, as such, be related to anything else in consciousness, and as if it must not always be related to consciousness itself; reflect on this relation, of the Sum of things to consciousness, and then that consciousness is included in the Sum of things, and the consciousness which reflects on both together takes the place of that consciousness now included in the Sum of things; repeat the process for ever, and nothing further comes out of it, never is an

Absolute reached, or a Sum of things represented not as an object of consciousness; a fortiori therefore the Sum of things cannot have a second intention out of consciousness; any second intention which it can have must be an aspect, or a differentiation, of itself in consciousness. I argue therefore that, if the universe is in its essence, or in one of its aspects, a contradiction, this is either to render it unintelligible, taken as a metaphysical explanation; or else it is to be taken as an ontological explanation, and then it rests on a misconception of what is possible. Consequently we can neither rest in contradictions remaining unsolved, nor acquiesce in Hegel's solution of them.

The mode, in which I propose to solve the apparent contradictions involved in the infinity and the finity of time and space, is to show first, that their infinity does not involve contradictions, and secondly, that this infinity is not contradictory to their finity, though there is a sense in which their finity is true; but that their finity and infinity are not predicated of them secundum idem, or from the same point of view. Now to instance in the extensibility of space, one c the four modes of infinity mentioned above, which I take as an example fairly representative of the other three, and as involving the rest in its fate. Mr. Mansel quotes from Werenfels such a proof as is mentioned above of the non-infinity of space in the notes to his Bampton Lectures for 1858. Lect. 2. note 15. p. 301. 3d edit.

Videtis hanc lineam b_____a_____c. Constituamus eam esse infinitam, et ultra terminos b et c in infinitum protendi. Dividatur hæc linea in puncto a. Manifestum est has partes inter se esse æquales; quia utraque incipit in puncto a, et protenditur in infinitum. Nunc te, Dædale, rogo; hæ duæ partes sunt-ne finitæ an infinitæ? D. Finitæ. Ph. Ita ex duobus finitis componeretur infinitum; quod repugnat. D. Fateor errorem. Infinitæ sunt. Ph. Jam in Scyllam incidis: ita partes essent æquales toti; infinitum enim infinito æquale est. Præterea vides utramque partem in puncto a terminari; non igitur finibus et terminis caret.

The argument proceeds farther, but rests always on the same principles which are here involved; and as I am not going to allege either the objection supposed by Werenfels, nor with Spinoza and Clarke that infinite quantity is not composed of parts, at least as an escape from this reasoning, I need not quote the rest of the passage. I agree with the remark quoted in the same note from Clarke, that infinites are not equals; and for the answer to this reasoning I look to the distinction between voluntary and involuntary modes of consciousness, which I hold to be the ground of the distinction between conceiving and imagining, a concept being an imagination or a perception seized and limited by volition, as will be more fully drawn out in a following chapter.

Διαιτητοῦ δεῖ. I find that umpire in the distinction between voluntary and involuntary, logical and intuitive, processes, between perception, representation, imagination, and these limited by volition. The strength of the argument quoted above lies in a covert passing over from one mode to the other, in substituting a definition for an intuition and in substituting a wrong definition, or in including in the object defined what was not included in it as perceived. What is the meaning of Infinity as maintained above in this Essay? It is, that space, in this case the line bc, cannot be so far extended in either direction as to be incapable of further extension. A fortiori, its limit cannot be assigned. But an assigned limit is requisite in order to compare it, as to its length, with another line, or to compare the two lines ab, ac, together, and to assert, Manifestum est has partes inter se esse æquales. They are not known as equals until a limit has been assigned to them, besides the common limit in the point a. This assumption of equality therefore violates the hypothesis, Ultra terminos b et c in infinitum protendi. But it may be said, Are not two infinites equal though we do not know their limits? I answer that they are not, until the objects to which the name is applied in each instance are compared. Thus there is substituted for the object of perception named infinite, that is, an object of which we can never see the whole, a defined object, of which, solely because it is defined, we are supposed to see the whole. The objects, the two lines extended from the point a, are not equal, but they have one property in common, that of being greater than we can present to ourselves in consciousness; they are equal not quâtenus objects, but quâtenus infinite; their infinity is equal, not their length; but the question is not about the length of their infinity, but about the infinity of their length; and about this, whether it exists at all. The definition of both from the same point of view, the logical category or genus under which they fall, that of infinites, is the same; but the objects are not the same, nor is their extent the same. If the matter of the comparison, instead of being the same, as two lines or two spaces, had been different, as for instance a line of time and a line of space, or a line and a surface, or a line and a solid, the fallacy would be seen in a moment. But the case is really the same, when two objects of the same kind, as when two objects of different kinds are compared. It makes no difference at all whether the two objects compared together fall alike under one or two or more definitions of kind. It is as objects that they are compared together, different in numero, and, in this case of the infinite lines, in order to see whether they are equal, or with reference to their equality in point of extent; and that they are both to be defined as infinite does not show that they are, but in fact precludes their being, defined as equal. And this appears to be Clarke's argument, or part of it.

Let us fix our attention on the facts as perceived. It is perfectly true that in making infinite space, or infinite time, a distinct object of consciousness, we are compelled to introduce a limit into them. To become a distinct object is to become subject to limitation. The object space, limited by consciousness, is not infinite so far as it is included within those limits set by consciousness, but the consciousness of space is extensible ad infinitum, we can go on being conscious of further and further portions of limited space without ever reaching a limit not set by ourselves, by weariness in exertion of consciousness; and all these further portions of space are still space in kind, each portion is limited only by another of the same nature. Here we have an infinite series of limited, finite, portions of space; but now comes out another fact in the production of this series. Wherever we are compelled to draw our line and stop, we perceive time and space beyond, which we resolve not to present in detail or as a distinct object to consciousness. It was shown in the preceding section, that a limit cannot be set without the objects on both sides of it being perceived. Thus before a limit is set to space, the unlimited space beyond it is perceived as well as the limited space within it. The object, infinite space, is space limited on one side of the last limit, and unlimited on the other side of it. If we stopped at the last limit, then it would be only the series of finite portions of space which was infinite, while the whole would be composed of finite portions; then space would be infinite indeed potentially but finite actually; there would be no contradiction, but space as finite would be the object of presentative perception, while space as infinite would be a mere potentiality. But as it is, a limit is not a thing which it is possible to stop at; a space beyond is perceived before the limit is perceived and while the limit is perceived; the limit is introduced into space, and does not confine space but a part of space only. Thus space as infinite is an object of presentative perception. This is what is meant by the infinite extensibility of space, and it is a fact of perception. And this fact is not impugned, though often supposed to be so, by the proof that none of the portions of space which have become distinct objects of consciousness, nor all of them taken together, are infinite.

It may put the matter in a clearer light, and exhibit the ground of the false appearance of contradiction between the two impossibilities, of regarding space and time as finite on the one hand and infinite on the other, to state the case thus. We cannot imagine time and space as finite. Why? Because our consciousness is limited in its nature, time and space being its modes. We cannot make time and space, as infinite, a distinct object. Why? Because our consciousness is limited in its degree of power. And again, keeping in view the distinction, to be hereafter more fully explained, between conceiving and imagining, we must conceive time and space as finite. Why? Because consciousness in one of its modes, namely conception, is voluntary limitation or imposing of a limit. We must imagine them as infinite. Why? Because so long as we are conscious we are conscious of time and space. Time and space are limited only by incapacity of exhausting them, that is, of continuing to be conscious of them; and the limit imposed upon them is imposed by our volition. Conception is imagination limited by a voluntary effort and for a certain purpose. But when an object is limited by volition, the object so limited is not the contradictory of an unlimited object, unless that object is voluntarily unlimited; for the two objects are then not limited and unlimited secundum idem. The object time, or space, is limited and unlimited at once, and is one object, but is not limited and unlimited in the same sense, or from the same point of view. Time and space as finite are concepts, that is, are limited by volition; as such they are not contradictories of time and space as infinite; this would require that their infinity should be imposed by volition, which it is not. Time and space as finite are modes of voluntary consciousness, of consciousness adopting a purposed limitation; as infinite they are modes of involuntary consciousness, which we can never transcend so long as we are conscious at all.

Aristotle tells us, Nat. Ausc. b. III. cap. 6. § 7. that the Pythagoreans and others, against whom he was arguing, defined the infinite, τὸ ἄπειρον, as that οὗ μηδὲν ἔξω ἐστί. He himself, starting from the contemplation of the infinite κατὰ διαίρεσιν, defines it as that οὗ ἀεί τι ἔξω ἐστί. But though neither definition is adequate or correct taken alone, yet taken together they are applicable to both modes of the infinite in time, and to both in space. Thus the true definition of the infinite is Quod nihil ultra se habet præter se ipsum. Time is never limited except by time; space never except by space; but both are limited by themselves always. Thus Hegel says, Logik, Book 1. Abschnitt 1. p. 136, Werke, vol. 3. Darin selbst, dass etwas als Schranke bestimmt ist, darüber bereits hinausgegangen ist. That is, all limitation involves an outside as well as an inside. This fact is nothing else but the fact of the infinity of intuition or imagination in time and space.

The problem of the infinity of time and space has been thrown into a complete shape in our days by Sir W. Hamilton and Mr. Mansel; and it must be remembered that prudens quæstio dimidium scientiæ est. The question is not simply, Is there an infinite in time and space or is there not? But it is: The infinite is impossible, therefore its contradictory only exists, namely the finite; yet the finite is impossible, therefore its contradictory only exists, namely the infinite; reconcile these reverberated contradictions. The way which has been taken here seems to offer a satisfactory solution of this problem, for it has shown on the one hand, that there is not only negative but positive ground for affirming the infinite in one sense; and not only negative but positive ground for affirming the finite in another sense; and on the other hand, that the infinite in the sense in which it is affirmed is not open to the charge of involving contradictions (for the infinite is not a concept but a percept), and thus necessitating the substitution of the finite; and that the finite also in the sense in which it is affirmed is equally secure from the same charge, and thus necessitating the substitution of the infinite. In other words, it has been shown that the finite and the infinite are not contradictories, but products of consciousness in two separate parts of its domain or in two separate functions.

But now, if it is admitted that the apparent contradiction, involved first in each view taken separately, and secondly and consequently in the two views taken together, has been dissolved, and that time and space are shown to be in one sense finite, and in another infinite, a further question arises, which is this: Of the two attributes finite and infinite, resting each on its own ground and predicated from its own point of view, which is the most essential, the most fundamental, expressing best the nature of time and space; or, what comes to the same thing, which point of view is the most commanding, which is that to which the other is subordinate? There can be but one answer. It is that point of view which keeps equally in sight both object and subject. Time and space when they are treated as objects only, their subjective character being lost sight of for the moment, when they are considered as having already become objects of consciousness, are then regarded as finite. The point of view from which they are called finite, is that from which they are regarded as objects of cognition only. That from which they are called infinite is one from which the moment of their passing into consciousness is seized and fixed on, in which their relation to consciousness in the very act of our being conscious of them is weighed and described. This point of view therefore, which keeps their subjective and objective character equally in sight, is that which is decisive of their ultimate or innermost character, and that to which the other point of view is subordinate. The finite character of time and space is subordinate to their infinite character.

Subordinate not contradictory, since the two characters are not predicated from the same point of view, as has been shown. The nature of our consciousness in presence of objects compels us to think of time and space as limited by nothing but themselves, and as always limited by themselves. Our incapacity to exhaust them is their infinity. But every step we make towards exhausting them is a limitation, all that we can distinctly include within our ken is finite. Nor is there any contradiction here to what has been said above, that the limitation of the degree of our power is the cause why we cannot present them to our conception as infinite. To conceive them as infinite would involve a contradiction. But though this cannot be done, yet it will be seen in the last chapter of this Essay, that we can imagine or represent it as done, represent it as an actual conception. There will then arise, not a conception of the infinite, but a conception of such a conception, a represented conception; and such represented, or anticipated, conceptions of the infinite are called Ideas.

CHAPTER III.

PSYCHOLOGICAL.

THE ORIGIN OF THE COGNITIONS OF TIME AND SPACE.

ἓν μέν τι γίνεσιν πάντων, τὴν δὲ οὐσίαν ἕτερον ἕν.
— Plato.

§ 18. HERE we leave that central point of view which embraces at once subject and object, and pass over into the objective kingdom, that of objects as such and their connections between themselves. We make abstraction of the principium cognoscendi, and consider only the principium existendi. Cognitions themselves are existences, for they are objects; the evidence of their existence is our consciousness. If what has been said in the preceding chapter of the nature and value of the two cognitions, time and space, as the starting-point of all philosophical analysis, and the ens unum in multis in all cognitions, is admitted, it is of secondary importance what theory is held as to their origin in the mind.

The objective kingdom is the kingdom of empirical, that is, complete objects, as opposed to elements of objects, or members of analysis of objects, which have become objects only in conjunction with each other. Such elements of objects can never be regarded as causes or the cause of the objects of which they are elements; for in the first place all the elements of the object give and receive meaning and existence from each other first in combination, and in this same combination the object also which they compose first exists; the object and its elements are simultaneous in existence, and not one precedent, the other subsequent; and in the second place, were the elements regarded as existing first and separately, a further cause would have to be sought, a cause of their being brought into conjunction in the object. All causation, all history, must accordingly be distinguished from metaphysical analysis, and must be conceived as obtaining between empirical or complete objects, considered as former and latter in point of time.

The result of the analysis in the preceding chapter was, that every instance of consciousness contained two elements, formal and material, that is, some particular feeling in some particular time and some particular space; which is equivalent to saying, that every object of consciousness contained two elements, formal and material, that is, some particular quality in some particular time and some particular space; for that which is feeling from the subjective point of view is quality from the objective. The elements in every cognition are time, space, and feeling, and in every object are time, space, and quality. Consciousness is feeling in time and space; objects are qualities in time and space. But when it is said, Consciousness generally is feeling in time and space, attention must be called to an ambiguity in the term feeling, as in all general and abstract terms. It is the same ambiguity which kept up the Nominalist and Realist controversy, and is so natural and almost unavoidable that its influence has long outlived, as it

PART I.
CH. III.

§ 18.
The object of psychology.

long preceded, that controversy. When an abstract and general term is used, for instance roundness, is it imagined by speaker or hearer to be an object itself apart from all and every particular and determinate instance of roundness, from which it is generalised? Every one will say that it is not; but not every one will be on his guard against so employing and imagining it. In the case of feeling, this abstract and general term feeling may be taken as indicating the class of all the particular and determinate feelings, without specifying any of them, or it may be taken as indicating feeling by itself, as a real substratum, but without any particular determinate feeling; it may be imagined either as having no determination, but still really existing, or as having some determination, but one not specified or expressed. In the latter sense it may be called a provisional image, but a provisional image doubly abstract, or doubly provisional; for first all particular modes of the formal elements of time and space are abstracted from, secondly the determinate feelings are abstracted from, that is, are retained provisionally only in the general and abstract notion expressed by the term feeling. And this is the sense in which the term will be employed here. See Hume, who refers to Berkeley, on this subject, Treatise of Human Nature, Part I. § 7.

Consciousness then being feeling in time and space, the three elements being in every instance and in every object inseparable, constituting one complete, empirical, object of consciousness, it follows that to assign the cause or invariable condition of the origin of its one element, time and space, is impossible without assigning also the cause or invariable condition of the origin of its other element, feeling; and thus the question as to the origin of the cognitions of time and space is bound up with the question as to the origin of consciousness itself as a whole.

But again consciousness as a whole, consisting of these elements, is one aspect of the entire universe, and, since time and space its inseparable elements are infinite, is infinite also, and no question as to its origin can possibly arise. It is not therefore concerning consciousness as the subjective aspect of the world of qualities that the question of origin is put, but concerning the mind, the conscious life of the individual consciousness, the object of psychology, distinguished from consciousness in the former sense, in § 13, as being those feelings which are localised and circumscribed by the body, which is a particular portion of the world of qualities. The mind, or consciousness as inhabiting the body, is the object of which the origin and the history is sought; not the whole, but a part of the world of feelings cut off from the rest by the fact of their having always the same set of qualities as their object, whatever other qualities they may have for objects besides, and limited to the space occupied by that set of qualities. This objective mind is sometimes taken as if it were the whole of the subjective aspect of the universe; the object of psychology, as if it were the object of metaphysic; and the error of so doing will become apparent in the course of the present enquiry, which seeks to discover the origin of the mind.

In the preceding chapter the distinction was drawn between elements and aspects of phenomena, and the distinction between the two aspects of phenomena, the subjective and the objective, was said to be a distinction perceived by reflection. The diagram there employed to make this clear was a circle, supposed to be seen from two sides by a person changing his point of view from one side to the other; and this person symbolised reflection. But in fact reflection arises within those very phenomena, and is one of them. It neither divides the aspects from each other, nor itself from either of them; but distinguishes them into feelings and qualities, every phenomenon being feeling and quality at once; and for reflection both feelings and qualities are objects, but only qualities are objects for direct consciousness; for feelings are perceived by reflection as direct consciousness itself. But in the mode of reflection which is entered on in this chapter, psychological not metaphysical reflection, the object of enquiry is the mind, an object consisting partly of feelings and partly of qualities; which latter must be included in the object, since the circumscription of the feelings is given by them; and since the former, the feelings of the mind, are circumscribed by the latter, the body, they are divided in space from other feelings. Psychological reflection therefore may be represented as standing between the two objects of which it examines the connection, between the mind on the one side and the world of qualities outside it on the other; the mind occupying a distinct portion of space by being placed in the body. Now any particular portion of the world of feelings may have an origin and a history, conditions of existence and of development, a place in order of time in the whole world of feelings, as well as a place in space; and the question of this chapter is, what are the conditions of existence, what objects, feelings or qualities, must invariably precede the appearance, of that portion of the world of feelings known as the mind. This is the sense in which alone it is legitimate to speak of the origin or conditions of existence of consciousness. But since I am about to examine some classes of already existing theories, and this distinction as here drawn is not recognised in them, but consciousness is treated as capable of isolation, as an object by itself, without reference to the condition of this isolation, namely, its inhabiting a particular portion of the world of qualities, I shall not at first insist on this point, but take consciousness in the way in which it is presented in those theories. And it will afterwards be pointed out how the want of this distinction enables theories, which are at least legitimate while partial and subordinate, to pass into theories of the same class which are illegitimate because put forward as complete; for instance, it will be seen how the partial and subordinate psychological theories, which refer consciousness respectively to a soul and to a brain, become theories of absolute idealism and absolute materialism.

§ 19. All theories, possible and actual, as to the origin of consciousness may be divided, first, into such as place its cause in an object outside of consciousness, inferred to be its cause from examination of the phenomena, and such as place its cause in an object within consciousness, revealed by an analysis of consciousness itself. Another division of such theories is the division into such as are idealistic, seeking the cause of consciousness in an immaterial object or essence, and such as are materialistic, seeking its cause in a material object and its properties. A third division is into such as place the cause of consciousness in an object or essence considered statically, and such as place it in a movement or an activity, which theories may be called dynamical. All theories must fall, since these divisions are each of them exhaustive, under one alternative at least of each of these three pairs.

Taking the first of these divisions as a basis, the theories of the other two divisions may be referred to it. Then under those theories which infer an object to be the cause of consciousness will fall those idealistic theories which assert an immaterial soul, considered as an object existing statically, and those materialistic theories which assert a material object, as the brain or nervous matter, to be the cause of consciousness, considered also statically, or as existing previous to its operation. Under those theories which hold that the cause of consciousness lies within consciousness, and is revealed by an analysis of consciousness, will fall those idealistic theories which assert an Ego, considered dynamically as pure or absolute activity, whatever may be the laws regulating the development of this activity; these theories are found in the works of Fichte, Schelling, and Hegel, among others. There will thus be three classes of theories: first, those which infer an external immaterial object, called a Soul, to be the invariable condition or cause of consciousness; secondly, those which find by analysis an internal immaterial activity, called by Fichte the Ego, by Schelling the Reason, by Hegel the Spirit, as the cause of consciousness, this activity being also the Absolute, the cause of all things as well as of consciousness, and the sum as well as the cause of all its effects; and thirdly, those which infer an external material object, such as the organised body, or the brain, or nervous matter, belonging to such a

OF TIME AND SPACE.   151

body, to be the cause or invariable condition of consciousness. Of course a description so brief as this of the different theories respecting the origin of consciousness is only to be regarded as an indication of them, not as a sufficient description. It would be impossible to do justice to them without a much more elaborate description and statement of their several views, and the ground and connection of them, than is possible here.* Besides which, each of these classes of theories has assumed a different shape in the hands of every independent writer who has supported it; and arguments which may be valid against one writer would lose their force when confronted with distinctions and theories invented by another writer to escape from similar arguments. I offer the present division of possible theories about the origin of consciousness as a framework to guide discussion, as the lines of latitude and longitude on the map are a framework and guide to the relative size, outline, and position of the countries over which they are thrown, to any one beginning to learn geography. It is very difficult, for instance, to determine under which of these three classes the Leibnitzian theory of the Monads should be placed. It is clear, I think, that it belongs to those theories which infer a cause, and do not reach it by analysis; but whether it is to be placed under the idealistic or materialistic branch of this class is not so clear; for first it appears to combine in the Monad both an immaterial and a material mode of existence, the Monad is said to be a simple substance without parts, Monadologie, (1); yet it has an interior, (7); and qualities, (8). If to be a simple substance without parts is to be immaterial, the Monad must belong to both the materialistic and idealistic branches at once, and my classification will be so far unsuited for the explanation of the theory. The Monads again (3) are said to be the true atoms of nature, the elements of things; and (9) those Monads which have perception more distinct and accompanied by memory are called Souls. Although therefore the above distinctions can be applied to all theories, yet they are not suitable to the explanation of all; if any one wished to explain Leibnitz's theory, he must do so not by pointing out these distinctions, but by pointing out other distinctions or principles which Leibnitz employed, or along which he moved, in traversing and obliterating these.

Again, it is difficult to bring under any single head of the present division the theory of M. Cousin; for although he maintains that the soul, le moi, is inferred as the supporter of consciousness, by a principle which is called the law of substance, loi des substances, yet he holds that it is inferred in every act of sensation, the first as well as subsequent acts. See, for instance, his Premiers Essais, Année 1816, v. ix. Since it immediately accompanies every act of sensation, it should be discoverable by the analysis of that act, notwithstanding that it is an inference and not a perception. M. Cousin maintains that we do not perceive the substance, but infer that something exists which we call by that name; and argues accordingly that it would be no valid objection to ask, What this substance itself was? for its existence only is inferred and not its nature perceived. But the act of inference at least must be known to us, which accompanies or is involved in the act of perception. I think it will become apparent as we proceed, that this substance supposed to be inferred is nothing but what I call the formal element in perception.

§ 20. To speak now of the first class of theories, those which infer an immaterial substance to be the cause of consciousness. In the first place, it is impossible to imagine a substance strictly immaterial according to the explanation of matter given in the preceding chapter, namely, as a particular feeling in a particular time and space; for nothing can be present in consciousness without being present as some feeling; the feeling in consciousness is the matter or quality of the object. I do not say that the feeling must be one of those of the five definite senses. The soul may be imagined as a substance which has qualities or a quality which have no objective names as qualities, but only subjective names as feelings. The soul may be imagined to be an object which, if we had presentative perception of it, would excite the feeling of joy, or pride, or love, or reverence, or suchlike. Nothing can possibly be more opposed to my theory than to deny the existence of objects of which we have not, or have never had, presentative perception. Such feeling would be the matter of the soul. But this would be to make the soul material, if my phraseology were adopted; it would be to make it immaterial, in the sense in which idealists have usually employed the term. Such is the notion which I frame to myself of the meaning of those who speak of the soul as an immaterial substance; and I think that this meaning is logically correct, that such an object is capable of being imagined or conceived without inconsistency.

But from this it does not follow that such an

object is the cause of consciousness; it does not follow that, because we can represent it as an object of presentative perception, it is actually at any time an object of presentative perception. It exists, true, but how? As an object of representation, imagined according to the requirements of an object of possible presentation. It is an object of possible, not of actual, presentation. From this a further step is requisite to imagining it as the invariable condition of the origin of consciousness. Two steps must therefore be taken by the idealist of this school, first from the possible to the actual, secondly from actual existence to existence in the relation of cause to a particular effect. I believe that it is the need of taking the latter step which has led idealists of this school to take also the first step; that the need of accounting for certain phenomena in consciousness has led them to infer the actual existence of the object, which seemed to them alone capable of explaining the phenomena in question. I will mention and examine the principal of these phenomena, and attempt to show, that the object inferred to account for them furnishes no better explanation of them than the material object does, the brain or nervous matter in an organised body, which is undoubtedly an object of presentative perception.

These principal phenomena of consciousness are, so far as I know, the following: 1st, the total difference in kind between consciousness and every other affection, or quality, or mode of existence, in objects; 2d, the unity or oneness in every moment of consciousness, no matter how multiform the objects of that moment of consciousness may be, or whether they are a combination of presentations or of representations, or of the two together; 3d, the unity or oneness of the individual consciousness throughout life, whereas the body of the individual has completely changed, that is to say, the sense of individual personality; 4th, the sense of effort or volition known as the Will; 5th, the sense of freedom or liberty of the will.

Now as to the first point, the total difference in kind between consciousness and every other quality of objects, it is a difference which really exists, but which cannot be lessened by imagining an object or a quality intermediate between other objects or qualities and consciousness; for, whatever object or quality we imagine as the condition of consciousness, that object or quality remains objective, and whether it is conceived as immaterial or material is equally objective and unconscious. If however this object is conceived as itself a mode of consciousness, it then is discoverable by the analysis of consciousness in reflection, and belongs to theories of the second class, it becomes an Ego and not a Soul. It is said, and truly, that all action supposes an agent, that consciousness therefore supposes a conscious object as its supporter, that thinking supposes a thinking substance. But of what kind is this supporter, 'Träger,' of consciousness, considered by itself? Whether conceived as immaterial or material, the gap between it and the consciousness which it supports is equally wide. No middle object between consciousness and its supporter can be conceived, the difference in kind can not be annihilated or lessened. The same considerations apply also if we conceive consciousness as the result or action, not of an immaterial substance simply, but of the action and reaction between such an immaterial substance and the material substance of brain or nerve. In this case, the soul is conceived as a force, analogous to the vital force and the nerve force, and this mind force is the supporter of consciousness; there is an immaterial substance, the soul, but it has a force or mode of action of its own, and on this mind force in reaction with nerve force depends consciousness. "All our perceptions originate in the action and reaction which take place between the nervous system and the mind," says Mr. Morell, Introd. to Mental Philosophy, page 106. At page 36 he had said, "The view we have taken in the previous chapter of the vital and mental forces is opposed to the common notion that the body with its functions is one thing, the mind and its functions another. Physiology has rendered this notion wholly untenable. The alternative of the old dualistic theory, however, is by no means to force us into materialism. So far from that, we may hold that there is already a nascent spark of intelligence in the primary cell, from which the individual man is developed, and that this is, in fact, the *soul* in its primary unconscious state, already commencing that series of acts which reach up, in one unbroken chain, to the highest efforts of reason and will." So that although it is a force on which consciousness depends, yet this force belongs to an immaterial substance as its supporter, the "spark of intelligence in the primary cell;" and the force belonging to it, supported or exerted by it, is objective and unconscious, whether it is considered as belonging to an immaterial or to a material substance; in short the same observations are applicable to this mode of conceiving it as to the former. Therefore, in whichever way the supporter of consciousness, the conscious substance, is conceived, whether as immaterial or material, or as the force of an immaterial or of a material substance, the gap between consciousness and objects is not bridged, the causation of one by the other is as inexplicable in one way as in the other. All that can be said of the causation of one phenomenon by another is,—after A, B. No two phenomena are perfectly similar. It may be that of two phenomena, equally invariable as antecedents of a third phenomenon, the one which is most similar to it is said to be its cause; but it serves no purpose to invent a phenomenon similar to the one to be accounted for, when there is already a phenomenon discovered as its invariable antecedent, on the ground that this actually existing phenomenon is not sufficiently similar to the phenomenon to be accounted for.

The second ground for maintaining the existence of an immaterial substance as the supporter of consciousness is the unity of consciousness, known by the name of the unity of apprehension. We are conscious of objects as units, and however diverse these objects may be, and whether they are objects of presentation or of representation, or contain both one and the other, they are still combined into one single object in a single moment of consciousness. The supporter of that consciousness therefore, it is argued, must be a single indivisible unit; and since no material substance is indivisible, it must farther be immaterial. Now if this indivisible and immaterial unit is itself an object of consciousness in the moment of consciousness, so as to be used as a standard for introducing unity into the objects perceived along with it, it must be discoverable by the analysis of consciousness in reflection, and becomes conceived therefore

PART I.
CH. III.

§ 20.
Theory of a
Soul

as an Ego and not as a Soul, it is directly perceived in consciousness and not inferred; it becomes in fact the unity of apperception and not of apprehension. But if it is conceived as a soul, and not as an ego, if it is inferred, and not directly perceived, to exist as a single indivisible and immaterial unit, then there is no way in which such an unit can be represented to consciousness except as a mathematical point; and no mathematical point has a complete, empirical, existence, but always involves an extended substance, of which it is a boundary or in which it lies. So far then from being capable of serving as the cause of consciousness, such an unit has no complete, empirical, existence of its own. Supposing it to be a point existing in an extended material substance, it becomes a mode of the existence of that substance, a differentiation or a property of it. So far from offering a better explanation of the unity of apprehension than is offered by a material substance, it cannot properly be said to offer any explanation at all. Is there any insuperable difficulty in supposing unity of apprehension to arise in a compound material substance, such as the brain or nervous matter? I cannot see that there is; there is indeed a great dissimilarity between consciousness and objects which are not conscious; but the unity of apprehension offers no such difficulty; the unity of apprehension fully corresponds to the unity of objects apprehended. What is the unity of apprehension? That an object is perceived as one, and that objects differing only in point of their times of being perceived are perceived as the same. The perception of difference precedes the perception of sameness both logically and historically. We start from the perception of a single object, from the perception of oneness, suppose a feeling of the colour red, occupying the whole field of vision and lasting one minute; if the next minute offers no change of feeling, we still say that we perceive one object; but if the next minute offers to us the colour green, then we have a perception of difference; if this is followed by the colour red again, we perceive sameness, the sameness of this object with that of the first minute. There must be a perception of difference before a perception of sameness; and logically the perception of sameness is more complex, and includes as part of itself the perception of difference. Sameness of objects is nothing more than oneness of feelings in difference of times. Unity of apprehension arises both in perceiving oneness and in perceiving sameness. But the oneness of a perceived object, in what does it consist? In the oneness of the quality in oneness of the time, or in the oneness of the space occupied by different qualities in oneness of the time, according as the object is perceived in time alone or in time and space together. The unity of apprehension is the subjective aspect of the unity of the object perceived; that is, unity of feeling, or unity of a complex of feelings, in unity of time. This is the analysis of the phenomenon called Unity of Apprehension. The question is, whether a better explanation of this phenomenon can be offered, than is offered by the fact of the continuity of time and space, when undivided by any difference in the feelings contained by them. Why should we infer a single indivisible substance, a substance which is truly "one," to account for the oneness of consciousness, when the oneness of this inferred substance must be explained to consist simply in unity of feeling in unity of time, that is to consist in the very thing which it is introduced to account for? This is nothing but the old process of doubling the phenomenon to be accounted for.

The third argument is the sense of individual personality, of personal identity throughout life. From this it is inferred, that there must be an immaterial soul, the supporter of this sense of identity. The body changes all its particles of matter during life, yet the conscious being feels that he is the same person from childhood to old age. If memory, it is argued, depended solely on the changing matter of the body, we should preserve no memory of what we were when our body consisted of a completely different set of material particles from those which it consists of at any present time; the particles would have vanished, and the memory attached to them and depending on them would have vanished also. To this it may be replied, that though the particles of matter in the body vanish and are replaced by others, yet the change is gradual enough to allow that quality, in the vanishing particle, on which consciousness and memory depend, to be communicated to the particle which takes its place; and this is true in whatever way we imagine to ourselves the connection between the material particles and consciousness, whether as wax and seal, or as some kind of movement mechanical or molecular or magnetic, accompanied or unaccompanied by heat or light or sound. All such figures are of course only aids to the imagination in default of knowledge. But whatever the nature of the operation which goes on in the brain may be, each particle, which takes the place of a vanishing one, has this quality or this nature communicated to it, becomes a part of the old structure, and bears its part in supporting the consciousness which the old structure supported. The body then is in one sense the same body from childhood to old age, notwithstanding the change in its particles; and it is in a sense exactly parallel to this that the consciousness of the individual is said to be the same throughout life. Particular feelings and thoughts vanish and are replaced by others; the body of the child does not more differ from the body of the man, than the thoughts of the child from the thoughts of the man. The unity of organic growth and development of the body is exactly parallel to the unity in growth and development of the consciousness which is attached to it. In the brain are stored up impressions, qualities, or modes of operation, the causes of memory, which are communicated to and then preserved by every fresh particle of matter which is taken up into the brain. The brain becomes richer in these impressions, qualities, or modes of operation, and they constitute one part of the life of the brain, and make with each other a connected whole. So also do the thoughts and images in consciousness, and this is what is meant by personal identity. If the supposition of an immaterial soul was adopted, we should still have to suppose that this immaterial soul was subject to changes, to the exchange of the thoughts of the child for those of the man; the binding of these together is all that the immaterial soul is adopted in order to explain. But this bond is found as readily in the organic unity of the development of the brain, as in the unity of an immaterial soul, and therefore it is superfluous to have recourse to the latter supposition.

The fourth argument is the sense of effort or volition, the consciousness of Will. Properly indeed this is an argument for the existence of an ego, not for the existence of an immaterial soul; the object is thought to be directly envisaged in the moment of volition, not to be inferred in order to account for the phenomenon of volition; but since this distinction is not always drawn, I will say a few words on it here. The sense of effort, l'effort voulu, as for instance in the phenomenon of attention, is among the simplest and earliest states of consciousness, perhaps as early historically as any; it is an immediate, not an inferred, fact of consciousness. Effort is a sensation which we perceive immediately, as we perceive anger, fear, hunger, warmth, and so on. This sense of effort has been thought, notably by Maine de Biran, to reveal to us immediately the Moi, or substantial immaterial Self; and it was thought that the self reveals itself to itself in its consciousness of its own volition. But the sense of effort, whether it is effort for a distinct purpose, or volition proper, or only indeterminate effort, reveals the self neither more nor less nor in any other sense than other perceptions do. They all contribute to self-consciousness, which is the first reflective act of consciousness, in which self and not-self are for the first time perceived. In other words, volition is not reflection. All reflection is volition, that is, involves sense of effort for a purpose; but all sense of effort for a purpose is not reflection. Attention involves sense of effort indeterminately, but it does not involve envisaging self as an object. Effort again is roused by an interest felt, but it does not require that we should be conscious that *we* are feeling an interest. This would suppose an analysis of the feeling of interest which can come afterwards only. The consciousness of the ego as an object is a particular, a reflective, mode of the consciousness of effort. An effort or a volition of which we are conscious is an object of perception, and an immediate object of perception, but it does not include the ego in itself as objective; we do not perceive the ego objectively in it, until we have taken another step, until we have reflected. The process of reflection will be examined shortly.

The fifth argument, which is the last I shall mention, is the sense of freedom in volition. We are conscious of freedom, it is said, in choosing how to act, and this is an immediate fact of consciousness; but since we know that all material objects are subject to fixed laws, that being which is conscious of freedom, and which therefore is free, must be immaterial. What the sense of freedom is, what we feel when we feel ourselves free, it must be left till the process of reflection is analysed to determine. But in whatever way freedom is conceived, whether, 1st, as freedom to act when a wish is formed; or 2d, freedom in forming that wish originally; or 3d, freedom of the judgment from the influence of desires; or 4th, freedom of the desires from the control of judgment; and also in whatever circumstance freedom of any kind may be supposed to consist; whether, 1st, in the absence of all controlling or causative influence, out of the agent which is free; or 2d, in the positive origination of an action, or feeling, or thought, in and by the free agent itself; or 3d, in the total arbitrariness of the proceedings of the free agent, that is, in the impossibility of predicting any of them beforehand; the moment freedom, in any way or in any kind, is conceived as existing objectively, the explanation of that freedom as a fact is quite as inadequately supplied by the supposition of an immaterial, as by the supposition of a material substance, as the ground and supporter of the attribute of freedom. It is as difficult to suppose an immaterial substance isolated from others, and originating actions by itself, as a material substance; it is as difficult to imagine an immaterial as a material substance producing actions entirely arbitrary, in the sense of following no law and being incapable of prediction; it is as difficult to imagine an immaterial as it is to imagine a material substance, producing judgments unaffected by desires, or entertaining desires uncontrolled by judgments, or originating actions which have no form and no content. I admit that to conceive these things in either way seems to me equally impossible; but what I contend for is, that it is as impossible in one way as in the other; and this being so, it remains only to attempt to throw some light on the phenomenon of freedom, as a fact of consciousness, by the analysis of the phenomenon of reflection.

§ 21. To come now to the second class of theories, those which place the cause of consciousness in an immaterial Ego, or an immaterial activity which is at once subject and object of every moment of consciousness, and therefore to be discovered by analysis of the object or of the moment of perception; foremost among the supporters of which Kant himself is to be reckoned. See his Transcendental deduction of the Categories, Kritik der Reinen Vernunft, Werke, vol. 2. ed. Rosenkranz und Schubert, page 90-116. He speaks of the transcendental apperception as being at once transcendental and a state of consciousness,—

"dieses reine ursprüngliche unwandelbare Bewusstseyn," page 99; and this I can conceive in no other way than as being what I call an aspect of a state of consciousness, but an aspect perceived at once in the same act by which the object or state of consciousness is itself perceived. He seems to have considered every state of consciousness to have had three such inseparable aspects, as containing or being at once a consciousness of the identity of self or the conscious Subject, of the identity of the function of being conscious, and of the identity of the empirical object perceived; of these three aspects the consciousness of the identity of the action or function, Handlung, was the condition of the other two, the transcendental unity of apperception. See the passage at page 100, Eben diese transcendentale Einheit —zuerst möglich macht. What Kant sought to explain to himself was, how was the fact of unity or oneness, anywhere and everywhere, to be accounted for. He saw that there was this cognition in all consciousness and in all objects of consciousness, universally and without exception. It must therefore have or be some transcendental condition in nature, common to all its instances, every one of which supposed it, and in every one of which it also was manifested. The conception was like that of Plato's, τὸ ἓν, τὰ εἴδη, and τὰ αἰσθητά, only reappearing in the kingdom of mind and consciousness instead of in the kingdom of existences. Like that too it was but a doubling of the phenomenon to be accounted for, a choosing of one aspect of the phenomenon and elevating it into the condition of the phenomenon. It makes no difference how that Unity is regarded which is conceived as the condition of phenomenal unity, for all unity which can be brought before our consciousness at all consists of two elements at the least, time and feeling; and any condition of these elements becoming united, or being referred to each other, must itself consist of these two elements. Every existence can be analysed into elements which have no existence apart from each other.

Kant's Ich denke is then the reappearance of Plato's τὸ ἕν, but it is after passing it through the crucible of Descartes' Cogito ergo Sum. It is the Cogito ergo Sum analysed and made into an actual and universal element of all knowledge and all existence, an element which is at once their cause and their consequent. But it was not this with Descartes. With Descartes it arose in answer to the question, What is the ultimate certainty of which it is impossible to doubt, or, What is that fact which contains its own certainty combined with its existence? The simplest fact containing at once these two elements, existence and certainty, is the fact or state of consciousness called reflection, and the simplest expression of this fact is Cogito-Sum, or Ich denke; a fact which may be combined with, or form part of, any other state of consciousness, but which is not essential to all. It is composed of elements which are themselves complete states of consciousness. It is therefore the central point of philosophy but not of experience, the starting-point of examination of consciousness and interrogation of nature, but not of consciousness itself. Yet in some way it is contained in all consciousness, for it is developed out of it, and is the return of consciousness upon itself. The question is, how and in what manner contained in and developed out of consciousness. Just as, in § 13, there arose a question about the mode in which the contents of space existed in space, whether as feelings here, qualities there, or as feelings and qualities everywhere,—so here the question is, not whether reflection is contained in consciousness, but as to the mode of its being contained in it, whether it is as a development of a new shape which did not previously exist, or as a previously existing ground or cause which can be discovered in the germ in all instances, and which may be consequently regarded as the necessary accompaniment and condition of all.

Some writers have maintained the universal presence of the consciousness of self in all instances of consciousness, by a direct appeal to the consciousness of themselves and others. Jacobi, for instance, describes the discovery of the Ego in acts of direct perception, in his David Hume, ein Gespräch, Werke, vol. 2. page 175. edit. 1812-26. He says: Ich erfahre dass Ich bin und dass etwas ausser mir ist in demselben untheilbaren Augenblick. Und in diesem Augenblick leidet meine Seele vom Gegenstande nicht mehr als sie von sich selbst leidet. And again at page 176—dass auch bei der allerersten und einfachsten Wahrnehmung, das Ich und das Du, inneres Bewusstseyn und äusserlicher Gegenstand, sogleich in der Seele da seyn müssen; beides in demselben Nu, &c. But the question is, As objects both, or as object and subject? I see an object; there is a simple feeling. Neither "I" nor "object" as counter-distinguished, each from other, is as yet contained in it to my consciousness. And attend to it as closely as I will, dwell upon it as long as I will, analyse it as accurately as I will, I can discover no "I" in it;

but by attention, dwelling upon it, and analysing it, I can distinguish its feeling from its form, its material and its formal element. Attention and its results must not be confounded with reflection and its results; the first rough perception without the analysis of attention can be distinguished, it is true, from perception together with such attention; but then this second analysing perception can be distinguished also no less from perception reflecting as well as analysing. Those who find the ego in direct perception seem to me to distinguish only two things, the first rough perception on the one hand from perception analysing and reflecting at once on the other. But there are three things, not two, to be distinguished, perception, attention, and reflection. By reflection I distinguish the "I," the feeling, from the "object," the particular mode of the feeling, the colour, sound, taste, &c. There is neither substratum of the colour nor substratum of the feeling. If in reflection I fix my thoughts on the feeling, I may call it the subject; if on the mode of the feeling, I may call it the object. In seeing an external object I do not feel that I am and that the object is, but I have a feeling under the forms of time and space; I am conscious, and am conscious of an object existing in time and space; I am aware of the feeling, of the space it occupies, and of the time it occupies; but before I can distinguish the feeling from feeling generally, the incomplete from the complete moment of consciousness, the act of consciousness from its result, I must have represented or redintegrated the feeling in consciousness and compared it with others, that is, I must have reflected upon it.

The question, how consciousness is related to, or

distinguished from, self-consciousness is one of the most difficult in philosophy. It is the most central and the most important question in philosophy, just as the Ich denke is the most central and important point in the system of Kant. There are two chief ways of answering it. Either self-consciousness differs from consciousness only as a developed, differentiated, whole differs from the same whole undeveloped and undifferentiated, for example as a plant from its seed, in which case self-consciousness would be capable of discovery in consciousness by a sufficiently searching and properly directed analysis, and all consciousness would be rightly described as self-consciousness; and this is the theory of Kant, Jacobi, and many others; or self-consciousness differs from consciousness as one phenomenon differs from another which it invariably, under certain conditions, supplants and succeeds, but which except for this relation can not be called the same with it, as for example one mode of physical force, such as friction, passes into another, such as heat, or as electricity passes into or is supplanted by light; and this is the theory which I wish to establish here. In both cases consciousness is potential self-consciousness, the δύναμις of which self-consciousness is the ἐνέργεια; but this distinction of Aristotle's is very wide and embraces many modes or instances. The question is this: Is consciousness the lowest mode of self-consciousness, but self-consciousness still; or is self-consciousness a differentiation of consciousness which cannot be traced at all in consciousness? When we are fully self-conscious do we merely analyse an object, and see clearly in it a circumstance which is already there, dimly present to consciousness, or does that circumstance first arise when we are first clearly conscious of it? And if the latter alternative in these two questions is true, and supposing it to be already established, is there not then, as a separate question, an easy explanation at hand, why the opposite alternatives should appear so probable as they have done, in the fact of the extreme difficulty we have in throwing ourselves back in imagination into a position once occupied but long since abandoned, the readiness with which we imagine ourselves always to have felt what we at present feel, the comparative inability, as it would be in this case, to separate direct consciousness from self-consciousness when we have long accustomed ourselves to speak of feelings as 'ours,' that is, as always combined with self-consciousness? Both sides admit that potentially self-consciousness is contained in consciousness; but to me it appears that it can only be said to be actually present in consciousness when it is clearly perceived as an object, and when self and not-self are counter-distinguished; and that this is first done in reflection, preceded by many instances of perception. The question is by no means one about mere words and nomenclature, but about the analysis of simple elementary feeling, the material element in direct perception, which I maintain cannot be analysed into a self and a not-self, does not contain a self and a not-self, though it does contain a formal element, and which comes to contain a self and a not-self in a particular act, later than and dependent on perception, namely, the act of reflection. Perhaps the decisive solution of the question awaits the clearer because more practised insight of the future.

No reflection, not even the transcendental apperception of Kant, if that is considered as a reflection containing an Ich denke, is required as a condition or an element of a simple perception of an object. Simple perception of an object may indeed require attention, a felt effort; that is, it is possible that the sense of effort may be involved in the feeling which is the material element of every object; but this has been already distinguished from reflection. I feel an effort as I feel any other sensation; I do not necessarily reflect that "I" feel it, any more than in the case of any other feeling. Supposing therefore perception of an object to require attention or effort either as a precedent condition or as an element of the object perceived, still it does not involve reflection, or an Ich denke, or an Ich bin. It may be said, How can I perceive an object as one and the same, unless I refer it to one and the same consciousness? The answer is, that consciousness is one and the same for the same reason that the object is so, namely, because it is a feeling in a continuous time. Different determinate feelings succeed each other without interval in different determinate times, the times are distinguished by the feelings which occupy them, and the series of determinate feelings is continuous. Call the series of feelings feeling simply, and the result is a single consciousness; leave undetermined what the determinate feelings are, and we have a provisional image, feeling generally existing in a continuous time, just as we might describe a particoloured silk thread, of which one inch was blue, the next green, the next yellow, and the next red, as a single coloured thread, without determining what the particular colours were into which it was divided; the thread which corresponds to the time and the colour which corresponds to the feeling are continuous, and the unity thus introduced into the series of determinate colours is the result of generalisation of the provisional image, colour, from the several determinate colours. When states of consciousness are the object-matter of the generalisation, the generalisation is called reflection, because it is the object itself which generalises from itself, because the same series of feelings prolongs itself in the act of generalising from its previous states, instead of having a series of objects before it different from itself. The unity of feeling generally, or in the abstract, in a continuous time is a fact in consciousness which is first discovered by reflection, cannot be given by a single perception, but must be collected from many perceptions before it is itself an object of perception. In other words, we do not perceive an object to be one and the same object by referring it to a continuous feeling, still less by referring it to an Ich denke; but we discover that there is a continuous feeling determined into many special feelings, after having many times experienced such special feelings connected in a continuous time. Feeling in a continuous time as a fact, and not the knowledge of this fact, constitutes the simple perception of every single object. If it should be asked, Why and how it comes to pass that feeling is continuous, that is, combined with time, at all, that we ever have the feeling of oneness, it must be confessed that no answer can be given. No cause of the fact can be assigned, but only the analysis of the fact. Oneness is an ultimate fact in consciousness, as it is in every single object of consciousness. The same question might be asked in the case of every thing, from the most concrete to the most abstract objects of all. Oneness in a material object and oneness in consciousness, or the feeling of oneness, are not different facts, one of which can be explained by the other as its cause, but they are the objective and subjective aspects of one and the same fact, beyond which, in the way of assigning causes at least, we cannot reach.

Did we go no farther than the stage of direct perceptions, however richly our senses furnished us with them, we should have no knowledge but of phenomena and the relations between them, whether these were phenomena in time alone, or in time and space together; we should have no knowledge of their relations to what we call ourselves, or of ourselves in relation to them. And in many animals, except man, and in man himself in his infancy, we may suppose this to be the case. The notion of Self is introduced by reflection, which itself contains and in essence consists of the same simple unity of apprehension, but of apprehension applied to a particular kind of complex object, an object composed of previous cases of consciousness, of an apprehension in which their one common feature is contrasted with their many diverse features, the general indeterminate feeling with the particular determinate feelings. It remains now to describe the process of reflection, in order to see how the notion of self is introduced by it, or superinduced upon the simple perceptions. The unity of apprehension in reflection is called Unity of Apperception. And here is reached the point so often referred to in the present and preceding chapters.

Reflection is a generalisation, differing from other generalisations in having modes of consciousness as such for its object-matter; it is consciousness of perceptions so far as they contain the common element of feeling, abstracting from their other differences. In point of being feelings they are all alike, however much one determinate feeling differs from another, a sound from a colour, a colour from a taste, or one colour from another, for instance. It is inevitable that familiarity with the perceptions should bring to light this ground-difference existing in all of them, namely, that what they all are in common should be distinguished from what some are and others are not. Reflection first draws, then follows up this distinction, and investigates the element common to all so far as it is common and not determinate. The method pursued by reflection in this is the following. The reflecting consciousness considers those feelings which are nearest to it in point of time, it gets as close to its object as it can; that is, it turns its look back on the feeling of the moment immediately previous to itself, that is, represents or redintegrates it in consciousness. Reflection is a particular kind of redintegration, distinguished from other kinds by its particular object, which object is the common element of feeling, the feeling common to all instances of feeling, a logical and provisional object. In following this course reflection perceives that it has produced the same phenomenon, in point of kind, with that which it set out to examine. Instances have been produced in the course of reflecting of the same phenomenon, of feeling of determinate kinds and in separate but continuous moments of time; and these instances have been produced by the same reflecting consciousness. The chain of feeling or the series of feelings has prolonged itself, and, since it has been prolonged in reflection, perceives that it has prolonged itself; the process of perception of the common element in past states is a prolongation of that element in a present state. One moment consciousness is a consciousness of having advanced or continued so far, the next moment of having advanced a further, and the next a further step. It has made out this fact concerning the indeterminate feeling which it set out to examine, namely, that it forms a continuously advancing line in point of time, continuing up to but not into or beyond that indivisible present moment which will the first become past. That it continues into the present, and will continue into future moments, is an inference from this reflection, not a part of this reflection itself. It is a further and a different reflection.

It is clear that of this continuous feeling or consciousness, so far as it is provisional and not determinate, no complete empirical existence can be predicated; that the fact discovered concerning it by reflection, namely, its continuity in point of time, does not warrant us in personifying the general term feeling, in assuming an ego or personality of which consciousness is the attribute. The ego or personality which we are warranted in assuming, which we are compelled indeed to infer from the facts, is one which is the complex of all the determinate feelings of apprehension and apperception, the varying as well as the fixed, of all the apprehensions and apperceptions which have been bound together as a continuous chain of feeling from the moment when it began to exist as feeling to the present moment of consciousness. The whole to which these apprehensions and apperceptions belong, which they constitute, is thus definitely marked; it includes, or may include if memory is clear enough, all past states of consciousness, but nothing which has not been consciousness. This whole is the Person, the identical man, the Empirical Ego, as he appears to himself as the object of consciousness, the object of that consciousness by which it has been produced as an object in its progress. The phrase Empirical Ego will be familiar to readers of Schelling. See his Vom Ich, oder über das Umbedingte, Sämmtl. Werke, vol. 1.

But a name must be found also for the general and provisional term Feeling, as existing indeterminate and in time, for its existence in time gives it continuity as a provisional image, and time is its substance when it is regarded as existing; but it must be a name which does not express more than the analysis warrants us in assigning to it, a name which does not imply that it has empirical existence; and for this purpose let the name of Subject be chosen, and, in order to distinguish it from the empirical ego, let it be called the Pure Ego. The name Subject will distinguish it from its objects, whether determinate feelings or determinate qualities; the name Pure Ego will distinguish it from the complex of those determinate feelings, the empirical ego. The name of Subject best marks the fact that the feeling intended by it is general and provisional, and never an object by itself. Whenever feeling exists empirically it exists determinately, and in a moment of time which is an empirical object and has empirical duration. If we divide in thought this least empirical moment of time, or feeling in time, the feeling vanishes, but the time remains; the time becomes an incomplete moment, a δύναμις, but it still remains as time present to our consciousness. But what has become of the determinate feeling? It does not exist as feeling any more, our sensibility is not acute enough to perceive it below the point called by hypothesis the least empirical moment. It has not become feeling generally or in the abstract, for this is a generalisation from all the empirical determinate feelings, and cannot therefore include a case which is not a determinate feeling. Sir W. Hamilton would perhaps say that the feeling had become latent; but what is a feeling which is not felt? To say that it is latent, is only to say that it is not a feeling. There is only one adequate mode of conceiving the phenomenon of the vanishing of feeling in an incomplete moment of time. It remains potential or latent, not as feeling, but as organ, or as a mode of the material organ to which it is attached; the sensibility of the organ is not divisible so far as the form in which that sensibility operates. Starting then from the incomplete moment of time and letting it continue till it is complete, that is, till it is long enough for feeling to arise in it, we see that a determinate feeling is the result of a completed moment of time, and that consciousness arises at the end of the moment. At that instant we have an object of consciousness. Suppose that the next complete moment of time is a moment of reflection, and its object will be the previous complete moment. In this way we may be always conscious, but never conscious that we are conscious but only that we have been so; except indeed, as has been already said, by inference, in which sense we may be said also to be conscious that we shall be conscious hereafter. The present moment of consciousness is the darkest spot in the whole series of moments of reflection. The fact that consciousness is fleeting in point of time, that it escapes observation in the moment of consciousness, so that we are never conscious that we are feeling but only that we have felt,—the fact that we are never able to seize consciousness itself but only its product, warrants us in distinguishing a Subject from an Object. Could consciousness be its own immediate object, could reflection and perception be one, could sensibility be as infinitely divisible as its form, then every thing would be indifferently subjective and objective, we should distinguish neither subject nor object in phenomena, the ultimate dualism of metaphysic would be done away with, and existence and consciousness would constitute a true Absolute.

If we were to follow up this clue, it would probably occur to us that the so-called substance of the soul is time, just as the so-called substance of external tangible and visible objects is space. Time has been called the form of the inner sense, space the form of the outer sense; but both inner and outer sense belong to one conscious being, and this one conscious being as an existing object is now under investigation. The question before us is, Does the reflection of this conscious being on itself discover, in its object, itself, a constant and complete object, to which its changing states are attached, or with which they are bound up, so that this constant and complete object may be considered as the invariable condition of consciousness and its changing states? The answer given by the analysis of reflection is, that the only constant element in the object of reflection is time, which is also the form of the inner sense. Time therefore is the condition of the subjective unity of the objects of the inner sense, of the series of states of consciousness, and also of the objective unity of consciousness considered as an existing object. But time is no complete or empirical object, it is but the formal element of objects; it cannot therefore be regarded as the cause or invariable condition of the existence of consciousness; no more is space the cause of the existence of external objects. But the time and the space, contained as elements in objects of the inner and outer sense respectively, are that which causes them to appear as possessing a substance or substratum, and which has thus given rise to the notion of a substance underlying external objects, and of a soul underlying states of consciousness.

The foregoing view is not open to Prof. Ferrier's objection, Inst. of Metaph. Epistemology, I. § 8. There is no *remembering* that feelings were ours which we were not conscious of as ours when we felt them first. Feelings *become* ours first in reflection. They belong originally to one continued series; this fact we indeed remember in reflection; and in consequence name the series 'our self,' and the several feelings composing it 'ours.' The perception of phenomena, as simple phenomena, precedes the perception of the Subject, of the empirical ego, and of phenomena as objects; apprehension precedes apperception, just in the same way as the perception of difference precedes the perception of sameness. The frequent conjunction of apperception and apprehension, of reflection and direct perception, in later states of consciousness, as Kant says, Das: *Ich denke*, muss alle meine Vorstellungen begleiten *können*, need not make us conclude that apperception, or with Kant that transcendental apperception, is requisite as the condition of apprehension. That which is a peculiarity of some states of consciousness is not to be erected into a condition of existence of all states of consciousness.

The same erroneous procedure is found in Schelling, the error of adopting, as the cause of a phenomenon, the differentia or the definition of it. It is seen in the first sentence of the System des Transcend. Idealismus, Sämmtl. Werke, vol. 3. Alles Wissen beruht auf der Uebereinstimmung eines Objektiven mit einem Subjektiven. But knowledge does not *rest upon* the agreement of an objective with a subjective, but may be described as being such an agreement; there is no causal connection between the two things, knowledge and the agreement of an objective with a subjective; each is another term for, or mode of regarding, the other. But let this be exhibited more particularly. In the same work at p. 367, vol. 3, Schelling says: Man überlasse sich ganz der unwillkürlichen Succession der Vorstellungen, so werden diese Vorstellungen, so mannigfaltig und verschieden sie seyn mögen, doch als zu Einem identischen Subjekt gehörig erscheinen. Reflektire ich auf diese Identität des Subjekts in den Vorstellungen, so entsteht mir der Satz: Ich denke. Dieses Ich denke ist es, was alle Vorstellungen begleitet und die Continuität des Bewusstseyns zwischen ihnen unterhält. On this it is to be remarked, that in every series of perceptions, in all consciousness, there is a continuity of the consciousness, of the feeling or feelings. In reflection this continuity of feeling is fixed upon by the attention, observed, and called the Ich denke. The fact is the continuity of feeling, the expression or characterisation of it, when isolated by the attention, is the Ich denke. The fact accompanies inseparably all the Vorstellungen; the expression for it arises afterwards, in reflection. But Schelling here maintains not only that the Ich denke accompanies all the Vorstellungen, which would be true in so far as this, that the fact now called Ich denke does so, but also that it is the cause of the phenomenon of their continuity, unterhält die Continuität des Bewusstseyns zwischen ihnen. But it is clear that this is not the case, since the thought Ich denke itself involves continuity of consciousness, and is only possible in a continuous time. Continuity of consciousness and Ich denke are two terms for the same thing; the first is a name for it as an object of perception unseparated from the phenomena, the second as an object of reflection, isolated in a provisional image from the phenomena; they are not two objects, but one object in two shapes. Continuity of consciousness is common to all possible modes of consciousness; but the thought Ich denke belongs to one mode of consciousness only, namely to reflection.

The Ich of the Ich denke becomes, according to Schelling, its own object in intellectual intuition, intellektuelle Anschauung. I admit that Intellectual intuition is a good name for reflection; but I deny that, under either name, it reveals any other Ego than the empirical ego on the one hand, and that general or provisional image, the Subject, on the other. There are two reasons why the Subject cannot be conceived as a complete or empirical object,— first, because it appears as abstract and general feeling, never given in perception except as an abstraction; secondly, because, when we try to think of it as existing separately, we must think of it as existing in an incomplete moment of time; for if we think of it as in a completed moment of time, it is no longer general and abstract but a determinate objective feeling, the material element in a perception.

The analysis of reflection is now complete. It will be observed that I have used the word objects in speaking of phenomena previous to reflection, both in this and the preceding chapter, although phenomena become objective and subjective, and feelings are distinguished from qualities, first in reflection. No other course was open to me, and for this reason, that language, the articulate language of men, is first formed when reflection has arisen, and thus describes objects and has names for objects only as they appear to a reflecting consciousness. Things as they appear to consciousness previous to reflection are not described in such language, but are, so far as the language is concerned, non-existent; language itself is a late product of consciousness, and expresses things as they appear at the stage when it arises. If any animals besides man were found to have a language grounded on generalisation, this would I think be justly regarded as a proof that they had reflected and were possessed of reason. For they could hardly have generalised so much and so fixedly as to possess a language, without having also generalised the common element of feeling. But though phenomena have been spoken of as if they were already distinguished into their subjective and objective aspects, into feelings and qualities, before reflection has arisen, this must not make us forget that this was only an imperfect way of speaking, and that the way in which this distinction arises in reflection had still to be pointed out. The cognitions which we have of objects have been spoken of as if they were already separate from their objects, and as such cognitions became the objects of reflection. But they are in fact as yet only phenomena, not feelings as distinct from qualities, but both together and undistinguished; they are states of consciousness and states of objects at once, if we describe them by words applied to them by reflection. How do they first come to be thus distinguished? To answer this question, we must turn to the analysis of reflection and the distinction which it draws, namely, that between the Subject and the empirical ego. It does not distinguish the Subject from the empirical ego after having first distinguished the empirical ego into qualities and feelings; but the distinction of the empirical ego into qualities and feelings is the consequence of the distinction of the Subject from the empirical ego, which is at that time another name for the phenomena. When the Subject is on the point of being distinguished from the empirical ego, this latter is nothing more than the complex of phenomena, in which feelings and qualities are yet undistinguished; there is but one complex of phenomena in presence of reflection. The distinction itself of the Subject from the empirical ego involves the distinction between the qualities and the feelings of the empirical ego, between the complex of phenomena as feelings and the same complex of phenomena as qualities. Let these two distinctions be clearly seen to be two and not one; and now turn to their identity in reflection, to the mode in which, or the reason why, reflection necessarily draws the second distinction in consequence of its having drawn the first. Reflection is the distinguishing of the course of feeling into pure and determinate feelings, in time alone, abstracting provisionally from space: no matter what space these feelings may occupy, reflection considers them only so far as they occupy time. Reflection abstracts provisionally from space, that is, from the particular space occupied by the feelings, the succession of which it examines. Though all these feelings occupy or are placed in some portion of space, yet this circumstance is abstracted from, and only their succession is considered. In this consideration arises the distinction between the Subject, the incomplete moment of time, and its objects, the whole series of determinate feelings. Phenomena have resolved themselves into this distinction; the objects of the Subject are a succession of feelings. But this abstraction was only provisional, for these feelings also occupy or are contained in space, — the comparatively constant feelings, which are the body, and the less constant feelings which surround it on all sides, and the feelings which accompany these two classes, such as the emotions, the position of which is difficult to determine. These all occupy space and time together, are a succession of feelings and a succession of feelings in space-relations. When I take the feelings, as a whole, in these two relations at once, as distinguished from the same feelings with provisional abstraction of space, I consider them as qualities; for they are considered as statical and fixed in space and in the whole of time; they become the universe of qualities but without ceasing to be feelings. When any particular set of feelings is fixed on and considered in these two relations at once, it becomes a complex of qualities, with a certain figure in space and duration of time, yet in this case too without ceasing to be a complex of feelings. When I take a succession of these particular objects, some occupying a larger and some a smaller space, some occupying an indefinite and some a definite position in space, I am said to have trains of thought or association of ideas; and this is the condition in which consciousness is normally found, and which is the groundwork of all its elaborate and completed reasonings.

Qualities in the metaphysical sense of the term are then to be distinguished from qualities in the psychological sense. In the former they are feelings considered as occupying space as well as time; in the latter they are feelings considered as occupying all or any space except that occupied by the mind, which is the place of their effects and of their evidence. Qualities in the metaphysical sense are the objective aspect of feelings, objective to reflection when, having drawn the distinction between Subject and Object, it proceeds to distinguish its method in doing this from the facts or objects in which its method is involved. Its method is to abstract provisionally from space; but the objects in which that method is involved all occupy space. Its method then is the subjective aspect of its objects. And this method is the subjective aspect of the empirical ego; the objects of it are the objective aspect. Both together are the object of reflection, and therefore both together are the object of metaphysical enquiry.

All thoughts which arise in reflection are modifications, differentiations of this thought, that the Object is different from the Subject; or, in Kant's phrase, they are accompanied by an Ich denke. The two aspects of phenomena, subjective and objective, are therefore in reflection as inseparable yet as distinct as the two elements, formal and material, are distinct and inseparable in direct perception.

It is impossible here, and I do not pretend, to exhibit even in outline the various idealistic theories of the Ego, or in any way to enter on their respective merits. Hegel's logical idealism will be in some measure discussed in another part. Here I have offered only an analysis of reflection, which seems to me to take away the common ground on which all idealistic theories of the Ego must stand. For whether the individual Ego is deduced from the Absolute, or the Absolute from the individual Ego, it is reflection in both cases which furnishes the content of the conception formed. It makes no difference whether the universe is considered as one vast person, or the individual person as the constructor of an ideal universe; reflection is equally the source of the conceptions applicable to both. If reflection is a mode of intuition, and if its analysis has been rightly given, an answer has been supplied not only to the incorrect conclusions of theories of intellectual intuition, but also to theories which do not recognise reflection as intuition at all. But the question of the possibility of a purely logical idealism, such as Hegel's, requires a more direct and express treatment, and must be postponed for the present; and for this reason, that Hegel is as careful to bring together the two domains of nature and history, οὐσία and γίνεσις, as I am to keep them apart; and as the γίνεσις is with him inseparably bound up with the οὐσία, and this οὐσία is of a logical nature, his theory of the origin of consciousness and of its forms cannot be understood until the nature of his logic is considered, and this will find its proper place in the second part. It would indeed be a triumph of philosophy, if the distinction between nature and history could be really traversed and obliterated; but this cannot be done unless the distinction between complete objects and their incomplete elements and aspects, that is, the distinction between empiric and metaphysic, is first done away. Nevertheless the attempt to obliterate this distinction between nature and history is one of the greatest charms of Hegel's system. That which, in Hegel's system, most nearly corresponds to the distinction between the nature and history of consciousness, is his distinction between the Logic and the two remaining parts of his Encyclopädie, first the Naturphilosophie which contains the Idea, or completed Concept-form, in its Andersseyn or differentiation from logic, that is, as percept or Vorstellung or series of Vorstellungen, and secondly the Philosophie des Geistes, which contains the combination of the two former, or the transformation of percepts and concepts in the actually existing individual consciousness. These three parts of his system then form, or exhibit, one complete actually existing Spirit, Geist, which is identical with the logical form of it, the Idea. Space, time, and matter are the three first of the percepts, the three first steps taken in the second part of his system, the Naturphilosophie; the Idea, which is the culminating point or completion of the Logic, passes over, in obedience to its moving principle, which is Negation, into its difference; and the simplest and most general form of difference is outness, Ausscreinanderseyn, and this is called Space. Space then differentiates itself and culminates in Time; and time and space together culminate in Matter. Consciousness in its simplest and most general form,

Empfindung, or feeling, is in a similar manner the completion of the first step in the return of the Idea to itself, out of its differential state, to its state of identity with itself, as Geist; that is, it is the first step in the third part of the Encyclopädie, the Philosophie des Geistes. So far from considering feeling as an ultimate element of consciousness, the material element, incapable of analysis, Hegel derives it ultimately from thought in some of its forms, and considers that the ultimate nature of feeling consists in the circumstance of what is general, allgemeines, becoming also particular or determinate, bestimmt, without losing its character of generality. Das Nichtanimalische, he says, empfindet eben desshalb nicht, weil in denselben das Allgemeine in die Bestimmtheit versenkt bleibt, in dieser nicht für sich wird. Das gefärbte Wasser, zum Beispiel, ist nur *für uns* unterschieden von seinem Gefärbtseyn und von seiner Ungefärbtheit. Wäre ein und dasselbe Wasser zugleich allgemeines und gefärbtes Wasser, so würde diese unterscheidende Bestimmtheit für das Wasser selber seyn, dieses somit Empfindung haben; denn Empfindung hat Etwas dadurch, dass dasselbe in seiner Bestimmtheit sich als ein allgemeines erhält. Philosophie des Geistes. Encycl. § 399. Werke, vol. 7, 2d div. p. 115. This is, first, to take feeling in one of its second intentions instead of in its first intention; and secondly, and consequently, it is to deduce feeling from what I should call the formal element of consciousness as it appears in thought.

Such is a very brief sketch of Hegel's system, so far as is requisite to understand the position which the question of the origin, or the history, of time, space, and consciousness occupies with him; and it is clear that nothing said in this chapter, from the point of view adopted here of the relation of the history of a part to the nature of the whole, can be an answer to a theory founded on such a totally opposite view as Hegel's. The answer to Hegel's theory requires an examination into the nature of logic, and the controversy must be a logical one. Nothing decisive can be brought forward therefore in the first part of this Essay. What I think has been now shown is, that self-consciousness is on the one hand not an element in all cases of consciousness, and on the other not a simpler but a more complex phenomenon than consciousness; and further, that self-consciousness does not reveal to us any Ego or Subject-Object, but only the empirical ego on the one hand and the pure ego or Subject on the other; neither of which can be regarded as the cause either of consciousness or of self-consciousness, still less of their forms, time and space, either generally or in the mind; and that self-consciousness, as the more complex phenomenon of the two, must be explained by a reference to consciousness, and the object of self-consciousness by a reference to the object of consciousness, by stating it in terms of time, space, and feeling, and pointing out the additional element, namely reflection, which it contains. The Subject, such as it is, indeterminate feeling in incomplete moments of time, lies within consciousness, is discovered therein by reflection; and on account of its incomplete nature is incapable of being the cause of consciousness. Psychology therefore is debarred from all theories of the Ego as the cause of consciousness, for the whole ground where the Ego could be found is searched by reflection, and the Ego not found there. But whether physiological psychology will ever succeed in establishing by inference the existence of an immaterial Soul, or, as I should prefer to express it, an intangible and invisible Soul, as the cause of consciousness, and in inserting such a soul between the material organ, the brain or nervous matter, and consciousness, or in placing it before both consciousness and the material organ as the invariable condition of both the one and the other,—this is a question which cannot perhaps yet be decided in the negative, and which it is not in place to discuss here. What science would gain by this being established is not clear; a more complicated cause would be substituted for a simpler one, but then this would be, by hypothesis, demanded by the facts. But until this has been done, it remains to the metaphysician to have recourse to that cause or invariable condition of consciousness which is an empirical object of presentative perception, to follow the physiological path as far as it leads him, secure that on that path he is at least on the safe road towards truth.

But before proceeding to consider the third class of theories of the origin of consciousness, let me be allowed to illustrate by a comparison the process of consciousness developing into reflection, a process which has already been described as accurately and unfiguratively as the language at my command permits. Consciousness in this process may be compared to a man walking backwards, who does not see each step as he takes it, but only immediately after it has been taken; who sees the ground beneath his feet only when he has passed over it, not while it is being passed over. He sees the past, but neither the present nor the future landscape. It spreads to his right and left and before his face, and ever a new crescent rises, and an old one drops out of view. Of the future landscape behind him he argues from that which is now past and before him, and he can guide his course by an anticipatory judgment. The step however which he is at any moment taking has no more certainty than any of his future steps, and it is only by an anticipatory judgment that he knows that it will not plunge him into an abyss. The past landscape which is now in view has been not only an unknown future but an unknown present landscape, and has become past only by going through the stage of the present. So it is also with consciousness developing into reflection, only that consciousness and reflection are compelled and do not choose to adopt a blind and backward course. First consciousness is conscious of the landscape right and left, including the path before its feet, then of the growth of the path before it (and it is in distinguishing its own path from the rest of the landscape that reflection is completed), then of the unknown portion of the path and of the landscape which will become known the next moment, and finally of the presence of the same unknown moment in every step of the past and future as well as of the present. The different phases of the landscape, as seen from different successive places in the path, represent the empirical ego, the unknown moment in every present step represents the Subject.

The fact of our never being, even in reflection, conscious of the moment of consciousness, but only of its result, the fact that there is this unknown moment in the very act of reflection, that the object of consciousness and of reflection is known only after and not in the moment of consciousness, in the completed and not in the uncompleted moment of consciousness, a fact first told to us by reflection, this fact seems to me to be one ground, at least, of the ineradicable sense of freedom, which we call freedom of the will. Das gebe ich dir, says Jacobi, ohne Widerrede zu: dass das Gebiet der Freiheit das Gebiet der Unwissenheit sey. Ich setze nur noch hinzu: Einer dem Menschen unüberwindlichen. Werke, vol. 2, page 322. But I do not know that Jacobi would have given his words such an application.

§ 22. I come now to the third class of theories, that class usually but wrongly distinguished as materialistic, and which ought properly to be distinguished as physiological. For the first class of theories is also materialistic according to the true meaning of the term. Some matter the Soul of those theories must possess, or it would not be an object at all.

> "If matter, sure the most refined,
> High wrought and tempered into mind,
> Some darling daughter of the day,
> And bodied by her native ray;"

this it may be,—but it is matter unmistakeably still. Both these classes of theories are materialistic in the same sense of the term, and both become equally objectionable, if it is objectionable to be one-sided, only if they are put forward as the whole account to be given of consciousness, if they profess to decide the nature of consciousness by an enquiry into its origin and history in the mind. On this point I must say a few more words before entering into the physiological theory.

The analysis of the phenomenon of reflection has brought us back to the conception of subject and object, as two aspects of the same thing, co-extensive and coeval with each other, the conception which was exhibited, though imperfectly, in the diagram in the preceding chapter. And since reflection is the last effort of consciousness, the final analysis which is reached by reflection must be the ultimate analysis and nature of the thing analysed; the conception exhibited by it cannot be overridden by, or made subordinate to, any other mode of conceiving objects. Accordingly, every thing that follows in this chapter, the enquiry into the history and origin of consciousness, must be entirely subordinate to that conception of the nature of consciousness and its objects, as two aspects of one and the same thing. But how is this to be done; in what way can the origin of consciousness be conceived, when it has been shown that it is coeval and coextensive with its objects, with its forms, time and space, and with its material element or feelings, these being infinite both in time and space? To enquire into the origin of consciousness is to suppose that there was a time when, and a space where, it did not exist; yet reflection has forbidden us to suppose that there ever was such a time and such a space. Can consciousness have a beginning in time and space, and yet be coeval and coextensive with time and space; or be coeval and coextensive with its objects, and yet be preceded by some of its objects as its causes? The individual consciousness seems to have an origin in time and space, before which objects existed; and to await its end in time and space, after a short life, after which objects will exist as before. Yet these objects before and after life are objects only of the individual consciousness, and when either of these two relatives are taken away, the other, which is only its relative, must it seems share its fate. Here is a manifest contradiction, or at any rate what seems to be such; and the proof of the difficulty being really felt is the fact of the many theories adopted in order to escape from it. Three ways have been struck into, corresponding to the three classes of theories exhibited in this chapter, and adopting the same principles respectively, in order to explain the origin and history of the world or of consciousness. Each of these ways is essentially a theory of an Absolute, and each transforms the theory of origin from a subordinate theory into a theory sometimes covertly and sometimes professedly complete and all-embracing. Corresponding to the first class of theories there is the theory of thorough-going Idealism. It escapes from the difficulty of supposing that the individual consciousness has an origin in time and space, and yet that time and space and objects exist only as objects of consciousness, by conceiving that the objective side of the equation or pair of relatives, that is, the objects of consciousness, are a mere appearance, a mirror, of the other side, consciousness itself; that consciousness is the only real existence, while its objects are a phantasm of consciousness, thrown off by it and lasting only while consciousness exists, consciousness existing absolutely and in itself, and out of reference to any object whatever. Corresponding to the third class of theories is the theory of thorough-going materialism; as idealism annihilates objects, so materialism consciousness. The origin of consciousness is here directly in question. Consciousness is conceived as a phantasm, or a mirror, of objects which exist really in time and space, of magnitudes which

to us are "as good as infinite;" certain combinations
of these objects, objects which are accepted as really
existing, without question as to their nature, that is,
as an Absolute, produce for a time a sort of phantasm
which has the capacity of consciousness, but which is
nevertheless a mode of objects. These two theories,
absolute idealism and absolute materialism, are the
logical results reached, or to be reached, by following
up the enquiry into the origin and history of the
world, or of consciousness, as if it was the whole
question; instead of keeping that enquiry subordinate
to the question of nature. The theories of the second
class are already theories of an Absolute. They do
not subordinate the enquiry into origin to that into
nature, nor that into nature to that into origin, but
they keep the two in balance and combine them at
every step. This class of theories alone has been
adequately worked out; it is represented by Hegel.
Neither consciousness alone nor its object alone is the
Absolute, the cause of the other, or the reality of
which the other is the phantasm; both are united inseparably, and only together are they the Absolute.
Thus the Absolute has a nature, it is to be subject
and object, consciousness and its objects, at once.
This nature of the Absolute is Der Begriff. Its consciousness is Der Geist; its object is Die Idee. In its
infinite and eternal development every one of the
forms which it throws up or assumes, however imperfect, contains this same nature; objects are never
the cause of consciousness, nor consciousness of objects. Such is its nature; but what is its history,
and what the origin of the forms of thought and of
objects which it throws up or assumes in its development? Its nature, der Begriff, is to develop itself,

PART I.
CH. III.

§ 21.
The physio-
logical theory.

to unfold all that it has in it, in Hegel's phraseology, to become an-und-für-sich all that it is already an sich. How so? Its nature is to be subject and object, two opposites always, and sometimes contradictories, at once. It is all subject, but it is all object; it is all object and subject, but it is neither alone; therefore it is Begriff, for a Begriff or Concept-form is that which is the Identity of contradictories. In other words, the nature of the Absolute, der Begriff, is to produce ever new forms because it contains in itself Negation. Negation is the essential point in the Begriff, and two negations complete every Begriff; and the Begriff itself is the τὸ τί ἦν εἶναι of the Absolute; negation therefore is the mainspring of its development or history. The history and the nature are one and the same thing; it is only the special determinate forms of existence, the inadequate Concepts, Begriffe, which have an origin. Such briefly and inadequately expressed is one view of the grandest idea which the mind of man has ever conceived.

Thus the theory of the second class has no partial theory of origin, of origin considered as subordinate to nature, corresponding to it, because it contains both itself, and precludes the possibility of a partial theory founded on the same principle. The two partial theories of origin are theories of the first and of the third class. Reasons have already been offered for rejecting theories of the first class; the third class of theories has yet to be examined. But the question remains to be previously answered, how the apparent contradiction is to be solved between the equal claims of nature and origin, the avoidance of which contradiction was the motive which caused the substitution of the theories of absolute idealism and absolute materialism in the place of subordinate and partial theories corresponding to them. On what principle can the question of origin be made subordinate to the question of nature? The true answer is the same in some respects with that of Hegel. It is, that the questions of nature and history of consciousness and its objects are, though not identical, yet inseparably combined; but that since both of them, nature and history, are infinite in time and space, no question of origin can arise about them; while questions both of history and origin arise with respect to any and every particular object of consciousness. The history of consciousness is founded in its nature as much, though not in the same way, as in Hegel's theory. The history of consciousness is founded in its nature, not because its nature is the Concept-form and contains Negation, but because Time is one of its forms; consciousness begins to have a history as soon as it begins to exist, and that is at any point you can reach the furthest, going back into infinite time. All particular objects of consciousness on the other hand have an origin as well as a history; and one of these particular objects of consciousness is the connection of the empirical ego with that small portion of the universe which is most frequently presented actually, and may be presented always to consciousness, that is, with the body inhabited by it. In other words the conscious life of the empirical ego is the object of the investigations of psychology. Consciousness is a term of very wide meaning, and therefore may embrace very different particular meanings. Hence the apparent contradiction. If consciousness is taken to mean either the

Subject or the subjective aspect of phenomena, it has no origin; if it is taken to mean the conscious life of the empirical ego, as distinguished from the universe, it has an origin, as a particular object of consciousness. The conscious life of an individual, or of the empirical ego, may be imaged as a ring sliding along a pole, from end to end, to which ring cords are attached going off from it in all directions, so as to make it the centre of a globe of which the cords are radii. During life, that is, from the time when the ring is put on the pole to that when it falls off at the other end, it is in connection with infinity by means of the cords. The cords represent the perceptions and their objects in infinite time and space. The ring and the cords in the comparison are both tangible objects, and similarly the empirical ego in connection with its body is itself an object of consciousness in just the same sense as other objects are, namely, it is one of the objects which constitute the objective aspect of phenomena; it is as much an object as those objects are which are farthest removed from it in space and time; before reflection entered there was no difference at all, both were phenomena; after reflection, both became objects, differing in space and time relations, the conscious life of the empirical ego occupying that portion of space which is always nearest to the centre, which the Subject always perceives, or may perceive, whenever it perceives anything in space, and that portion of time which immediately precedes the moment of reflection. The connection of this portion of time and space with the more distant portions of both is the question of psychology.

Any moment however short in the course of the

ring along the pole is sufficient to allow the Subject in the empirical ego to perceive an infinity of time and an infinity of space. The Subject in the empirical ego is the correlate of all objects whensoever and wheresoever they may be, whether objects of psychology or objects of metaphysic. Existence is the sum of those objects; existence is presence in consciousness. Consciousness however has, through its objects, a fixed position in time and space, in the living body. Time and space are the forms with which it operates, perceives, or is conscious. Feelings filling those forms and moulded into them are the objects which it perceives. Those objects in space which are the farthest off are often the last to be perceived, a wider and wider range of the heavens is taken in by means of astronomical instruments; objects which are farthest off in time are often the last to be perceived, witness the problems of geology. Now with reference to space there is not likely to be any difficulty; but with reference to time it may appear strange to some, that what is perceived first should not always be conceived as existing first. The reverse is the rule, giving rise to the expression, "last in order of knowledge and first in order of existence." As we go on and on in investigation, we go back and back in order of nature. Instead of making the object last perceived the object last produced, we conceive it as having preceded the object perceived before it. Yet it was said in the preceding chapter and repeated here, that to be perceived was to exist, that existence was presence in consciousness. If so, it may be said, ought not the order of existence to be the same as the order of perception? This is the case when future objects or events are in question; when we imagine the future, that is, follow the chain of effects instead of causes of existence, that which is last in order of perception is also, as a rule, last in order of existence. Both the past and the future, the past dating back from the time of birth, and the future dating forward from the present moment of consciousness, are objects of the imagination, and are both constructed out of the same fund, namely, the fund of perceptions presentative and representative, which have been present from the time of birth to the present moment of consciousness. The life-time, being a fixed moment in time, with time before it and after it, causes those objects which are imagined last to be placed at the furthest point of time from itself; that is, earliest in past time, latest in future time; and thus the apparent anomaly, of what is last in order of knowledge being first in order of time, is removed. There is thus a double order, of knowledge and of existence; a progress in two directions at once, for the order of knowledge is itself a prolongation of the order of existence in a forward direction, while the objects which it imagines as existing in past time are a prolongation of the order of knowledge in the reverse direction. This is what I understand to be in Hegel's mind when he speaks of the progress of the development of the Begriff being a progress at once in two directions, a Rückkehr and a Fortgang, a Vertiefen into and an Entwickelung out of its essence. Everywhere what Hegel says must be interpreted, as alone it can be expressed, by a reference to the forms of time and space. The forms of time and space lie at the root of all the conceptions he forms of the universe and of thought. I do not say only that the language he employs and must employ involves, depends on, and expresses those forms, for this is by no means conclusive; but that the meaning of that language itself rests entirely on time and space, and the thoughts represent objects only in those forms.

Every thing which is not contained in the incomplete moment of consciousness, the Subject, is an object of consciousness, and every thing has existence in the same sense; the objects of existence previous to birth are objects of imagination, that is, objects not simply represented, but constructed out of objects represented, representations in a new shape. Past and future objects, each kind dating from the present moment, are present in consciousness as past and future, because time and space are forms of every moment of consciousness. Past and future objects are revealed to us and exist in present consciousness as the long line of Banquo's descendants are revealed by the glass carried by the eighth of the royal phantoms in Macbeth. Their existence as past and future objects includes in it a reference to the present moment of consciousness. The empirical ego belongs to past, present, and future time. The connection of the empirical ego with the body belongs, as an object of representation and not of imagination, to the present and part of the past time only. All objects without distinction have the same title to existence, namely, presence in consciousness; but all have not the same certainty, duration, or truth. That there has been a course of existence prior to the birth of the empirical ego into the body, or, what is the same thing, of the body into the empirical ego, no consciousness can doubt. Although this is an object of the imagination, it is not on that account uncertain. It is the province of reasoning to decide on the certainty or the truth of objects and classes of objects. Up to the present moment of consciousness, then, there has been a series of objects and events, empirical, taking place in the order of existence, and of which the connection of the body with the empirical ego is part. The invariable connections between the objects and events contained in this series, and in the future as well as in the past, since "Cujus rei ordo est, etiam prædictio est," are the field of enquiry of the special sciences. Psychology investigates the invariable antecedents of the conscious life of the empirical ego; not what consciousness is, but which objects of consciousness are they which invariably precede, in order of existence, those feelings or objects of reflection which exist in the body during life, and the removal of which invariably precedes the cessation of those feelings. The physiological class of theories on this question remains to be examined.

According to the physiological theories, the existence of the conscious life of the empirical ego, or of the connection of the empirical ego with the body, depends on the existence of nervous matter, and its degrees of development depend on the degrees of development of that nervous matter in quantity and complexity. Broussais in the 1st chapter of his work De l'Irritation et de la Folie, vol. 1. page 4. 2d edit., expresses himself thus: On voit que l'irritabilité est commune à tous les êtres vivants, depuis le végétal jusqu'à l'homme, et qu'elle est continue ; tandis que la sensibilité est une faculté propre à certains animaux, qu'elle n'est pas continue, et qu'elle ne se manifeste que sous des conditions déterminées. Ces conditions sont l'existence d'un appareil nerveux, muni d'un centre, c'est-à-dire d'un cerveau,—et un état particulier de cet appareil; car il n'est pas toujours apte à donner à l'animal la conscience des mouvements qui se passent dans ses tissus. Nervous matter, organised, possessing a centre, that is, a brain existing in a particular state or condition, is here pointed out as the invariable condition of conscious life. Taking the word brain as a brief expression for un appareil nerveux muni d'un centre, the invariable condition of conscious life will be, briefly expressed, a brain in a particular state. What this particular state consists in has not been determined, but what it consists in and what it is caused by are the great secrets, yet undiscovered, of physiological psychology. On these two questions increasing light may be expected to be thrown by physiological investigation, and to such an extent that they may be ultimately answered as fully as any other questions of physical science. Differences in the solutions offered or attempted of these questions make the differences between the several physiological theories of psychology, which all start from the one common basis above indicated. Against this common basis I think there are no valid objections; I believe it to be established beyond doubt by scientific research. The brain is an object which may be perceived presentatively; and the only question is as to the invariability of the connection between it and the feelings of the conscious life of the empirical ego. That it is the cause or contains the causes of those feelings is an inference, and in this respect the physiological theories agree with those of the first class; they both seek the causes of the conscious life of the empirical ego in something which is not included in that conscious life itself; they both infer a cause, and do not find it by analysis of the feelings caused. Consequently no physiological theory can logically confuse the brain with its feelings or thoughts; the separation of the two things in kind is provided for by the metaphysical distinction between feelings and qualities. Feelings can never be qualities unless they are considered as gathered up into fixed portions of space. The brain itself is such a complex of feelings, but the feelings supported or caused by the brain are by the hypothesis, by the condition of the enquiry, exempted from such a transformation into qualities, for it is their connection as feelings with the brain as a complex of qualities which is being examined. The inference of a cause supposes it to be different from its effect, and not contained in it.

Four things are to be distinguished,—the Subject; the empirical ego, or the world of feelings; the universe of objects, or the world of qualities; the brain, a particular object consisting of certain qualities, as the cause of the connection of the empirical ego with a small and distinct portion of the world of qualities. The Subject is no empirical or complete object, any more than time, space, and feeling are. The union of the three last constitutes empirical or complete phenomena; the union of phenomena with the Subject constitutes empirical or complete objects. The Subject taken alone would be necessarily conceived as out of all time and space, in other words, the attempt to consider it as an object is directly self-contradictory; the moment it is conceived as an object by union with phenomena, that moment it is conceived as fixed in time and space, as belonging to the empirical ego. The natural tendency of every one is to conceive every thing as an empirical object, to make even the elements and aspects of phenomena empirical, and to deal with them as such. Pure metaphysic, which refuses to hypostasise ultimate elements and aspects of phenomena, has thus necessarily an unsatisfactory because incomplete appearance; and there will always be a tendency to transcend it, and make some of its elements and aspects empirical, and therefore absolute. An idealist who should hypostasise the Subject might say, If the Subject is a necessary aspect of phenomena, and phenomena are eternal and infinite a parte ante, must not the Subject be so also? But this is to make the Subject into something which, besides being a member of a relation, has a separate and complete existence of its own; just as, for instance, master and servant are members of a relation, and one cannot be a master without having a servant, nor a servant without having a master, yet a man who is a master can exist as a man without having a servant, and a man who is a servant the same. Here the existence separately as men is a prior condition of the subsequent relation of master and servant. But the Subject has no such prior separate existence, the only existence which it has is as an aspect of phenomena; and this does not require that it should, alone, exist in the time and space relations which the complete phenomena exist in. The often employed comparison of light and darkness is much more to the point in this case. The first act of creation in the book of Genesis is "Let there be light: and there was light." The arising of light created an infinity and an eternity of darkness a parte ante; at that moment, fixed by the arising of light, there began to be darkness which had existed from eternity. Light created darkness in the sense of giving it a meaning and a nature; for darkness is one of those things which have meaning only in reference to something else, the first intention of which is a second intention. Darkness is the negation of all feeling of sight; light on the contrary has a first intention, it is the feeling of sight; in its second intention it is the negation of darkness. Hence light gives existence to darkness, which nevertheless occupies an eternity and an infinity previous to the existence of light. So must the relation of the Subject and objects prior to it be conceived; the Subject gives existence to objects, which have existed previously, in the sense of giving them a meaning and a nature; for though contained in all phenomena it is not observed to be contained in them, and the moment of its being first observed is called the moment of its first coming into existence; and it is thus treated provisionally as a finite object which has a beginning, notwithstanding that its nature is to be no object at all, and consequently to escape from all notion of beginning and ending. What is true of the Subject is true also of the empirical ego and the world of qualities, the two members of the distinction between the subjective and objective aspect of phenomena, for the Subject is that moment of time on the completion of which this distinction, and consequently the two members of it, arise. These three, the Subject, the empirical ego, the world of qualities, are coexistent and coeval aspects of phenomena, and constitute the entire metaphysical analysis or logic of phenomena. When any one of them is taken and considered as an object in relation to other objects, and as existing at any point of time or of time and space together, which is done when they are considered as connected with a body or with a brain,—this is treating them provisionally as particular objects, for the purposes of reasoning, since we must reason in the forms of time and space, and assume time and space to be wider than any object which we limit by them in volition for the purpose of reasoning. But this assumption and this voluntary limitation cannot alter the nature of the objects, in this case the metaphysical members of analysis of phenomena, which are reasoned of; they must come out of the crucible of reasoning with the same nature with which they entered it, and the assumption which alone introduced them into it must be laid aside when they quit it. The very reasoning process itself, which limits them provisionally, is a part, and an extremely small part, of the things which it assumes to limit and to make into particular objects for itself. In such reasoning only can the Subject and the empirical ego be considered as arising or coming into existence at a particular moment in the existence of phenomena; and when they are so considered they become, ipso facto, the mind, the conscious life of the empirical ego, the object of psychology, instead of what they truly are, the empirical ego and the Subject.

Difficult as it may be to become habituated to the distinction between the Subject and the conscious life of the empirical ego, or the mind, and to the consideration of the former as an aspect of all phenomena, and of the latter as an object among objects, it is yet not a self-contradictory theory; as those theories are which take mind for one thing and its objects for another, yet without resorting to an Absolute. In those theories the question of nature and the question of history hold an equal rank. Empirical objects make mind what it is as its causes, and mind makes objects what they are in their nature. Both mind and its objects are empirical objects, and yet each is the cause of the other. Objects are the cause of the existence of mind, and yet mind is the cause of the existence of objects, since without mind objects would not be what they are, and therefore we could not tell that they were the cause of mind. And if it is said that objects cause mind first, and then appear to it in a new shape, as the objects we are acquainted with, this is to have recourse to an Absolute in the shape of the Ding-an-sich. Each claims to be the cause of the existence of the other, that is, the cause of the other in the same sense in which that other makes the same claim. These claims are not only incomplete taken separately; that would be, by itself, no objection; but they are contradictory and incapable of combination, unless by making one or the other of the two objects, or both together, an Absolute. Transform however all objects into modes of consciousness, that is, into the objective aspect of mind, and transform mind into the subjective aspect of objects, and the question of history and origin is at once subordinated to the question of nature. What is an object, a quality, time, space, motion, causation, the series of objects in time, the series of objects in space? Take each separately and think of it, and the answer must be—a mode of consciousness. But in this the question of history is decided; the history or the sequence of causes of any object, however far back it may go, is a mode of consciousness; that is to say, is included in the question of nature. There is nothing previous to consciousness, for those things which were supposed to be previous to it are modes of itself; the laws which govern the sequences and coexistences of these modes are all that can be enquired into. There is nothing but time beyond time; nothing but space beyond space; the sum of things, existence, which is the objective aspect of consciousness, has no second intention, for it has nothing outside itself or before itself, in relation to which it stands. Consciousness and its objects are coeval and inseparable, two aspects of the same thing, which have no cause of existence out of themselves, but only a law of existence within themselves. Thus the question of origin and history, dealing with empirical objects, is subordinate to the question of nature dealing with metaphysical elements and aspects of objects.

It is not only in this part of psychology that difficulties arise from the separation of mind from its objects, as two empirical objects different in nature. Here the difficulty is to see how objects can be the cause of consciousness as an object, when consciousness is the cause of them at the same time. Later on, a difficulty will be suggested by the course of the discussion as to the mode of the action and reaction of mind on objects of sight and touch, and these objects on mind; how for instance a feeling of pain can cause the shutting of an eye, or the withdrawing of a hand, from a sunbeam or a candle. It is not only the physical action of the sensitive and motor nerves that is present and operative here; the feelings of pain are not only present by the side of and along with these physical processes, but are links

p

in the chain of events, are caused by the action on the sensitive nerve, and produce the action on the motor nerve. If not, why should exactly those actions be produced which withdraw the eye and the hand from the source of pain, the sunbeam or the candle? To escape from the pain, a final cause, is plainly the directing power, the motive, in these actions; feelings are a causative link in the series of phenomena, not merely an accompaniment of a series of phenomena in the nerves and muscles. Here then mind must react on physical bodies. How is this to be conceived? It is clear that mind and physical bodies must be brought under some common category, or have some common nature.

§ 23. After the physiological theories of the origin of the conscious life of the empirical ego comes the consideration of the physiological theories of the origin of the formal element in the cognitions of the conscious individual mind, namely, of the cognitions of time and space. These theories may be reduced, so far as I know, to three, all of similar nature and distinguished only by their respective degrees of completeness, according as they are founded on a single class of circumstances, or on the combination of this with a second, or with a second and a third class. They all seek the causa existendi of the cognitions of time and space, during the conscious life, in objects; they all consider time and space, existing in objects, as the cause of their existing also in the cognitions of the individual. The first of these three theories is, that time and space being universally present in objects of presentative perception, in every state of the consciousness of an individual from birth to death, and being the only points in which all objects, however dissimilar otherwise, invariably agree, become so habitual to the mind and assume such an exceptional degree of persistency, that, although they differ from other objects only in point of frequency of recurrence, which indeed is so great as to be universal presence in objects of presentation, they are soon regarded by the individual who experiences them as essential parts of his mental structure, and in fact become such.

The second theory agrees with the first so far as it goes, but adds a further circumstance in support of the conception common to both, namely, the circumstance of the strength of inherited impressions. If all the individuals of any generation are impressed as above described by time and space, those of succeeding generations will receive and transmit them with ever increasing accumulations of certainty, until they become inborn modes of consciousness, attached to and dependent on a particular inherited nervous or cerebral structure, which structure was produced originally by presentative perception of objects only in the first generation of men, as described in the first theory, and then being transmitted is fortified by the same constant perception in succeeding generations. This second theory is insisted on and adopted by Mr. Spencer in his Principles of Psychology, Part IV. chap. 7. This theory, I may remark, is quite in accordance with that circumstance in which, as I have maintained, consists the true meaning of the term necessity, in the cognitions of time and space; but others I am aware have considered that this explanation of the origin of that necessity in cognition reduces it to an apparent necessity only, and in fact explains it away. In my view, the theory of origin in the conscious life of the empirical ego is but the complement of the theory of the nature of these cognitions, so far as they are necessary; while in the view of many of those who hold, or reject, such a theory of their origin as the present, it is considered to be antagonistic to and destructive of that theory of their nature in which they are exhibited as necessary; and this in consequence of not keeping clear the distinction between the questions of history and nature. Similar has been the case with other doctrines in other subjects, for instance in anthropology with the doctrine of development of species by natural selection; the dignity and nature of man has been thought to be endangered by any theory of his origin that did not consecrate a special creative act to the production of mankind; but the question is here also, what man is, what his powers and endowments are, not how he or they came to be what they are, what the steps are by which his present actual position has been reached. It is of the greatest importance to keep these two questions, of history and nature, distinct; and the question of the history of any particular thing includes that of its origin, as the first link in its history. In psychology and metaphysic it is especially important, for the careful distinction of these two questions can alone prevent us from falling into the onesidedness which is the reproach of a materialism which has treated the question of origin as if it was the whole question, overriding, superseding, or supplying with a ready-made answer, the question of nature; which has thus given half truths for whole truths, and in doing so prepared the way for a falling back into two opposite errors, the transformation of objects into a deceitful appearance on the one hand, and into an absolute existence on the other.

According to this second theory, the cognitions of time and space are, with the life of the empirical ego of which they form a part, functions of the brain, and appear as a kind of intellectual instinct; nor is there any thing absurd in regarding cognitions, as well as feelings and actions, as functional or instinctive. It is very probable that the phenomena which we call instinct, the actions which we class as instinctive, are due to transmitted habits, actions performed so invariably during countless generations, that, though at first performed with consciousness and discovered by a tentative process, they are at last performed unconsciously and spontaneously, for instance the action of the young of mammalia seeking the breast. Instinctive actions include both reflex and consensual nervous actions; those are instinctive which appear to be performed for a purpose, in order to an end, but yet without apparent knowledge or perception of the end for which they are done, or in which the knowledge of the end is not the motive of the action. The terms instinct and instinctive are thus popular rather than scientific; they are the results of a crude and not an exact theory of the phenomena to which they are applied; and it was this character of an end being sought blindly, and without apparent knowledge of it, which attracted attention, and caused the phenomena to be attributed to some divine or supernatural or unknown power; a power which inspired the action, as it were, in its own superior wisdom and knowledge of what was fitting and requisite for the ends of nature. And what reason is there against supposing that a mode of cognition as well as a mode of action has in this way become habitual and functional? Nothing or very little is indeed known of the process which takes place in the nervous matter of the brain in consciousness; but it is impossible to suppose that consciousness takes place without action or movement of some sort in the nervous matter. It has been shown in the last chapter that movement is an all-pervading phenomenon belonging to the kingdom of objects, though not an ultimate element of objects. The movements to which some cognitions are attached may, for aught that is known to the contrary, and in accordance with much which is known, have become habitual and functional, so that the cognitions attached to them may share in their habitual, that is, their functional nature; or to put it in another light, that part of the movement essential to cognition, which is appropriated to the formal part of the cognition, may be the same in all cases of cognition, and then the cognitions attached or resulting, namely, time and space, will derive their universal or functional property from this part of the movement.

The third theory I will put in the form of a suggestion. The brain has been singled out as the cause of the conscious life of the empirical ego, yet not in isolation, without the concurrence of, and action and reaction with, other objects, but in such a sense that the entrance or addition of a brain to other objects completes the series of circumstances on the completion of which the conscious life arises. Both the constitution of the brain and that of other objects are contributors to the existence of the conscious life with its properties such as have been described. Now it is well known that the nerves of the special senses conduct only feelings each of its own special kind. The optic nerve gives only feelings of light, the auditory nerve only feelings of sound, and so on, whatever may be the means by which they are excited to activity. Touch the optic nerve and a light is perceived, touch the auditory nerve and a sound is heard. Conversely, no other nerves but those specially adapted for the purpose transmit special sensations; the optic nerve will not transmit sound, nor the auditory nerve light. "Electricity may act simultaneously on all the organs of sense,—all are sensible to its action; but the nerve of each sense is affected in a different way,—becomes the seat of a different sensation: in one the sensation of light is produced; in another, that of sound; in a third, taste; while in a fourth pain and the sensation of a shock are felt. Mechanical irritation excites in one nerve a luminous spectrum; in another, a humming sound; in a third, pain. An increase of the stimulus of the blood causes in one organ spontaneous sensations of light; in another, sound; in a third, itching, pain, &c." Dr. J. Müller's Elements of Physiology, Dr. Baly's transl., book iii. sect. 4. The sensations therefore of the special senses depend upon the particular constitution of the nerves of those senses. But on the other hand the sensations conducted by these nerves depend for their particular modifications upon the objects which excite them; what particular colour shall be seen, what particular sounds shall be heard, depends upon the waves of light and of sound in the air, outside the organism. The properties of the nerve and those of the external object limit and modify each other. Thus the matter of perceptions, the qualities of external objects, or the sensations in the perception of them, depend upon the constitution of the nervous matter together with the constitution of the object perceived; that a sound or light shall be perceived depends upon the nerve, that it shall be such and such a sound or light depends upon the object. May not the same hold good in the case of the formal element in the same perceptions? Why should we attribute the appearance of sensations in the forms of time and space solely to the object, and not also to the constitution of the nerve? It is true that the time and the space occupied by perceptions in the brain are not the same as the time and the space occupied by those same perceptions in the rest of the world of qualities; in a short moment of consciousness we can represent to ourselves a year, a century, or an age; in a short moment of consciousness and in a small portion of nervous matter, the surface of the retina, we can present to ourselves a large portion of the expanse of heaven; in a short lifetime and in a confined abode we can reproduce, and even produce in imagination, the perceptions of a great part of the worlds of history and astronomy. But may not the same conception hold good here which held good in the case of the matter of perceptions? May it not depend on the constitution of the nervous matter that we have time and space at all in our perceptions, and on the particular constitution of the objects perceived that we have this and that size, length, figure, and order in the perceptions? It is true that, if we consider the perceptions as they exist in the brain, the relations of the time and the space which they occupy there to the time and the space occupied by them in the rest of the world of qualities have not been determined; that, though the time they occupy in the brain is definite, yet the space is indefinite except in the cases of the extremities of the nerves of sight and touch. But the same may be said of the sensations or matter of perceptions; in the brain these are indefinite, and irrespective of the particular sensations of particular objects; the nerve-constitution supplies only a limit to the kind, that is, to the variations of the particular objective sensations. So also the brain can be conceived as supplying a limit to the kind or to the variations of the particular size, figure, length, and order, in time and space, of the perceptions of objects. The constitution of the brain, as possessing extension and duration, determines that objects shall appear as possessing time and space relations, while the constitution of the objects, in the rest of the world of qualities outside the brain, determines what particular relations these shall be.

Thus the time and space and qualities or matter of objects come equally from within, equally from without, the brain; and owe their origin equally to the constitution of the brain, equally to the constitution of other objects. This being supposed to be their first origin in the conscious life of the empirical ego, room is then left for the habit of the first theory and the inheritance of the second to operate, to continue the work, and to give the sense of necessity to these elements of perceptions. But the question of origin in the conscious life, of conditions of existing of both elements, formal and material, since both elements are equally necessary, should be decided by analogy. If the material element is due partly to the constitution of the brain irrespective of other objects, it is according to analogy to suppose that the formal element is so too; and that objects appear in consciousness, in the conscious life of the empirical ego, as

PART I.
CH. III.
§ 23.
Origin of the formal element.

extended, not only because they have extension themselves, but partly because the nervous matter has extension; that they appear as having duration partly because the nervous matter, as well as the objects, has duration. It is more according to analogy to suppose the cognitions of time and space coeval with the conscious life, because the nervous matter in which it arises occupies time and space, than to suppose the conscious life, so far as relates to the form of its perceptions, existing first as a tabula rasa or sheet of white paper, which is first modified and written on from without; for the nervous matter in which it arises is not such a tabula rasa, but has both form and duration. Or if the figure of a tabula rasa is adhered to, it ought to be employed with the addition of a "per impossibile," for even a tabula rasa has extension and duration. Indeed it appears to be impossible to suppose conscious life arising in an extended and enduring material substance, and yet arising not modified or conditioned by the properties or modes of that substance, as well as by the objects which excite that substance to reaction.

CHAPTER IV.

PRESENTATION AND REPRESENTATION.

Nun ist aber in der Anschauung nicht die blosse Wirkung eines Gegenstands, sondern der Gegenstand selbst unmittelbar gegenwärtig.

Schelling.

§ 24. THE analysis of consciousness and of phenomena is now complete; the elements and the aspects of all phenomena and of every phenomenon have been pointed out. It remains to exhibit these elements and aspects in conjunction, as constituting empirical objects and the complex of such objects in the universe of feelings; that is, first, to analyse the composition of the empirical ego statically; in other words, to examine the combination of the elements of consciousness in states of consciousness in which the time and the space are considered fixed and limited, abstraction being made of the states of consciousness which precede and follow the one under examination; and secondly, to analyse the composition of the empirical ego dynamically; that is, to examine the laws of change from one state of consciousness to another. The empirical ego and the laws of its constitution and of its progress, of its nature and of its history, are the object of enquiry henceforward; not, as before, the nature of its constitution and the history of its laws, but the laws of its nature as exhibited in the combination of its elements, and in the history or progress of its development; the general and sometimes the universal laws to which its combinations and its development anywhere and everywhere are found to conform.

The empirical ego is the complex of all feelings or states of consciousness, as distinguished by reflection from the qualities which are their objective aspect. These states of consciousness are either direct or reflective perceptions, or they may contain both direct perception and reflection. Reflections or reflective processes in consciousness are therefore themselves part of the empirical ego, and the objects of a further reflection; they hold two positions, bear two characters, first as phenomena of the empirical ego, states of consciousness simply, or direct perceptions, second as processes of reflection, inasmuch as their objects are other states of consciousness which have preceded them. In the present chapter abstraction will be made of this their second character, or their character as reflective, and they will be considered only in their first character as direct perceptions or states of consciousness. The eighth chapter will be devoted to consider them in their character of reflective processes. It must be remembered that an investigation like the present is itself an exercise of reflection.

The empirical ego must on the other hand, for the purposes of the present enquiry, be distinguished from objects as qualities which do not enter into it as feelings. The body, to which the consciousness of the empirical ego belongs, enters into it as a complex of feelings, and as such is combined with every one, or nearly every one, of its states of consciousness; but the brain which is the cause of its conscious life does not do so; it may be represented in some unfrequent states of its consciousness, but it is not commonly present as a feeling in the empirical ego. It is universally present as a contributing cause of the existence and continuance, and its changes are present as contributing causes of the changes, of the feelings in the empirical ego; but this is a fact known by inference, and when we draw this inference or examine the connection between the brain and the empirical ego, that is, reason psychologically or as psychologists, then first the brain is present as a feeling and an object of representation. The brain therefore, as a complex of qualities, has no more to do with the analysis of the combination and development of the feelings of the empirical ego, than the air we breathe, or the food we eat, or the earth we stand on; all these are particular objects of the empirical ego, necessary to its existence indeed, but forming an infinitesimal part of the complex of its feelings. To make these into objects of enquiry, in enquiring into the empirical ego, would involve giving a history of the objects of consciousness in all its branches, such as astronomy, geology, civil, political, and philosophical history, chemistry, anatomy, physiology, and so on. But it is the laws of development of the empirical ego, not the history of that development, which is the purpose of the remainder of this Essay. Leaving then the brain and its connection with consciousness apart, I shall endeavour to exhibit an accurate picture of the complex of feelings presented or represented in the empirical ego.

Of the four things distinguished from each other

in § 22, one, the empirical ego, has now been distinguished more at length from two of the others, the Subject or reflection as such, and the brain; the fourth is the world of qualities, which is in fact the objective aspect of the empirical ego. The world of qualities and the world of feelings are identical. There is no division between two objects, the feeling here, the quality there; but both are the same. It is nevertheless with the subjective aspect only that we have to do here; though it might appear that, since both were the same, it would be indifferent which aspect should be chosen for examination. It is not indifferent, for this reason. In their subjective aspect objects can be presented in their first intention, as they are to consciousness alone, without reference to their relations to any other objects; the same objects as qualities are very often incapable of being presented in their first intention, and without a reference to their causes, or effects, or some other relation to other objects. The ultimate analysis of any object will always be found presented in the form of a feeling and not of a quality; when any quality is named, there will always the further question arise, And what is that? The answer will be a feeling. Heat is a quality; it may be analysed into motion, and a particular kind of motion or combination of motions is heat; that is, one kind of motion is produced by another or composed of others, and the first kind of motion, heat, when described as so produced or composed, is described by a second intention. Heat in its first intention, however, when it is so produced, what is it? The only answer possible is, that it is heat as a feeling. Beyond this we cannot go. The subjective aspect includes the objective in it, which can be evolved out of it by reflection. The subjective aspect, feelings and not qualities, are the kingdom of first intentions and of ultimate analysis at once, and therefore the object-matter of metaphysic.

In investigating the laws of any special set of objects or portion of phenomena, that is, in any special science, the reverse is the method proper to be adopted; the objective aspect of things, or objects as qualities, are the most proper to be kept in view; for, first, the relations of objects and qualities to each other in time and space are the object-matter of investigation, and not the ultimate analysis of each separately, nor the comparison of this ultimate analysis with that of all other separate objects in other special sciences. Each special science works in a portion of the objective world, with only partial reference to other special sciences. What objects and qualities are towards each other, in what portions they will combine with each other, what they will produce when brought together, what changes they will produce in other objects; these and the like are the questions of the special sciences, not what they are for consciousness alone. Consequently the special sciences make abstraction of this their subjective aspect, and treat objects as collections of qualities, without reference to the feelings which they may at any moment be translated into.

There is a well known dictum of Bacon's which seems at variance with the view here taken of the entire correlation of the subjective and objective aspect of things. This dictum is to the effect, that the subtilty of nature far exceeds the subtilty of the human intellect, and seems therefore to imply that the latter is no perfect correlate of the former. The dictum is undeniably true, but it does not for all that destroy the correlation. The subtilty of nature is a fact of inference and representation; wherever it has not been completely fathomed and perceived by, or translated into, the subtilty of the intellect, there it is inferred and represented as existing, and as remaining to be some day perhaps perceived and fathomed. It exists no doubt; and exists as an inference and a representation, not yet translated into subjectivity in its completeness. The existing subtilty of the intellect is far inferior to this represented subtilty of nature; but on the other hand, the subtilty of the intellect, completely adequate to the subtilty of nature, exists also in representation and by inference, only that it is referred to the future, as that of nature to the past and the present. Some day or other all the subtilties of nature will be perceived, and the subtilty of the intellect brought up to a correlation with them. Both subtilties are inferences and representations, only one is represented as past and present, the other as future. The present degree of subtilty of the intellect is certainly far inferior to the present, inferred and represented, subtilty of nature; and man is regarded as the discoverer of a previously existing object; and in this sense the dictum of Bacon is true, without doing any violence to the conception of the perfect correlation of the two aspects of phenomena.

Since the world of qualities is the correlate of the world of feelings, and the general laws of both are under examination, if any general laws of one of the two correlates are discovered, they must also appear as general laws of the other. There cannot be general laws of consciousness which are not general laws of objects; and this it will be found there are, and that they bear both characters, objective and subjective. Since however these laws are discovered by reasoning, the proper place for their statement will be when the reasoning process is examined, that is, in the chapter on voluntary redintegration. Every universal law of consciousness is also an universal law of objects; and every law of objects, universal in a particular field, such as chemistry or mechanics, is also an universal law of consciousness when occupied in that field. Presentative perceptions are the source from which all others are derived, and from their vivid and inevitable nature they give the law to all others. Yet they are not entirely constant and unchangeable; on the contrary, they are capable of modification by representative perceptions to which they have themselves given birth. Two kingdoms thus arise, one of objects, presented and represented, considered as constant and unmodified, whether previous to or in consequence of modification; the other of objects, presented and represented, considered as subject to, or in course of, modification; the first is what is commonly meant by the term laws of nature, the second is what is commonly meant by the term man's empire over nature. It would be more correct to call the first the world as it is at any particular moment; and to call the second the world as it might be, or as capable of modification in certain ways. The second is entirely subordinate to the first, for the very circumstances and laws, which constitute and govern the modification of the world, are circumstances and laws which belong to, and are part of, the world as it actually is. Presentative and representative perceptions, inseparably mingled together, constitute one universe of qualities and of feelings, one universe governed by laws under which it functionates in one unchangeable course, but in the bosom of which, and among those very laws, there are found some which modify the operations performed under the guidance of others; and, since the proportion of the latter set of laws is small in comparison to the former set, the latter appear to be changers of the general order of the universe; the truth being, that the laws which govern the entire order of the universe embrace both sets of laws, both the modifying and the modified; and this order of the universe, this unchangeableness including change, it is, which alone deserves the title, or can be expressed in the terms, of universal and necessary laws of the world of empirical objects.

The change and modification here said to be introduced into the world as it actually is, at any particular time, is not the change or modification of one set of objects in nature by another set, such as, for instance, the change introduced into the nature of plants or animals by transplantation into different soil, climate, or circumstances; or such as the change introduced into inorganic matter by the implanting of organic matter, or vice versâ; or the evolution of force or motion of one kind from force or motion of another kind, and the reaction of the one on the other. All such cases of change, however striking, are instances of the regular and general course of nature, of the first of the two sets of laws mentioned above. The distinction here intended between those two sets of laws, the change apparently effected in the former by the latter, is a change and a distinction which arises from certain feelings of the empirical ego which are localised within and not without the body; it arises from the feelings of pleasure, pain, effort, or volition; and the distinction is therefore correctly drawn, though not correctly expressed, in saying that it is the distinction between the laws of nature on the one hand, and man's empire over nature on the other. The foregoing remarks will serve as an introduction to the remainder of the Essay.

§ 25. Presentative perception is never found by itself unmixed with representative perception; indeed the greater part of any state of consciousness, except the very earliest in life, is composed of representations. Representative perceptions are repetitions of presentative perceptions with a decrease in vividness. When an object has once been presented it has a tendency to be presented again, that is, represented, in other circumstances, and with decreasing vividness; and a store of representations is thus laid up, some of which are always present in consciousness. Since it is impossible to find states of consciousness which contain presentations only, it is necessary, in order to examine presentation, to consider cases of it in provisional images, abstraction being made of the representations involved in them; and this was the course taken in §§ 13, 14, where presentations of objects were examined apart from representation. But hitherto the enquiry has been limited to objects which may themselves be directly presented to consciousness, without requiring other objects to be represented previously; that is, it has been limited to the examination of objects of sensation internal and external; and the world of objects, of qualities and of feelings, has been described as a whole composed of presentations and representations of sensations mingled together. But there are certain feelings which arise and are presented to consciousness first in the representation of objects of sensation external and internal. These are the emotions. On their first arising they are presented, but they arise first in the representation of objects of sensation. When we begin therefore with objects, or the world, of sensation, we soon come to a point, namely, the representation of its objects, where feelings of a new order enter into consciousness; and these, though presented, yet belong to representation, if representation is taken to mean representation of the world of sensation. These new presentations, the emotions, give a new character to the world of objects. First the representations in which they arise are modified by them, and then indirectly future presentations of objects of sense are modified also; such presentations of objects of sense as are not in harmony with the emotions are destroyed or avoided, and such as are in harmony with them are produced or procured. It is necessary to take a view of the classes of the material element in cognition, in order to see the bearing of the following enquiry.

Feelings were divided, in § 12, into sensations and emotions, and the former into sensations of definite organs and sensations of indefinite organs. Of these three classes of feelings, emotions arise only in representation of objects belonging to the other two classes; but this does not imply that they are composed of the feelings of those other classes. However complex an emotion may be, whether it can be analysed into simpler emotions or not, it cannot be analysed into sensations; nor can it be analysed into sensations and imagination of them as past or future, probable or improbable, although perhaps imaginations of this kind may be necessary as conditions of the arising of the emotion; for instance the emotion of hope is very different from the sensation of health, or any other pleasure of sensation, combined with the expectation of enjoying it; the feeling which we call hope is something different from this, though it may arise immediately and be inseparable from it. The same may be said of desire and aversion, of love, anger, fear, and I believe of all the feelings which we call emotions and passions. The same is true of moral approbation and disapprobation of others, and of a good and bad conscience in ourselves.

There are two other feelings, or modifications of feeling, which accompany or can accompany all others, whether sensations or emotions, and arise indifferently in presentation and representation of sensible objects, I mean the feelings called pleasure and pain. If these arise in presentation and accompany sensations, they are commonly, but to the confusion of all accurate thought, called physical pleasure or pain; if in representation, accompanying emotions, they are commonly called, but with equal confusion as a consequence, mental or moral pleasure or pain. Every feeling if it has a certain considerable degree of intensity, or if it lasts for a certain considerable length of time, is accompanied by the feeling of pleasure or of pain; and even a feeling accompanied by pleasure, if it attains a certain further degree of intensity, or lasts for a longer time, begins to be accompanied by pain; and the pleasure and pain, which accompany other feelings, are so mixed with them that they seem to make but one complex feeling; and this might lead us to suppose that all feelings were but modes of pleasure and pain, were not this forbidden by the difference in kind which is always observable between them by analysis. Pleasure and pain never are observed pure, that is, separate from other elements of feeling, together with which they compose a complex feeling; to separate them in thought from other feelings is to represent them in a provisional image, of which the other feelings are the parts abstracted from and provided for.

Pleasure and pain are the boundary line between cognition and emotion, for some sensations are without pleasure and pain, but no emotions are so. Emotion may be defined as feeling arising in representation, involving pleasure or pain. Those feelings which are not accompanied by pleasure or pain belong to cognition and not to emotion. Cognition extends over all feelings whatever; feeling extends over all cognitions whatever; but the addition of pleasure or pain to feelings (and it must be remembered that all feelings may be accompanied by pleasure and pain) makes of feelings two classes, one class to which interest attaches, the other to which interest does not attach. These two classes of feelings and cognitions, distinguished from each other by the presence or absence of pleasure and pain in presentation, and of interest in representation (for interest is represented pleasure and pain), are the respective contents of speculation and practice; and the distinction between these two classes is the ground of the distinction between the two domains of speculative and practical knowledge. All action, operation, function, considered as a series of circumstances or events, leads us to consider the motive power, that is, what circumstance or event in the series or without it is the invariable antecedent of another circumstance or event in the series. In all voluntary actions, or series of events produced voluntarily, when we look for such invariable condition, we find that it is always a pain or pleasure or an interest of some kind. No one can name a voluntary action of which pain or pleasure or interest, that is, pain or pleasure presented or represented, is not the condition. Pain, pleasure, and interest are on this account called motives of actions, so far as they are voluntary; just as other circumstances are called motives, or forces productive, of events so far as they are not voluntary. Pain and pleasure when represented and considered as the motives of voluntary actions are called final causes; and as all causes productive of events or objects are called efficient, these causes are final and efficient at once; that is, their being final is the mode of their efficiency.

Does any one feel inclined to remark here, This is Utilitarianism? I reply: The term Utility, properly applied, is a term which indicates only mediate and subordinate ends. That which possesses utility, be it of ever so noble a kind, is by that very circumstance constituted subordinate to that for which it is useful; whatever possesses utility belongs not to practical knowledge generally, but to that wide section of it which is properly called pragmatic, or the knowledge of means for ends. Now I grant that things which are ultimate ends not only may be but always are also useful or productive of ends, which are less noble than themselves but still very desirable; for instance in the proverb, Honesty is the best policy, honesty which is an ultimate end is also useful, that is, productive of certain tangible advantages; but this is not its claim to our esteem. And it is in vain to apply the logic of utility here, and to say that the claim of honesty to our esteem is its utility in producing an approving conscience, for honesty does not produce but is such an approving conscience, the happy frame of mind called an approving conscience is included in the state of mind called honesty; that is, there is no more desirable state of mind produced by honesty than honesty itself; not what it produces or leads to, but what it is, is what the value of honesty and of all ultimate ends consists in. So again with Prayer. The logic of utility has been applied to prayer, and it has been argued that, if prayer does not produce rain or sunshine, it is of no value; or again that, if it only produces an effect in the mind of the person praying, it is either useless or useless and hypocritical both. But the truth is, that prayer is a state of mind which is valuable for its own sake, or as an ultimate end; and instead of asking what it is useful to produce, the question ought to be, what it is in its analysis, and its worth determined accordingly. Utility implies that all ends are subordinate, whereas some are ultimate. Interest is a term which includes both, and which is therefore coextensive with the term Practice in its widest sense. To judge of objects which are ultimate ends, like honesty and prayer, by the properties they possess of producing other objects, to which as producing them they are subordinate, whether those other objects are more or less noble than themselves, is to judge them by an inadequate and therefore a misleading standard; from which, I may add, the application of the distinction of first and second intentions would have saved us. Yet the term Utility would be legitimate instead of Interest, if we could adopt a theory of consciousness being one thing and its objects another thing in kind; for then all objects of consciousness might be represented as existing for the sake of something else, namely, of consciousness itself.

Here then, in Interest, is the great boundary line between Ethic and Metaphysic, between practical and speculative knowledge. It is not coincident with the distinction between the formal and material elements of cognition; if it were, our systems would be much simpler, but as it is they are perhaps better morticed, their parts lying over one another as bricklayers lay their bricks; but the distinction between speculative and practical knowledge falls a little on the material side of the distinction between the formal and the material element. Pleasure and pain, or interest, almost universal modes of feeling, are the boundary line within which all practical knowledge consists; the little more which speculation possesses over and above practice, the feelings which do not contain pleasure or pain, is the circumstance which assures speculation its supremacy over practice, a supremacy the same in kind as that which the judicial functions have over the administrative in a well-ordered state, a supremacy which we justify to our imagination by the epithets of calm, disinterested, unimpassioned reason. All emotion lies within, or on the practical side of, this boundary line; and while all practical knowledge is also theoretical, there is a small part of theoretical knowledge which is not practical, namely, feelings which do not contain pleasure or pain originally, or from which they have been purged. Putting this small class of feelings aside, and using it only to remind us that there is such a thing as perfectly disinterested cognition,—though I am far from doing such a contradictory thing as holding that such perfectly disinterested cognition is an ideal to be admired or aimed at;—contradictory I hold it, because it would be adopting as an ideal an opinion which condemns adopting ideals at all, for what is an ideal but a conception to which the greatest degree of interest is attached?—keeping then this small portion of feelings in mind only as a proof that speculative knowledge has a wider foundation than practical, and comparing together the two domains of speculative and practical knowledge, the two elements which each contains are found to be the same in kind, material and formal, but the material element in practical knowledge is always considered so far only as it contains or consists of pleasure, pain, or interest. Practical knowledge is speculative knowledge the material element of which contains, and so far as it contains, pleasure, pain, or interest. Speculative knowledge is practical knowledge abstracting from that part of its material element. That is to say, all knowledge is both speculative and practical, in two different respects; all knowledge has a speculative aspect and a practical aspect, each always at the least provisionally present in the other. In the proportion which the two elements hold to each other in any moment of consciousness, that is, in the proportion which the feelings of pleasure and pain hold to the feelings in which pleasure and pain are abstracted from, and vice versâ, in that proportion will the moment of consciousness be reckoned to be, predominantly or equally, practical or speculative, a piece of conduct or a piece of reasoning.

There is one other feeling which must be mentioned in order to complete the picture of the elements which come forward in representation as well as in presentation; it is one which belongs to the same class as pleasure and pain, and is also like them an accompaniment and an almost universal accompaniment of other feelings,—namely, the feeling of effort. It is not the feeling of muscular tension or exertion that is here meant, though that is a special kind of the feeling of effort, but it is the feeling of effort taken in a wider sense than as being confined to muscular action. It is difficult to imagine that any combination of two feelings in time, or in time and space together, can originally and in the first instance take place without being accompanied by a sense of effort, which afterwards vanishes when the combination of the feelings into one object or succession of objects has become habitual. All new objects are accompanied with a sense of effort, in comprehending them, or conceiving them in the relations of their parts, for the first time. Whether the phenomena which are to be combined in consciousness are all presented, or all represented, or partly one and partly the other, the object, that is, the phenomena in combination, involves a sense of effort until it has become familiar; and this sense of effort is part of the object, which on that account is called strange, odd, or incomprehensible. We are perfectly familiar with this circumstance in daily life, and it is difficult to avoid the conclusion that all objects, which must once have been new, must also have been accompanied originally by the sense of effort. This sense of effort in cognition is called Attention, and the quality which corresponds to it in the object is strangeness or incomprehensibility; when we call any thing strange or incomprehensible, we mean to assert that it would take a greater or less degree of attention to make it harmonise with our previous knowledge, or that it would take more attention than we could give to it, in order to make it do so. Generally then it may be said, that all phenomena, whatever other feelings they consist of, include or may include the feeling of effort, as well as those of pleasure and pain; and that even the simplest states of consciousness are originally or may become, in their material elements, highly complex. The arising of the sense of effort in any object is the arising of the phenomenon of attention. Previous to this the object was confused and obscure; it now begins to become distinct and clear. The difference between these two stages consists in the addition of a feeling, the sense of effort, a part of the material element of the object, which thus is differentiated and developed. Why such a process or such an addition takes place at all is not to be explained, but must be regarded as an ultimate fact in consciousness, like many others inexplicable, an ultimate element in analysis of the phenomena. It is probable besides that this sense of effort never arises but when accompanied, and never ceases but when it ceases to be accompanied, by pleasure, pain, or interest. Every object of perception contains both or neither. To attend to any object or any sensation supposes either that I feel pleasure in it, or that I feel forced to attend to it by the pain it causes; yet in both cases without having a distinct purpose in view, either the purpose of retaining and increasing the pleasure, or that of removing and lessening the pain. When there is such a distinct purpose in view, it is a final cause of the attention, and such attention may be designated by the name voluntary, as distinguished from the original and spontaneous attention out of which it sprang.

Besides the feelings already mentioned, there is the formal element to be taken into account; and then we shall have before us the entire object of reflection, the empirical ego, the world of feelings, both presentations and representations, exhaustively described in its general outlines. This yet remains to be done, by showing the mode in which presentations and representations are combined, so as to form new and more complex objects. The same formal elements which presentations and representations separately contain, the same formal elements which hold them together before combination with each other, these same formal elements, time and space, perform the same office for them when they are combined. No categories of the understanding, except so far as time and space themselves are such, are required to combine presentations and representations into new objects.

§ 26. It was said in § 10 that all perception, and consequently all representative perception, involved combination or synthesis, and that all the more complex perceptions involved comparison. As we have now before us all the elements of representation, we are in a position to enquire into this point. When I see before me a variously coloured surface and regard it with attention, fixing my view now on one part, now on another, I represent one part while another is being presented; if I recall sensations of touch at the same time and combine them with the sensations of sight, the surface appears in three dimensions, and breaks up into objects separate in space and at different distances from the eye and from each other, and the entire surface becomes an object of representation as well as presentation, it is presented to sight and represented to touch. Now in the process so described there are two stages; first the visible surface is partly presented and partly represented, when I traverse it in different directions with the eye; secondly, it is represented to touch while presented to sight. In both stages comparison is involved. In the first stage, suppose, red in one part of the surface is separated from red in another part of the surface by a bright light; the red in two places is perceived as red in each of them, and the sensation of red is distinguished from the sensation of the bright light between the two places. Instead of three moments of sensation, red, light, red, there arise two, red and light; that is, the red in one place and the red in the other are classed as the same sensation. It makes no difference whether I see the two places of red, or recall one while I see the other, or recall them both; there is no difference in the sensation, there is difference only in the place, or in the time and place together. No category or concept of unity or sameness is here applied; the surface is distinguished, difference is introduced into it, by the difference in the material element, in the sensations of red and of light. The perception of the sensation red in two places is the first foundation of the notion of sameness. Where is the difference? In the sensations of red and of light. Where is the sameness? In the sensation of red in two places. There is no sameness in the sensation of light, for there is no difference in the formal element, a difference first introduced by the material element. But why do I proceed in this way at all? why do I class the red in two places as the same sensation? The answer is found in the pain accompanying the sense of effort, the effort which accompanies the new phenomenon. The more the phenomenon is simplified, the less effort it involves. Tentatively, not at first with conscious purpose, I find that it is less effort to perceive red once than twice. But on what rests the power, the possibility, of perceiving red once instead of twice, as the same instead of different? The answer of Kant, and I believe of most so-called Platonising philosophers, would be, On a category or concept of unity, or sameness, as a form of thought, of which no further account could be given. The true answer is, On the unity of space itself. Physiological psychology gives no answer to this question; it is indeed not properly a psychological but a metaphysical one; and therefore psychology stops short with the answer to the previous question, namely, with saying that I do class certain sensations together, and that I do so because it is easier and simpler to classify than not to classify. It does not proceed to ask, What classification is in its ultimate analysis? The true answer to this question, which may also be expressed in a formula similar to Kant's, How is classification, or synthesis generally, possible? is, The Unity of space and time. Since space is one, and difference is only introduced into it by the different sensations, or by differences in the material element, it follows that, when there is no difference in the material element, there is no difference at all; when there is difference only in the

PART I.
CH. IV.

§ 26.
The immediate
and remote
object.

position of the material element, that is, in its relation to other sensations in space, there is unity in kind and difference in position, that is, there is sameness. Thus the concept Sameness first arises, as a consequence, not a condition, of the process; and the process which ends with classification is called diagnosis or comparison, a putting asunder different sensations and putting together similar sensations.

In the second stage of the process also a comparison takes place. Suppose the surface seen to be an open window with two red curtains on either side of it. The parts of the surface which I can touch, suppose one of the curtains, I have presented to two senses; two sensations characterise that portion of the surface, and distinguish it from the other portions; I now move and touch the other curtain, that is, after certain other muscular sensations I find the other red portion of the surface become distinguished by sensations of touch, and sensations of touch of the same kind as those distinguishing the other curtain. And from the place where I now am I can repeat the same experience with regard to the first curtain. The two curtains then become by comparison the same in every thing except in position in space. But the light between them either cannot be touched, or if I put my hand out I find sensations either of warmth or cold, or wind, or rain, very different from the sensations of the curtains. Still the open space is part of the visible surface, and if it does not contain sensations of touch, it contains sensations of sight. Notwithstanding the difference of the sensations in different parts of the visible surface, these parts are all alike in point of containing sensations; there is sameness between all the parts in this respect, and unity of the entire surface or object. Thus the second stage is a repetition of the same process of comparison as before, only with sensations of two senses instead of with sensations of one sense. And I think it will be admitted that, if this explanation is valid for the cases now examined, it is valid also for cases in which the material element is more various, for cases where the material element includes sensations of the definitely known organs, of the indefinitely known organs, and feelings which arise first in the representation of these sensations. All these form complete states of consciousness, portions of time and portions of space occupied by different feelings. Anger, for instance, is a state of consciousness in which a certain series of objects and events are represented, which bear the character or quality of being unjust, cruel, painful, or the like. The emotion is combined with the representation, and makes a part of it, corresponding in consciousness to some quality or circumstance represented as existing in the events or causes of them. If this circumstance, or this quality, is separable from the events, and in proportion as it is separable from them, the emotion of anger ceases or remits.

The same remarks apply to phenomena which occupy time alone; the only difference being that here nearly all the sensations are represented, whereas in space a great number are presented at once. An instance of representation of objects both in time and space at once, and on a large scale, is Gibbon's treatment of the history of the Decline and Fall of the Roman Empire. He there represents events not in the order of their actual occurrence, but of their affinities for each other, relating separately several series of events which occurred simultaneously, and disintegrating the one complex cable of events into many strands. But this is a process which requires a preliminary examination of the original complex series, in order to discover which are the events which belong to each separate strand; and this is only possible by observation of the similarities and dissimilarities in the material element of the events themselves. War, religion, wealth, law, race, and so on, become the heads under which the events are classified, according as they contain elements which predominantly bear upon such and such feelings or emotions in mankind.

Objects are phenomena combined in time and space, whether the material element is of one kind or more than one. One feeling in time, or in time and space, makes an object; and also any number of feelings combined in, that is, considered as occupying, one portion of time or one portion of time and space together, is one object also; but these two cases require distinction, for in the former case the object is simple and indecomposable empirically, in the latter case it is empirically, but perhaps provisionally, decomposable into simpler objects of which it is the aggregate. The former may be called the immediate, the latter the remote object. In the former case, the material element limits the formal; in the latter case, the formal element, already limited by one of the material elements which it contains, is the limit to within which other material elements are referred. Take any feeling in a certain time and space, and then see what other feelings are contained in those boundaries; in this way a remote object arises. Take the time and the space so limited and contrast it with the material element of all kinds which it contains, that is, with the feelings which occupy it, and there arises a notion which is the truth, or true modern and philosophical representative, of the old Greek and Scholastic notion of Substance and Attribute, or Substance and Quality. Time, space, and feeling are, taken objectively, time, space, and quality, or ποιότης, of that portion of time and space. Time and space are that in which alone the ποιότης can be said to inhere; and time and space are common both to feelings and to qualities. And not only sensations of the first class are qualities, but also sensations of the second class, such as the sense of effort, the sense of muscular tension, of heat, of cold, of hunger, and thirst, the last being qualities of our own bodies only, arising in certain circumstances. Lastly, emotions are qualities; for we always attribute to those objects of the senses, on the representation of which the emotions arise, some constitution or nature in consequence of which we desire, or fear, or hate, or love them; just as we attribute to visible and tangible objects some constitution or other, in virtue of which we see them and touch them. And we do this notwithstanding that it has never been possible to point out, in any objects on the representation of which emotions arise, any qualities which could make any claim on the ground of similarity to be regarded as the direct cause of the emotions which they were supposed to excite. Qualities and sensations are the same, two aspects of the same thing, and not cause and effect one of the other; so also with emotions; they are the qualities on the perception of which they are supposed to arise. The quality of being injurious to our interest is not, on being perceived, the cause of the emotion of aversion, but this quality and the aversion are one and the same thing, one arises and ceases and remits as the other does. This will probably be met by a denial, and instances brought, such as that of poison; poison, it will be said, is injurious to my interest, yet it does not inspire me with aversion unless I perceive it to be poison, that is, unless I perceive that it has this quality of producing death. This quality remains whether I perceive it or not, whether I consequently feel aversion or not, whether I consequently drink the mixture or not. Well, let us examine this instance; and I hope to be excused if I dwell at some length on it, as such instances are well adapted to set the relation of presentation and representation, and of object to subject generally, in a clear light.

By quality is meant here, as it has been throughout, perceived quality. The poisonous quality of a potion when perceived is aversion in consciousness. The existence of the quality unperceived (that is, imagined or assumed only by us now and here for the sake of argument) is not the cause, or at least not the only cause, of its being perceived by the person who is about to drink the potion; whatever may be the cause of the quality being perceived by him, when it is perceived by him he feels aversion, and feels less aversion the less certain he is that it is poisonous; when he is certain that it is not poisonous, he feels no aversion at all. The question is not as to the expediency of enquiring and feeling certain about the existence of the poison, but as to the nature of the phenomenon of the aversion when it arises. The question is, whether the perception of the quality of being poisonous is the cause of the emotion of aversion, or whether that perception is the objective aspect of the emotion. The quality of being poisonous is perceived in representation, an odour or a colour presented is combined with a representation of an injurious or fatal effect on the body; of course it is highly important that I should so represent it (supposing it to be poisonous); it is highly important that I should feel aversion and not drink the potion; but the only question here is about the connection between the emotion of aversion and the representation of the potion presented as poisonous. I maintain that they are one and the same thing; that it is impossible to have the representation and not to feel aversion, and impossible to feel aversion and not to have the representation of some injurious quality. If it is said that some people may have the representation and not feel the aversion, the answer is that, if so, it will be in consequence of their having a representation of some overbalancing benefit, as for instance of a release from suffering by death. The representation of the effect the potion will have on the body is the object, of which the emotion is the subjective side. There is no other object but this representation; experience, or the result of drinking the potion, has to decide whether that representation was a true one, whether the object as presented will act in one way or another; if it produces death, we then say that it before contained the poisonous quality, and that the representation was true. There is no other object but the representation. If there is, what is it? The poisonous quality itself. But this is the object of the representation, or the object as represented. Let us examine this point. We say that it *was* poisonous after it has been proved to be so. But we speak proleptically, if we say it *is* poisonous before the poison is represented as contained in it. Suppose the glass before us; is it or is it not poisonous? That we can doubt about it shows that it is not presented as poison. It is, then, represented as such. When it shall have produced death, then we say that it *was* poisonous all along; a representation of what it has been, not of what it is, even now, presented as. The proleptical manner of speaking is very common and very convenient, but in the one case it expresses an anticipation, even though there may be strongest evidence, in the other case a retrospection. In both cases the quality of being poisonous is an object of representation. When we say that it is poison, we mean that it will be followed in certain circumstances by death. The word "is" covers two meanings, it expresses either a fact of presentation or a fact of representation, and gives no distinguishing token as to which of these it is used to express. The quality of being poisonous is a fact of representation, when inferred before the fact of producing death; and, however certain we may feel about it, we still are speaking by prolepsis if we say that the potion is poisonous, as if it were a fact of presentation. After the fact of death, the quality is again inferred to have been present, as a cause of the subsequent death, a representation again, but one referred to the past time. The quality of being poisonous is never an object of presentation, unless the potion should be seen in the operation of producing death; this operation is that on which the whole business hinges.

Emotions being attached to representations;—and this admits of no exception, for suppose that we saw a murder committed before our eyes, the horror felt by us would not arise from the facts of presentation, but from the representation of their meaning and importance, that is, from our knowing that it was a murder we saw;—emotions being attached to representations and not directly to presentations, they appear to have an arbitrary origin, to be, as the current phrase goes, subjective, and incapable to a great extent of prediction; whereas the qualities to which they are commonly referred, e. g. the quality of being poisonous in the above case, seems to be capable of actual proof, subject to strict physical laws, and, in the current phrase, objective. The fact is that the quality and the corresponding emotion are equally subject to strict law, equally capable of prediction. The opposite mistaken opinion arises from confusing our knowledge, the knowledge of observers who now discuss the question, with the knowledge of the empirical ego under discussion. To him, to that empirical ego, the knowledge of the poisonous quality and the emotion of aversion are one and the same thing, equally subject to strict law, equally capable of prediction. To us, the observers, his emotion and his knowledge are two objects, and the fact of which he has or has not knowledge is a third object, which we may have means of discovering and being certain of, without his having any such knowledge. This third object, when known to us, is that which seems to possess such objective certainty when contrasted with the ignorance of another man, the empirical ego. But in this chapter, and in metaphysic generally, we are employed not in enquiring into the advantages observers have over combatants, or into the difference between the general knowledge of an observer, that every thing is subject to law, and the particular perplexities of a combatant as to what will be the particular events which will occur in obedience to general laws; but into the nature and proceedings of consciousness generally, in the empirical ego, irrespective of what others may know about them. It is perfectly true that, to a third person, the opinions and feelings of another man are more uncertain and less capable of prediction than many facts in physical nature; and generally speaking objective qualities are more easy of prediction than subjective feelings; the history and prediction of things from the subjective side, as they will appear to another person (the empirical ego) is a more complicated affair than the history and prediction of them as they will appear or actually are appearing as objects to the observer himself. The observer has two sets of objects before him, the objects or qualities of nature perceived by himself, and the objects or qualities of nature perceived by another man; no wonder the emotions and representations, which belong to this second set of objects, appear disconnected from the qualities of objects which belong to the first set. These two sets of objects ought never to have been compared together, or brought into connection with each other; nothing but confusion can result, or could possibly have resulted, as indeed has been the case, from such an illogical procedure. The objects of nature and the feelings of the mind, as they are to one and the same individual, are the object-matter of metaphysic, that is, of the branch of knowledge or enquiry which aims at investigating the connection and relations of consciousness to objects, of knowledge to things known, and of mind to the objective world. We are then right in judging of emotions by sensations, right in making both of them objective as well as subjective; but the error lies in assuming occult causes, or occult qualities, as the ground of either. Not even in visible and tangible objects is it possible to point out any qualities which are not resolvable into sensations. Both emotions and sensations are the qualities of which they are supposed to be only the evidence and image.

So far as to the analysis of representations considered as complete wholes, completed moments of consciousness, or complex objects. The following chapter will be devoted to the process by which they are produced, the course of their arising, or their genesis; yet not their psychological as distinguished from their metaphysical genesis, not their connection with the tangible organ, the brain, and the changes or processes which take place in it; nor yet their history as an entire series, either in the race or in any individual, which would be the application of metaphysic to history; but the principle of their genesis, the nature of the bond which is common to all, that is, their metaphysical genesis, or analysis as states of consciousness dynamically, as members of a succession of moments; in other words, the connection and relation of moments of consciousness to each other, not, as in the present chapter, the analysis of them separately and for themselves.

The moments of consciousness form a series, in which each moment is an object containing feelings, or qualities, occupying a portion either of time alone or of time and space together; and this series of moments, in their connection and concatenation with each other, will be the subject of the following chapter. It is true that the concatenation of the moments

§ 29.
The immediate and remote object.

of consciousness depends on that of processes or modifications which take place in the tangible organ of consciousness, the brain, just as each moment of consciousness by itself, that is, presentations and representations separately, depends upon states or a state of the brain; but to investigate this dependance belongs to psychology, which is in its earliest infancy in this branch, since nothing at all or very little is yet discovered of the condition of the brain either in perception or in redintegration of perceptions. The psychological causation of redintegration I shall leave entirely aside, and busy myself with attempting to discover the order in which moments of consciousness as such precede and follow each other, so far as these consist of representations and of presentations depending on them; for to investigate the order in which the original presentations occur, presentations independent of representation, would be to investigate the ultimate laws of nature themselves. These objects of redintegration at least we are acquainted with; and if any invariable order can be discovered in them, we shall be entitled to call that phenomenon which invariably precedes another its cause in consciousness; and those phenomena which invariably precede others, that is to say, that property or quality (whether belonging to the material or to the formal elements of the object) which determines what the succeeding object shall be, or from knowing which we can predict what the succeeding object will be, that property in objects will be correctly designated as their motive power in consciousness, or the efficient cause of their redintegration. This whole subject is commonly known by the name of the Association of Ideas.

§ 27. Man lives in a world of remote objects, at least from the time of the arising of reflection in his consciousness. These remote objects, as it has been shown, are composed of presentative and representative perceptions, presentations being vivid and original perceptions, and representations being less vivid repetitions of presentations. But when the word repetition is applied to them, it is implied that the same object is twice present in consciousness, once as presented and once as represented. Sameness means unity of feeling in diversity of time or of space, or of both together. The representations therefore are also different from the presentations which they repeat. The same thing is true of the remote objects which constitute the world in which we live. For instance, I pass to-day for the first time through a certain street in London; the street is a remote object composed both of presentations and representations; to-morrow I pass again through the same street, and on entering it I perceive that it is the same as that which I passed through the day before. What is it that takes place in consciousness, in this perception? First, a presentation of the street; secondly, a representation of the street passed through yesterday; thirdly, a perception of the unity of these two objects, which would be perfect unity were it not that twenty-four hours intervene between the two. If the feeling differed, for instance, if some houses had been burned down in the night, I should doubt if it was the same street or not, for it would partly renew and partly not renew the first presentation. The object of my perception the second day consists therefore of an object composed of a presentation and a representation, lasting twenty-four hours, counting back from the second presentation of the street.

There is another class of cases in which the progress is not from a presentation to a representation, but from one representation to another. Suppose that, instead of passing again through the street the second day, the street is suggested to me by something else. Then the second day I have a less vivid perception of the street than I had in passing through it the day before, but I still have a representation of it in my mind now, and a representation of it as having formed part of the presentations of twenty-four hours ago; and these two representations melt into one, just as in the former case. I refer however the certainty of the existence of the street in both cases to the presentation. In the first case I say, The street certainly exists now, though I may have dreamed it yesterday; in the second case I say, The street certainly existed yesterday, though I only represent it now. In the second case too, the places occupied by the presentation and the representation are different, as well as the times; for on the second day I am in another place, and the representation of the street does not fit in with the objects of the present landscape. This change of place requires accounting for; and this is done only by the events which have happened in the course of the twenty-four hours during which the street is represented as existing in its own landscape, its landscape as an object of presentation.

Presentations and representations differ from each other only in degree of vividness, which includes distinctness in arrangement of their parts. But any particular object as a representation differs from the

PRESENTATION AND REPRESENTATION. 253

same object as a presentation, when the two are compared together by a subsequent reflection, at least in point of position in time. These two objects however make together but one object, occupying the whole of the time which separates them; not indeed occupying the whole of it with equal certainty, but some parts with greater or less degrees of probability; as, for instance, I am certain of the existence of the street when I see it presented;—when I recall it next day, I am certain only of its existence at the former time; nor am I so certain of its having existed then, as I should be of its existing now, if I were again to have it presented; for the fact of its having been presented is now only a representation. Such is the account in general terms of the world in which we live, or in other words, of the empirical ego, considered as distinguished into presentations and representations.

All our representations have been once presentations, or have been formed out of their elements differently modified and combined; a difference which is capable of an infinite variety. But here arise two questions, which it is well to state, but which are both unanswerable in metaphysic or as metaphysical questions; first, why there are presentations at all; second, why they have a tendency to become representations, or to be repeated less vividly in consciousness. The first question is equivalent to asking, why there is a world or an existence at all; as to which it has been shown that we can analyse its nature, but not assign its cause. The second question admits only of a psychological or partial solution. Given the fact of representations following presentations, or the tendency of presentations to be repeated as repre-

Part I.
Ch. IV.

§ 27.
Remote objects in connection.

sentations, then the existence of the brain, its connection with the rest of the world of qualities, and its consequent modifications, is to be regarded as in some way or other the condition of this reproduction. The sequence of the representations depends ultimately upon the sequence of the presentations, so far as these latter are unmodified by volition; and the sequence of the representations, either modified or unmodified by volition, reacts again upon the presentations, in a degree slight by itself but important in its accumulation, for it is this accumulation of mental wealth which transforms and improves the world.

Two other questions arise however with reference to presentations and representations, which may be answered partially now, and perhaps completely in the far distant future. The first is, What is the law which determines whether such and such a particular presentation shall be repeated as a presentation or not; for instance, whether a man who has seen a particular street in London to-day shall ever have it again presented to him. The answer to such questions as these depends upon the inductive examination of the course of nature, and cannot be given by any knowledge of the laws of consciousness; not because the laws and the phenomena of nature are not equally phenomena and laws of consciousness, but because the phenomena require experimental observation and comparison in their relations to each other, and their investigation has accordingly hitherto treated the phenomena as belonging to the world of qualities and not to the world of feelings. And in this investigation the results hitherto reached have been very general, and men have not yet succeeded in reducing to knowledge the complicated contingencies of everyday life; in other words, we know many of the laws, but very few of the facts which would fall under them, the greater part being hid from observation.

The second question relates to the sequences of representations, without intermixture of presentations; and these have always been considered as phenomena of the world of feelings and not of the world of qualities; the examination of them has been hitherto psychological, and the results have been held to belong to psychology. The question is, Why such and such a representation should be followed by such and such another representation; or what is the element in any representation which is the invariable antecedent of such and such another, or determines what the next shall be; for instance, why, when I am thinking of St. Paul's, the name of Brunelleschi occurs to me. The enquiry is equally experimental and determinable by observation as in the case of presentations, and equally incapable of being determined by any previous knowledge of the laws of mind. The suggestion which I offer in solution of this question will be found in the following chapter.

CHAPTER V.

SPONTANEOUS REDINTEGRATION.

Ἆρ' ἥσθου τι προσδεῖσθε ἐν τῇ ξυγχρήσει;
                                            Plato.

§ 28. Sir William Hamilton has shown, Lect. 31, 32, vol. 2, p. 233, referring besides to Aristotle and St. Augustine, that the laws of association are all of them cases of the single law of redintegration. Of any past state of consciousness, whether highly complex or comparatively simple, any part, member, or element, recurring again either separately or in connection with other objects, and whether it be in presentation or representation, has a tendency or power of calling back and redintegrating in consciousness a part larger and more complex than itself, or the whole, of the past state of mind in all its completeness. And since the whole of the past conscious life of an individual is one connected whole, any object or any moment of this connected series has the tendency or power of beginning a redintegration, which might continue itself until the whole conscious life was lived over again in representation. Any object which has formed part of a complex state of consciousness may also have formed part of other complex states, and have occurred in an infinite variety of combinations. It will have a tendency to redintegrate all of these; but it is obvious that it will not redintegrate nearly all, perhaps not even one completely; for it will commence redintegrating one, and while this is going on another object may come into prominence, in the half-finished redintegration, which will change the course of thought and become the starting point of a new redintegration. It becomes necessary therefore to enquire what are the particular laws of redintegration; what laws determine the preference of redintegrations, or the tendency of particular objects or states of consciousness to redintegrate other particular states of consciousness.

Turning for a moment to the psychological order of causes of redintegration, in order not to forget its position and the relation it holds to the metaphysical order, a homely comparison may perhaps be of service in connecting the two orders. Many people will remember seeing children "watch the congregation go out of church," or doing it themselves as children. A child burns a newspaper and throws it beneath the fire-grate;

> "The flame extinct, he views the roving fire,
> There goes my lady, and there goes the squire;
> There goes the parson, oh illustrious spark,
> And there scarce less illustrious goes the clerk."

But Cowper's lines do not give a full picture of the vagaries of the "illustrious sparks;" they often return on their steps (having forgotten perhaps a prayer-book), and shine where they had shone before; they linger (having forgotten perhaps a prayer), and others join them to see what they are about; they illuminate the deserted benches, and different parts of the church are perhaps many times refilled with their former occupants; they traverse the church again and again, and only after many partial reilluminations the whole becomes finally dark. It is to these partial reilluminations of the newspaper tinder that I compare the process of redintegration. The brain is the tinder, the perceptions and aggregations of perceptions are the sparks and masses of sparks, the redintegrations are the reilluminations, only not so short-lived. Of course this is not to be pushed too far, but only employed to assist the imagination in representing the process of redintegration as arising in its tangible organ, the brain.

The law or laws of association are thought commonly to have been already discovered; causation, resemblance, contrast, contiguity in place and time. All of these Sir W. Hamilton reduces to one general law, that of affinity. It is true that all moments of consciousness, all objects of consciousness, have affinity with each other; for all are feelings, all occupy time, or time and space together, and all are parts or portions of one series of moments of consciousness, and of one corresponding universe. If however, in order to come nearer to particulars, we distinguish this general law of affinity into cases of contrast, resemblance, and contiguity in place and time, or go farther still and add causation to the list, this gives us no law of the preference of contrast to resemblance, contiguity in place or time, cause or effect, or in short of the preference of any of these to any other of them; still less does it give us any law of preference within the selected category, or point out which among the causes, or effects, or objects resembling or in contrast, is to succeed to the object with which we start. Any object whatever is connected by affinity with all other objects whatever; and any object whatever stands in relation of either contrast or resemblance, cause or effect, contiguity in place or in time, to any other object whatever; so that, if the two connected objects do not readily fall together under one category, they do under another; and consequently to point out that they stand in some one or more of these relations, when they occur in redintegration, is no explanation at all of the process of redintegration, is no discovery of the link between objects in redintegration, of that quality in any object which determines what the succeeding object shall be.

Besides the foregoing objection, this explanation of the laws of association is open to another not less serious. It is, that they are calculated to form links only in voluntary and not in spontaneous redintegration, nor yet in those cases of redintegration which having been originally voluntary have become spontaneous, but solely in those which are still actually voluntary. For the explanation supposes that I pass from one object of consciousness to another through the representation of a relation of a certain kind, a relation either of cause or resemblance or so on. Suppose it is the relation of cause which is the link, why is this relation distinguished from others, unless it be that we already have a purpose in view, and know where to look for the object to be redintegrated? And in this case the volition, the choice of the category of cause, is the real explanation, the determining element, in the object redintegrating, determining first the redintegration of the notion of cause, secondly the particular objects which fall under that notion. Neither in spontaneous nor in voluntary redintegration are these categories of cause, resemblance, contiguity, &c. a real explanation of the determining element in the objects redintegrating.

Again, supposing that we did pass from one object to another through some one or other of these notions, as the connecting link, we should still require an explanation of the link, which connects that link itself with the redintegrating object, or object beginning the redintegration, and to account for why this relation and no other is fixed upon, retained, and employed as a link with other objects. Why should the sight of a table redintegrate the notion of cause, or effect, or resemblance, or contrast, or contiguity in time, or contiguity in place? Why should we pass from any object to this class of six general notions? Why should we single out one of the six in preference to the rest? Why should these or any one of them be supposed to be the determining element in the object, table, by means of which it calls up or redintegrates in consciousness, say, a pen, a chair, a dinner, a Bench, or a Board?

To take an instance; if my bookcase calls up the notion of the carpenter who made it because he is connected with it as its cause, this must be because I go through the notion of causation to reach that of the carpenter; for if it calls up the notion of its carpenter before that of its cause, it is clear that carpenter rather than cause should be the name of the link of association; and the question still remains, What determines me to go in this particular instance from the notion of the bookcase to that of causation, in preference to the other five notions or any others besides them? All notions of objects may be connected together by or under some or all of these categories; but this very fact disqualifies them for being considered as the leading threads or motive power in producing or calling up the notions of particular objects out of, or in consequence of, the notions of other particular objects.

There is no exciting, suggesting, or calling up of like notions by like, of cause by effect, of neighbour by neighbour; this is no true account of the process of redintegration. There is no affinity between separate objects or their representations, in virtue of which one produces or reproduces the other. It is true indeed that something like this may appear to have taken place when we reflect on the redintegrating process, and first begin to ask after the laws of connection of objects supposed to be separate and independent. We have, however, not really been stepping from object to object, contiguous, similar, or dissimilar, like the Shadowless Man, in Chamisso's tale, from island to island. There is no power or quality in the representations, considered as images of objects, by which they can summon each other. The general notions which bind them together, such as causation, contrast, contiguity, and resemblance, though undoubtedly they form a common element pervading them, yet have no generative power, and cannot impart any such to the perceptions which they bind together. Time and Space are indifferent to the particular empirical objects they may contain. The whole chain, network, or pile of network, to which our past states of consciousness may be compared, and to which we may consider every new moment of consciousness, whether of presentation or representation, as adding a new mesh, is one connected and closely netted whole, any part of which may come into consciousness again, and some part of which must come into consciousness again, in every new moment of consciousness. Not because notions have been together in the objects, or world of qualities, but because they have been together in consciousness, the feelings of the empirical ego, do they reproduce each other.

How came it to pass that these categories were fixed upon, as the links connecting objects in redintegration? It appears to have been because objects were considered separately, one by one, and not as modifications of one world or one consciousness. Just as objects of perception were considered separate, a table, a chair, a Roman Emperor, a star, for instance, as so many distinct separate objects, the conjunction of which in one space made the world in which we live, so the representations of these objects were considered not as moments in one and the same series, and one and the same consciousness, but as separate objects in the mind, each existing for itself, and connected, not in kind as parts of one whole, but by mere juxtaposition in time, in the empirical ego. The connection between the parts of the series of images in the mind was then sought in the images so far as they were representations of external objects, that is, in the time and space relations of the images to each other, instead of in the images as moments of consciousness, or as feelings of the empirical ego. Thus not only were the representations, or ideas as they were called, images of external objects; for instance, my idea of a Roman Emperor an image of that Roman Emperor as he once existed in the external world; but the connections between the ideas were images of the connections between the external objects; which circumstance lent great completeness and plausibility to the theory. As the external objects were subject to certain laws of sequence and coexistence, so also their images in the mind; and the laws of sequence and coexistence of the images in the mind were the images of the laws of sequence and coexistence in the external objects. The mind in producing her images in association thus was imitating and repeating, in her own domain, the operations of nature, making use of certain general laws which she derived originally from the observation of the sequences and coexistences of external objects; not that the two, or the three, or the six, laws of association, however they might be counted, were supposed to be a representation of all the general laws of sequence and coexistence in external objects, but that they were a selection from them, or a general expression and image of them, adopted by the order of nature for the mind to conform to in her operations; whether it was that the mind was determined so to operate by the physical laws or constitution of the brain, or whether the mind imposed the laws on herself in consequence of original observation of, and abstraction from, the external objects.

But when once the conception arose of consciousness being one connected series, lengthening itself each moment, and growing out of its former self and out of its previous content, as a plant out of its seed, so that the moments of consciousness are not separate objects, calling up each other in virtue of similarity or contrast, but organic parts of one living whole; when once attention was called off from what representations are as images of objects in perception, and fixed on what they are as members of a subjective series of moments of consciousness, as containing feelings and not as containing qualities; which is virtually what Sir W. Hamilton has done in his reassertion of the general law of Redintegration;—then the enquiry was directed into its proper channel, and the process of lengthening of the chain of consciousness in redintegration was exhibited in a manner favourable to investigation.

§ 29. Brown, in his Philosophy of the Human Mind, lect. 35, in pointing to emotions as a source of association, and James Mill, in his Analysis of the Phenomena of the Human Mind, chap. 3, in pointing to vividness and frequency as the causes of strength in association, and connecting vividness with pleasure and pain, came very near to what seems to me to be the truth. Referring to the analysis of representations in § 25, there will be found only two which can be regarded as the elements or qualities determining redintegration. If the redintegrating object is a representation, the factor in it which determines the redintegration of the next object is the predominant interest which it contains; if the redintegrating object is presented, then either the pleasure or pain, or some represented pleasure or pain, that is, some interest, is the determining factor. Sir W. Hamilton too, in note D*** to his edition of Reid, p. 913, states as a "Secondary or Concrete principle—what may be styled (under protest, for it is hardly deserving of the title Law):—IX. The Law of Preference:—Thoughts are suggested, not merely by force of the general subjective relation subsisting between themselves, they are also suggested in proportion to the relation of interest (from whatever source) in which these stand to the individual mind." This however, taken as it must be in connection with its context, goes but a small part of the way which the principle it states is capable of going. The method in which this principle operates must now be examined, together with the other operations which concur to the result.

In every object there is a part which is either pleasing or painful, or may become so by the continuance of the object in consciousness; if it is pleasing, that alone rivets the attention; if it is painful, the attention is drawn to it equally, but with an interest in its absence. Pleasure in presented objects, interest in represented objects, is that which occupies the attention, and causes that part of the object to which it is attached to linger in consciousness and to exclude the other parts of it from consciousness. It is true that in objects of presentation vividness fixes the attention, irrespective of the pleasure or pain attached to the part of the object which is vivid; but then this very vividness while it lasts prevents us from passing on to another object, the part which is vivid must lose its vividness before we can have a new object in its place; but the pleasure which belongs to any part of an object is carried on into the redintegrated object. Vividness would suffice to account for the first step in redintegration, but not for the second, as will be seen when the second step is described. Vividness is the cause of an object remaining in consciousness, not of its melting into another object; pleasure on the other hand we dwell upon, while the object to which it was attached is let go. Pleasure first fixes the attention on an object,

then covers its departure, by remaining while the other parts of it vanish. Objects of presentation come and go entirely irrespective of our wishes, our likings and dislikings; so long as an object of presentation or representation is vivid, it remains in consciousness and begins no series of representations. But when once it pleases us to dwell on it, we begin immediately, in spontaneous, not in voluntary redintegration, to forget the object, and think only of the pleasure, and a series of representations is set on foot. The object originally presented, or represented, is then the first in the series of represented objects; though we may be looking at it with our eyes, it is an object of representation. We exercise no volition, but spontaneously redintegrate what we may. The motive power in this series, the secret spring which effects the changes in it, the invariable factor antecedent to every new object in it, is interest; the interest felt in the antecedent object determines what its form shall be, and consequently how the next moment shall differ from it when it arises out of it.

Two processes are constantly going on in redintegration, the one a process of corrosion, melting, decay, and the other a process of renewing, arising, becoming. Unless by an effort of volition, which is here out of the question, no object of representation remains long before consciousness in the same state, but fades, decays, and becomes indistinct. Those parts of the object, however, which possess an interest, that is, those which are attended by a representation of pleasure or pain, resist this tendency to gradual decay of the whole object. I do not say those parts which are most vivid; that would be a tautology; but those parts are most vivid, or resist decay, which are attended by the feeling of interest. This inequality in the object, some parts, the uninteresting, submitting to decay, others, the interesting parts, resisting it, when it has continued for a certain time, ends in becoming a new object. The old object by reason of its inequality, of the lasting nature of the interesting parts and decaying nature of the uninteresting parts, has changed into a new object, a new object consisting of the parts which had an interest for us in the old object, together with an environment of some sort or other, but as yet quite indistinct and provisional. The question now is, how these new parts are filled up, that is, how the second object in the series of redintegration arises.

I recur now, in order to take this next step in the redintegration, to the general law of redintegration, namely, that every object, which has occurred in a variety of combinations, has a tendency to redintegrate, or call back into consciousness, all of them. The combination of the interesting parts with others, in the original object, kept their combination with other, that is, former, objects out of consciousness. But now that the uninteresting parts of the original object have vanished or decayed, the interesting parts of that object are free to combine again with any objects, or parts of objects, with which they have at any time been combined before. All the former combinations of these parts may come back into consciousness; one must; but which will? There can be but one answer; That which has been most habitually combined with them before. This new object begins at once to form itself in consciousness, and to group its parts round the part still remaining from the former object; part after part comes out and ar-

PART I.
CH. V.
———
§ 20.
Analysis of
redintegration.

ranges itself in its old position; but scarcely has the process begun, when the original law of interest begins to operate on this new formation, seizes on the interesting parts and impresses them on the attention to the exclusion of the rest, and the whole process is repeated again with endless variety. I venture to propose this as a complete and true account of the whole process of spontaneous redintegration.

Several well known phenomena are accounted for by this analysis of the process of redintegration. First, the difference in kind of the objects represented in redintegration according to the cheerful or melancholy mood we are in. For though it has always been a well known fact, that cheerfulness and melancholy were accompanied by representations of very different kinds of objects, yet no one, so far as I know, has pointed out any other cause of this accompaniment than the supposed suitability of objects like darkness, storm, confusion, slow music, to melancholy, and objects such as sunshine, flowers, quick music, to cheerfulness; a suitability of which no other ground could be discovered than the fact of the accompaniment, so far as it was a fact of presentation; which accompaniment, accordingly, as a fact of presentation, Mill, in the work already quoted, substitutes for the supposed suitability as an explanation of the phenomenon of the accompaniment in redintegration. The connection between the two circumstances, the mood of mind and the objects redintegrated, appears now to be a causal one, the interest felt being the common element in the two objects, the redintegrating and the redintegrated. When melancholy we do not redintegrate such objects as storm, darkness, war, &c., because we know beforehand that such objects will satisfy an interest, and this must be the case if suitability is the cause of the redintegration;—this would be to make the redintegration voluntary; nor yet because melancholy objects, such a storm, darkness, slow music, war, and so on, have in presentation occurred together, and so are reproduced together in redintegration; the order of redintegration is too different from that of presentation, and that of presentation too varied, to allow of such an account being accepted as sufficient; but the interest in such objects of representation is greater in moments when we are melancholy, and this is one of the signs of a melancholy mood; and then the interest is the motive or efficient cause of their redintegration. The question is not, Why such and such objects have an interest for us when we are in a melancholy mood, and such and such other objects when we are in a cheerful mood; this is an immediate and ultimate empirical fact of consciousness, which we can no more explain or account for than we can for the sweet or sour taste of some objects, or for the red or green colour of others. But the question is, Why certain classes of objects are redintegrated when we are in one mood, and certain other classes when we are in another mood; and the answer is, not only that they are of a melancholy or cheerful nature, which may be called their suitability to our mood, but in addition to this, that the interest we feel in them, arising from this suitability, is the determining motive in spontaneous redintegrations, the element or factor which is common to both the objects in redintegration. Other sensible qualities of objects are fixed and constant in them, but the interest they possess for us is not fixed and constant in them, at least is much less so than those sensible qualities are; and thus, when the interest becomes the fixed point in any phenomenon or series of phenomena, the other qualities of those phenomena become pari passu unfixed and inconstant; and, since this is the case in redintegration, the series of objects in redintegration loses that particular regularity and order which its objects possessed as presentations, and acquires another regularity and order determined by, or turning as it were on the pivot of, interest.

Another thing accounted for by this analysis is the apparent melting of one object into another, a well-known phenomenon in dreams. Scenes and faces, and even objects not visible but inferred, change imperceptibly into other forms and characters, in dreaming. One moment you see one face which you know, the next you see that it is not that face but another; yet this excites no surprise, though you are conscious of the change. Objects imagined to be present but not seen in the dream change their character in the same way. The unity of the interest prevents surprise; if the interest changes its character, if for instance, in the dream, a face, which excites interest of a pleasant kind strongly, is succeeded, in consequence of some external change of circumstances, by another, the interest of which is strong but painful, then surprise is felt.

Thirdly, this analysis accounts for the balance between habit and interest; people who have few or weak interests are decided predominantly in their redintegrations by habit; those who have many or powerful interests have redintegrations of more variety and more apparent originality. Interest is the source of what is called character. What a man's character is depends on his interests, that is, on what he habitually takes pleasure in, on the habitual trains of his spontaneous associations, and derivatively from these of his voluntary associations. If I know what he habitually takes an interest in, I can predict what the character of his associations will be, and know what his character is. But interests, if at once few and powerful, have a tendency to coincide with habit, for then they both run in the same groove; it becomes a habit to feel certain interests; and the same series of redintegrations revolves day after day, unless the objects of presentation are unusually new and various, as for instance in travelling. Old age brings with it a lessening of the number of interests, and of the intensity of many that remain; consequently it also brings an increasing domination of habit; and this the rather, if the interests that remain are few and powerful.

To go back now to the instance of the bookcase; if I go from the notion of the bookcase to the notion of the carpenter, the reason is because in the particular instance of representing or presenting the bookcase I am interested by some circumstance in the material, or the measurement, or the construction, with which the carpenter has been connected previously in consciousness. I do not call up the representation of the carpenter because I am interested in him, but because one particular part or aspect of the bookcase, which interests me most and excludes or survives the rest, has been particularly connected with the carpenter in a previous presentation. That part of the whole previous state of consciousness now again represented to me, to the exclusion of other parts of the bookcase, by a temporary feeling of interest in it, reillumines the whole state of consciousness, and recalls it as a whole, of which it was a part in the original presentation. There are cases no doubt in which the interest felt is a purely intellectual one, and where any object at once leaves standing out, to the exclusion of its other parts, notions of relation or cause, and these again call up objects which have been most habitually presented or represented as instances of such causes or such relations; here the intellectual conception of a cause or other relation, such as contrast or resemblance, is the most interesting thing, and its interest is its title to prominence, and the circumstance which makes it the link between two objects in the redintegration.

Dreams and reveries are the instances of the most purely spontaneous redintegration, without the admixture of volition. When in dreaming we are conscious of a purpose, of a preference for having or for not having such and such a representation, before it actually arises, then we must be in a state very near waking. Very often in redintegration we do not represent the redintegrated objects as familiar remembered objects, but they come before us as quite new. This is called productive imagination, and the most perfect instances of it are dreams. No one doubts that the apparent novelty of the representations is due to the novelty of the combinations in which their parts are represented, and this apparent novelty is quite as intelligible on the theory now suggested as on any other. The more insignificant and unessential the interesting part of any object is, the more different will the object which it redintegrates probably be from the former object, and the wider will be the range of possible objects habitually connected with it; again, the more habitual an object is, the less likely is it to impress consciousness and dwell on the memory as one of the links in the redintegration, and thus the points of interest alone will be those which will appear afterwards to have composed the series. There is another phenomenon, which occurs sometimes, of the very opposite character to this of apparent novelty. It is when we have a strong feeling of the sameness of objects, or states of consciousness in redintegration, with some object or state of consciousness which has preceded, but what or where we cannot remember. I allude to cases of dreams, and more rarely of waking perceptions, where we have a strong conviction of having been before in the same place or the same circumstances as those of the present presentation or representation, but nevertheless can recall no other circumstances which confirm the conviction. Sometimes we dream of a place which appears perfectly familiar; sometimes we see a place, waking, which appears familiar, though we know we have not seen it before, and then, perplexed, say we must have seen it in a dream. Here are cases of an inexplicable sense of familiarity and recognition obtaining in dreams, in waking, or in cases which perhaps consist of both. It seems to me probable, that this sense of familiarity depends on the rousing of the same particular feeling of interest by two or more different perceptions; and that from the identity of the interest we infer the identity of the objects of presentation or representation.

§ 30. The laws of spontaneous redintegration, according to what has been said, are three; 1st, the general law of redintegration, that consciousness is one connected whole, and that any object may call up, either directly or indirectly through other objects, any other object or the whole of past objects of consciousness; 2d, the first law of the method in which this is done, namely interest; 3d, the second law of the method, namely habit. The question now arises whether either of these latter laws can be reduced to, or subsumed under the other; whether habit is a particular case of interest, or interest a particular case of habit, or whether both fall under a common category. The latter appears to me to be the truth. Habit so far as we are conscious of it, or consciousness of the series of objects so far as they are habitual, is a pleasure. What the physical cause or ground of this may be is a psychological question, as, for instance, whether it depends on physical changes in the brain which continue the same until some cause arises to turn them into another channel; this would be habit as a fact in tangible matter. But habit as a fact of uniform succession in states of consciousness is a pleasure; it is the pleasure of the sense of ease and facility, or the absence of the sense of effort. That is to say, habit, so far as we are conscious of it, is a kind of pleasure, and in this sense is a motive power in redintegration; as a law of consciousness it is the law of minimising effort, of moving in the direction of least resistance, exactly parallel to the physical law expressed in these same terms. Resistance in consciousness is expressed by the term effort.

Interest is the representation of pleasure or pain; so that both habit and interest are referable to a common notion, pleasure, of which habit is one particular kind, and of which interest is the representation. That is to say, pleasure, either directly as habit or indirectly as represented, is the source and spring of all redintegration. For interest, as the representation of pain, is not a motive in spontaneous, but only in voluntary, redintegration; pain in representation is not a motive but a resisting power, unless it is accompanied by volition and a purpose of avoiding it. The only way in which interest, as a representation of pain, is a motive power in spontaneous redintegration, is when the interest is of an intellectual character, and when the pleasure in representing pain is the pleasure of wonder or curiosity; as, for instance, when we are said to be fascinated by painful images. So that, when interest is defined as the representation of pleasure or pain, and then besides called the motive in spontaneous redintegration, a further limitation is requisite, namely, the limitation of it to those cases where the representation of pleasure or of pain is itself a pleasure; and this must be, if pain is the feeling represented, to cases where the pleasure is intellectual, arising from knowing rather than from feeling.

The result is this, that pleasure contains in it all the determinative power in spontaneous redintegration; the link which connects one object with another in spontaneous redintegration is always some mode of pleasure. But pleasure is so wide a term that it requires limitation, and the particular modes assigned in which alone the determining power is exercised. These are, first, the mode called ease, absence of effort, or habit; second, the mode of representation called interest; but then, interest being a representation both of pleasure and pain, it is easy to see how a representation of pleasure should be itself a pleasure, but not so easy to see how a representation of pain should be so; accordingly, interest as a mode of pleasure is of two kinds; first, where it represents pleasure it is a pleasure arising from the matter, or feeling, contained in its object; secondly, where it represents pain it is a pleasure arising from the form or cognition of its object; in the former case it is a pleasure simply, in the latter it is a pleasure of intellect. It must be added that cases of the latter kind are rare, and that generally where interest as a representation of pain is the motive of a redintegration, it is so only through volition or voluntary effort, and the redintegration is to that extent not a spontaneous but a voluntary one.

Pleasure as limited above is the determining power of the movement of objects in spontaneous redintegration, a determination of the character of the series in every succeeding moment, or a motive if we consider the objects or moments separately. The law of redintegration is, that it is determined by pleasure limited as above; this is the general fact in all redintegrations, that is, the efficient cause of their movement or determination, in other words, their determining law. It is hard, I grant, to banish from the mind the notion of physical impulsion or attraction, that is, of tangible bodies pushing or pulling each other, when motion, force, power, determination and so on are spoken of; and even harder perhaps to avoid thinking of force and power as some occult or unknowable Thing-in-itself, behind or under the phenomena, that is, the feelings in time and space. The common inability to do the former, that is, to banish the notion of actions of tangible bodies on each other, when the terms motion, force, and power are used, gives rise to the difficulty which has been felt and which will probably be felt again, the difficulty of representing to oneself how pleasure, a mode of consciousness, can be a cause, or motive, in trains of spontaneous redintegration. The difficulty is not usually felt at all, though it ought to be more acutely felt, in the case of voluntary redintegration; the will is a phenomenon so familiar, that we accept a volition, as a cause of other phenomena, as readily as we accept a tangible body as the cause of motion in another tangible body. Accordingly, where the will cannot be regarded as the efficient or motive cause, ἀρχὴ κινήσεως, as it cannot in spontaneous redintegrations, there recourse is usually had to a tangible, psychological, cause, namely, the changes in the brain, as the efficient cause of redintegrations, and to the so-called laws of association, contrast and resemblance, cause and effect, contiguity in time and place, as a framework applied by ourselves afterwards to the phenomena, as a means of reducing them to some order and making them intelligible to ourselves, not as laws imposed on the brain by nature, but on the redintegrations, after they have arisen, by our logic. For, as it has been shown in § 28, if these categories are regarded as in any way efficient, or existing in consciousness previously to the production of the object redintegrated under them, they can only be causes of a voluntary and not of a spontaneous redintegration, they can only be causes employed by some one who has already a purpose, more or less definite, in redintegrating one class of objects and not another. If on the other hand they should be regarded by any one as efficient, but yet not existing in consciousness previously to the production of the redintegrated object in consciousness, then they must be regarded as laws of the operation of the tangible organ of consciousness, namely the brain; but, if so, then only in the sense that they are expressions of the result, in redintegration, of certain laws of the operation of the tangible organ, which in their own shape as laws of that operation are unknown, or at least unexpressed by these laws of association; that is, they do not describe how the brain operates in producing redintegration, but only how the result is constituted which that operation has produced. Spontaneous redintegration is a process in consciousness which requires a further analysis than these laws of association furnish; and this further analysis has been supplied by pointing out the invariable factor in it, namely, pleasure limited as above.

Thus the old theory of the laws of association, so far as it is a theory of spontaneous redintegration, is intelligible and complete only when supplemented with a psychological theory of the action of the brain in consciousness. To this action of the brain it refers for the motive or determining power of the course of association. The redintegrated states of consciousness are not produced by previous states of consciousness, but both are produced by the action of the brain; and, conversely, there is no ground for saying that the redintegrated states of consciousness react upon the brain or modify its action, so as to cause that action to produce another state of consciousness. But the relation between the states of the brain and the states of consciousness must be conceived as similar to that between the ivory keys of a pianoforte and the striking of the strings by the hammers, when I run my finger along the key-board. The strings are struck in a certain order, and this order indicates the order of the striking of the keys on the key-board; but the striking of each hammer on its string depends on the striking of its key on the key-board; and does not cause either the striking of the next string by its hammer, or the striking of the next key by my finger. Such is the only explanation which the old theory has to offer of the phenomena of spontaneous redintegration; and that there is such a distinct class of phenomena as those of spontaneous redintegration, the existence of dreams is sufficient to prove; for no one can pretend that dreams are instances of redintegrations which once and originally were voluntary, but which have become so habitual as to be performed without the sense of effort. The old theory therefore is imperfect; it not only requires the supplement of some psychological theory of the action of the brain, but also it offers no account either of the mode of production of states of consciousness by the brain, or of the reaction of the redintegrated states of consciousness on the brain itself; consciousness must be conceived by it in some such way as the foam thrown up by and floating on a wave, and having no reaction on the motion of the wave; so consciousness must float, in its spontaneously redintegrated states, on the surface of the brain. It is therefore only a part of a complete theory, and the connection with the other part is not worked out.

Those who, in addition to holding this theory, hold also a total difference in kind between consciousness and its objects, would find such a connection of the two parts of this theory of the laws of association very difficult. And this difficulty can not be avoided in the case of voluntary redintegration, whatever may be done in that of spontaneous. In them both, the production of states of consciousness by states of the brain has to be conceived; and in voluntary redintegration, certainly, the reaction of states of consciousness on the brain has to be conceived besides. It is impossible there to suppose consciousness to be a mere foam, aura, or melody, arising from the brain, but without reaction upon it. The states of consciousness are, in voluntary redintegration, links in the chain of physical events or circumstances in the external world. When the sun in June shines in at the window, I lift my hand and pull down the green blind. The sensation of heat is painful; representing this I feel an interest in obviating it; this is a purpose, or final cause, which as efficient produces the sensation of effort in lifting my hand and pulling down the blind, and a more agreeable state of sensation is the result. The whole proceeding is capable of analysis into states of consciousness which follow one another according to regular observable laws. There is first the feeling of the sun, the blind, and the window, and of my own body near it; these objects are states or a state of feelings in time and space together; in this state arises, or into it is introduced, a feeling of the heat being too great; I feel an interest in representing the painful sensation and its removal; I fix the representation of the removal of the painful sensation in consciousness; here is voluntary effort; the representation so fixed completes itself by the general law of all redintegration, and becomes completed with the representation of the objects which must be presented to consciousness, if the painful sensation is to be removed; those objects, represented, become familiar and involve an effort which is less painful, as represented, than the sensation of heat, as represented; the least painful representation remains alone in consciousness, that is, consciousness takes the direction of least resistance; and the new object exists with greater vividness than when balanced by the opposite representation, that is, it becomes a presentation, namely, the presented fact of my hand moving and pulling down the blind; on which the heat, as presented, ceases. External objects, tangible and visible, are modes of feeling, and the brain among them; the brain is not introduced into the series just described, solely because it is not included in it as an object of consciousness; its being of a visible and tangible nature would be no obstacle to its introduction, any more than it is in the case of the blind, the sun, and the window. The action of the brain may be inferred to exist and accompany and condition every step of the process; but that will not alter the facts as they at present stand, nor introduce the brain into them as a presented object. But it is impossible to explain the phenomena of voluntary action, as for instance the case just described, by the mere production of consciousness by the brain; for, unless a reaction of consciousness on the brain is introduced, the particular actions performed are meaningless, and no special cause for each or any of them can be assigned; for instance, what determines the brain to guide the muscles to pull down the blind? Can we conceive that just this phenomenon and no other would follow, if every other circumstance remained the same, except that the feeling of pain from the heat and representation of the means to avoid it were absent? If spontaneous actions are explained as automatic, or as results of the action of a material organ alone, still voluntary actions cannot be explained so; and this explanation of spontaneous actions involves the assumption of the action of external, material, tangible objects on consciousness; while the corresponding explanation of voluntary actions involves, besides this, the further assumption of the reaction of consciousness on those objects; that is, involves twice the notion of influence or impulse exercised by one heterogeneous object on another; the two objects being at the same time conceived as so heterogeneous, that the notion of their having an entirely different and independent origin was adopted solely to escape from the supposed difficulty of conceiving either of them as arising out of the other.

I argue, therefore, that keeping consciousness and its so-called material and tangible objects apart and treating them as separate and heterogeneous objects of existence is a course which leads to insoluble contradictions; for though we may disguise their incongruity at starting, that is, in the theory of perception, if we start on a materialistic basis, yet we soon require to employ not only the tangible objects as the cause of consciousness, but consciousness as the cause of the tangible objects, a result which might indeed have been perceived as inevitable from the first; and if we start from an idealistic basis, we have this latter difficulty at the very first setting out. If it is maintained that neither can be produced out of or by the other, because they are heterogeneous, then also their mutual action and reaction, when they have been produced, must be admitted to be inconceivable. Nor can they exist separately from the very first, for then we have the same inconceivability in the very first intercourse between them, an intercourse which nevertheless is an admitted fact of experience. It follows that we must conceive them to be different aspects of the same phenomena, that is, that qualities are feelings and feelings qualities in their subjective and objective aspects respectively; that the series of states in the one are the same with the series of states in the other, only on its other side or aspect; and that each series is complete in itself, containing an interminable succession of causes and effects, belonging to itself, and not borrowed from the opposite aspect of the phenomena.

§ 31. The sense of effort may be included in all cases of spontaneous redintegration; but the sense of effort is not volition. Volition is the sense of effort fixed to a particular object with pleasure or pain; and these are the elements of liking or disliking, choosing to have or to avoid, any thing. In the instance given above of a voluntary redintegration, the action of pulling down the blind to avoid the heat, the moment of volition was that wherein the removal of the sensation of the heat was fixed upon, a moment in which effort was involved in representing the sensation of heat. The moment of external action, of the arising of the cognition, or the feeling, of my hand being extended and the blind drawn down, is not a moment of volition but of action consequent upon it. No volition exists at this latter moment, at the moment when the representation becomes a presentation; this happens in consequence of the absence (in obedience to laws of spontaneous redintegration) of the opposing feeling, the representation of heat. Yet it is at this latter moment that volition is commonly supposed to be exerted, and not at the former moment; or rather the two moments are not distinguished from each other, and the line between feeling, or cognition, and action, or volition, is drawn at the moment of arising of the external event, at the moment when the representation becomes a presentation. But in this account of the matter it is not made clear how a feeling, or cognition, becomes an action, how things so different as these are commonly supposed to be, a supposition which leads to the line being drawn where it is commonly drawn, can pass one into the other. For the interest in the former moment is the cause of the physical, presented, event in the latter moment, and this interest contains the volition. The true account must be, that the representation of the interest is an action in the same sense in which the subsequent presented event is. When an interest of this kind is included in redintegration, the interest is still the determining factor of the redintegration; but the knowledge of the particular object sought or avoided, anticipating the presentation of it if obtained, and preventing the presentation of it if avoided, is the new element which distinguishes voluntary from spontaneous redintegration. Volition is anticipation of a result, and all interest in redintegration which is anticipatory is a volition, and makes the redintegration voluntary from being spontaneous. The interest is the efficient, the anticipation the final, cause of the remainder of the redintegration. Anticipation in an interest makes the interest a final as well as an efficient cause; interest in an anticipation makes the anticipation an efficient as well as a final cause. Volition, which is an interest in an anticipated object, for instance, either the increasing of an experienced pleasure, or the decreasing of an experienced pain, or the procuring of an imagined pleasure, or the preventing of an imagined pain,—volition, which in some or other of these ways is interest in an anticipated object, is a final cause which has become efficient, according to the scholastic saying, Causa finalis movet (that is, becomes efficient, or an ἀρχὴ κινήσεως) non secundum suum esse, sed secundum suum esse cognitum.

There are three degrees of complication in redintegrations: first, when there is pleasure or interest but no sense of effort; second, when there is both effort and interest; third, when there is effort, and interest, and anticipation. Redintegrations are perfect when there is interest and anticipation in a high degree, and effort in a low degree; the minimising of effort is the perfection of redintegration; when to will is to perform, to wish is to obtain. Redintegrations of the first degree of complication, where there is interest but no effort or very little, are pure enjoyment; those of the second degree, where there is effort and interest but no final cause, are more or less painful and bewildering, and of these there are very few and rare instances, since they at once and of themselves pass into redintegrations of the third degree, the pain being at once perceived as an object to be avoided. Redintegrations of the third degree, containing effort, anticipation, and interest, that is, voluntary redintegrations, are the highest and most important class; and under this class fall all reasoning processes, all action and conduct of reasoning beings, and all happiness of which such beings are capable, as such. In the history of the development of an individual from infancy, the sense of effort may have been involved in some of the earliest instances of consciousness, and volition the same. To trace the history of the development of an individual consciousness is not the purpose of this Essay, but to analyse particular states and particular processes of consciousness into their component elements; and for this purpose the logical order of increasing complexity is followed, since metaphysic is the applied logic of consciousness and of the universe.

§ 32. The point which has now been reached is one at which the two elements of consciousness, formal and material, appear to have developed into distinct functions, or modes of operation, of the conscious being; and this is a consideration which deserves to be dwelt upon. Nearly all enquirers into the nature of man agree in distinguishing in him three general or cardinal functions, and three only, to which either separately or in combination all operations of consciousness may be referred. These are, to adopt Sir W. Hamilton's nomenclature, Feeling, Cognition, and Conation; and man is accordingly considered in a threefold aspect, as a feeling, thinking, and acting being. Now the first thing that strikes the attention in this division of functions is, that it is threefold, while the elements of consciousness are never more than two, feeling and form. When the feeling or material element of consciousness is made the object of consideration, in a provisional image or series of images, then man is said to be a feeling being and to possess a function of feeling. When the formal element of consciousness is made the object of consideration, in similar provisional images, then the cognitive function of man is in question. But where has the function of conation its source? And what is its claim to rank with the other two functions? It is founded on and includes feelings of a particular class. The sense of effort is conation; the sense of effort attached to a definite object of desire or aversion is volition. The material element of consciousness, the feelings, have accordingly two great branches; the first including feelings so far as they do not determine a series of redintegrations, actions, or reasonings; and the second including feelings so far as they do determine such a series; and this second branch is again divided into such feelings as are final causes as well as efficient, and such as are efficient only. Hence we distinguish among feelings, first conations, secondly volitions. But both the original branches of feeling, namely, feelings proper and conations and volitions, together constitute the material element of consciousness, and not one of the three taken alone is entitled to an equality of rank with the formal or cognitive element.

Very different is the view usually taken of these three functions. The tendency to hypostasise is nowhere more deeply rooted than in the case of conation and volition. To hypostasise is to assume an unknown essence, substance, cause, or ground, behind or below phenomena; and not only is this the case in phenomena so far as they exist in space, but also in phenomena so far as they exist in time. The terms motion, power, force, are used not to express the phenomena in particular arrangements of time and space; for instance, the term motion is not used to express feelings in space changing in time, power and force not to express the rapidity of the change, or the quantity of the phenomena changed, but to indicate or imply some unknown and unknowable cause, underlying and producing the change; and while scientific writers warn us against understanding them to employ the words with such a meaning, and explain that they use them only to express phenomena, and not such occult substances, essences, causes, or grounds (which is, if I rightly understand the phrase, the distinguishing mark of the "positive" method of philosophising), they still assume or suspect that there may be such essences, only without the capability of being known to us, and of corresponding to our capability of knowing them. On this assumption or suspicion it is not the province of special and positive science to enter; but it is the province of metaphysic; and especially in cases where the hypostasising of phenomena interferes with and opposes positive results of actual analysis.

Just as motion, power, and force cannot be hypostasised, so neither can conation or volition. That things move or change more or less rapidly, that they move and change at all, is an ultimate empirical fact in consciousness, which is resolvable by analysis into its elements, time, space, and a plurality of feelings. No cause or antecedent state to time, space, and feeling generally is conceivable; time, space, and feelings together constitute change or succession in feelings. Consequently, not the cause of change, motion, power, or force generally, but the cause or invariably antecedent phenomenon of this or that particular change or object, arising in the place of or after another, is conceivable. But this is a cause not of change or motion, but of the determination of change or motion; it is a determining cause, and if not final is efficient, the ἀρχὴ κινήσεως of this or that object or feeling. But as motion, force, and power have been hypostasised in the external and tangible world, so conation and volition have been hypostasised in the empirical ego; and as the universe generally has been regarded as nothing but an exhibition of Power, so all human actions and thoughts have been regarded as nothing but exhibitions of a particular kind of power called Will, subject however to restrictions and limitations arising from the universe, or exhibition of other power, in which the human being was placed. Hence the Will took its place by the side of Feeling and Cognition, as their equal at any rate, and sometimes as their source. The conception of the beginning of motion generally, as distinguished from that of the determination of motion, is a provisional image, or a conception, introduced by volition itself for the purposes of facility of reasoning, and supposes motion already both before and after the point where it chooses to assume the beginning. Motion generally is coeval with a plurality of feelings in time and space; the first difference of feelings in these forms together is motion; there is no empirical fact previous to motion. Volition is no beginning or source of motion, but a determination of it, and the beginning or source of a new and separately characterised portion of it. Volition impresses a character on motion and succession of feelings, it is no beginning of motion or succession.

The normal state of consciousness is a spontaneous state; it is that from which consciousness starts and to which it tends, passing through the intermediate state of volition founded on conation. The vast importance of this intermediate state to us practically, since it occupies in the ordinary business of life our whole attention, and is hourly increasing in the extent and complexity of its objects, and absorbs our interest in the character of a search after practical

PART I.
CH. V.
§ 32.
Division of functions in consciousness.

and theoretical truth, hides from our view the states which are its source and its issue. Yet, as the mind progresses in its search after truth, it lays behind it a series of spontaneous states, which though forgotten in themselves, forgotten in the form in which they appeared when new, are yet the lever, as it were, and the instrument of all future progress; they have become part of the mind itself, which thenceforth is what it has become. The mind is always taking a fresh start, and considering itself as having always been, as necessarily being, that which it now finds itself to be. It forgets the origin of its opinions and principles, and considers them only as produced "from its own fund;" as a trustee, who mixes his own and his cestui-que-trust's moneys at his banker's, forgets how much is his own and how much his cestui-que-trust's.

Voluntary redintegration is not more independent of the laws of spontaneous redintegration than walking is independent of the laws of gravitation. As walking (I borrow the illustration from Coleridge, who applies it in a similar manner) is a constant interruption of, and a constant returning to, the law of gravitation, so the conscious guiding of the train of representations in voluntary redintegration, by reference to a purpose, is a constant interruption of, and a constant returning to, the laws of spontaneous redintegration. In the former we keep rejecting the representations which the latter keeps offering to our notice, if they do not appear conducive to the end we have in view, the question which we propose to ourselves to answer; and the perceived non-conduciveness of the rejected representations becomes our guide in fixing at last on representations which are conducive. But we work always through and with the laws of spontaneous redintegration; our most artificial, most independent, and boldest steps are only leadings into other channels of the same trains which took a course of their own previous to the interference of volition. Not only are the representations the same in kind in both cases, but they are also the same in point of the possible number of them. No course can be taken under the guiding of volition, which could not have been taken without it; volition cannot increase our knowledge; it can only choose between different branches of it; it cannot produce what is new, it can only select from the old. At any moment a certain number of courses are open to our thoughts; according to the degree or kind of the volition, the train of the redintegrations takes this course instead of that, plunges, suppose, into the fiftieth instead of into the first. At another time, returning to the same point, it might without volition take the very same or a different direction. As many courses are open without as with volition. In other words, the laws of spontaneous redintegration embrace every possible case of trains of representation. The conscious volitional guiding of thought can create nothing, but can deal only with the representations or perceptions which are already, perhaps only in their elements, present in the web of the redintegrations waiting to be woven anew into this or that pattern.

In psychology and in other special sciences the threefold distinction, of feeling, cognition, and conation, is very serviceable, because, first, the distinction between the two branches of feeling, one of which is conation, is strongly marked and easily seized, and secondly, the effect of men's volitions or conations on other men is for other men most important. It is well therefore to mark off from others those states of consciousness, which at once involve a sense of effort and produce the effect of external actions or events towards other men or on other objects, and to consider these states of consciousness, that is, volitions and conations, together with the effects or events which they produce in external objects, as single but complex phenomena. But if this is done, and if volitions and conations together with the events produced by them are considered as single phenomena, under the name of actions, then the distinction must also be retained by which actions are divided into immanent and transitive, that is, into those which do not produce a change without the mind, or in external objects, and those which do pass on to such production. In metaphysic, however, conations and volitions are nothing more than particular kinds of states of consciousness, which like all other states of consciousness are resolvable into feeling, the material, and time and space, the formal, element. And as feelings are empirically inseparable from cognitions, so also are conations and volitions; and though there may be feelings and cognitions which are neither conations nor volitions, there cannot be conations or volitions which are not both feelings and cognitions. When feelings, sensations, emotions, conations, volitions, and cognitions are spoken of as separate objects or separate states of consciousness, the terms must always be understood as provisional and abstract, and as implying a quâtenus, or indicating the character and circumstance which is particularly intended to be made the object

of discussion in the phenomena in question. As such
provisional images, cognitions alone are the special
objects of metaphysical, feelings and volitions of
ethical, enquiries; and it is as belonging to feelings
and volitions, that is, to the domain of Ethic, that all
knowledge and all cognitions have a final cause or
serve an ultimate purpose,—a truth expressed so
often by Aristotle in the famous words οὐ γνῶσις
ἀλλὰ πρᾶξις. Cognitions and feelings exist each with
reference to the other and for the sake of the other,
just as the material and formal elements in the least
empirical moment of consciousness exist for each
other and by each other alone. In volition first an
end, a sake, a final cause and purpose, is discerned;
in volition first it exists. As object and subject
exist first in reflection, so final causes exist first in
volition. Potentially both are contained in phenomena, before they exist actually for consciousness;
we discover afterwards that they were provided for.
We represent them as having been potentially present in the past; and in the same way, in the future,
higher and wider powers than we have yet any idea
of may exist already in the states and modes of consciousness, and of existence, which have already been
developed in man, and in the universe which is now
actually his. Who shall limit the "endless resur-
rections" of faculties yet dormant, whose very seeds
may be yet uncreated? Who shall imagine bounds
to the endless power of development, which has
already, in the universe as it is already known to us,
produced such phenomena as could not possibly have
been anticipated until the fact itself declared them,
yet all following one law, and consisting of the same
elements? Not those assuredly who contend for the

infinity of that law and those elements; not those who see unity underlying all phenomena, and existence and consciousness of a piece; for this is the very condition of understanding the lowest as a prophecy of the highest, a grain of sand as the anticipation of the moral law, and the moral law itself as the promise of its own fulfilment.

CHAPTER VI.

VOLUNTARY REDINTEGRATION.

Signifer, statue signum: hic manebimus optime.
Livy.

§ 33. It has been shown that the whole field of consciousness is occupied by perception and spontaneous redintegration; that the latter may or may not include a new perception, but that, if it does so, the new perception is a very small part of the entire process of consciousness; and that time and space are as necessary to spontaneous redintegration as to perception. Spontaneous redintegration is the subject-matter of all more elaborate processes of consciousness; and these more elaborate processes, which are all included under the general term voluntary redintegration, are applications of a form to spontaneous redintegrations, are workings up of spontaneous redintegrations into shapes, and guidings of them into directions, under the influence of some end or purpose, more or less clearly seen by the person who performs them. It is the purpose of the present and the following chapters to show, that all these shapes and directions depend ultimately upon, and are capable of being analysed into, the forms of time and space and nothing else; in other words, that understanding and reason, in all their branches, are nothing more than modes of time and space applied to perceptions and redintegrations, and that the laws of logic themselves are founded on, and are an application of, the same forms.

To explain this position more fully it should be recalled, that perception is the minimum of cognition, the subjective name for an object. But consciousness cannot rest with merely having formed objects, it is compelled to work them up into systems, and this it does in spontaneous redintegration; but it cannot stop here; it is compelled also to dominate its own spontaneous systems, to remodel, organise, and complete them, which process is called the search after truth. All this organising and completing requires no further formal apparatus, no other a priori furniture or instruments, than those cognitions of time and space, which have already presided at the production of the subject-matter, the perceptions and spontaneous redintegrations which are to be completed and organised.

In the simplest cases of perception the procedure is entirely synthetic, a combining of separate sensations into a single object of perception; but in spontaneous redintegration the foundation is laid for analysis, by the omissions which accompany representation. Thinking is nothing more than a voluntary combination of synthesis and analysis; we are employed both in dismembering the objects we have, and in forming others from their fragments. An abstraction may arise either by attention, by fixing the consciousness on an attractive part of the object presented to us, or spontaneously and without effort by the mere forgetting of some of the features of the object. But by an abstract notion is usually meant a notion formed by voluntary attention to some parts of an object, to the exclusion of the other parts; and this sense of the word will be retained here. Suppose that we have a perception or a redintegration of some external object before us, for instance a house. We are attracted by some part of it which stands in relation to some feeling, perhaps intellectual, as curiosity, perhaps æsthetic, as sense of beauty of outline, perhaps of a moral or sensuous nature, as if one room contains persons or things which interest us. In these cases we are first attracted and then determined to abstract, or withdraw the attention, from all other parts of the object, and to fix it on that which interests us. The result of this process is an abstract notion. It is voluntary if we suppose that the abstraction has involved a choice between two attracting parts, that is, a conscious effort to fix the attention on one instead of on another. From this point we may again proceed either spontaneously or voluntarily, by spontaneous or voluntary redintegration. If by the former, no further effort or attention is required for the performance of the redintegration; if by the latter, we must have a purpose in view, an interest beyond that of merely dwelling on the single abstract notion which has interested us. The redintegration itself must be instituted for a purpose, and with an end in view. This purpose involves the comparison of two abstract notions, of the general sameness of which we have had a perception in the course of spontaneous redintegration. The result of the comparison of abstract notions is a general notion, and this is formed out of the abstract notions by a voluntary redintegration of them. Say for instance that, in the case of buildings, we are attracted by one which has a colonnade of pillars attached to it, that this feature attracts our attention by exciting our æsthetic interest. In the first colonnaded building we see, we attend to the pillars, abstract the pillars from the other features of the building, and make of them an abstraction. The term pillared is an abstract, but not yet a general, term. It becomes a general term only after two further steps have been taken. The first is a renewed perception or a spontaneous redintegration. We see the same building again, or a picture of it, or have it represented in spontaneous redintegration. We must have seen several pillared buildings, or had such buildings several times represented in a redintegration. The several instances are requisite to give us the content of the voluntary redintegration. In spontaneous redintegration there is no reason why one pillared building should redintegrate another; the interest in the pillars sets the redintegration going, but then gives way to another circumstance of interest; but when we have had several instances of pillared buildings presented or represented separately, and then feel an interest in this circumstance of being pillared, for its own sake, then we keep rejecting all the objects offered by spontaneous redintegration except those which resemble the object with which we started; yet not because they resemble that object, but because the interest attaching to them is the same; and indeed, if it was their resemblance, and not their interest, that led us to fix upon them, general notions would precede and condition voluntary redintegrations and not vice versâ. This voluntary redintegration is the second step; volition guides the redintegration to represent all the pillared buildings we can think of, because the interest in this circumstance is kept before the mind, and the result is, that we become conscious that it is present, as the same feature, in different instances, that what attracts us in the different instances is the same circumstance; we make a conscious effort to bring them all again before us, and, having tested them by comparison with each other, the term pillared then becomes a general, as well as an abstract, term. Volition has been employed in forming a class of objects, in abstracting the notion of pillared from numerous instances of buildings, instead of the circumstance of being pillared from a single instance. General notions are thus the first result of voluntary redintegrations.

It is true that we may have voluntary redintegration of a single object of perception, whether abstract or concrete; we may have both spontaneous and voluntary redintegration of it; but of this simple kind of voluntary redintegration, the simple recalling of a single object, it is not here the place to speak; here we have only to treat of voluntary redintegration so far as it is a dynamical process, so far as it is employed in recalling several abstract objects and reilluminating trains and aggregates of association. The simple case will be considered in the second Part under another head. Here too I shall speak only of those voluntary redintegrations which give rise to general as distinguished from abstract notions. General notions cannot be formed without voluntary redintegration. We cannot hold fast, for instance, two or more cases of perception of pillared buildings, and fix our mental vision on them alternately, without a purpose in view and a conscious effort to attain it.

PART I.
CH. VI.
¶ 53.
Abstract
and general
notions.

Spontaneous redintegration does not include that alternating process which is implied in the words holding together two or more instances of perception. A second effort in addition to the original act of attention, if so we call the being attracted to a single point of interest, is required in order that we may move backwards and forwards, so to speak, on the lines of redintegration. Yet the new process employed in making general terms, the process of voluntary redintegration, differs only in point of greater intensity and complexity from the act of attention with which we start in spontaneous redintegration. The new object of perception which interests us, the aggregate of instances of pillared buildings, instead of the single instances, is too large to be comprehended by one glance of the mental vision, and too complicated to be satisfactorily explored by traversing it once only and in one direction. It is the interest of the object, its attractiveness for us, which is the motive or determining power, both in spontaneous and in voluntary redintegration; but in the latter case the nature of the object forbids the easy and immediate satisfaction of the interest, interposes obstacles in the way of seeing all we wish to see, the interest in the object still remains when we have seen a single instance of it; in the instance of the buildings these obstacles consist in the number and remoteness of the objects, the faintness of the perceptions, their unfrequent recurrence in spontaneous redintegration; and we thus become conscious of a purpose, and of a second effort, a greater attention, necessary to master our purpose. The attracting interest in spontaneous redintegration is transformed into a foreseen purpose in voluntary redintegration, is changed from an efficient into a final cause, as an interest the knowledge of which, and not its mere existence, causes us to make the new effort of attention.

The description of the process of voluntary redintegration harmonises with what has been already said of the nature of volition, since voluntary redintegration is but an instance of applied conation. Volition is conscious effort for a purpose of which we are conscious. Every process of nature, our whole life, is activity; when that activity meets with a felt resistance, there is effort; and when that effort is persisted in with a purpose, there is volition. Not conscious effort, but conscious effort with a purpose, is volition. Nor is it requisite to volition that the purpose should be clearly seen or understood; it is enough if it be represented to the mind as a future pleasure, near or distant, a pleasure to be retained or a pleasure to be acquired, whether in thinking or acting or feeling, a pleasure which is not fully attained by the actual rapidity of advance made towards it, or which is denied to us by obstacles or by a movement of our own in the opposite direction. There then arises a discrepancy between the wish and its accomplishment, and we are conscious of the progress we make in satisfying the wish.

§ 34. Having seen how general notions are acquired, let us now see more closely what their nature is. It is one peculiarity of them to fill no definite space and no definite time, in the way that the objects do from which they are abstracted; so long as they remain abstract they cannot be brought before us in a complete and definite image. And since there is no such thing in presentation as a horse in general, or a man in general, many persons are continually ready to exclaim, with Wordsworth's Wanderer, but with a technical meaning foreign to his intention,

> Give us for our abstractions solid facts,
> For our disputes plain pictures.

Nevertheless the process of abstraction is indispensable to all objective thinking; and since all generalisation is abstraction, what is true of the latter is true also of the former, so far as it is comprehended under the latter. In abstracting however we never carry the process to the limit of annihilating in thought the parts which we abstract from; but we place the object or the part of the object to which we pay attention in relation with some other parts or some other object, and consider it never as independent but always as interdependent with other parts or objects which we leave undetermined and provisional. When we abstract the colour red, for instance, from a certain number of coloured objects, we think it away from all of these, but we place it in another object which we either imagine or represent for the purpose. But this new provisional shape of the abstract notion red we consider as having no necessary connection with the colour red, and therefore as capable of easy dismissal at any moment that a true claimant arises. The difference between an abstract and a concrete notion is, not that the former has not, while the latter has, definite or particular shape or duration, but that the former has these properties provisionally only and momentarily, the latter has them constantly and securely.

It is often said, True, we can conceive such and such a thing, but we cannot imagine it; or, True, we can imagine, but cannot conceive it. Such a distinction between conceiving and imagining is in my opinion unsound. There is no such essential difference between them. When we can do the one, we can do the other; and what we cannot imagine we cannot conceive, and vice versâ. The difference between them is this, that conceiving contains an additional element to imagining; a concept is an image fixed by volition. We can imagine both a concrete and an abstract object, but in both cases alike the object imagined must be in relation to our sensations, must contain matter, or the material element in cognition. Imagination does not relate to the sense of sight alone but to all the senses, and is properly so extended in its meaning; we imagine a sound, or a touch, as well as a colour. Unless the object imagined contains a material element, it is either purely formal, or it is not an object of cognition at all. Except one object alone, time and space as the pure object, when they may be considered as mutually and alternatively matter and form to each other, though even then their divisions are derived from feelings,—except in this one case, the material element is as necessary an ingredient in objects as the formal element; and every object, in order to be cognised at all, must contain something which is in relation to our sensitive nature, or some determinate feeling. Abstract conceptions are no exception to this rule, for purge them of the material element and they lose their meaning. On the other hand, there is no imagining the material element in any cognition apart from form. Some shape and some duration in relation to our senses that material element must have; and the process of abstraction gives to it a provisional shape and duration, both liable to alteration on the occurrence of a new instance, and made provisional in order to include new instances.

An abstract or general or provisional image or concept may be dealt with in two ways; either it is kept before the imagination, and then it is represented as part of an object, all the other parts of which are liable to change, in the way just described; and this is the only way in which any use can be made of it in reasoning properly so called; or it is dismissed entirely from consciousness, as an image, care only being taken to have the means of recalling it when it is wanted for comparison; and this is done by means of names. We name a quality, or an operation, an image or a conception, and then we can at any moment recall by means of the name the representation signified by it. And when representations are so recalled they appear in the shape before described, that is, as the fixed part or parts of objects, to the other parts of which we attach the further quality of being removable at pleasure. We thus hold the general notion as it were in solution, ready to combine with the other parts of the objects to which reasoning or presentation shall manifest that it truly belongs. In whichever of the two ways just described representations are dealt with, that is, to use Kant's terms, whether we reason ostensively or apagogically, whether we reason with the objects before us in representation or presentation and by comparison between them, or reason with their names or other marks only before us, unconverted into their significates, our reasoning must be conformable to the Postulates of Logic; Logic as a formal science embraces both methods of reasoning. But ostensive reasoning alone properly deserves that name; apagogic reasoning is rather to be called computation or calculation; and ostensive reasoning accordingly falls under two heads, first as a series of complete or empirical phenomena, as a process of voluntary redintegration, and secondly as subject to purely formal laws, or as containing a purely formal element; or, as it may also be expressed, first with reference to its motive or determining force, the course or courses which it takes, and secondly with reference to the laws which that force is subject to, whatever may be the course taken. It is treated as the first in the present chapter, and will be treated as the second in the following chapter, the first of the Second Part.

§ 35. Reasoning, so far as it keeps within the limits of what has already been observed and does not attempt to discover or establish new truths beyond the limits of already observed facts,—for there is another field of reasoning, which will shortly be described, and another sense of the word generalisation, namely, an application of knowledge already gained to facts not yet observed, in anticipation of them,—reasoning within these limits is nothing more than testing and completing general notions by applying them to new presentative or representative perceptions, and comparing the latter with the former. The general notions are then modified according to the result of the comparison, and the name by which the general notion is signified henceforth resumes the entire process, that is, expresses its result, as it before resumed the process without the new presentative or representative perception. Many general notions have been so fixed that their meaning is henceforth not subject to modification. Black and white are typical, in common parlance, of this class. Others are still in process of modification, as for instance in the popular theology of the present day, the general notion signified by the word Inspiration. When the qualities and processes have been determined which are properly to be included in this general notion, the name inspiration will express and recall these, always however in a floating, provisional, shape; and thenceforth all qualities and processes which differ from those so included in this general notion will be excluded from it, and will either find a place in some other general notion, allied to that of inspiration, and signified probably by a cognate name, or will be confined to those other general notions to which they have hitherto belonged in common with that of inspiration. Reasoning, limited as before, is nothing more than this dealing with general notions, keeping them before consciousness, and applying to them ever new and new characteristics supplied by experiment and observation, to see if they will harmonise with the old, and, if there is one with which they will not harmonise, determining which of the two best harmonises with the rest. The canon of this process of harmonising, or rather the form of the canon of reasoning, which is applicable to it when it is conceived in this general way, abstracting from its particular methods of induction or deduction, is this: That conception or general notion is the true one which expresses all the facts of the case, without exception, in the simplest possible shape; or, that which provides a place for all the phenomena with the least expense of classification. This is called the Law of Parcimony. It is subjective, it relates primarily to our knowledge of objects and not to their existence, to our representation of them, not to their existence as represented. What objects will harmonise, and where they will best harmonise with the rest in a conception, must be left to the particular cases of reasoning to determine.

To give an instance of this harmonising in general notions, we may go back to our old instance of the pillars. Is this conception, pillared, to include buildings with those bas-relief imitations common in shop-architecture? Those who have been supposed above to have formed the general conception of pillared buildings from an æsthetic feeling will now have to compare that conception with this new presentative perception of the bas-relief pillars on the shop-front. If they find the separate and independent existence of each pillar, so as to form a passage between the pillars and the rest of the building, to be a necessary ingredient of the pleasure which attracted them in making the general conception, they will exclude the bas-reliefs as incapable of harmonising with some of the essential ingredients of that conception; if not so necessary, they will extend their general conception to embrace such instances of bas-relief pillars, and will exclude from it on the other hand the qualities of independence and of forming a passage between the building and the pillars. Nor is the process in this æsthetic example at all different from what it is in scientific conceptions; only in the latter the reason for admitting new perceptions into the general conception is drawn, not from taste, but from a scientific interest. The general conception of Man from a physiological point of view is still, I believe, undetermined and sub judice. On the side of his relation in organisation to inferior animals, instances are still being sought to show what precisely it is, what difference of composition, structure, or function of his material organism it is, which is invariably and exclusively present with all the other essential characteristics which at present constitute the general conception. When such a difference is discovered, it may possibly compel the modification of some of the other characteristics now included in the conception.

A passage from the Logique of Destutt de Tracy expresses admirably this modification of general conceptions, which is reasoning. Chapter I. near the end. "On doit donc suivant moi se représenter chacune des idées qui sont dans nos têtes comme un petit groupe d'idées élémentaires réunies ensemble par des premiers jugemens, duquel, au moyen de tous les jugemens postérieurs que nous en portons, il sort continuellement dans tous les sens, des irradiations pareilles à ces tuyaux qui s'allongent. Ce petit groupe quoique gardant toujours le même nom, celui qui en est le signe et le représente, change donc perpétuellement de figure et de volume, d'autant plus que souvent une nouvelle addition en détruit beaucoup d'autres plus anciennes; et cela fait varier continuellement ses rapports avec les autres groupes qui le touchent par différens points, et qui, de leur côté, éprouvent des altérations semblables. Cela peint très bien à mon avis ce qui se passe dans notre esprit tant que nous vivons, et la cause pour laquelle divers individus, et le même dans différens temps portent des jugemens différens des idées exprimées par les mêmes signes."

Is there more in the law of parcimony, so far as it is of a formal character, than the well-known forms of time and space? This is the question which must be answered here, at the first stage of the description of voluntary intellectual processes. Its analysis will show what its constituent parts are. It is a practical command to consciousness to take the shortest route in representing the relation of two points, and to embrace different objects by the simplest possible outline. So far as this command describes what the nature of the thing to be done is, it is merely time and space again; the same formal element which appeared in perceptions, and no other, appears again when these are worked up into conceptions; time relations and space relations between objects, this is what the formal part of conceptions consists of. But this would equally be the case if the command had been to take the longest instead of the shortest route, the most complicated instead of the simplest figure. What remains is a law for conation, not for cognition. All reasoning cognition involves an activity, or an effort, resting on, and proceeding from (in order still to keep in view the psychological order of causes), the material organ of consciousness, the brain; an activity which has its modes of operation and its degrees of energy to expend upon them. The better the modes of operation, the more available is the energy, and the more it can perform. The law of parcimony is nothing more than saying, husband your energy, choose the shortest road, and the simplest figure. There is no other stringency of an intellectual nature in the law of parcimony but the stringency of practical, not theoretical, good sense. It is found by experience that less energy is expended in imagining a straight line than a crooked one. Thus so far as the law of parcimony is a law of cognition, it is nothing more than the well known forms of time and space; what other stringency it has is derived from the nature of conation and the pleasure which consists in minimising effort.

The law of parcimony is expressed well in the words employed by William of Ockham, *Frustra fit per plura quod fieri potest per pauciora.* Summa Tot. Logicæ, Pars I. cap. 12. Its characteristic of being a law for conation, not for cognition, is common to it with all Postulates; all postulates are laws for conation, are laws of reasoning so far only as reasoning is a voluntary, that is, a conative process. Thoroughgoing scepticism, such as is exhibited by Sextus Empiricus, rests on the refusal of a postulate of reasoning as a voluntary process, namely, of the postulate that the result of reasoning will be truer than its commencement, that we shall be in a better position with regard to truth by means of reasoning than we were without it. Scepticism does not deny the reality of facts, but the reality of truth; for the reality of truth is an assumption involved in all reasoning; and this assumption the sceptic will not make. It is obvious that all volition involves the assumption of the attainability of that which it seeks to attain; otherwise it would not seek to attain it, that is, the conation involved in the volition would cease. In reasoning, truth is that which conation seeks to attain; therefore the assumption of the attainability of truth, that is, of greater truth than that from which we start, is involved in every instance of reasoning. All reasoning was rejected by the Sceptics as involving this assumption; they neither reasoned themselves nor accepted the reasoning of others, except hypothetically and as a concession to convenience. All kinds of voluntary conation too as well as reasoning they rejected on the same ground; and this was the meaning of their phrase ἀταραξία, as the aim of life, and of living ἀδοξαστῶς, that is, without expressing an opinion of the truth or falsity, right or wrong, of what they said and did. "Let us not dogmatise" meant with them, "let us make no assumptions." And thus the Sceptics are to be classed together with the Stoics and Epicureans in point of making the practical part of life the chief part of their philosophy; all three schools considered primarily man's nature and capacities, his position in nature, and what he should do in life; and subordinated to this consideration, as means to an end, the investigation of speculative truth. But the Sceptics did so more thoroughly than the others, and eliminated volition even in practical questions; for all practical questions are speculative. Thorough-going scepticism is only saying "I don't care about speculative truth."

§ 36. This process of the formation and re-formation of general notions, so as in the shortest and simplest way possible to express and combine all the separate phenomena, is an operation of consciousness with two aspects or functions, inseparable one from the other, well named by Dr. Whewell in his Philosophy of the Inductive Sciences, Book XI. ch. I, the Explication of conceptions and the Colligation of facts. General notions perform both these functions at once by exhibiting phenomena as cases of general laws. In a general notion the facts explicate or are the content of the notion, and the notion unifies the facts. And this kind of generalisation I call criticism, or critical reasoning, in order to distinguish it from the following kind of reasoning or generalisation, which I shall call acquisitive. Critical generalisation looks backwards only, looks only at facts which have already been objects of presentation, or already inferred from such objects, and remodels them in redintegration, in order to find the general notion which will express them all in the briefest formula, or colligate the facts in the simplest possible image. Acquisitive generalisation, on the other hand, looks forwards into the future as well as backwards into the past, and endeavours to deduce from objects and their already known effects new objects and new effects, whether these are to be introduced into the groups of objects already known, or whether they are to take place in the historical future, whether it is a divination of objects and events, belonging to groups of already observed objects but not yet observed in those groups, or a divination of objects and events which are yet to arise and constitute future experience. Critical generalisation explains past knowledge, acquisitive generalisation foretels future knowledge; critical generalisation is representation only, acquisitive generalisation is imagination in addition.

The line of demarcation thus drawn between critical and acquisitive reasoning, besides the inherent evidence it may be thought to possess of being a truly drawn line, acquires some additional probability from its being coincident with two other lines of demarcation in cognate matters. It coincides with the line of demarcation between facts considered as contingent and facts considered as necessary. It is admitted that all facts, in so far as they are links in the complex chain of causation, are necessary; that their contingency arises from our not knowing in any particular case either what the cause of an event is, or whether that cause will itself take place. All facts which have not only happened but are known to have happened are necessary, cannot be undone, cannot fail to have happened; knowledge and the fact known coincide, and the apparent contingence of the fact vanishes. Of facts, objects, and events, all that is known and all that is unknown is necessary; all that is unknown is contingent besides. The future and unknown is in itself equally necessary with the known and the past; but particular things which are unknown, whether in the past or the future, are as such particular things contingent; what is known, whether particular or not, and whether it is in the past or in the future, is necessary. The known or necessary facts are on one side of the line of demarcation, and are objects of critical generalisation; the unknown or contingent facts are on the other side of the line, and are the objects of acquisitive generalisation, the aim of which is to bring them over from one side to the other.

And, in the next place, just as the case stands with other objects of knowledge, so it stands also with the object of self-consciousness in its own actions, that is, with the sense of the freedom of the will. Our sense of freedom arises from the fact of our knowing that our action will, when it arises, be a determination of the object of self-consciousness, but not knowing in what way it will be determined, what line it will take, in what way its self-consciousness will be coloured or will feel. That is, its determination is unknown and, being also a particular thing, is contingent. Those of our actions which we have already done are necessary and known, and fall on the side of critical generalisation; those of our actions which we have not done, though equally necessary as actions, yet as particular and unknown actions are contingent besides, and fall on the side of acquisitive generalisation.

Since critical generalisation has two aspects or functions, that of explicating conceptions, and that of colligating facts, but consciousness operates in order of time, it follows that there are two modes of proceeding in critical generalisation, one starting from a general notion subsumes individual, particular, or less general notions under it; the other, starting from individual, particular, or less general notions, superinduces a general including notion upon them. These modes of proceeding may be regarded as the exercise of what is called by Kant die bestimmende und die reflektirende Urtheilskraft (Kritik der Urtheilskraft, Einl. iv. Werke, vol. 4, p. 17); and analogous modes of proceeding will disclose themselves in the operations of acquisitive generalisation. These are the two modes in which the double-faced operation of critical generalisation is carried into effect; but in whichever of the two ways we approach the matter, both aspects and functions of critical generalisation are involved. Whether we go from less to more wide, or from more to less wide, notions, the process as a whole will be both an explication of a conception and a colligation of facts. As an instance of the subsuming process may be taken the general notion of being combustible, starting from which we subsume under it diamond and coal, the notion of combustion having been current before either diamond or coal were found to be combustible substances. And as an instance of the superinducing process may be taken the construction of a type of formation in the animal kingdom, from the grouping together of individual animals which all resembled each other more closely than any one of them resembled any other animal, where the general conception results from the comparison of particular instances, and is not imposed from without.

Critical reasoning in its two modes, subsuming and superinducing generalisation, rests on the assumption of a law of nature and of consciousness which, from its extreme simplicity and universality, it appears almost superfluous to mention, but which nevertheless for the sake of completeness of systematisation it is proper to state. It has been shown that all redintegration includes the consciousness of the sameness of the objects redintegrated, the sameness of the objects of presentation and representation. This circumstance, which in spontaneous redintegration is a fact universal, common to all states of consciousness, and underlying all redintegrations, is in voluntary redintegration and all its processes an assumption. The certainty of all critical generalisation depends upon it. It may be named the fact of the Stability of Nature, by which is meant, that observed phenomena remain what they were when we have ceased to observe them; and that when we shall again observe them, they will appear what they were before. When I pass from particular phenomena, such as crows, ink, hats, to a general notion colligating them all, such as black, I assume that the general notion black has still a meaning, that black objects are still possible in presentation, that it refers to and rests its truth upon objects of the same character, black, as before, and that this characteristic of blackness is a constant general phenomenon in nature and in consciousness. If there were no sameness in presentations, the sameness in representation would lose its truth, and soon cease altogether; for it would be equivalent to this, that no empirical, particular, feeling would be presented again to consciousness. The stability of nature therefore, derived from presentation, continued as an universal fact in redintegration, is assumed in all voluntary redintegration, and therefore in all critical reasoning. It is besides a law relating to the matter and not the form of objects, to the feelings of consciousness not to the times and spaces which they occupy; or rather it relates to empirical objects and not to their formal element alone.

§ 37. Acquisitive reasoning rests also on the assumption of this same law, but not on this only; it rests besides on a further modification, or addition to it, namely, on the law known as the Uniformity of the course of nature. See Mr. J. S. Mill's System of Logic, Book II. ch. 1-2. The term uniformity of the course of nature means the stability not of objects but of their sequences, that the same impressions will be followed by the same; for instance, that the visual impression of fire to-morrow will be followed by the impression of burning if I touch it, as it was followed by it when I touched it to-day; while the term stability of nature means that the visual impression of fire to-day is the same as the visual impression of fire to-morrow, and the burning of to-day as the burning of to-morrow. Acquisitive reasoning, in assuming as its starting point the law of the uniformity of the course of nature, assumes implicitly the law of the stability of nature; but it does not explicitly assume it, because it is busied with sequences only, for all passing from a known to an unknown is a sequence.

But the law of the uniformity of the course of

nature is not the whole of what is assumed in acquisitive reasoning, as the principle or canon on which it rests. It is only the material, or rather the empirical, portion of the whole principle; it is founded on the material in conjunction with the formal element in cognition, and not on the formal element alone. It expresses a general fact concerning sensations and feelings, not concerning the properties of time and space in which these feelings appear. It supposes indeed everywhere that the feelings exist solely in time and space; how otherwise could it predicate uniformity of them? but it is not this fact which it sets itself to express. What it states is, that among the feelings filling time and space uniform sequences are everywhere observable; that similar feelings, or objects so far as they make themselves known by feelings, in similar circumstances, will be followed by similar feelings and similar objects. Though it thus abstracts from the formal element in cognition, it does not therefore shake off its authority. On the contrary, it will be found hereafter that it owes a great part of its validity to the formal element. It will be hereafter shown that the necessity of having some antecedent to every consequent, and some consequent to every antecedent, that the validity of the canon or law of Causality or Ratio Sufficiens, which is the formal side of the law of the uniformity of the course of nature, is nothing else than the form of time joined to and existing in the form of space; the proof of which has been already given by Sir W. Hamilton. It would seem to be this canon of causality which has given to the canon of the uniformity of the course of nature its appearance of necessity, wherever such a character has been ascribed to it. It is the necessary

PART I.
CH. VI.
—
§ 37.
The principle
of acquisitive
reasoning.

preliminary consideration which gives strength and importance to the canon of uniformity; it assures us that this latter stands on firm ground, and works in a legitimate direction; for it shows that we are compelled to look in the direction where the canon of uniformity looks, and for something which that canon professes to find. Here again comes out that same distinction, between form and matter in cognition, between empirical objects and their metaphysical elements, which has been observed in all the phenomena yet described; in the present case revealing itself in the law of acquisitive reasoning.

§ 38.
Induction and
deduction.

§ 38. Acquisitive reasoning has two processes, Induction and Deduction, analogous to the superinducing and subsuming processes of critical reasoning, and which may like them be treated either as two sides of one and the same operation, or as distinct processes preceding and following each other. First, induction precedes, deduction follows, taking up the operation where induction relinquished it. Induction is the establishing a general law from particular cases, valid not only for those particular cases, but for all cases, yet unobserved, which resemble them; as, for instance, from the observed cases of the death of creatures possessing fleshly bodies a law is established that all creatures possessing fleshly bodies are mortal. Deduction is the application of such laws to instances yet unobserved, thus bringing them under the general law established by induction, as when it is concluded that an infant to be born to-morrow, because he will possess a fleshly body, will be mortal. Now of these two processes it is to be remarked that they are fundamentally the same, two stages of one and the same process; and that the essential character common to both is, that they are both ultimately deductive.

First, they are parts of the same process; the second, deduction, is a part of the former, induction, and included in it. For, when I say that the child to be born to-morrow will be mortal because he will possess a fleshly body, I say not more but less than what was said in the general law established by the former part of the process; I state a fact already included in that general statement, that all creatures possessing fleshly bodies are mortal. The same observation which justified me in making that general statement, and not that general statement when made, justifies me in asserting of the child to be born to-morrow that, if he possesses a fleshly body, he will be mortal. So that the second part of the process, though called deduction, is but a specification of the first part called induction. (It is hardly necessary to refer the reader to Mr. J. S. Mill's System of Logic on the subject of induction.)

But secondly, this inductive process itself is deductive, and in the following sense. The general law which it asserts is not only a description of the observed cases, but an anticipation of all cases which are or shall be of the same nature, though not yet observed; as in the above instance it is asserted, not only that all the observed cases of creatures possessing fleshly bodies are mortal, but also that all cases, observed or not observed, of creatures possessing fleshly bodies will be cases of the same kind in the property also of mortality. Now the observed cases alone cannot justify such a generalisation; there must be some other consideration involved in extending the assertion to comprehend unobserved cases. This consideration is, That the course of nature is uniform, that is, that an object which remains similar in its relations to the senses will also remain similar in its effects, or will be followed by objects similar in their relations to the senses. That is, in this instance, that the object which we call a fleshly body will always be succeeded by the same object, namely a decaying body. This general law is the ground of all inductions; that is to say, all inductions are founded on or deduced from this assumption. It is the ultimate major premiss to which all particular inductions, such as the above, stand in the position of conclusions. The latter are applications of the former, subsumptions of a case under a given rule; and in this sense all inductions are in their nature deductions.

The tables are turned; but they must be turned again. This primary principle of all inductions, from which all inductions are deductions, is itself an induction. It is a generalisation from many cases, in which similar objects have been followed by similar, to all cases of objects followed by objects yet unobserved. Though it may be true that all subsequent induction is deduction, yet it is deduction from a former induction; its ultimate ground, the law of the uniformity of the course of nature, appears to be an induction which rests on no prior deduction.

But the tables must be again turned, and for the last time. For on what rests this first induction, prior to the particular inductions founded on it, this first induction of the uniformity of the course of nature? The uniformity of the course of nature is a generalisation from many cases, in which similar cases have been followed by similar, to all cases of objects followed by objects yet unobserved. We have not observed the uniformity in all cases, but extend it from the observed to the unobserved. What justifies us in generalising at all in unknown cases, in going out beyond the actually observed, in assuming that uniformity of effect from uniformity of cause holds good in other cases besides those observed? That which justifies us in so doing is a state of consciousness in redintegration. We go out beyond observed facts, that is, beyond presentations, because in spontaneous redintegration presentations are completed, are supplied with their effects, before those effects are presented in consciousness. Spontaneous redintegration anticipates the effects of presentations; and thus the assertion of the effect is a deduction from our state of mind in spontaneous redintegration. A child who has burnt his fingers to-day dreads the fire to-morrow. This is apparently an induction; he generalises the first instance of fire followed by burning, and to-morrow he assumes before the fact that fire will burn him. Why does he do this? Because the sight of the fire the next day redintegrates the total impression left by the fire the day before; the visual sensation to-day is the same as that yesterday, and redintegrates the sensation of heat. In other words, his induction that the fire the next day will burn him is a deduction from his association, in redintegration, of the sight of the fire with the feeling of burning. That association is the link between the two cases, the first, where the effect has been observed, and the second, where it has not been observed. It is true that mere association is an untrustworthy guide, but previous to verification it is the only one we have. Previous to verification, it is our only guide to truth in unknown instances; and in passing from a number of instances of uniformity of cause and effect to other instances, in generalising the law of uniformity, in making that induction which is the ground of other inductions, this process of spontaneous redintegration, confirmed into a habit, is the ground or moving cause of the generalisation. Its validity depends on the fact proved a posteriori, on the verification supplied by a constant experience; but the assumption of its validity depends on spontaneous redintegration and is an a priori assumption. Ultimately therefore all induction is deduction from a prior state of consciousness or cognition.

Not only in the inductions made previously to the establishment of the law of uniformity is the link, between the known and the unknown, due to the anticipation of the event in redintegration, but also in inductions made after the establishment of that law. For however certain we may be of what is past, however much previous anticipations have been confirmed by later experience, so that we can assert that, in all past experience, the course of nature has been uniform, what is there in experience to justify us in extending this certainty to future or unknown cases? Why should not the course of nature cease to be uniform at the point at which we have arrived? What certainty have we that the sun will rise tomorrow; or why should not events henceforth follow each other without reference to their antecedents? Since we do not know the cause of the uniformity of the course of nature, and since that uniformity is no necessary law or form of thought, it is clear that we can suppose it to cease at any moment; for we can think it away, and we know of no prior condition from which it follows. The only possible answer accordingly is, that the sense of certainty is due to the habit confirmed by experience of associating phenomena with their observed sequel, of completing presentations in redintegration with the effects which they have had in presentation, and imagining the effects when we imagine the causes,—in other words, to the strength of association. It is consciousness in redintegration which takes the step from the observed cause to the unobserved effect, and links together observed and unobserved phenomena. Redintegration, not presentative perception, is the source of acquisitive generalisation, or of extending a conception to embrace objects not yet observed. Presentative perception verifies or supplies the verification of this process, as it originally supplied the objects which are redintegrated. When we do this with a conscious effort and for a purpose, we employ the forces of spontaneous redintegration and direct them; we fix upon one image and redintegrate it, but the redintegration proceeds by the same means as when it was spontaneous and unguided by the will.

The point under consideration is important enough to warrant a somewhat longer discussion. Mr. Mill in his System of Logic, having laid down this law of the uniformity of the course of nature, says of it in Book II. chap. 3, "This fundamental principle or general axiom of induction is no explanation of the inductive process." He holds it to be "on the contrary itself an instance of induction," and "one of the latest in attaining strict philosophical accuracy." But it is with the nature of the inductive process itself that we are here engaged; and I think it will appear, as well from what precedes as from what follows, that the nature of the inductive process, when regarded as a process of consciousness, that is, from the subjective side, and as a chain of cognitions rather than as a chain of objects of cognition, when we look at how we know rather than at what we know, is, that each step in it is dependent on and subsumed under a previous cognition, that is to say, is deductive; and that while objectively, or with reference to what we know, the whole process is properly called induction, being a superinducing of particular facts which as particular facts cannot be known previous to or independently of the process itself, at the same time subjectively, or with reference to how we know, the whole process is properly called deduction, since it consists of anticipations founded on previous knowledge. Verification too is either a deductive process, or a process of presentative perception and not of reasoning at all. The whole process of acquisitive reasoning or generalisation will then be divided as follows; in its subjective aspect it is deduction, in its objective, induction; both of these aspects being inseparably connected, every generalisation possessing both. Then two stages of this double-faced operation will be distinguished; the first moving from particulars to generals, and called specially Induction, the second from generals to particulars, and called specially Deduction.

When the canon of the uniformity of the course of nature was established, on what depended its validity? On the law of nature which it expressed. This law of nature is the ground of the validity of all inductions, both of those made before and of those made after the discovery of the canon. But upon what depended the feeling of certainty with respect to those inductions made before the discovery and without knowledge of the canon? That these inductions were valid is true; but how were they known, or assumed, to be valid is the question; how came they to be depended on? The ground of certainty with respect to those prior inductions is really also the ground of certainty with respect to the later inductions, and to the canon of induction itself. This canon when discovered throws back light, it is true, on the validity of the former inductions, the steps by which it was itself reached; but the felt certainty of the former inductions was necessary to produce the felt certainty of the canon of induction. There are here two questions, subjective and objective respectively in their reference; the first regarding the causa cognoscendi of induction, the latter the causa existendi, the possibility or condition of such certainty existing. The latter question is answered by the canon of induction itself, which gives the objective ground of certainty, that is, which shows the validity of the inductive process, by stating the general law of nature on which it rests. The former question, which relates to the certainty of the inductive process, is as yet unanswered, except so far as the preceding remarks are an answer. How came men to trust in results reached by the inductive process before the discovery of the inductive canon; how came men to employ without hesitation the process of induction, before they knew the general law that the course of nature is uniform? This is the question.

The answer cannot be found in the canon of causality or ratio sufficiens, deduced from the formal element in cognition, for the question relates only to sequences in the material element or in empirical objects. And if there were no uniformity in the material element, if objects followed each other at random and not uniformly, still they would be subject to the laws or forms of time and space. Nor can it be found in any constitution of material objects, as objects only, for the question relates to something subjective, to the sense of certainty attached to certain processes of reasoning. It must be sought in the modes in which consciousness deals with objects as objects of consciousness; and this points out to us the phenomena in which the answer is to be found. It will be found in the phenomena of spontaneous redintegration, dependent on, and repetitions of, presentative perceptions. The sense of certainty in induction depends on the law of consciousness which represents together phenomena or parts of objects which have been presented together in perception; and the more frequently and closely they have been presented together in perception, the greater is the tendency to represent them together in redintegration. It is the tendency which I have called the second law of redintegration, the law of Habit. This tendency causes us to expect that, when one of such phenomena is presented to us, the others will be presented immediately. Why? It is commonly said, because we have found it so presented before. But this is not enough. We want to know how this circumstance, of having found it so presented before, operates; why this circumstance is the cause of the expectation. And the reason is, that all consciousness is of a piece, that one fragment reilluminates the wholes of which it has been a part, and first of all those of which it has most habitually been a part; that the spontaneous working of consciousness, going deeper and beginning earlier than its voluntary working, makes us complete the phenomenon presented by the addition in redintegration of its constant companion in presentation, and thus anticipate the conclusion, that is, anticipate in redintegration the completion of the phenomenon in its new presentation. This is but a description of what Hume assigned as the cause of our ascribing necessity to the law of causation, which cause he named habit or custom. It affixes a distinct meaning to his explanation, and the term which he employed to express it; and at the same time it shows the limits within which alone that explanation is true, namely, not as an explanation of the whole law of causation, but of a part of it only, namely, of the subjective aspect of the material or empirical canon of acquisitive reasoning, or induction and deduction.

When the conclusion drawn by spontaneous redintegration has been often justified by the event, by the completion of the phenomenon in presentation as expected; when it has been justified by the event in cases where at first, from the completion being delayed or withheld by some unforeseen cause, it seemed to be contradicted by it; we then at last see that, as the spontaneous redintegration was produced by the objects in presentation, so it is also supported by them even in cases where it outruns them, and that, if the expected completion is delayed or withheld, it is so in consequence of some fact, unobserved in the antecedent, which alters the consequent phenomenon in accordance with the same law of uniformity; and we then adopt voluntarily the course which we entered on spontaneously, and carry over into voluntary redintegration the method which spontaneous redintegration offered us. But this involves the discovery and adoption, is nothing else than the discovery and adoption, of the canon of induction, if not in all its fulness of certainty in all possible instances, yet in a manner able to serve as a basis for future inductions in matter not very dissimilar to that of those inductions which we have already made, though not perhaps at first for inductions in very dissimilar matter. For to say to ourselves that the method offered by spontaneous redintegration (though not by that name) is good and serviceable, and to resolve to adopt it, is in fact to draw a conclusion as to the uniformity of the course of nature in limits wider than we have yet had experience of. This brings the process of induction under the phenomena of voluntary as opposed to spontaneous redintegration, though it shows at the same time that its roots are in the latter.

The certainty of the canon of induction depends, according to what has been said, on the laws of spontaneous redintegration, and these again on the phenomena of presentation. This certainty, therefore, however great it may be, can never be so great as not to be liable to be overturned by a change in the presented phenomena. If the phenomena presented to consciousness, the immediate and remote empirical objects, should cease to follow unvarying laws, and should be presented instead in unfixed sequences, a state of things which we can easily imagine possible, this sense of certainty would decrease and at last vanish; the validity of the canon of induction would vanish, and there would be no more inductive reasoning. But the formal element in cognition would remain unaltered, both in existence and certainty, both in universality and necessity; and the canon of causality founded upon it would be equally valid as before, every phenomenon would still necessarily have some antecedent and some consequent, only not the same always, but always varying. We should have no special sciences but formal logic and formal mathematic; these would lose their interest, and the whole intellectual world as well as the physical would be a chaos. These two laws, then, of the stability and the uniformity of nature are those which were anticipated in § 24, where it was said that some such laws, of presentations as well as of representations, must be discoverable, which are beyond man's control, and which, unchangeable themselves, should admit of or command changes within themselves.

It can now also be seen in what the difference consists, and where the line is to be drawn, between cognitions, objects, facts or states of consciousness which are strictly universal and necessary and those which are so only apparently, partially, or conditionally. Strictly universal and necessary is the implication or conjunction of the metaphysical elements of objects or states of consciousness, form and matter, time and space with the feelings which they contain, because no state of consciousness whatever exists which does not contain these two elements; the very question itself, or that state of consciousness which attempts to dissociate them, contains them in combination. But apparently, partially, or conditionally universal and necessary are any habitual conjunctions in time and space, successions or coexistences, of two or more complete or empirical objects; such as, for instance, are the laws of the stability and uniformity of the course of nature, and any more particular associations of empirical objects; for in all such cases the associated objects can be dissociated in thought, and represented apart from each other, without the representation itself being an instance of their combination. Here then is apparently the solution of this long vexed question in philosophy.

According to what has been said, all acquisitive reasoning is, in its nature and from the subjective side, a deductive operation, a subsuming a new case under a previously known rule, and this whether the cases brought under the rule are whole classes or particular objects, whether the proposition established is general or particular. All reasoning which goes beyond actual observation, and anticipates either facts or laws, is ex præcognitis et præconcessis, notwithstanding that it is also a rebus, per res, ad res. What constitutes it acquisitive reasoning is the subsuming or superinducing of unobserved facts. Consequently all acquisitive reasoning, including all induction, rests on a law which is also the law of syllogism, which is, that a concept contained in another concept is contained also in a concept containing the latter; for syllogising is nothing else than the connection of present with past states of consciousness, so as to exhibit the present state of consciousness as a modification or a part of a past state. Hence all true deduction is syllogism, and can be exhibited in some form or other of syllogising, or in a particular syllogism; and if all induction is deduction, it follows that all induction is syllogism, and capable of being exhibited, if true, in syllogistic form. The inductive proposition, All men are mortal, is a case subsumed under the law of redintegration, What has happened in the observed cases of creatures possessing fleshly bodies will happen also in cases where the issue has not yet been observed;

or, as we may say when the canon of induction has been established, the law, That the course of nature is uniform. The remainder of the process is saying, The case of possessing a fleshly body is part of the course of nature, therefore it is uniform, i. e. followed by the same result in unobserved as in observed cases.

Both induction and deduction, if considered as stages of acquisitive reasoning, are deductive in their nature as processes of consciousness; consciousness alone, in a broad sense, that is, including redintegration as well as presentative perception, and not presentative perception alone, or, as it is commonly called, experience, furnishes the ground for anticipating experience; in other words, all anticipations of experience are deductions from data of consciousness. And it is with these processes as processes of consciousness, or from the subjective side, that we have to do in metaphysic. The correctness of particular instances of these processes, the truth of the propositions in which they issue, where it cannot be shown by presentative perception in observation or experiment, must be tried by tests furnished by logic; the ground of that correctness, the condition of existence of logical truth, is all that has to be given here. That ground is in the presentations, but the ground of our certainty of its correctness, the condition of our arriving at logical truth, is in the redintegrations. Whether we apply our previous knowledge rightly, so as to assert what future presentations will confirm, depends not only on the accuracy of previous observation, but also on the skill employed in guiding trains of voluntary redintegration, in choosing crucial instances, eliminating immaterial circumstances, and other rules of sound reasoning; and then future presentations will be the test of the truth of present redintegrations.

§ 39. Such are the two great divisions into which reasoning or voluntary redintegration develops itself, and such the principles, formal and material, on which it rests. Critical generalisation precedes acquisitive in logical order, as being the simpler of the two. But if we look to the completion of science in these two methods, it will appear probable that this very character of superior simplicity, in critical generalisation, will be its title to rank last in order of cognition, acquisitive generalisation being a connecting link between two stages of critical generalisation. As soon as new facts are proved by acquisitive generalisation, so as to rank as facts of experience, they ipso facto become part of the domain of critical generalisation, and are included in the whole body of known facts which criticism has to explain and find the simplest conception for. They pass into the domain of philosophy from that of science, into the patrimony of those who, in whatever field, cultivate knowledge for its own sake and not as means to a further end; for science is the servant of all the needs of man, not only of his bodily and his moral, but also of his intellectual, needs. The fewer and simpler the mental formulas are in which the phenomena of nature can be arranged, the richer those formulas will be, the greater command will man have over his knowledge, the more will each conception bring with it, and the more organic will be its whole system. If we could suppose it possible that all possible effects could be foreseen with certainty, acquisitive generalisation would be entirely merged in critical, and science in philosophy. But this is the ideal goal of science, always to be aimed at and never fully reached.

§ 40. All things may be classed in a threefold order, in order essendi, existendi, and cognoscendi; that is to say, in their logical, historical, and scientific order, λόγῳ, καὶ χρόνῳ, καὶ γνώσει. Arist. Metaph. VI. 1. The first is the order of philosophy, the second is the order discovered by science, the third is the order pursued by science. When any series of facts has been discovered, the business of philosophy is to arrange them in their logical order, and this is a function of critical reasoning. When the mind is discovering new facts, general or particular, it starts from facts already known, and these known facts are first in order of knowledge. The new facts discovered are discovered in the order of their existence; their order of existence, their dependence on each other through causation, is what is discovered by science; to know the causes and effects of objects is the aim proposed to itself by science. There is nothing contradictory to this division in the fact that all objects are objects of consciousness, and that existence is equivalent to being present in consciousness. For of this being present in consciousness there may well be more than one order, the objects present in consciousness may be arranged in more ways than one. They may either be arranged according to their order of development in the consciousness which arranges them, and then we have the history of that particular consciousness, and we have the facts in the order cognoscendi, γνώσεως, the order pursued by science; or they may be arranged in the order in which they have been discovered to exist towards each other, and then we have them in

the order existendi, χρόνου, or historical existence, in which order the facts which are placed farthest from the reasoning consciousness, in past time, are first, and those placed farthest from it in future time are last; or they may be arranged in the order of increasing complexity and decreasing generality, as a system the truth of which depends on the Law of Parcimony, and then we have them in order essendi, as a system of conceptions or definitions, λόγῳ, or logical order. This latter order is that followed and exhibited in this Essay, and in all merely philosophical writings.

These three orders must be carefully kept apart in thought, and what is first in one order not confused with what is first in another order. The greatest difficulty is to keep apart, not the order of knowledge from that of existence, but that of existence from that of logic. It does not follow that what is simplest and therefore first in order of logic is therefore first in order of existence; for instance, that those animals which stand lowest in Cuvier's Animal Kingdom, and exhibit the smallest differentiations of the characters common to all animals, have been the first produced in order of history. And again, it may well happen and be proved by science, following Mr. Darwin's method, that more complex animals are modifications by natural selection, in order of history, of less complex organisations; that vegetable structures have developed into animal, and inorganic substances into vegetable structures. But facts of this kind do not follow from the logical order of priority between simplicity and complexity. Nor would this logical order be affected by a reversal of the historical order of existence, if this should be done by further scientific discovery. If for instance it should be discovered, that this universe, which, on the Nebular hypothesis, has exhibited a series of stages of development, beginning with absolute disorganisation, and differentiating itself at each stage into a structure of always increasing complexity of function and character, the latter stages of which we have indeed means of observing only in our own planet,—if it should be discovered that this universe, at a time previous to that Nebula of the hypothesis, existed in the form of a more organic, more highly organised structure, than any thing we have witnessed in the world as it is at present known, from the dissolution of which prior world that Nebula of the hypothesis itself arose, in that case, though the order of historical priority would be reversed, the order of logical priority would remain the same, the simple would still be prior to the complex. For the simple and more general is prior to the complex and less general in order of logic, because it is the key to the comprehension of the whole of the latter by the mind at one glance. Having the general conception, all or any of its differentiations are understood; but having one or several or all of the differentiations, the whole is not understood. Logic, as a function of critical generalisation, consists in comprehending the whole and all its parts together, uno ictu; and therefore the simple and general, and not the complex, is the bond of union and, as such, the first in order of logic. Otherwise we are thrown back into the order of knowledge, where one thing is known before and without the knowledge of another.

In philosophy, the confusion of the order of logic with the order of existence is one source of ontology, of the conversion of metaphysic into ontology. Metaphysic is the applied logic of the universe, ontology is the attempt to assign the absolute cause of the universe. Such a confusion of the logical order with the historical order, leading to the transformation of metaphysic into ontology, is found in Aristotle; and it is interesting to watch the method in which this transformation was effected, in his mind, and how he was led to retain an ontological side by side with a metaphysical system. A passage which shows this is found in Metaph. Lib. XI. cap. 7. § 1. ὥστε ἀΐδιος ἂν ᾖ ὁ πρῶτος οὐρανός. ἔστι τοίνυν τι καὶ ὃ κινεῖ. ἐπεὶ δὲ τὸ κινούμενον καὶ κινοῦν καὶ μέσον, τοίνυν ἔστι τι ὃ οὐ κινούμενον κινεῖ, ἀΐδιον καὶ οὐσία καὶ ἐνέργεια οὖσα. He argues thus, Because an empirical object which is moved is always found as a member of a series of objects, three at least, the first of which moves it, and the last of which is moved by it, this series may be regarded as a complete series and as a representation of every series of moving things. The first object in the series however is, so far as it belongs to this series only, a mover and not a moved; there is therefore, in the phenomena of motion generally, such a thing as a phenomenon which moves other things, without moving or being moved itself. Because in this series the first object is the representative of one of the logical elements of motion, namely, moving others without moving oneself, therefore the logical element has an empirical existence. The first object in the series is κινούμενον as well as κινοῦν when regarded as an empirical object, and not only as the representative of the logical element. The logical elements of τὸ κινούμενον, namely κινεῖν and κινεῖσθαι, if exhibited as logical, ought to be exhibited as simultaneous; they are not so exhibited by Aristotle; and why not? Because, taking these two logical elements, he removes them into an empirical, or historical, series,—ἐπεὶ δὲ τὸ κινούμενον καὶ κινοῦν καὶ μέσον (and the words καὶ μέσον show that he is thinking of an empirical series); because the thing moved is mover as well as moved, and is besides a mean between a mover and a moved; because it, as an empirical whole A, is moved by an empirical whole B, and moves another empirical whole C; therefore the empirical whole B, which moves A, is not moved itself by a previous empirical whole, or by any thing else;—τοίνυν ἔστι τι ὃ οὐ κινούμενον κινεῖ, there is something there which moves others without moving itself. How can such reasoning be brought about? It is because the term B bears two characters; first, as an empirical whole, it is first in the series of three; secondly, as the mover, distinguished from the moved, and from the moved and mover, of the series, it is a logical element, and exists only quâ mover. The logical element, quâ mover, κινοῦν οὐ κινούμενον, is carried over or erected into an empirical whole containing this element only. Then, because the logical elements of moving and being moved are separable in thought,—notwithstanding that, as such, they are simultaneous and interdependent relatives,—they are separable and independent empirical wholes; and because in a series of three empirical objects, say three billiard balls, the motion of the first is the cause of the motion of the third, transmitted through the second, therefore the logical element of moving is prior in order of existence to the logical element of being moved. Nothing κινοῦν οὐ κινούμενον can be obtained without recourse to the logical analysis of τὸ κινούμενον, and nothing first in order of time can be obtained without recourse to the empirical series of which τὸ κινούμενον forms a part. But by the union, or confusion, of these two methods, the logical and the historical, an empirical and independent existence of a κινοῦν οὐ κινούμενον can be produced. And as this is placed in the οὐρανὸς which is ἀΐδιος, it follows, τοίνυν ἔστι τι ὃ οὐ κινούμενον κινεῖ, ἀΐδιον καὶ οὐσία καὶ ἐνέργεια οὖσα. Aristotle separates the logical quality of moving without being moved, and erects it into an actual cause of motion historically, or in order of existence. His next step, in § 2, is to look about him for something which answers to this description; and he finds it in that which is at once ὀρεκτὸν and νοητὸν, an object of desire and an object of reason, and this is with him the first cause and mover of the universe, its ἀρχὴ κινήσεως, or efficient cause. The latter part of the Metaphysic of Aristotle insists on the necessity of empirical objects being prior to logical objects. Δεῖ ἄρα εἶναι ἀρχὴν τοιαύτην ἧς ἡ οὐσία ἐνέργεια. XI. 6. § 4. The οὐσία of the cause of the universe, the very essence, logical definition, or nature of it, must be ἐνέργεια, complete or empirical existence. Yet the distinction between logical and empirical existence, between οὐσία and ἐνέργεια, is not hereby destroyed; but an instance of a thing imagined, which is both at once, the essence of which is to be a complete object. When you have such an object in your thoughts, you cannot help asking the question, What is it? or, What does it exist as? And if the answer is,—As a complete object, this nature of it is shown, by your asking the question, to be different from the mere fact of its being present in your thoughts. So that empirical existence and logical existence,—the latter including all inseparable elements, aspects, and relations,—are two distinguishable things, a fact capable of experimental proof at any moment; and any attempt to resolve one into the other is to create a contradiction which does not exist in nature; the assumption of their being one thing, when they are not, makes them, so long as that assumption lasts, contradictories, and their assumed unity a contradiction.

The same confusion attaches to the conception of consciousness itself, a confusion which the present distinction of the three orders, of logic, of history, and of knowledge, enables us now finally to clear up. Consciousness has three meanings, and a place in the three orders, of logic, history, and knowledge. In its first meaning and in the order of logic, it is the correlate of all existence or all objects whatever, at once of the empirical ego on the one hand and of the universe of qualities on the other, being itself no object but present inseparably in all objects whether before or after reflection. In this meaning it is called the Subject; and it distinguishes itself as such from its objects first in reflection, or its act of distinguishing itself from its object is called reflection, for it is never separated from its object but consists in the development of a distinct subjective aspect in it.

Consciousness in its second meaning is the empirical ego, the subjective aspect of all objects in their detail and completeness. It is the correlate of the objective aspect of objects, or of the universe of qualities in all its parts; and these two aspects together, the world of feelings or cognitions and the world of qualities, are the correlate of consciousness in its first meaning, that is, of the Subject. The empirical ego belongs to the order of knowledge, for it is the complex of all feelings or cognitions in the order in which they arose and connected themselves with each other as such. Its history, as an object for the Subject, is a history of feelings or cognitions, and their historical order is the order of their connection as feelings or cognitions, that is, in many cases, the reverse of the order of facts or qualities of which they are the subjective aspect. Thus the empirical ego has two sides or aspects; first, it is an object for the Subject, and as such has a history, or exists in the order of history; and secondly it is the subjective aspect of the world of qualities, in which character its historical order becomes the order of knowledge. All partial sequences of cognitions or feelings are parts of the whole sequence of the empirical ego, and the empirical ego contains and constitutes them in its own order as sequences of cognition.

The third meaning of the term consciousness is the conscious life of the individual being, that is, the feelings or cognitions of the empirical ego together with those feelings or qualities which are called the body, and with which they are constantly connected in experience. This object is heterogeneous, consisting of a part, as it were, of the empirical ego enclosed or circumscribed by a part of the world of qualities, or, as it is commonly expressed, of a soul dwelling in a body. Briefly it may be said, the third meaning of consciousness is the soul. The circumscription of the soul by the body gives it a place in the order of history properly so called, that is, in the history of the world of qualities, the correlate of the empirical ego. The confusion noticed above is the confusion of the Subject with the soul, the confusion of that which, as being no object, is out of all relation to the order of objects in time, and something which is supposed to arise in time as an empirical object. The Subject exists only in order of logic, and not in either the order of history or the order of knowledge. It is the limit, point, or line of demarcation between the empirical ego and the universe of qualities, existing potentially before reflection and actually afterwards, potentially in phenomena, actually in their subjective and objective aspects; but, whether potential or actual, included alike in phenomena and in objects, and alike necessary in order to the possession by these words of any meaning whatever.

Confusing the Subject with the soul, or conceiving the Subject as an empirical object, I suppose an enquirer to ask, 'How can my consciousness be necessary to all existence, so that without my consciousness there is no existence, and yet I be able to point to the time when my consciousness began to exist, by being born into a previously existing world, existing before and independently of my consciousness? The world must have existed before my birth, either as it exists now or in some way unknown to me, and my consciousness must have had then no existence in any sense.' The answer has been already given. The soul may have had then no existence, true; but the Subject? The same existence as it has now, that is, neither an empirical, nor an objective, but a logical one, in the world which you assert existed before the birth of the soul. Its existence depends on the existence, and is inseparably involved in the existence of that world, irrespective of the soul, and both world and Subject exist, or vanish, together. Time and the Subject being coeval and inseparable, since time is a mode of consciousness, no question can arise about the origin of the Subject any more than about the origin of time; and no question can arise about the origin of time, because the notion of origin is derived from the notion of time, and can be conceived to exist only within time.

TIME AND SPACE.

PART II.

CHAPTER VII.

METALOGICAL.

DIVISION I. THE POSTULATES AND THE CONCEPT-FORM.

οὐ κατὰ συμβεβηκὸς τὸ ὅτι.

Aristotle.

§ 41. METAPHYSIC is the science which considers existence in its most general aspect, so that the few most general laws which are to be established in this science must be capable of conforming to all the laws of the special sciences; and conversely, all the laws of the special sciences must agree in being capable of harmonising with the general laws of metaphysic, before they can be admitted as proved laws of existence. The starting point, therefore, of metaphysic is the most abstract, generalised, notion of existence, which can be found in consciousness; or, as it would have been commonly expressed before the development of philosophy due to the Cogito ergo sum of Descartes, the starting point of metaphysic is existence itself, in its most abstract shape, existence as such and nothing more; or, in Aristotle's phrase, τὸ ὂν ᾗ ὄν, καὶ τὰ τούτῳ ὑπάρχοντα καθ' αὐτό.

Of this abstract existence two things are certain, first, that it is always determinate, never entirely indeterminate, existence; secondly, that it has no logical contrary, that is, no contradictory. The proof of both facts is experimental. As to the first, it has been already said that the highest abstraction must contain, at the very least, the cognition of time and some feeling occupying it, that we cannot be conscious and not be conscious of feeling and time. The object therefore of consciousness is always a determinate object, even if it contains no further determination than the mere form of time. As to the second, existence has no logical contrary, or contradictory, because nothing but existence can be present in consciousness. Existence and consciousness are coextensive; suppose consciousness, and it is consciousness of an object, that is, of existence; suppose existence, and it is existence in consciousness, that is, an object. Logic, however, is a process or mode of consciousness. If Hegel's pure Seyn was pure Nichts, it would be the cessation of consciousness altogether. It will be admitted that both these proofs are experimental.

As a consequence of this reasoning, I distinguish two senses of the concept-name, Non-existence; one, in which it has an object or concept signified by it, the other, in which it has none, but is a concept-name only. When non-existence is opposed to the abstract existence which is coextensive with consciousness, it is a name without an object named by it; for if there were one, it would be out of consciousness. In this sense the words are true which Aristotle uses to express the opinion of Parmenides, Metaph. I. 5. Παρμενίδης δὲ παρὰ τὸ ὂν τὸ μὴ ὂν οὐθὲν ἀξιῶν εἶναι, as are also those expressions which Parmenides himself employs in his eloquent verses:

ἡ μέν, ὅπως ἔστιν τε καὶ ὡς οὐκ ἔστι μὴ εἶναι,
Πειθοῦς ἐστι κέλευθον, ἀληθείη γὰρ ὀπηδεῖ.

* * * *

οὔτε γὰρ ἂν γνοίης τό γε μὴ ἐὸν (οὐ γὰρ ἐφικτόν),
οὔτε φράσαις. τὸ γὰρ αὐτὸ νοεῖν ἐστίν τε καὶ εἶναι.

The working out of these thoughts of Parmenides is philosophy; which then first became possible when Descartes approached them and examined them from the subjective side.

Non-existence in this sense, or pure nothing, is a concept-name and not a concept. It is a name without an object, such as there are many; for it is one function of words to serve as signs or marks of objects, but not their only function; words have a suppositio materialis vel naturalis, as well as a suppositio personalis vel formalis (Gerson, in his Concordia Metaphysicæ); that is, they are things and objects themselves, as well as the marks of other objects, and as objects themselves, independently of things signified by them, they have their laws of production, modification, and destruction. And it is a concept-name without an object, inasmuch as it is produced by an extension of the same process by which it was formed in its legitimate sense, in which it has an object signified by it. What now is this legitimate sense?

In the legitimate sense of the word non-existence, it signifies the negation, that is, the absence from consciousness of one or more particular objects, not, as in its illegitimate sense, the absence from consciousness of all objects, as if that were possible. But within this limit, short of excluding every thing from consciousness, any thing can be excluded or can be absent. Each absence is the ground of, or the thing expressed by, a particular negation; is the non-existence of a particular object or set of objects. As existence is determinate, so also is non-existence. Existence includes non-existence within it, the latter is a mode of the former. Also existence precedes non-existence in point of time, whether we take existence in its more abstract or in its more particular sense; for, until we have been conscious generally, we cannot be conscious of the absence of any object, and, until we have been conscious of this or that particular object, we cannot tell what it is which is absent when we are not conscious of it. It follows from what has been last said, that all negation has reference to the past, or to the future, and not to the present; that it is not the expression of a present feeling of the absence of any object, but of that feeling as past, it may be but a moment ago. We recall the feeling, or the object, in denying it; in the moment of feeling its past absence it becomes present. The past absence is the thing said or predicated by the negation; the negation is the expression of the present feeling of a past absence of feeling; the feeling being present, while we deny it to have been present formerly.

It may be well, perhaps, to sum up what has been said in a definition of existence, although I am aware that high authority has said that it is one of those matters which are obscured rather than explained by defining them. Werenfels, in De Tempore, Opuscula, Vol. 2, says, Existentiæ conceptus simplicissimus, nomen clarissimum est; plane ut existere quid sit, si definire velis, rem obscuraveris potiùs quàm explicaveris: actu, in rerum naturâ, extra mentem,

extra causas esse, omnia aut obscuriora sunt magis‑
que ambigua, aut certe clariora non sunt. Certainly
none of these definitions will agree with what has
been here maintained. Existence in fact seems to be
a striking instance of the difference between the fami‑
liar and the known, in which it offers a parallel to its
counterpart consciousness, according to what Shake‑
speare says of man, in *Measure for Measure,*

> Most ignorant of what he's most assured,
> His glassy essence.

Plato assumed οὐσία or Being as the transcendent or
at least the transcendental cause of the existence of all
determinate objects. In the Parmenides, Steph. 151,
he says of this determinate and actual existence, τὸ δὲ
εἶναι ἄλλο τί ἐστιν ἢ μέθεξις οὐσίας μετὰ χρόνου τοῦ παρόντος;
So long as the objective point of view is adhered to,
no definition is possible; for on the one hand no
higher abstraction is known, to which to refer exist‑
ence, distinguishing it at the same time by its specific
difference, and on the other it would be impracticable,
as involving a progress in infinitum, to give all the
particular objects which exactly occupy the same
field as existence, and to name all the particulars
contained under it. But let the point of view be
changed, and a definition of the latter class becomes
possible at once. We no longer have to seek within
existence itself, as such, for its definition, but another
character discloses itself pervading its entire sphere,
as if a crystal globe should suddenly assume a rosy
tint, without losing any of its crystalline clearness; a
difference without a division, which pervades and dis‑
tinguishes every particle of the sphere; each charac‑
ter, therefore, being coextensive and simultaneous

with the other and with the whole. Such was the change wrought by the magic spell, Cogito ergo sum. My existence, what is it? Thought, consciousness,—cogitatur. For this is the meaning of that phrase, it means the phenomenon of consciousness; not that a soul or an ego is included in the cogito. See Descartes, Objectiones Septimæ in Meditationes, § II. Notæ. Sed mente concipitur nihil hic aliud significat quàm cogitatur; et ideo malè supponit fieri mentionem mentis quatenus est pars hominis. The question of the existence of the mind is not prejudged by Descartes in the starting point of his philosophy. Existence and consciousness are identical in point of extension, they have exactly the same particulars contained under them; one defines the other. But of two coextensive objects we always call that the definition of the other which is the more familiar of the two, since definitions are always used cognoscendi causâ. We call therefore consciousness the definition of existence, and existence the object defined by consciousness. Consciousness, and not existence, is the true ne plus ultra.

§ 42. If now, standing at our present point of view, we were to substitute one of the functions of consciousness for the whole, the logical function of conceiving for consciousness in all its branches, and the formal part of that process of conceiving for the process and the objects of it together, that is, the formal concept, considered as a concrete object, for the really concrete concept, which consists of a material element, feeling or sense, as well as of a formal element; and if we were to erect this formal process of conceiving, and the results to which it leads as its deductions, into the subjective counterpart of the world of existence, in place of the whole richly endowed consciousness which is its true mirror; it is manifest that we should obtain a totally false system of existence, although we might describe with faithful accuracy the formal process of conceiving, and deduce correctly the results of that process. In analysing now this formal process of conceiving, it will I think be made evident that it is totally unfit to sustain such a part. And while all must recognise in Hegel his profound insight into the formal part of this process of conceiving in and by itself, no one is bound to accept also the ontological system which he has founded thereon, and which he considers as its equivalent. Hegel says, in the Introduction to the Encyclopädie, § 3, that die Philosophie *Gedanken, Kategorien,* aber näher *Begriffe* an die Stelle der Vorstellungen setzt. Vorstellungen überhaupt können als *Metaphern* der Gedanken und Begriffe angesehen werden; and in § 5, that the true content of our consciousness is preserved and exhibited in translating it into the form of the thought and the concept; by which he does not mean that truth is attained by reflection, or by comparing old notions with new evidence (Nachdenken), but that thought, which supplies itself both with form and matter, is the only true thing, as opposed to sensible perception, of which it is entirely independent, and which, so far from furnishing the matter of truth, derives from thought all the truth it may possess.

Yet it is equally true, that perceptions, presentative and representative, can no more be without form, than thoughts or concepts without matter, and matter of the same kind in each case. And here lies the distinction which I wish to establish. Every thing that is in consciousness is real, though it may not be a thought or a concept. Truth indeed depends upon the distinct comparison of perceptions, that is, upon thoughts and concepts, and upon the forms of their comparison; but this requires completing by the additional statement, that thoughts and concepts derive their reality from perceptions which become true first in comparison, that is, in the shape of thoughts and concepts. Without thought no truth, without perception no reality. By reality I understand the actual existence of any object, its actual presence in consciousness; this is not greater after thought than before; thought has transformed it into a different shape, has given it new relations, but has added nothing to its real existence. Truth, on the other hand, is the product of thought, the form which an object assumes after investigation, and thus is greater after thought than before. Reality depends on the relation between objects and consciousness, truth on the relation between objects in consciousness. The true and the real have constantly been confounded, or rather I do not know that they have ever been distinguished. As reality has but one source, so also has truth but one; as consciousness gives reality, so its form gives truth. The formal process of consciousness must be one, consciousness must have unity of function. Denkend ist der Mensch immer, auch wenn er nur anschaut, says Hegel, Encyclopädie, § 24, Zusatz 1. This is what is profound in Hegel's system; he sees that there must be unity of function in consciousness. But where are we to find this unity; what is its form; and in what does it consist? Hegel's reply is, In that process, and in that form of it, which conceives and deals with concepts, that is, in the form of thought as opposed to that of intuition; and if so, then both the form and the matter of intuition must be generated out of the form, the matter, and the process of thought, belonging to it in its own right underived from intuition.

This Essay takes the opposite route, and, equally recognising the necessity of an unity of function in consciousness, makes the attempt to deduce the forms and the laws of thought from the forms and the matter of intuition. One mode of consciousness has no greater reality, nor gives us objects of greater reality, than another. But the understanding, and reflection so far as it is its development, is the fabricator and producer of truth. It was natural to suppose that the understanding and its forms were the source of reality; and others besides Hegel might be tempted, on other grounds than his, to strike first into this way, since it was universally recognised that the understanding and its forms were the organs of truth. In thought we are occupied with the relations of objects to each other, and the attention is called off from their common relation to consciousness; it was supposed also that reality resided solely in the objects, and not, as must be imbibed from Descartes, in the relation between the objects and consciousness. Reality therefore, it would be argued, must be the product, the discovery, of that function of consciousness which deals with the objects as they truly are, whether in themselves or to each other. Moreover it had always been remarked that the changes in the conscious subject, the object of psychology, were the most fertile source of uncertainty; that different habits of mind and of body caused objects to be seen in very different lights, and that it could never be known for certain whether two men

A A

saw or felt exactly alike. This caused the attention to be withdrawn from the modes of intuition as sources of reality, and fixed upon reasoning and thought, since these were the methods of producing agreement out of disagreement, and exhibiting an object in the same light to all observers; and when many observers saw but one object, and agreed in their description of it, must they not see it as it really was, independent of the subjective peculiarities of each observer? If to see objects truly was to see them as they really were, independently of consciousness, the process of thought must be the discoverer of real existence. But it must be replied to such reflections as these, that in fact we do not get rid of subjectivity, nor even of subjective variations, by adding to the modes of intuition those of thinking, and by considering, as is done in thought, the relations of objects to each other, abstracting from their relations to ourselves. The objects, which are proved to be true, remain as thoroughly subjective as before; and error still exists in the memory, though recognised as error.

Perhaps the account which would be usually given of the relation of truth to reality would be this, that truth is subjective reality, and reality objective truth, reality being entirely independent of the mind or consciousness, and truth being the knowledge of that reality. Those who so conceive the matter are entirely at one with Hegel on this one point, namely, that true knowledge is a knowledge of an absolute: every piece of true knowledge, for instance one of Kepler's laws, would be a knowledge of the real and independent, that is, of an absolute. The assumption of a gulf between the objective and the subjective, which I think is no uncommon assumption, is in this one respect entirely in unison with Hegel's doctrine, that truth and reality exist in thought and not in perception. Both doctrines are doctrines of an absolute; both systems reach the same goal by different routes; both maintain, that only what is true exists, and that this existence is an absolute existence. On this common doctrine being held, forthwith it must either be maintained, on the above distinction between objective and subjective, that erroneous notions, since they correspond to no object, have no existence at all; for even true notions are only shadows of reality, and where there is no reality there can be no shadow (and this doctrine is so vague that I am at a loss to state it without a metaphor); or it must be maintained, with Hegel, that true notions are themselves reality and absolute existence. But if Hegel's doctrine should for any reason be rejected, then the only alternative is either to reject the doctrine of an absolute altogether, or to maintain that nothing subjective, as such, has any existence. But this latter course is not only repugnant to the common use of language, but involves us in inexplicable difficulties of thought; for we not only say but feel, for instance, that a pain exists and is real, and that an opinion exists and is real, when we argue it in our own minds, or combat it in others. There remains, therefore, no course open but, at once, to deny the absolute and to distinguish between reality and truth; calling every thing real that comes forward in consciousness, and every thing true which, being in consciousness, will stand the test, or be the result, of that mode of consciousness called thought.

§ 43. The first thing which strikes the attention in the phenomenon of logical conceiving is, that it is a voluntary process. No one forms concepts without an effort, nor without a purpose in view. We are conscious of an effort to fix the attention and to hold fast one peculiarity in an object or set of objects. Conceiving then belongs to that stage or kind of consciousness which is conscious of purpose in addition to its other objects, however much the original effort may afterwards be forgotten when use has rendered the concept-name familiar. It was shown in § 31, that volition is a particular form of the sense of effort; that it is the sense of an effort combined with the feeling of an interest, that is, of purpose in the effort. One mode of this volition is the function of logically conceiving. But as volition differed not in its nature from the spontaneous activity of consciousness, but was itself that spontaneous activity carried to a new development, so also the form of volition called conceiving is not essentially different from the forms of the spontaneous activity of consciousness, called perception, imagination, and representation. It is a repetition voluntarily of the same processes and with the same machinery, that is, in the same forms or formal elements, which were employed in the spontaneous and intuitive functions of consciousness. This process of conceiving has already been described in the concrete, in the chapter on voluntary redintegration. It remains to examine the formal element as it appears in that process, and to see whether it contains any new characters not derived from the formal element in perception, namely, time and space.

When volition is applied to modify the objects of perception, the results are concepts and the postulates. The means at the command of volition are the power of making an exhaustive division, and of fixing the attention on one branch and withdrawing it from the other. It has been shown in § 16, that this power of being exhaustively divided is an essential characteristic of time and space, and that it arises from the presence of a material element in those forms. This property the will now takes possession of, and enforces a point or a line of demarcation between the objects which have excited its interest. This distinguishing is conceiving. It is a holding fast any content, no matter what, and distinguishing it from all others. It is determination and limitation, and depends, as already said, on the power of making an exhaustive division; for in order to distinguish an object from all others we must be able to embrace both the one and the others in our view. It matters not that the particular object, determined and distinguished from all others, which we had in view when we formed the concept, is found to be the same with other objects which we were at that time expecting to find among the all others; nor that, among the all others, are found particular objects which are afterwards properly included in the one. For instance, it matters not to the concept, white objects, as distinguished from objects not-white, that some swans are found to be included in the all others, or not-white objects. The concept, white objects, is provisional, anticipatory, potential, so far as regards its extension over the particular objects of perception included in it, but it is the most strict and fixed mode of thought possible, so far as regards its own nature as a concept. White objects and not-white objects are fixed and unchanging in their significance, in spite of this or that object passing over from one to the other category.

PART II.
CH. VII.
DIV. I.

§ 61.
Origin of the Laws of thought.

All concepts include their proper object and exclude all others. The formal nature of concepts, apart from the proper objects of them, is therefore inclusion and exclusion; when we conceive, we include and exclude, and the object included is the proper object of the concept. The postulates arise in the same way. For the possibility of including and excluding, as a concept does, is founded on the possibility of making an exhaustive division, and this is expressed by the words Either — Or, by the words This—Not-this, and by the logical postulate of excluded middle. The other two postulates have the same reference. The first, or the law of Identity, A is A, envisages the first branch of the exhaustive division, the inclusion or object of the concept, and affirms that all included by the concept is included in the proper object of the concept. The second, or the law of Contradiction, No A is Not-A, envisages the opposition between the two branches of the concept, its inclusion and its exclusion, and affirms that all which is included in the one is ipso facto excluded from the other. The third is the law of Excluded Middle, Every thing is either A or Not-A, and envisages the two branches ab extra, and affirms that this identity and contradiction are exhaustive, and that nothing exists which is not included either entirely in the one or entirely in the other. The three postulates or ultimate laws of thinking logically, that is to say, properly, are expressions of one and the same mental fact or fact of consciousness, which is at once objective and subjective in its reference, namely, the fact of the existence in all things of an entirely exhaustive division, which is drawn out into distinctness so soon as we begin to think about them. To

THE POSTULATES AND THE CONCEPT-FORM. 359

think, to conceive, is in its ultimate and most abstract shape to divide exhaustively, to include and exclude; or, looking to the content, the object of thought, the concept itself, which may be permitted here for a moment, for the sake of completeness, it is to compare one thing with another, the content of the concept with other contents excluded from it; in other words, that which is division as to its form is comparison as to its matter. This process of exhaustive division is expressed in all its significance by the three postulates of logic; they bring out its value and its nature in all their bearings, and fit it for application to the purposes of formal and controversial reasoning. As postulates too they have another significance. I have called them indifferently postulates and laws; they are laws, when drawn out into shape, so as to be made the major premises of syllogisms; they are laws of formal thought, when formal thought, or logic, is considered ab extra, as a phenomenon to be studied, or when they are used as a test or canon, by which to examine a train of reasoning. But they are in their ultimate nature practical rather than theoretical laws, inasmuch as they emerge, as logical principles, only in a voluntary process of consciousness, as part and parcel of every instance of reasoning, and thus are laws of volition, that is, are postulates rather than simply laws. The logician says, Let it be granted that we must divide exhaustively, or that A is A, No A is Not-A, Every thing is either A or Not-A. But why let it be granted? Because to fix the attention on one object involves and is conditioned by an exhaustive division. Thinking is a conscious movement or movement of consciousness, and farther it is a voluntary movement; no one forms concepts involuntarily. Its ultimate laws are imposed by, though not produced out of, the will. The postulates express a resolution, 1st, when I say A, I mean and will mean A; 2d, and nothing else but A; 3d, whatever that "else" may be. In controversy, or thinking in company with others, the postulates impose this resolution on others; they are the preliminaries of all argument; if you argue, you must do as I do, and mean, by A, A and nothing else.

§ 44. The same act of thinking, the act of dividing exhaustively, which finds one expression in the three postulates of logic, finds another expression more brief and more concrete in the concept-form. The concept-form is capable of analysis into the postulates; it contains them implicitly, it expresses them as a single fact. Every concept-form does two things, include and exclude. Its inclusion is its proper object, which I call simply the concept; its exclusion is the contradictory of its inclusion. The concept-form contains two contradictories. Contradictories are the creatures of logic; they are expressed by the word "not." White and Not-white are contradictories. This results from the voluntary nature of conceiving; I express in this way, namely, by the word not, my assumption for the moment of an object, no matter what, and my exclusion from it of all other objects, no matter what. If I assume A, then to call it Not-A violates the hypothesis, for this was the very and only thing which I resolved to avoid by naming A. If I assume White, every thing is primâ facie admissible as a predicate of it, except one thing, namely, Not-white. Contradictories are violations of the hypothesis which we begin with, reversals of the resolution which we have taken.

Omnis determinatio est negatio, says Spinoza. Nothing more true. To determine, define, limit, is to affirm the inclusion,—but at the same time to deny the exclusion. Every concept-form denies as certainly and as essentially as it affirms; negation is included in it as necessarily as affirmation, the negation of one, the affirmation of the other, of the two contradictories. Since it is a single act, the act of exhaustively dividing, which produces both the inclusion and the exclusion of the concept-form, both contradictories are equally necessary to the concept-form, and equally necessary to each other. Since a third point is taken, to which the two contradictories equally and alike refer, namely, the concept-form itself, or the act of dividing which constitutes it, the two contradictories become contraries; and we may call them logical contraries, since contraries are objects contrasted with each other by reference to one third object, or one single third point of difference, as right and left are contraries with reference to the person between them; and as contraries also the contradictories of the concept-form are amenable to the rule, Contrariorum eadem est scientia. The whole which they constitute, the concept-form itself, is the point of view from which both are contemplated at a glance. The contradictories are also relatives, necessary to each other; A involves Not-A in its mere assumption. They go together in thought for the purpose of mutual contradiction, just as relatives go together in existence for the purpose of mutual affirmation. Father and son, Master and servant, Sovereign and subject, are relatives which are necessary both to the existence and to the intelligibility of each other. A and Not-A are relatives which are necessary to the intelligibility but not to the existence of each other. The same necessity exists in destruction as in support, for in both cases it is a logical necessity.

Each of the two contradictories in the concept-form involves the other; and the concept-form, which may be called indifferently by the name of either, involves them both. A, if we take it as the name of the concept-form, includes Not-A; and Not-A, if we take it as the name of the concept-form, includes A. And each of them, taken as a limb of the concept-form, involves but excludes the other. In other and more Hegelian words, the concept-form is the unity and the identity of contradictories; a later negation denying an earlier negation; the negation of the negation of A by Not-A; the perception that each contradictory is involved in the other. The act or phenomenon of exhaustive division, giving rise to the contradictories and their identity in the concept-form in voluntary processes of consciousness, is what I understand Plato to mean by the phrase τὸ ἐξαίφνης, near the conclusion of the Parmenides, and what Hegel expressed by his "nicht übergeht sondern übergegangen ist." The division by itself occupies no time nor space, for a division is a distinction between two objects which occupy time and space, no portion of time or space intervening. The division does not exist, cannot be presented to consciousness, by itself; it must be presented as two objects different from each other. But the weight of this view of the matter, this fact of consciousness as it truly is, bears not against the necessity of the cognitions of time and space, but in favour of it. Plato might be justified in taking his τὸ ἐξαίφνης out of time, but no one writing after Kant is justified in doing the same. The two contradictories of the concept-form are mutually essential, but they are connected together in time; they are modes of consciousness and require time for their envisagement, and that whether we envisage them together in the concept-form, or separately as contradictories.

There are then, as will be evident from what has been said, three things to be distinguished in the process or phenomenon of thought or conceiving. First, there is the concept-name, which may be empty of object or content; meaning to express a concept, or an object as conceived, we may express nothing; the instance given above was that of pure nothing, which points out, as it were, the direction in which the object of it would be found, were it possible to find it. Other instances are, Iron-gold, a Round-square, and so forth. Secondly, there is the concept-object, which is properly called the concept simply, which will be considered in the following Division; it is the object or content included in and assumed by the concept-form. Thirdly, there is the concept-form, which has just been examined. And this concept-form it is, which is the sum and substance of Hegel's system of philosophy. Concept-forms are with him the only real existences, from the most abstract of all, Seyn-Nichts, to the most concrete of all, Die absolute Idee, that in the formation of which no other concept-form has been omitted, and in which they are all originally contained. The origin however of the concept-form itself has been here pointed out, and it has been shown that it is derived from the nature of time and space being exhaustively divisible, and from this divisibility being adopted and enforced by the will, for the purpose of investigating objects.

§ 45. The course of enquiry has now brought us to a position, from which a brief criticism of Hegel's Logical System may be attempted; a task which, it will be remembered, was postponed in Chapter III. I cannot offer the following as a complete examination of Hegel's Logic, still less of his whole system of philosophy of which the Logic is the foundation; at the same time I think that it will exhibit all the essential and fundamental points of it; and as a preliminary I distinguish in the Logic four things; its starting point, its goal, its content, and its method, or principle of movement; which distinctions, if kept in view, will serve as the framework of the following remarks.

Hegel's Logic lays claim to a double character; it is proposed as at once a system of metaphysic or ultimate logic of the universe, and as a system of ontology or absolute existence. It might be supposed that a system bearing the latter character was ipso facto disqualified from bearing also the former, since it has been shown that ontology, or a system of absolute existence, is a chimera; and accordingly that, if it could be shown that Hegel's Logic laid claim to be an ontology, it must abandon its claim to serve also as a system of metaphysic. But this would not be examining the case on its merits; for it might be justly replied, See first whether the system is valid as a metaphysical system, and, if it proves to be so, then the character of the system itself will decide whether it is also an ontology, and the existence there exhibited an absolute existence; you cannot decide generally that ontology is a chimera, until you have first weighed the evidence offered by this system of metaphysic. The question, then, before us is,

What is the validity of Hegel's Logic as a system of metaphysic, or applied logic of the universe? Hegel's Logic is one great concept-form, of which the inclusion, the exclusion, and the connection of the two are the Absolute Idea. Der Begriff is the term which I translate Concept-form; and Die absolute Idee is its completed content, or object, including in that phrase both the object included, the object excluded, and their connection in the concept-form. The absolute idea is involved in the concept-form, and vice versâ; form and matter in this sense are inseparable. In the concept-form and the absolute idea together lie the essence, the nature, the explanation, of all existence whatever; they are the logic of the universe, explain why things exist at all, and why they exist as we see and feel them. For the absolute idea, involving in itself the concept-form, is not inactive, but proceeds to evolve from itself the world of Vorstellung, or phenomena in time and space. "Die reine Idee, in welcher die Bestimmtheit oder Realität des Begriffes selbst zum Begriffe erhoben ist, ist vielmehr absolute *Befreiung*, für welche keine unmittelbare Bestimmung mehr ist, die nicht ebenso sehr *gesetzt* und der Begriff ist; in dieser Freiheit findet daher kein Übergang statt, das einfache Seyn, zu dem sich die Idee bestimmt, bleibt ihr vollkommen durchsichtig, und ist also hier vielmehr so zu fassen, dass die Idee sich selbst *frei entlässt*, ihrer absolut sicher und in sich ruhend. Um dieser Freiheit willen ist die *Form ihrer Bestimmtheit* ebenso schlechthin frei,—die absolut für sich selbst ohne Subjectivität seyende *Aeusserlichkeit des Raums und der Zeit*.— Insofern diese nur nach der abstracten Unmittelbarkeit des Seyns ist und vom Bewusstseyn gefasst wird, ist sie als blosse Objectivität und äusserliches Leben; aber in der Idee bleibt sie an und für sich die Totalität des Begriffs, und die Wissenschaft im Verhältnisse des Göttlichen Erkennens zur Natur." The external world of nature, or Vorstellung, or as I should say of feelings in time and space, is thus represented as flowing directly and necessarily from the absolute idea, and from that alone. The existence of the formal element, time and space, is accounted for by the freedom of the absolute idea, since time and space have something free and unlimited about them. But the existence of feelings, the material element as I call it, is not accounted for at all. The germ of them, or the logical reason for them, however, is given in the Logic, as also is that of time and space. This Entschluss, or development of the absolute idea into an external world, is the object-matter of the Naturphilosophie, which thus contains the separation of the idea from the external world which is its product, and examines the product apart from the parent. But now farther, since the idea evolved this product because it contained the concept-form, the same reason compels it also to connect again its product with itself; for the external world, being the product of the idea, contains also the concept-form. It proceeds therefore to evolve out of itself, returning to the idea by the evolution, the absolute mind, der absolute Geist, who is to the absolute idea just what the absolute idea is to the concept-form, its absolutely existing content, or object, but from the subjective side. There is one absolute mind, with one absolute idea, connected by one absolute form of thought. The passage already quoted proceeds as follows: "Dieser nächste Entschluss der reinen Idee, sich als äusserliche Idee zu bestimmen, setzt sich aber damit nur die Vermittelung, aus welcher sich der Begriff als freie aus der Aeusserlichkeit in sich gegangene Existenz emporhebt, in der *Wissenschaft des Geistes* seine Befreiung durch sich vollendet, und den höchsten Begriff seiner selbst in der logischen Wissenschaft, als dem sich begreifenden reinen Begriffe findet." This is the concluding passage of Hegel's Subjective Logic. Werke, vol. v. p. 342-3. There are thus three divisions of the whole of philosophy; 1st, that which shows how the form of thought raises itself or develops itself into the idea; 2d, that which shows how the idea develops itself into the whole external world; 3d, that which shows how the whole external world develops itself into the mind which is the concrete and existing counterpart of the form of thought in its absolute idea; the result being, stated shortly and in non-Hegelian terms, that there is one supreme existence only, the absolute mind; which is, not contains or possesses or perceives, but is, all its ideas, the external world and its laws among the rest; which is therefore the absolute idea, and that in one mode of existence, as inseparable from the mind as the mind from the idea, namely, the concept-form. Thus the absolute idea, the absolute mind, and the absolute concept-form are exactly that which I designate by the term aspects. They are inseparable and coextensive characteristics of each other. To examine one of them is to examine the other two, and to examine two of them is to examine the third. The absolute concept-form cannot be examined alone, for that would be to separate it from all content. Hegel accordingly takes the absolute concept-form and the absolute idea together, and makes them the object-matter of the Logic. The Naturphilosophie and the Philosophie des Geistes together make up the content, objectivity, existence, or reality of this object-matter of the Logic, of the absolute concept-form together with the absolute idea. The Logic contains the principles of the two other parts of the system; and therefore an insight into the Logic, that is, into the form, the content, and the method or principle of movement of the absolute idea, is an insight into the whole system.

The Logic contains three moments, Das Seyn, Das Wesen, Der Begriff. In the last is completed the concept-form; for Hegel does not start with the assumption of the concept-form as such, but with the assumption of a concept, in which indeed the concept-form is included implicitly, an sich, but not yet proved explicitly, an und für sich; this is part of the logical development itself. The distinction between the concept and the concept-form, such as I have drawn it in this chapter, is nowhere found in Hegel. He distinguished indeed between der Begriff and die Begriffe; but when he uses the singular, der Begriff, it is left uncertain whether the attention is meant to be drawn to the object, or to the form of the object, mentioned. So that in assuming a concept, das Seyn, as the starting point of logic, Hegel assumes both concept and concept-form, but reasons only from the former. He starts in the Logic from the assumption of a concept, because it was proved in the Phänomenologie that all true knowledge is conceiving, and that in concepts, Begriffe, and not in Vorstellungen, intuitions or perceptions, is truth. "In dem Wissen," says Hegel, Phänomenologie, page 588, "hat also der Geist die

Bewegung seines Gestaltens beschlossen, insofern dasselbe mit dem unüberwundenen Unterschiede des Bewusstseyns behaftet ist. Er hat das reine Element seines Daseyns, den Begriff, gewonnen." But how, it may be asked, does Hegel manage to reach der Begriff, as the conclusion of the Phänomenologie, without deriving it from, or at least including in it as essential constituents, the cognitions of time and space in their proper shape? Do not these cognitions oppose him at every step of his progress to a pure concept, a concept to which they are, in that shape, considered unessential? They would do so, it must be replied, if he had not put them aside at first, and transformed them into a shape suitable for further transformation into the pure concept. These cognitions must, if they are universal and necessary, meet him at the very first step of the Phänomenologie; and accordingly the very first step of the Phänomenologie is to abolish or transform them, pages 71-97. How is this done? By striking at once from the very beginning into the route of second, as distinguished from first, intentions; that is, by neglecting to analyse objects as objects for consciousness alone, and seeking instead for general notions under which to group them, and general terms by which to characterise them; and this characterising Hegel calls perceiving the truth, or Wahrheit, of the object. He begins with the whole field of immediate impressions of sense; the knowledge which we have of them, he says, is the most abstract and poorest truth; it says of its object only this,—it exists. This is to neglect the analysis of the object, and to ask what can be said *about* the object, taken as a whole. The next step is to observe the distinction, in this

BB

whole object, into general and particular, general consciousness and particular instances of it, and to notice the only circumstance common to all the particular instances, namely, that they are relations of a Subject, an Ich, to an object, or that they consist in an object and a Subject, mutually conditioned, or conditioning each other. Then the objective side of this relation is first examined, the object being taken as a present object in time, das Jetzt, and a present object in space, das Hier. Every such object has the common property, common to it with all the rest, of being present; in other words, the Hier and the Jetzt are an allgemeines. The same is then shown of the other or subjective side, of our consciousness of the object, as was shown of the object itself. Allgemeinheit or das Allgemeine is the next object investigated, into which the previous objects of sense are represented as transformed, or, what is the same thing, which is represented as their truth. This general object then comes before us as das Ding von vielen Eigenschaften, the subjective side of which is Wahrnehmung. The mode of coexistence of these properties, Eigenschaften, is then examined and characterised, and the object transformed into the concept of forces acting in polar opposition to each other; and the subjective side of this object is Verstand. In this way, no sooner does an object arise for consciousness than it is characterised or described in terms borrowed from some other objects; and the new object thus produced is treated in the same manner. The analysis of the objects as they exist for consciousness alone is never seriously entered on. Thus it is that time and space, as the formal elements of all objects, are put aside from the first, and the pure concept, as the mode or form of das absolute Wissen, which is the result, and therefore the truth, of the whole of knowledge, is established in their stead, as containing and therefore superseding them. But such a method of proceeding starts from a previous assumption, the assumption that descriptions instead of definitions are the truth of objects; and also disobeys one essential condition of all investigation of truth, namely, to keep steadily and directly in view the object which is being investigated.

Such is the foundation laid by Hegel in the Phänomenologie, upon which he proceeds to work in the Logic. In the Allgemeine Eintheilung der Logik, Werke, vol. 3, p. 47, he says, "Der Begriff der Logik aber selbst ist in der Einleitung als das Resultat einer jenseits liegenden Wissenschaft, damit hier gleichfalls als eine *Voraussetzung* angegeben worden. Die Logik bestimmte sich danach als die Wissenschaft des reinen Denkens, die zu ihrem Princip *das reine Wissen* habe, die nicht abstracte, sondern dadurch concrete lebendige Einheit, dass in ihr der Gegensatz des Bewusstseyns von einem subjectiv *für sich Seyenden* und einem zweiten solchen *Seyenden*, einem objectiven, als überwunden, und das Seyn als reiner Begriff an sich selbst, und der reine Begriff als das wahrhafte Seyn gewusst wird. Diess sind sonach die beiden *Momente* welche im logischen enthalten sind. Aber sie werden nun als *untrennbar* seyend gewusst, nicht wie im Bewusstseyn jedes *auch* als *für sich seyend;* dadurch allein, dass sie zugleich als *unterschiedene* (jedoch nicht für sich seyende) gewusst werden, ist ihre Einheit nicht abstract, todt, unbewegend, sondern concret." In order to understand this passage, it would perhaps be as well to refer to a corresponding passage in the Phänomenologie, Einleitung, p. 65, a passage beginning, Dieser Widerspruch und seine Wegräumung. He means to say, in the passage here transcribed, that thought, which is the truth of all modes of consciousness, or into which all must be resolved, must be now examined for itself; not in its conditions, as containing an object and a subject, but as consisting of a nature of its own, as I should say, thought in its first intention, abstracting from all particular things thought of, and leaving only the process or thing itself, Thought, as an Existence. So considered, he asserts that it has two inseparable moments, or aspects as I should call them, namely, Seyn and Reiner Begriff, pure thought and existence or being. The fundamental distinction in Hegel's Logic is indeed a distinction into a material and a formal element or aspect; but not into the material and formal elements of perception, feeling and time and space, nor yet into what I call the two aspects of phenomena, Object and Subject; but into two elements or two aspects of thought, namely, existence and pure thought, or, as I should call them, the concept and the concept-form. It is from this that he starts; and this must always be remembered, namely, that das Seyn is thought; for, when he makes his first beginning with das Seyn, he abstracts from the circumstance that it is thought, and treats this aspect or moment for itself, in its first intention as a concept, and does not deduce any thing from the fact that it is a thought, or a concept-form. Out of the mere das Seyn he deduces die absolute Idee, not by comparing it with thought, or bringing the two together at all, but solely by attending to what the thought, das Seyn, is.

THE POSTULATES AND THE CONCEPT-FORM.

Now I shall try to show, 1st, that all the concepts and all the steps taken by Hegel involve an element which he does not acknowledge, the form of time; 2d, that from a certain point onwards they involve another element which he does not acknowledge, the form of space; 3d, that the account given of the thought of matter and of the arising of this thought is insufficient; 4th, that the forward movement depends on the relation of the first and second intention of objects, and that the appearance of contradictions and their solution is removed by attending to this distinction; and 5th, that, so far from negation being the moving principle of thinking, or of the process of thought, it is the mere expression of a limit imposed by volition, which is another element not acknowledged by Hegel.

The first, fourth, and fifth of these points must be treated together, at least it is impossible to treat any of them separately without mixing up the others. I will, however, take the fourth, and show how the Hegelian movement depends on the difference of first and second intentions, which not being acknowledged gives an appearance as if a contradiction and its solution had taken place. In the first book of the Logic, Das Seyn, all the triplets which compose it contain, each of them, 1st, an object in its second intention; 2d, the same object in its first intention; 3d, an object composed of these two intentions, which thus becomes a new object, is called by a new name, and is the first object or moment of the succeeding triplet. The first triplet of all begins with Seyn, reines Seyn. This is the bare thought of existence, presence in consciousness; it is undetermined only because it is a voluntary abstraction from all determination. It is the mere thought about objects, ὅτι ἔστιν, without any particular object thought of, the characterisation of all and any particular objects as existing. Turn now to this abstract existence, the thought of existence, and ask what it is for consciousness, or what it is in its first intention, and the answer must be, that it is Nichts; as an abstraction it has no first intention, but is a mere abstraction, nothing. But the first and the second intention are one and the same thing; to think of abstract existence and to think of nothing is the same, and yet not the same; thought passes from one to the other, and each becomes the other, from whichever you start. Seyn and Nichts together are Werden. Now here the elements of time and feeling are present at every step. There can be no becoming, no change, without time, and there can be no thought of existence, and no thought of nothing, without occupying time. The time involved in the Werden is involved in each moment of it; and to have a thought of Seyn or Nichts is to have consciousness affected in a particular way, that is, to have a feeling. See a criticism on Hegel, from a somewhat similar point of view to mine, in Herr Trendelenburg's Logische Untersuchungen, vol. 1, p. 36, 2d edit. See also, for an account of the nature and drift of Hegel's philosophy, Mr. Stirling's Secret of Hegel, 2 vols. 1865.

Werden, or Becoming, is the unity of existence and nothing; but what is it in its second intention? How is it to be characterised? It is certainly a determination; namely, of Seyn by Nichts and of Nichts by Seyn. It is determined existence, Daseyn; and thus there arises a starting point for the next triplet, which is Daseyn als solches, Qualität, Etwas.

Determined existence, in its first intention, or for consciousness alone, what is it? Answer, Quality; the quality of a thing. A determinate existence, determined to a quality, is however a particular something, Etwas. Das Daseyn becomes Etwas, Daseyendes.

The third triplet begins by treating Etwas as a second intention, Etwas und ein Anderes, something and something else. The first intention of this concept of comparison is, that it is Bestimmtheit, Beschaffenheit, und Grenze; something and something else, taken together, are a determination of nature and a limit. Take these two moments together, and there arises the notion of the finality of every thing, die Endlichkeit.

The fourth triplet begins with Endlichkeit, that all things are limited and cease at a certain point, because something else begins; this mutual limitation is a bound, over which each is trying to pass, das Sollen; and the finite thing is limited by the finite, that is, by itself; it sets itself a bound, and passes over its own bound, for it is itself on the other side. The limitation and the passing over it, taken together, are therefore die Unendlichkeit; or the finite things have the nature of infinity.

This process goes on through all the first book, Das Seyn. A second intention, then its first intention, then their union. The principle of movement, then, is this, that you begin with a second intention, by exercising volition in making abstraction; this is itself a concept, or an inclusion and an exclusion; a negation, for you have yourself fixed your object, and excluded other objects from it; and since it is a second intention, it has a first intention, or has some content. In the case of das Seyn, this content is obviously Nichts; and so you have not only a first intention of abstract existence, but one which contradicts it. If it had been seen that das Seyn was already a second intention, it would have been replied to Hegel, Das Seyn is not Nichts, but all things whatever, without attending to their qualities; all things whatever are the first intention of das Seyn; but if you propose to us the abstraction, das Seyn, the concept, das Seyn, and treat this, which is a second intention, as if it were a first intention, as if it were an object for consciousness by itself apart from its content, then no doubt its abstracting or conceptual nature must be taken into account, and such an abstraction is Nothing. The apparent contradiction arises from treating a second intention as if it was a first intention.

The place where notions involving the cognition of space are first introduced is in the third chapter of the Section of Quality, entitled Das Fürsichseyn. Fürsichseyn becomes Unity, das Eins; then the unit, das Eins, is in its first intention das Leere, "das Leere ist so die Qualität des Eins in seiner Unmittelbarkeit," p. 176. Now, taking the quality of unity together with a single unit which excludes every thing else, there arises the notion of units excluding units, that is, of Plurality of units; and this is Repulsion. Repulsion involves attraction, and this is the passing over of quality into quantity. Now it is impossible to have a notion of repulsion or of attraction without the notion of space, just as it is impossible to have the notion of becoming, Werden, without that of time. The passing over to the notion of space is concealed by the simplicity of the notion of an unit, which may be a mere unit or moment of time; plurality of units also may be conceived as existing in time alone; but repulsion and attraction, a reciprocal action of these units on each other, even though it should be conceived as taking place along a single line, involves the visibility or the imagination as visible of that line, and makes it a line of space, a line on which there is a movement both forwards and backwards at once. But here there is no real deduction of the relations of space from those of time; the passage from one to the other is merely concealed, by the Unit, so that you do not know how you come to find yourself in a world of externality, outness, or space relations. The three chief divisions of the section on Quantity are, first, Quantity as a second intention, simple, continuous, unity; second, the same as a first intention, Quantum; third, the relations of Quanta, as quanta, to each other,—das quantitative Verhältniss. This relation becomes proportion, das Maass, which is the object-matter of the third section of the first book, Das Seyn.

The Logic has to account for the existence, that is, to give the concept or thought, of every thing that comes forward in the external world, or in nature. The Logic is the genesis of the thoughts, the concepts, the true essences, or natures, of the phenomena of sense. The thought of time, in this sense, would be produced by the very first negation, the negation of Seyn by Nichts, and would be contained in the thought of Werden; so that we should not be surprised, in the Naturphilosophie, to find phenomena of sense existing in time, seeing that the concepts, in the Logic, have existed in the same way; similarly the thought of space is quantity, and the existence of space in phenomena of sense is provided for and explained by our having had the thought of quantity in the Logic. Hitherto, in the two sections of Quality and Quantity, we have had nothing as content but time relations and space relations, and nothing as form but the negative movement of thought, out of which and the concept, das Seyn, the content has been represented as arising, this content being time and space relations and the proportion obtaining between them. But now the phenomenal existence of matter has also to be accounted for, the existence of solid, tangible, visible, and otherwise sensible bodies; the thought or concept which makes them possible, and is their essence and truth, has to be given. This is done at the end of the first chapter of the third section, Das Maass, p. 406, under the head, Das Fürsichseyn im Maasse. The passage begins, Es macht aber die weitere Bestimmung aus; and the thought or concept in question is that of Selbstündigkeit. Henceforth, in the two remaining chapters of the first book, Das Seyn, Hegel must be understood as having in his mind tangible and otherwise sensible objects, and their chemical composition. He speaks indeed of the laws of chemistry, chemical affinity, and so on; but he has really given no account or reason why matter should arise, why there should be colours, sounds, odours, hardnesses, roughnesses, and so on. He has included them in his concept, Selbstündigkeit, without naming them. Selbstündigkeit may be a good logical expression for tangible matter, when tangible matter has arisen, but it is no cause of any thing being tangible, or an object for any of the senses. Chemical relations may, it is true, be resolved into time and space relations, but the relations suppose the matter. I think there is no other course to take but to assume the existence of feeling in all its kinds, as an ultimate fact, as an element in all consciousness, and seek to discover the formal element in it, its modifications and laws of modification; not to assert that feeling, or matter, as existing in nature or the world of Vorstellung, is a poor imitation of thought; for the question then will be, How comes there to be just such an imitation as this is?

In the third chapter of this section, the last step, that in which das Seyn reaches its completion, is, that it appears as Substance and Attributes, as Indifference towards all its own modes of existing, and as the sum total of all. Here it would seem that all progress was impossible, the sum total of all attributes having been reached. But here comes in the reflection, or the fact, that das Seyn is a thought. All the objective relations and forms of das Seyn have developed themselves necessarily, one from the other, to their utmost; but what is the nature of this movement of development itself, its formal side, as it may perhaps be called? The different steps, the three movements in each triplet, have developed themselves necessarily, inevitably, one after the other; but what is the nature of this necessity, this inevitableness? In other words, what is the essence, das Wesen, of the world which has thus arisen? It is the movement by contradiction, a movement to a result which is thereby also overleapt, a movement which posits something and at the same time transcends or denies what it posits. The view is turned back on the series of concepts now completed, and in them is discovered a law of development as well as a series of concepts developed.

The second book of the Logic, entitled Das Wesen, exhibits this movement of thought as thought. In it four things may be remarked; first, that it treats of the laws of thought or of logic, the postulates; second, that it traverses the same ground as the first book traversed, but in a different way; third, that the law of the movement is different from that in the first book; and fourth, that the notions of time and space relations, or dynamic and static relations, are every where involved. To begin with the law of the process itself. This process is that which was exhibited in the first book, but there as involved in existences or concepts, Seyn, Werden, Qualität, Quantität, Verhältniss, Maass, and so on. Here that process is exhibited in itself, abstracted from these stages of its course, or objects produced in its course. But it has stages of its own, and an evolution of its own, apart from those objects. Its analysis is the dynamical analysis of the process which, in the first book, was exhibited as a succession of statical concepts. There the concepts were compared and analysed, here the movement between and connecting the concepts is analysed; and the concepts which are the stages, or halting places, of the movement are named, or characterised, by their relation to the movement itself; so that they seem to be different but are the same as the concepts in the first book. The movement and the concept reached by it, in this book, are what I should call the incomplete and the completed moment of consciousness. Hence the law of the process is not, as in the first book, a triplet consisting of a second intention, its first intention, and the union of the two, but a triplet consisting of the incomplete moment or movement, its completion in a concept, and the union

of both in a third concept. It might be expected
that the movement of thought would be one and the
same in all instances, or in all moments of Seyn; that
it could therefore have no moments of development
of its own, but, when pointed out, would be pointed
out once for all, as the single law of movement and
development of all possible concepts. This might
have been the case, if Hegel had simply turned his
attention to the formal character, the concept-form,
contained in every concept, as it was shown to be
contained in the concept, das Seyn, at the beginning
of the first book. But such is not Hegel's procedure.
He develops every thing from das Seyn as a concept,
and not as a concept-form. Consequently das Wesen,
the formal element of das Seyn, has itself a particular, concrete, shape; it is not Wesen in the abstract, but the Wesen of the Seyn, of the series of
concepts of the first book. From this relation of the
Wesen to the Seyn are developed all the series of
particular relations or essences, which are the categories of thought. This is consistent and logical, and
the result is a series of concepts which are relations
of other concepts, which are the relations of the concepts of the first book to each other.

The last step taken in the first book was to exhibit das Seyn as the substance of all its attributes,
their indifference and their sum. That is to say, das
Seyn is already a relation; das Wesen is relation, and
this relation is the first and simplest moment, or particular relation, in all the future series, is the Wesen
with which the second book begins. The first triplet
of the book shows the relation of Wesen to Seyn, and
throws light on the second point remarked above,
namely, that the ground traversed by both books is

the same. First chapter, p. 8, vol. 4. "Das Wesen ist das *aufgehobene Seyn.*" All that is not Wesen is unwesentliches; except the pure relation, or pure movement of thought, every thing is Schein, mere appearance. "Der Schein ist der ganze Rest, der noch von der Sphäre des Seyns übrig geblieben ist." p. 9. But all the Seyn was taken up into the Wesen; what then can the Schein be? It is a mode of the Wesen; "der Schein ist das an sich Nichtige; es ist nur zu zeigen, dass die Bestimmungen, die ihn vom Wesen unterscheiden, Bestimmungen des Wesens selbst sind," p. 11. And again, "Der Schein ist also das Wesen selbst, aber das Wesen in einer Bestimmtheit, aber so dass sie nur sein Moment ist, und das Wesen ist das Scheinen seiner in sich selbst. Das Wesen in dieser seiner Selbstbewegung ist die Reflexion." p. 13-14. As I should express it, the Schein is the completion of the incomplete moment of time, Wesen.

The next triplet analyses Reflexion. The movement itself exists, or is setzende Reflexion, the incomplete moment; secondly, it thinks or posits something,—äussere Reflexion, the completed moment; thirdly, this something is itself, bestimmende Reflexion.

The second chapter treats of the essentialities, Wesenheiten, or Reflexions-Bestimmungen. They are in fact the postulates of logic, or rather correspond to what are called the postulates; for Hegel takes the movement itself and not its stages as the essential thing, imposing the postulates on itself, or creating them in its course. The three moments are, Identität, Unterschied, and Widerspruch, p. 26. "Das Wesen ist zuerst einfache Beziehung auf sich selbst; reine Identität. Diess ist seine Bestimmung, nach der es vielmehr Bestimmungslosigkeit ist." By Identity, I think, what Hegel meant, or had in his mind, was two successive moments of time, the content of which was exactly the same, and which are therefore only arbitrarily distinguished as two, by stopping short and reflecting that the same content has continued. This pure reflection is therefore equally pure distinction, Unterschied, of the identical moments. Identity is the character of the pure movement of reflection; its goal, or the completion of it, is to have established a difference, or a distinction, between the two moments. Each moment is at once like and not like the other. When the second moment is like the first in content, then the two are the Positive; when unlike, the Negative; and in this latter case, one moment is positive, the other its negative, and each exists only by virtue of the existence of the other, that is, each both includes and excludes the other, its opposite. This at one and the same time, and in one and the same respect, exclusion and inclusion is the contradiction, der Widerspruch. Every moment of thought is identity as movement, and difference as result; the two things are inseparable, exist in every movement of thought; that is, contradiction is the movement of thought. I explain this phenomenon, of which Hegel was the first to see the importance, by attributing the distinction to the material element, the feelings and volition among them, existing in and dividing the formal element; there being two sources of every empirical movement of consciousness, the whole movement is continuous or identical in one respect, and divided or different in the other respect, and thus no contradiction arises. Hegel, who admits only one pure movement of thought, without any double element, can only attribute the phenomenon to this pure nature of thought itself, and say that it is its nature to be contradiction.

The remaining chapter of the first section treats of der Grund and die Bedingung, which may be considered as corresponding to what is commonly called the Ratio Sufficiens. And in these the time and space relations appear to me to be every where supposed and tacitly employed. Der absolute Grund bears a statical character, der bestimmte Grund a dynamic character, and die Bedingung combines the two methods. The two remaining sections of this second book, Die Erscheinung and Die Wirklichkeit, require also, as it seems to me, notions of time and space relations to be present, in order to their being understood. The law of development is the same in these three sections of the second book, as in all their subordinate triplets. Das Wesen, the object of the first section, is in its completion die Erscheinung, the world of phenomena, the object of the second section; and this together with the movement which produced it is die Wirklichkeit, the object of the third section. The Wirklichkeit of the second book corresponds to the Maass of the first book, and is the essence of the Maass. The last stage of Wirklichkeit is die Wechselwirkung, the action and reaction of the universal Substanz, taken as a single moment; and this grasp of the whole as a single moment is der Begriff, the Concept-form, which has no further distinctions within itself, but only, as I should express it, distinction of aspects as a whole.

THE POSTULATES AND THE CONCEPT-FORM.

The third book of the Logic treats of, or rather exhibits, the Concept-form, the Begriff, as the evolution of its three aspects in their relation to each other; it unites in itself the Seyn and the Wesen of the two former books, traverses the same ground as they do, but in its evolution constructs a world out of them, which is the world of reason and of truth, the world as it really is. This is done in the third section of this book, Die Idee; and die Idee is what Hegel calls the Reason, Vernunft, as distinguished from the Understanding, Verstand. "Die Idee kann als die *Vernunft* (diess ist die eigentliche philosophische Bedeutung für *Vernunft*), . . . gefasst werden." Encyclopädie, § 214.

In this book we have no longer before us the successive stages reached by pure thought, the concepts of the first book, nor those of the movement of pure thought itself, as in the second book; but we have the concrete action of thought, the movement and its concepts together, the concepts as produced by the movement and not as produced by each other. That is, we have first the logical forms of thought themselves, as distinguished from the laws of the movement, the postulates; these forms being the conceptform itself, the judgment, Urtheil, and the syllogism, Schluss. These are the three chapters of the first section of the book entitled Der Begriff. The second section contains the object or content produced out of, and corresponding to, these forms of thought; it contains 1st, the world of mechanism, as conceived by thought, or the mechanical laws of the universe; 2d, the world of chemistry, as conceived by thought, or the chemical laws of the universe; and 3d, the totality of these two spheres, their τέλος or completion, or adequateness to the concept-form which they express; and this is called Teleologie, "der Zweck ist seiner Form nach eine in sich unendliche Totalität." vol. 5, p. 206. The third section contains the union of the two former, namely, the subjective process of thought and the objective content, or aspect, of it, a content or aspect which has come, in the Teleologie, fully up to the form or subjective aspect or process. The two things, subjectivity and objectivity, are henceforward united; they were originally what I should call aspects of the whole, that is, each of them was the whole Concept-form from its own point of view; or, as Hegel expresses it, the Objectivity is the Besonderheit des Begriffes, the Subjectivity is the Allgemeinheit des Begriffes. The remaining section, called Die Idee, is the Einzelnheit des Begriffes, or the Concept-form as an actual existence, subjective and objective at once, all of whose actual forms of existence are forms or modes of consciousness, the living personality thinking and feeling. The chapters of this section are 1st, Life; 2d, Cognition; and 3d, the unity of both. In or as the Absolute Idea, which is the unity of both, says Hegel, vol. 5, p. 317, "der Begriff ist nicht nur *Seele*, sondern freier subjectiver Begriff, der für sich ist und daher die *Persönlichkeit* hat,—der praktische, an und für sich bestimmte, objective Begriff, der als Person undurchdringliche, atome Subjectivität ist,—der aber ebenso sehr nicht ausschliessende Einzelnheit, sondern für sich *Allgemeinheit* und *Erkennen* ist, und in seinem Andern *seine eigene* Objectivität zum Gegenstande hat."

As to the law of the process followed in this book, it still moves by negation, and negation of that negation, as in the two former books, but its law differs from theirs, as much as theirs differ from each other. Each of the moments of the concept-form, namely, Allgemeinheit, Besonderheit, Einzelnheit, is the whole of the concept-form; in my phrase, an aspect of the concept-form;—"die Momente des Unterschiedes unmittelbar die Totalität des Begriffes sind." Vol. 5, p. 33. Each of these movements cannot be compared with, cannot exclude or include, any thing that is not already part of itself. The law of the development of the concept-form is therefore analysis; its negation is the negation of one of its aspects by another, and the negation of that negation by showing that they are both the third aspect.

Such is my interpretation of the dream of this king of thought; which, according to this interpretation, is an attempt to derive, first, that which I call matter, or feeling in all its variety, from form; not from that which I call form, time and space, but from the form of thought in conceiving; and secondly, to derive that which I call form, namely time and space, from the same source. My purpose in the present § has been to show that he has not succeeded in doing this, but that, at every step, that which I call matter and that which I call form must be included, in order that his reasoning and his terms may be even intelligible. The rest of the chapter is an attempt to show that the reverse of this theory is the truth, namely, that the form of conceiving is a product of the forms of time and space together with matter or feeling. In this way we possess, in the concept-form, not only a particular mode of consciousness, but one which can be used as an Organon, or test of the truth of other modes of consciousness. Unless logic can be used as such an organon, there is no test of the truth of any thing left, except of logic itself; and no man can be sure of having mastered any fact securely, or as true, unless he has mastered the whole of logic, that is, of metaphysic, and seen the relation which that fact bears, and the niche which it occupies, in the logical or metaphysical system. All empirical and particular phenomena of sense, or Vorstellungen, can only be known by being referred to their proper head in one of the Books, Sections, and Chapters of a Logic; and what is the science or the principle which teaches us to refer these to the right head in the Logic? Since the empirical and particular facts in all the special sciences are changing in relation and increasing in number every day, we shall want some general science, with general rules, to guide us in referring them to their proper head in the Logic, without which they cannot be understood; that is, we shall still be in want of a logic as an organon. Hegel's Naturphilosophie and Philosophie des Geistes might indeed serve as useful guiding examples, but we should still want some general rules, applicable to all cases. Hegel's Logic, in becoming a metaphysic or applied logic of the universe, has ceased to be an organon, or a test of the correctness of particular processes of thought. It has virtually, in this point, gone back to the station of the Platonic Dialectic, before Aristotle produced the system of formal logic; for in that system of Plato's there was one thing, and one only, to see, namely, the εἴδη. If you could understand these, you had truth; if not, you were involved in hopeless error. Reason as I reason, said Plato, admit the εἴδη, and distinguish them in phenomena, or you do not reason at all; reasoning is to apply my system. Aristotle however showed that to apply Plato's system, or any other, was but a particular kind of reasoning and not the whole; true or false, it was a metaphysical and a complete system, and as such not a Logic; containing more than the mere laws of reasoning, it was not adapted to serve as an organon. The same objection applies to Hegel's Logic; true or false, it contains so much, that, as a whole, it offers no standard for judging of extra-logical matters. It is a complete system, ready made to the hand of the reasoner; who, before he has accepted it requires some organon by which to examine it, and, after accepting it, some rules of applying it to future circumstances.

But Hegel's Logic is not only a metaphysical but an ontological theory, a theory of the Absolute. It does not profess to say what the subjective, or any other, aspect of existence is, but to say what existence as a whole is, to transmute existence into the concept-form, as the truth of existence, of which truth existence is a moment. How comes it that Hegel's metaphysical theory, which has just been examined, appears in this other character of a theory of the Absolute? This is not a necessary consequence of being a metaphysical theory; all metaphysical theories are not ontologies; but it is a consequence of the particular phenomenon fixed on by Hegel as the key of his system. It is because the concept-form is the ground and substance of his metaphysical analysis that his metaphysical analysis is also an ontology. Every concept is a logical whole. If the entire phenomena of the world can be reduced to the concept-form, they constitute a whole from which nothing can be excluded, but in which every thing is provided for. If now the concept-form is a product of other modes of consciousness, and a product which arises only to be transcended, a limit which is itself overleapt as soon as set, then whatever may be included in a concept-form is but a part of the world of phenomena and not the whole, and the concept-form itself is a part and not the whole of consciousness; it is a particular way of representing phenomena, the effect of volition, looking to a further purpose, and capable of use as an organon; which is the view taken of it in this Essay. But if the concept-form itself, the essence of which is to be a limited whole, is the ground, substance, and truth of all things, from which nothing is excluded, then the universe must be regarded as an Absolute, as something which has nothing beyond it and yet is limited. Now although Hegel includes Infinity itself in a concept; and the concept of infinity, or infinity as a concept, is what I understand him to mean by his expression true infinity, as opposed to false, or the schlecht-unendliches; and though this is the same thing as that which I mean by the idea of infinity, there is this difference between the two cases, namely, that the idea of infinity, as will be seen in the chapter on Ideas, is a mode of expressing or trying to grasp the phenomenon of infinity, Hegel's schlecht-unendliches, an attempt which confessedly fails, and names its failure in naming the object it attempts to grasp; while Hegel's concept of infinity, on the other hand, professes to have grasped the infinite, because it has included it in a concept-form. The circumstance that there is something which exceeds our power to grasp, this circumstance is the infinity of that something, be it time, or space, or feeling; infinity is the concept-name of that circumstance, and when we present that circumstance to ourselves in thought we have the concept of infinity. Assume now that the concept-form is the truth of every thing, that a circumstance as conceived, or as a concept, is what that circumstance really is, and then in having the concept of infinity we have grasped infinity, and made it finite; which is Hegel's assumption and Hegel's result. But if the concept-form is only the mode in which we represent a circumstance to ourselves for a particular purpose, then in grasping the concept infinity, we only grasp the circumstance that there is something which exceeds our power to grasp. This circumstance, called infinity, is a fact of perception, which is not altered in its nature by fixing it steadily in view and distinguishing it from other facts as a concept.

It is therefore the concept-form which makes Hegel's Logic an ontology. But even the concept-form itself is not the Absolute; for we cannot help, so imperious is the form of time, putting the question even to this, Why does the concept-form itself exist? Why does Negation exist? Why does a concept-form exist which begins with Seyn and ends with der absolute Geist? The necessity of putting this question brings down any ontology whatever to the rank of a metaphysic: and as metaphysic the system must stand or fall. As, in order of logic and metaphysic, the last thing arrived at is always a metaphysical element or elements, which are not empirical objects, so, in order of history or genesis, the last thing arrived at by cognition, beyond the earliest empirical object in the series, is always a question and not an answer to a question. You can characterise the whole series within its own limits, but never enclose it without leaving a period before it uncharacterised.

I share with Hegel his grand and profound conviction, that What we know, that we are. See this expressed in the Encyclopädie, § 239. "In der That aber ist die Natur das durch den Geist gesetzte, und der Geist selbst, ist es der sich die Natur zu seiner Voraussetzung macht." We make the world by knowing it; for the time which is past, which we imagine as independent of us, is a representation, or representative perception, of some present moment. We call it into existence according to the laws which govern consciousness; that is, the world is produced and developed according to the laws which govern consciousness; the principle, or principles, of the process of knowing are the principle, or principles, of the process of existence in the world. But what are those principles? This is the question on which I diverge from the Plato of our days, ὁ Πλάτων ὁ ἀληθινός, ὁ διάδοχος τοῦ Διαδόχου, Hegel. His theory is stated in one word,—Negation, or rather, Contradiction. One single principle explains every thing, and moulds all into one grand and comprehensive system. The fewer are the principles employed in explaining any thing, the more difficult and complete is the explanation; but the richer, the more complex, those principles are, and the more they require and admit analysis, that is, the more elements they contain, so much the more does the explanation, which they offer, become easy and incomplete. Now contradiction is certainly one single principle, but it contains many elements. What are these elements? Time, simple feeling, feeling of will. Contradiction containing these elements will carry us wherever we can make abstraction from an external world; but it will not explain the existence of such an external world. To explain this, another element must be added, the form of space. There are then deeper and simpler principles than contradiction; and the simplicity and completeness of Hegel's system are apparent only and not true. Make time, space, and feeling the principles of the world, and a system is obtained, less apparently complete and promising less, but, in my opinion at least, more able to perform what it promises.

It will be well perhaps before leaving this subject to give a few instances, in which Hegel attempts to explain phenomena of the world of qualities and of the world of feelings by referring them to their logical "truth," or to explain them in their first intention by giving their "truth" or second intention, in which it will be seen how unsatisfactory such explanations are.

Nature itself, the external world considered in the abstract, what is it? It has been already said that this is the first production of the last stage of the Logic, of the Absolute Idea. Hegel answers this question in the Encyclopädie, § 247, Werke, vol. 7 (1), p. 23. "Die Natur hat sich als die Idee in der Form des *Andersseyns* ergeben. Da die *Idee* so als das Negative ihrer selbst oder *sich äusserlich* ist, so ist die Natur nicht äusserlich nur relativ gegen diese Idee (und gegen die subjective Existenz derselben, den Geist), sondern die *Aeusserlichkeit* macht die Bestimmung aus, in welcher sie als Natur ist." "Negative *or* external to itself;" but whence the notion of externality or outness, and whence the equivalence of this outness to negation? Why should the negation of the idea be outness? Is it not clear that there must already be outness, before it can be perceived as different from the idea? An external world is already there before it can be explained as being the negation of a world conceived as only in itself, the idea. Mere negation of the idea does not explain the fact that outness is the object which negatives the idea. Why does the idea determine itself to evolve from itself *dieses* Andere, this and no other negation of itself? No answer is possible except that the external world already exists.

The explanation of space labours under the same difficulty, Encyc. § 253,—"Das Aeussersichseyn als positiv." This is a description of space, and supposes space already there. It is the same with time,— "Das Aeussersichseyn als negativ." It is evolved from space as the negation which space contains in itself, § 257. It is "das Angeschaute Werden," § 258. It has been shown however above, that time is involved in the concept Seyn itself, previous to Werden, so that it is insufficient to say that the concept Werden is the truth, ground, or explanation of time.

Matter, in § 261, is the union of space and time, the existence in which their ideality becomes reality, or as Hegel expresses it farther on, § 448 at the end, "Raum und Zeit durch die ihnen immanente Dialektik des Begriffs sich selber zur *Materie* als ihrer Wahrheit aufheben;" and this their passing over into concrete Daseyn, says Hegel, is inconceivable for the mere understanding, and consequently is always represented by it as an ultimate fact, a gegebenes. He adds that the current notion is to represent space and time as empty, and then to let them be filled with matter; which remark shows that he had no notion of them as metaphysical elements of objects, a conception to which his remarks do not apply. But can matter, either as feeling or as the quality of tangibility, be explained by such an analysis as this into space and time?

I pass over all the remainder of the Naturphilosophie, since only one acquainted with the physical sciences could examine it to any purpose; and to this extent my knowledge and consequently my criticism of Hegel's system is defective. I turn to the point at which it passes over into the Philosophie des Geistes, the point at which it makes the first step towards evolving the absolute mind, or the absolute idea as a concrete and real existence. At this point the living animal organism, which has gathered up into itself all the less complete forms of external existence, is represented as passing into a state of pure abstract generality, in death, der Tod des Natürlichen, Encyc. § 376, vol. 7 (1), page 694. At the completion of the Logic, the Begriff threw out its own Aeusscrsichseyn, which was Nature, and was itself its Insichseyn. This nature itself, die concrete Allgemeinheit, is now, at the end of the Naturphilosophie, aufgehoben, that is, has become an abstract universality, and this in presence of the idea. There remain then only the idea, or Insichseyn, and its abstract objectivity in presence of each other, that is, abstract subjectivity and abstract objectivity; and this is the existence which remains existing, the Subject-Object, mind in its most abstract shape. Such is the starting point of the Philosophie des Geistes, the object-matter of which corresponds perhaps as nearly to the empirical ego as to any thing that comes forward in this Essay, just as Hegel's conception of nature corresponds most nearly to what I have called the world of qualities.

Having in § 395, vol. 7 (2), page 81, gathered up into a focus the general characteristics of the mind, into the focus of an individual Subject or mind, Hegel proceeds to the development of this individual mind. The first instance I will notice is his explanation of Empfindung, sense in its most general shape. What is sense or sensativeness? I have already quoted part of his answer to this question in § 21, from Encyc. § 399, p. 115. "Durch das Empfinden ist somit die Seele dahin gekommen, dass das ihre Natur ausmachende Allgemeine in einer unmittelbaren Bestimmtheit für sie wird. Nur durch diess Fürsichwerden ist die Seele empfindend." This is a description, not an analysis or an explanation. The phenomenon of sense must be present before it can be described, and the description cannot be regarded as its cause.

Begierde, desire; what is the explanation given of this? Answer, in § 426, page 270. When any thing which is identical with itself feels a contradiction with itself, there arises a Trieb, or impulse, to remove the contradiction, and this impulse is desire. This may serve as a description of desire when once the feeling is there; but the question of why there should be such a feeling at all, or why a felt contradiction should be such a particular feeling, is not answered; the feeling has no explanation but itself; it is no explanation to say that it may be described as a felt contradiction with oneself.

Similarly it is attempted to explain the phenomenon of feeling, Gefühl, in § 471, page 363, by saying that it is "nichts Anderes als die Form der unmittelbaren eigenthümlichen Einzelnheit des Subjects, in der jener Inhalt, wie jeder andere objective Inhalt, dem das Bewusstseyn auch Gegenständlichkeit zuschreibt, gesetzt werden kann."

Again in § 472, page 364, the phenomenon of pain is explained by saying that it is "die Unangemessenheit des Seyns zu dem Sollen."

These instances are enough for the present purpose; and if it should be replied that all these objects and feelings are included, as content, in the concepts as exhibited in the Logic, the answer must be, that in that case these concepts themselves are capable of analysis and analytical explanation, and that their explaining power is due to the elements of which they severally consist, for that every concept is a compound, complete, or empirical object.

It remains finally to notice the way in which Hegel resolves again the individual mind, which he is examining, into the general or absolute mind, with which the treatise ends. This is done virtually, that is, the first steps are taken in §§ 426-429, Die Begierde, and the two following §§, Das anerkennende Selbstbewusstseyn. In the phenomenon of desire, the objects in reference to which the desires arise are recognised as of the same nature, an sich identisch, with the Subject. They are therefore, if not capable of being immediately taken up into the Subject, considered necessarily as so many independent subjects, so many instances of an alter ego. Thus the Subject creates out of its objects, in the phenomena of desire, a world of other individual minds, all of the same nature with itself, and separated from it only by the bodies which they inhabit. Instead of considering every object as unconscious till reasons have arisen for considering it conscious, the mind, on this theory, considers every object as conscious till reasons have arisen for considering it unconscious; and this follows from the assumption that originally all consciousness depends on self-consciousness. This view appears to be supported by many facts in the early history of science and religion, so far as it is known to us, namely, by fetichism in the earliest states of civilisation, by polytheism, and by the explanation of physical events by reference to the inner feelings of men, such as φιλία and νεῖκος. These facts however do not render necessary the explanation of them by supposing self-consciousness to be prior to consciousness; for it is sufficient to suppose that self-consciousness was developed prior to the development of these early modes of thought, and there is nothing to show that these early modes of thought were contemporary with consciousness itself. If then all consciousness is self-consciousness, and all objects of consciousness are of the same nature as consciousness, which latter is no doubt the case, then not only all objects are objects of self-consciousness, which is true in a certain sense, but also there is but one self-consciousness in the world, the absolute mind; for the objects of consciousness are themselves instances of self-consciousness, each mind recognises itself in all its objects, and the one common object, or complex of objects, which all the minds recognise as themselves, is itself self-consciousness, and the separate minds are in their turn its objects. This one common Subject-Object is the absolute mind, and other finite minds are the modes of its self-consciousness. Assume self-consciousness as the starting point, and it will also appear as the goal; there as absolute logical form, here as absolute existing mind. This is Hegelianism. But, on the other hand, assume consciousness as prior to self-consciousness, consciousness in the forms of time and space as prior to, or the condition of, self-consciousness, or consciousness reflecting on itself in those forms, and this self-consciousness will only arise in connection with a body in space, and as placed in the centre of a world of qualities as well as of a world of feelings. All instances of self-consciousness that exist, or may exist, without having this one body as part of their inseparable objects, that is to say, all other minds except the Subject, are objects of inference to the Subject, inferred from changes which take place either in the bodies to which they are referred or in other parts of the world of qualities, and inferred from the similarity of those changes to those which accompany the self-consciousness of the Subject in its own body. And not only are they objects of inference to the Subject, but they are also objects of imagination to it, imagination of a feeling similar to its own, dwelling in a body which is one of its own external objects. All other instances of self-consciousness are to the Subject objects of consciousness and not of self-consciousness. In the same way it must imagine that it is, to these other Subjects, an object of consciousness and not of self-consciousness. There is no self-consciousness taking place between them, they do not reciprocate self-consciousness; there is between them, considered as Subjects, no common Subject.

It is worthy of remark that there are many points of resemblance between the Logic of Hegel, the protagonist of ontology, and the Philosophie Positive of Comte, the protagonist of positivism. There is first the similarity of Hegel's Absolute Mind and Comte's

Vrai Grand Etre, or Humanity; each of which is the concomitant result, if I may so speak, of the evolution of the world-history; each of which is personified as a single individual; and each of which is the object of divine honours; and these three points of similarity suppose several minor ones. Then again there is the progression by triplets in Hegel, in which the first member is the an sich, the last the an und für sich, and the middle the transition between them, while the last stage, when reached, throws back light upon the nature of both the previous stages, not understood before they had produced their results. To this answers Comte's doctrine of a triple stage in the actual history of all development, the middle of which is but a transitional state, which cannot be judged of till the last stage has been reached, for which it was a preparation; for instance, in the fields of the intellectual, the active, and the affective functions of man, three stages may be observed; in the first, the fictive, the abstract, and the positive stage; in the second, the conquering, the defensive, and the industrial; and in the third, the domestic, the civil, and the universal. Politique Positive, vol. 4, chap. 3, page 177. Progression by triplets in all reasoning has been shown to depend on the will first setting, and then overleaping, a bound, whereby a second object is distinguished from a first, and then seen to have something in common with it, the result being the concept-form, the form of all reasoning. This law is Hegel's discovery. But it is very remarkable, though perhaps not surprising, when a positive philosopher discovers, on quite independent grounds, a law of progress in actual history so closely corresponding to the law of progress which a metaphysical philosopher deduced from the discovery of this logical and abstract law of reasoning in general.

I will finally notice a similarity or rather sameness of principle which is the most comprehensive of all, a principle which is common to both philosophers, and which belongs, in my judgment at least, to what is true and not erroneous in their two systems. Both writers, each from his own point of view, and in his own half of the world, move round the same centre; for the principle which they share is the central truth of their two systems. This truth in Hegel is, that the universe can only be described, analysed, and known within itself. In the Philosophie Positive, the ruling thought, as exhibited in the Law of the Three States and elsewhere, is, that the search after causes is vain, and is superseded by the search after laws. In other words, analyse the order of coexistence and the order of sequence of phenomena within the world of phenomena, but seek no cause for any of them that is not itself a phenomenon. Both conceptions are the same, namely, to keep within phenomena, to analyse their order and interdependence, and to abstain from going beyond or seeking the Why of the universe; instead of this, to seek only for the necessary or universal antecedents of particular objects, as parts of the whole. A difference between them there is, and a wide one, namely, that this mode of philosophising is in Comte a renunciation of an attempt as useless, while in Hegel it is a claim to have succeeded in that attempt,—the attempt to seize the Absolute. Look only for laws and not for causes, say they both; philosophy is the discovery of laws and not of causes; the absolute is not to be seized, remain within your fixed limits. But why is the absolute not to be seized? With Hegel, because it has been seized already, is defined, and contains all causes within it; with Comte, because it cannot be seized at all, and we must content ourselves without causes. Equally however in both cases is the search for causes given up. The way in which I should be inclined to express the same truth would be by the ancient formula, Operari sequitur esse, or by saying That the question of history is subordinate to the question of nature.

CHAPTER VII.

METALOGICAL.

DIVISION 2. THE CONCEPT.

συμπλοκὴ γάρ νοημάτων ἐστὶ τὸ ἀληθὲς ἢ ψεῦδος. τὰ δὲ πρῶτα νοήματα τίνι διοίσει τοῦ μὴ φαντάσματα εἶναι;

Aristotle.

§ 46. THE present division of this chapter has to treat of the inclusion of the concept-form, its object, the concept itself. A concept is an abstract notion, adopted by the will, and implying a reference to other objects excluded from it, which are not specified by it. We must go back and place ourselves again at the point of view taken up at the beginning of Chapter VI., where abstract notions were considered as passing into general notions. There it was shown how, by the addition of the element of volition, general notions were formed out of abstract. But it is clear that volition can fix on an abstract notion, whether in presentation or representation, and retain or repeat it in consciousness without redintegrating other objects besides the one fixed on. If this only is done by volition, the volition ends with the abstract notion, without proceeding to the formation of a general notion, and the abstract notion is a concept; for it is fixed on by the will for the purposes of comparison, and this makes it a concept. Or volition may proceed beyond the original abstract notion, and form a general notion by redintegration of other objects in consciousness which contain as a common factor the original abstract notion. The abstract notion appears thus in two shapes, both alike due to volition, but one more elaborate than the other, the simpler of which is a particular abstract notion, and the more complex a general abstract notion. To both of these I give the name Concept, which has thus two kinds under it, the particular and the general concept. The latter alone has been usually treated as a concept; it has been considered that concepts must be general terms, that they contain and include a comparison, and express the result of a comparison;—concipio, capio hoc cum illo, said Coleridge;—but the distinction between the general and particular nature of the inclusion of the concept-form appears to me comparatively unimportant, by the side of the essential nature of the concept, which is the implied reference it contains to the objects which it excludes. This implied reference is due to the will, and is common to both kinds of concepts, the particular and the general. The general concept is the result of a comparison, for it is a general notion; but as a concept, as used for the purposes of logic, it is an unity; and as such it matters little whether, as an intuition, it is a simple or compound object, the result of one act of perception or of a series. An unity in consciousness need not be a minimum of consciousness; the will may adopt an object of greater or less extent, complexity, or duration, and make it an unity for the purposes of logic; we must not understand, by the term unities, unities of equal magnitude. Again, no object of perception is so simple as to be incapable of analysis; the particular abstract notion contains parts which would come into prominence by dwelling on it; although it is the product of perception or of spontaneous redintegration, before it is fixed on by the will, it is not simple and uncompounded in itself, but receives its unity from the will, just as the general notion does, for the purposes of reasoning. It is not therefore the simplicity or the complexity of the inclusion that makes a concept, but the nature of the relation of the inclusion to the exclusion. The concept is an abstract notion, either general or particular, adapted for comparison with other objects.

The concept includes general and particular concepts. It includes also first and second intentions; that is to say, both objects in their first intention and objects in their second intention may be concepts. In § 10 it was shown that an object in its first intention is an object for consciousness alone, and that an object in its second intention is an object in its relation to other objects in consciousness. For instance, steam is an object for consciousness alone, an object of the senses of touch, sight, and so on. But it is difficult to think of steam without including in it its motive power, or power of reaction on a surface compressing it. If this is included in the notion of steam, we have a new object before the mind, steam in its relation to other objects; this is steam in its second intention. Or take the object called a straight line; here is an object of presentation or representation, familiar to every one, in its first intention; but if I include in the object the notion of its being the shortest way between two points, I have compared it with other lines connecting those points, and now have before me an object in its second intention. Either of these two objects may be fixed on by volition for the purpose of being compared with other objects; that is, either of them may become a concept. But when this has been done, and the concept formed, then that concept is used as an object in its first intention, for the purpose of being compared with other objects; or concepts, as such, have a first and second intention, and the distinction between first and second intentions is applicable to concepts as well as to percepts. Objects in their second as well as objects in their first intention may be taken by the will and made into concepts; but whatever is taken and made into a concept is taken and treated as an object in its first intention, with a reference to objects excluded from it but not yet thought in reference to it. Steam, for instance, whether in its first or second intention, when adopted by the will as a concept, is taken as an object in its first intention, present to consciousness, and all other objects are excluded from it, as being not-steam. This reference to other objects excluded from them is impressed upon the objects taken as concepts by the will, and not by the actual knowledge of the excluded objects. When used in this way these objects are concepts. As abstract notions, the objects in question have a single and direct reference to consciousness, which may be called their first intention, and an independent existence; as concepts they have a second existence, a second reference, to all other objects besides themselves, white to not-white, pleasure to not-pleasure, pain to not-pain, and so on, which is impressed upon them by the will for a particular purpose, and this may be called their second intention. From this second reference possessed by concepts it has been sometimes argued, that the two sets of objects, one implied, the other expressed by them, are equally real and lasting, that in fact they are relatives in nature as well as in logic, and that the existence of the one involves the existence of the other in the same mode of existence; for instance, pain of pleasure or not-pain, happiness of misery or not-happiness, white of not-white, and so on; whereas, as far as logic is concerned, it might turn out that the exclusion not-white had no objects included in it, but that all the world was white, and white alone. It is clear that this reasoning does not relate to the objects in their simple reference to consciousness. Not-white objects may exist, but their existence out of logic does not depend on the existence of white objects. White exists as a concept, and not-white exists as its exclusion; whether it exists as a percept is a question for perception. When we know one or more percepts which are excluded from the concept, that is, when the exclusion as well as the inclusion of the concept is supplied with an object of consciousness, the concept is said to be thought. The concept white, for instance, is thought, when we envisage it in contradistinction to red or gray.

It may be said, from the old point of view in logic, that more is requisite to the thinking of a concept, or of any object, than that some object of those excluded from it should be supplied in consciousness to contrast it with; that it is requisite that this supplied object should be of a particular kind, that it must stand under the same general notion with the concept or object thought; that both together must be referred to a common class, or common larger concept, which includes them both under it. Thus white would be thought when it was contrasted with red, because both fall under the common class of colour; but white would not be thought if it was contrasted with any object which did not fall under a common class with it, for instance, with hard;—"heterogenea non comparari, ergo nec distingui possunt." But this objection vanishes on closer inspection. The rule, heterogenea non comparari, ergo nec distingui possunt, is admirable as a maxim of practical argument; it means that, to come to an useful conclusion, you must come to close quarters with the notions employed; that you must narrow the class of notions, common to both subject and predicate of your propositions, narrow your middle terms, till you come to one single point of difference between them. It does not mean that there are notions which have no common notions with others, under which they both stand. It is useless to distinguish white from hard, not because there is no common notion under which they stand, but because this common notion under which they stand, that of sensation, is too remote for most practical purposes. When it is said, therefore, that it is a notion of a particular kind which must be supplied to a concept in order that it may be thought, it must be replied, that it is so only for the purpose of thinking it usefully or profitably; but that it is really thought, whatever may be the notion supplied to contrast it with. For all notions whatever stand under some common notions, or at least under one common notion, that is, have two or more points in common. I mean of course that they all without exception stand under the common notions of time, space, and feeling; and that they should be thought under these notions is, in fact, what is essential to thinking; not however because time, space, and feeling are concepts, or names of a class, not because they are categories, but because class names, common notions, and categories, are derived from and are modifications of feelings in the forms of time and space; a point which the present division of this chapter is designed to elucidate.

Although the concept involves a relation, yet the relation itself is not the object of the concept. Relations may be themselves objects, as existing between other objects, or as being modes of objects, and as such may be the objects of abstract terms, and therefore, as such, the objects of concept-names. For instance, the relation of duplicity is, in relation to consciousness alone, expressed by the abstract term duplicity, as a first intention; it means an object doubled; and also the relation of this very object to others, to simplicity, triplicity, and so on, in which it is a second intention, is expressed by the same word, and is a concept. The relation which is expressed by the concept-name is itself an object in relation to another or to others excluded from it, not now any longer to objects or relations included in it. Concepts are not relations except incidentally. A relation may be, like other objects, a concept, the object of a concept-name in its first intention, but as a concept it has a relation, beyond its inclusion, implied by it as its exclusion. Every concept is a first intention and implies a second intention.

Concepts are of the same nature with abstract and general notions; what these are, concepts are also. But these are objects, or parts of objects, or objects composed of the parts of other objects of perception, either presented or represented, either in immediate intuition or in redintegration. That is to say, they are images, Vorstellungen. Every image is a feeling or a complex of feelings of a certain kind and of a certain degree of intensity, bound together for a certain time in a certain figure or in a certain place. A particular abstract notion is an actual image, a general notion is a provisional image. It is not the result of a single act of abstraction, but of several compared together, and therefore it is an image which was never given actually in presentation as it appears in representation, when the general term is applied to it. This circumstance, together with the fact that we use general terms apagogically more often than ostensively, has made writers fancy that the general term, which they called a concept, was something different in its nature from an image, instead of being, and not merely being capable of translation into, or proof by means of, an image or object of perception. It is a provisional image, which is presented again to thought as an image of which there are many parts waiting to be filled up, and which therefore is still liable to modification by the results of investigation. Fries, in his System der Logik, § 24, says, Das Denken der Begriffe ist immer vom Schematismus der Einbildungskraft abhängig, denn jedes abgesonderte Bewusstseyn allgemeiner Theilvorstellungen erhalten wir ursprünglich durch die Abstraction der Schemate in der Einbildungskraft. To his expression Theilvorstellung corresponds mine of provisional image. I think it will be admitted readily that the particular abstract notion, as described here, is an image, but not so readily that the general notion is so. At the same time, if my remarks establish the point with reference to the general notion, they will a fortiori have done so with reference to the particular.

Objects of consciousness, it has been here asserted, are all without exception capable of being analysed into two elements, the material or feeling, and the formal, time and space. It would follow that, if general notions are objects of consciousness, they also must be capable of analysis into these elements and no others. Here however appears to arise a case which is an exception from this law; for general notions, τὰ καθ' ὅλου, or universals, are certainly in some sense objects of consciousness, but never was one of them yet given in presentation. They seem to elude the laws of time and space. It would seem that they must have some other nature, or ratio essendi, apart from time and space, that they must constitute a region of consciousness apart, where they live under their own laws, a domus exilis Plutonia of shadowy forms without a body.

That which appears, however, as an impossibility of being brought under the forms of time and space lies in reality not in the form of the general notion, but in its matter. The unreality of general notions consists in this, that they are objects which do not occur in presentation, that they contradict what is commonly called experience. They are combinations of objects, or skeletons of objects, which it goes against our habit to assign existence to, because we know that it is against universal experience of the senses that such abstractions should be presented to them; the object of the general notion is too absurd or too imperfect to exist. This however does not destroy in them either their form of time and space, which they had in the concrete, nor the material element or its modes, which they then also possessed. The elements remain the same though combined again, or though reduced to a minimum of power of being perceived. This I call a provisional image. If not this, then the concept-name or general term has no object of consciousness signified by it. But it is clear that it has an object signified by it, or it would be of no use in reasoning. And when we voluntarily perform the process of abstraction, at what do we stop, what is the state of our mind when we have completed the process, and are looking about for a name to fix the result by? We have before us an abstract or a provisional image, in which the parts of the object abstracted from are represented by a blank space, and the parts attended to remain in their own colours. This is the object of the abstract, and this in more complicated cases is the object of the general term, universal, or concept-name. The case is exactly the same as that of the division which separates two spaces or two times. It has no existence by itself, but only as involved in the two spaces, or times, which it limits. When we think of a division in the abstract or by itself, we represent the spaces or the times which it separates as existing provisionally and not definitely.

What has usually been understood by the word Concept is a compound of the properties of this provisional image and the term which designates it, the concept-name. As the former, the concept was not an image, that is, a complete one, and as the latter it was capable of being employed in reasoning. Reasoning appeared consequently to be a process independent of the forms of time and space, which are the forms of all images; though at the same time it was admitted that it was only valid when it could be applied to images; in other words, that the concept must always admit of being tested by objects of a possible intuition. But if it can be shown that all reasoning is employed with images, actual or provisional, the only valid distinction in this matter will be that between the concept and the concept-name, the general notion and the general term, and between the two kinds of reasoning employing them respectively, ostensive and apagogic, the latter being the representative of the former. Abstract and general notions therefore are images, though provisional; and concepts differ from images solely in being held fast by a conscious effort in consciousness, and this cannot change their nature as images.

§ 47. There are however some instances of concepts which seem at first sight not to be capable of analysis into images modified by volition. I will examine those given by Werenfels in the Dialogue De Finibus Mundi, which has been already quoted. In that dialogue this point is argued at length. Werenfels says in effect, Infinita pæne sunt quæ non imaginamur, concipimus tamen, — Universalia, numerum millenarium, mille-angulum, circulum perfectum, icosa-hedrum, globum penitus rotundum, motum aut velocem nimis aut lentum, materiæ in infinitum sectionem. Now these all bear one character. In them the concept is an assumption that the task of imagination has been completed; they are abbreviations, compendia, of imagination; not because imagination is unfit, but because it is too weak to perform the whole task of representation. The failing of the imagination is in degree, not in kind of efficiency. The number 1000, for instance, is a whole consisting of 1000 units; the 1000-angled figure is a figure containing 1000 angles. We begin by imagining the synthesis of a few units and a few angles, but being wearied have recourse to an "and so forth up to 1000." Without the beginning in imagination, we could not conclude by a concept. But how is the stopping-point reached, the number 1000 itself? This concept, 1000, which is assumed as the goal of the "and so forth," must be first attained. This concept is the gathering up into unity of several syntheses of imagination. First units are added together, up to 10, then the sum 10 is added to itself 10 times, then to the sum 100 is added another sum of 100, which has been reached independently by another similar process, till it has been added to 9 other sums of 100. At each step there is a gathering up into a single unit, 10, 100, 200, &c., a synthesis of the units effected by the imagination. Each of these gatherings up into unity is a concept, a brief expression of the result of imagination, in order to keep hold of the ground which has been won. The number 1000 is originally reached in this way; and, when the meaning of the concept-name 1000 has been explained to any one, he appropriates the result of the original imagination without himself going through the whole process, and deals thenceforth analytically with the amount 1000, which was attained originally by a synthetical process.

The perfect circle and the perfect globe are also concept-names expressing the anticipated fulfilment of the task of imagination in analysis, in abstracting the material element from empirical circles and globes, so that what remains is a pure intuition of a figure in space. The so-called concept is a pure intuition of space. It says no more than this. Let it be granted that we can have pure intuitions of figure. These cases differ from those previously examined in having no definite goal assigned which is assumed to have been reached, as was the case with the number 1000. They simply say the perfect circle and the perfect globe; and perfection is a very indefinite notion. These cases exhibit the poverty of the concept; for where the goal cannot be supplied, as in the case of the number 1000, by the imagination, there is nothing definite in the concept.

Motion too swift or too slow to be seen, felt, or imagined, and the infinite division of matter, are concepts which differ somewhat from both of the former classes. They turn upon the old question of infinity in time and space. Motion and matter are objects of presentation; and as such are always presented in certain quantities, certain minima of presentation. Beyond these minima of presentation we can go, in dividing them, by representation, and have representations of motion much swifter and much slower, and of matter much smaller, than we ever have in presentation. But representations are images, not concepts; let volition fix on any image and it becomes a concept. Now to conceive motion infinitely swift or slow, and matter as being infinitely divided, is to imagine our own power of representing motion and matter as too weak to go beyond a certain point, and to fix on that circumstance in the phenomenon of imagination or representation as the one we wish to consider. Either this fact in the phenomenon of representation is the content of the concept-names in question, or they have no content at all. For if they are taken as meaning a motion and a division beyond the point where consciousness becomes incapable, from whatever cause, of penetrating, they manifestly contradict themselves by expressing an impossibility performed, a finite-infinite, a divisible-indivisible. In the first case, the fact of weakness exhibited in certain modes of imagination is seized on and expressed as a concept; in the second case, there is a concept-name without a concept. The contents of these concepts are images, and their infinity is another name for the weakness of the imagination.

There is another concept mentioned by Werenfels and quoted with approval from Descartes, that of ipsum nihil, pure nothing. We can conceive, he says, but not imagine, pure nothing. This must be connected with other concepts which he mentions, one of which is the limit or end of any thing; "manet hoc fixum et immobile nos fines nullius rei imaginari posse." And again he says, Ita licet imaginari non possim nihil esse extra mundum, concipere tamen possum. These three instances show the true nature of a concept, its derivative nature, and its limited nature. The concept is a limitation of the process of imagination, the imagination stopped at a certain point by volition. Imagination gives no last limit, because its form, time and space, has no limit. Imagination is never without an object, since it contains always time and space. The concept is an assumed limit, assumed for practical purposes by the will, — Signifer, statue signum, hic manebimus optime. The relation between imagination and the concept is similar to that between a whole of extension, a general notion, and a whole of intension, any particular object contained under it. The general notion or class, animal, has fewer qualities than any individual animal has; and in this sense the individual animal contains more than the class; but, on the other hand, the class animal contains more than the individual, for it contains all the individuals. If the class or general notion, animal, were a concrete phenomenon, any individual animal would be a modification of it, adding some modification or other, and in this respect surpassing the thing modified; but the modification would itself belong to, and be a part of, the phenomenon modified. So it is with imagination, which is a particular concrete process of consciousness, and the concept. The concept is a modification of imagination, but it never exceeds the limits of imagination; all modifications of imagination are imagination. Now as to these three instances of concepts; if the concept is a form of consciousness, simply of consciousness, not of imagination, it cannot be without an object, it cannot have pure nothing for its object. If we suppose ourselves to conceive pure nothing, we are mistaken, and mistake the concept-name Nothing for an object. To suppose that we can conceive Nothing is to suppose that consciousness can exist without being consciousness. Because we can conceive limits within the field of objects, we suppose that we can conceive the limits of that field itself. As to the "fines nullius rei imaginari posse," —it is not the case, if by res is meant an object with a material as well as a formal element; such empirical objects are limited in perception itself. If, on the other hand, by "fines" are meant limits which have pure nothing beyond them, then conceiving them is nothing more than abstracting the attention from what is beyond or excluded from those limits; and the limits in this sense are as little conceivable as they are imaginable. The limits, in their true sense, exist both in imagination and conception. As to the "nihil esse extra mundum," it will be clear from what has been already said, that it is a mistake to apply the limitation of particular objects by others to the whole of the world, where the expression "whole of the world" assumes that no particular object is to be imagined outside it; whereas it is a law of imagination, wholly independent of our will, that no limit can be perceived, without there being perceived at the same time the existence of something beyond that limit, an existence involved in the fact of limitation itself.

If this criticism is correct, it follows that the fundamental doctrine of Werenfels must be rejected, "Imaginatio longe angustior est conceptu puro." In fact, reality is whatever can be given in imagination; the field of the concept is limited by that of the imagination, while the limits of particular objects in that field are given by the imagination and adopted by the conception. The statement of a limitation is a concept. But the limits of the whole can be neither imagined nor conceived; it is not true to apply to the whole, as if it could be perceived, what is true of the parts, which are perceived. But the very function of limiting, in which conception consists, provides concept-names which have no objects; and it is here only that imagination is really outstripped, namely, by the concept-names which are mere words. Nothing exists to which it is not easy, so far as words go, to prefix a "not." Again, the fact that all division increases the number of objects, since it makes two where only one existed before, shows in what sense only it can be said, that many things can be conceived which can not be imagined. If you break up a statue, you have a heap of fragments instead of a single image. The whole is of the same extent in both cases; the parts, membra dividentia, though introduced by conception, are evolved from, and remain parts of, the whole of imagination; imagination is not transcended but modified.

§ 48. Intuition in its two shapes, presentative and representative perception, supplies limitation of particular objects in the forms of time and space; that is, the limitation of particular objects is given in and with the objects themselves, and in perception, of which imagination is one form, previous to and independent of conception. The function of conception is to hold these limitations fast, in order to compare the included object with others which are excluded. This is the first step in logic, and it is a step taken by the will. The will leads us to dwell on a particular, limited, content of perception, as fixed for our purpose of arguing about it. In other words, when we treat a name or an object as a concept, we are exercising not merely cognition but volition, and are making a conscious effort. This view is not opposed by the fact that afterwards we may become so familiar with the concept that we use it and understand it without effort. To fix on a particular object, in contradistinction to other objects, requires more than a spontaneous movement of consciousness; it requires a conscious effort and a conscious purpose. In intuition no contradictories are found, but only contraries; the sensibility is conscious of being affected in a particular way at one time, in another way at another time; but these two objects are not yet contraries, but only differents; they become contraries when perceived to belong to one and the same consciousness; these two objects, so given, are contraries; they are as yet only compared with each other as different states of the same empirical ego. When they are held fast, each by itself, and compared with reference to the same time and space, that is, to the same moment of the empirical ego, then the same two contraries appear as contradictories. The assumption of the one is then contradictory to the assumption of the other, because we cannot at the same time and place cognise both one and the other; and this involves their comparison also secundum idem, for to adopt two points of view, or two respects, is to place the objects in two moments of time. If one is held fast, as it is in a concept, the other must be let go or assigned to another time and place. Approaching from the side of the concept, contradictories precede contraries and are their condition; we distinguish first an A and a Not-A, and secondly refer these to their common parent, a third thing, the concept-form, which is at one time one of them, at another time the other. Approaching from the side of perception, contraries precede contradictories; consciousness is differently affected at different times, and these affections or objects of perception are contraries, inasmuch as they are different and yet united in a third thing, their common parent, consciousness, the common element in all its moments. They become contradictories when one object of perception, simple or complex as it may happen, is fixed on by volition and assigned to one moment of time in consciousness, long or short as it may happen; then this object in this moment is the contradictory of all other objects referred to that moment. Assign those other objects to other moments of the same consciousness, or to that same moment considered from another point of view, which is the same thing, and the contradictories become contraries again, and a new quality is added to the object perceived. Contradictories belong only to logic; and since logic can only be applied to objects in time and space, contradictories are valid only within and not without time and space, and can only be applied to particular objects of cognition, and not to a supposed whole or universe of those objects, for such a whole is not possible in time and space.

The word Not is a word of logic, and not a word of intuition. It is the turning point of all conception; it expresses distinction, being borrowed from the greatest distinction known to reflection from cases of intuition alone, the distinction between being conscious of particular objects and not being conscious of them. We are conscious of objects only in empirical moments of time, and volition excludes from those moments the objects from which it abstracts. In volition we are conscious only of one object, however complex or however simple that object may be. Logical contradiction depends upon the nature of our consciousness, which can cognise objects only in empirical moments of time, that is, on the incompressibility of time in consciousness, in conjunction with the incompressibility of time and space in objects of consciousness. Thus the law of contradiction, together with the two other forms of it, the laws of identity and of excluded middle, known as the postulates of logic, is no law of intuition as such, but is a law, and indeed the first and fundamental law, of logic; at the same time, it is founded on the laws of intuition, the forms of time and space in consciousness, and is the expression of these forms, as soon as they are adopted and applied by volition. If an Hegelian should reply, that contradiction creates time and space, by constantly denying itself; contradiction being nothing else than the necessity of a constant division and casting off of a logical opposite; and that in this way, since the logical opposites cannot remain together, they are thrown apart, out of one another, and this outness is time and space; the answer is, that contradiction cannot throw objects out in time and space, unless the objects already exist in those forms; and all objects do this; the forms of time and space are in the contradictory objects, not in the contradiction, and are in the objects as such, and before the contradiction is perceived. There is nothing in contradiction which can make time and space intelligible to us; but, given time and space, then the addition of the feeling of volition is the explanation of contradiction.

It may appear perhaps, at first sight, that only the form of time, and not that of space, is employed in logical thinking; this, however, is not so, but both forms are involved. The perception even of internal feelings, as was shown in § 13, is always connected with perceptions occupying space; those internal feelings are always felt in connection with a body, and that body as a part of an external world. It is possible to fix the attention on the internal feelings only, and to abstract from the body and the external world; but the moment we place those feelings in relation to others, which must be done in logic, they must have a position assigned them, the position they occupy in the body and the external world. Even if we consider the internal feelings as an isolated series, so that each feeling is compared with those only which precede and follow it in the same series, thus occupying time alone, yet the whole series is connected in experience with other feelings occupying space, and has a position assigned to it with reference to them, so that the line of time, which the series occupies, becomes a line of space; and consequently each moment or feeling of the series occupies a part of that line of space, in other words, becomes a part of a series of modifications of objects existing in and occupying space. Therefore the form of space is necessary for the logical thinking not only of objects which are perceived as occupying space, objects of the senses of sight and touch, but also of the internal feelings themselves. When we think of anger, for instance, we think of it as an emotion belonging to a complex of feelings, among which are a body and objects outside that body, in relation to some of which feelings the emotion of anger arises; in other words, we think of it as a quality or modification of the empirical ego which exists in space.

But not only does space enter into logical thinking in consequence of the constant coexistence of objects of space in perception with objects of time in perception, but the line of time itself becomes treated as a line of space by having one portion of it fixed on by volition, as a concept, and contrasted with other portions of the same line. A line of time differs from a line of space in this circumstance only, that in the former nothing once presented is ever presented again, but only represented, while in the latter every part of the line may be presented again, and we may move backwards and forwards between the same presentations. Whenever a portion of a line, or series of feelings, in time is fixed on as a concept, that portion is taken to be examined as a whole, simultaneously; it is indeed a representation, but we move backwards and forwards in it, and treat it statically, as a simultaneous or statical object, as if it were a part of a series of feelings in space. Every representation, whether of simple or complex content, when treated as a concept is treated statically, that is, as occupying a portion of a line on which we move backwards and forwards; is treated as if it were an object of presentation in space; and, since all feelings are part of an empirical ego which occupies space, every representation, when treated as a concept, is treated as occupying a portion of space as well as a portion of time. The concept expressed by the A of the postulates occupies a certain portion of space existing for a certain portion of time.

Every concept is the logical τὸ ἄν and the logical τὸ ἕν. It is assumed to exist at the moment of thought, and every thing else to be non-existent at that moment. Concepts as such have only an assumed existence; objects which do not exist may be assumed to exist for the purpose of being disproved. By giving a name, the existence of something named is assumed; hence we can say without absurdity, Iron-gold is not; for as a concept we choose to assume it for the purposes of argument, and then we deny that it exists for perception. To say, Iron-gold is not, is exactly equivalent to saying, Iron-gold is a concept-name and not a concept. Concepts as such, or concepts in their form alone, have no reality, and differ not in point of existence from concept-names;—both have an assumed existence only. The concept is thus the logical existence. It is also the logical unit. It is the expression of a single empirical moment of time. No matter how long a time may be occupied by the existence or the consciousness of the particular objects comprehended under it as a general term, the understanding them all as comprehended in the concept makes them into a single empirical moment of time in consciousness; they are gathered up into a provisional image, and assumed to be all one thing for the purposes of argument.

§ 49. The concept as an object is a provisional image, and as such contains no other elements than those found in images and objects of perception; and it owes its character of unity to the exercise of volition in the forms of time and space. Volition is a mode of consciousness, and subject as such to its forms; in fixing on any object of consciousness by a voluntary effort, we fix on it as occupying a certain portion of time and a certain portion of space; and all the shapes which an object of consciousness can take are modes of these two ultimate forms of time and space. No other modes of unity but these would seem to be possible, and certainly no others are required. It is superfluous to look for any pure or a priori forms of thought as thought, different from these two well-known forms of perception. For the will is not limited in its choice of objects, or parts, or shapes, or durations of objects, nor in its power of combining them, farther than in point of degree of energy. If, however, such other pure and a priori forms of thought as thought are assumed, as existing independently, and not as elements of the objects to be thought by means of them, then it may be shown, by a mode of argument known as the τρίτος ἄνθρωπος, that these forms are similar to the objects which are thought by means of them, and that some third concept or form is required to which they in their turn may be referred, and by reference to which their relation to the objects thought by means of them may be explained; for without such a reference no explanation has been given, but the form of thought is a mere duplicate of the object thought; for instance, plurality as a form of thought is but a general expression for many objects of the same sort taken together, and the fact is as much an explanation of the form as the form of the fact. If, then, there are forms of intuition and forms of thought side by side, with distinct origin, then some third form of consciousness must be assumed in order to regulate the application of one set to the other; and this journey in infinitum Kant found himself compelled to enter on, for, having established time and space as forms of intuition, and the categories as forms of thought, he introduced as mediators between them, first, the Schemata, by which space relations of objects were transformed into time relations, and so brought closer to the subjective process of thought, supposed to exist in time alone, and, secondly, the system of Principles of Synthetic Judgments a priori, by which schematised objects, or objects reduced to the form of time, were subsumed under their proper category. On the other hand, if these forms of thought are taken as elements already existing in the objects of perception, which formal elements it is the office of logical conception to bring out distinctly and apply to the objects in which they are involved, then it may be shown that such formal elements are all capable of analysis into the forms of time and space, in union with the material element which is their content. And this may be shown of all forms of thought, whatever their origin may be supposed to be; and, for instance, it may be shown of the Kantian Categories, which are the following:

	I. QUANTITY.	
Unity.	Plurality.	Totality.
	II. QUALITY.	
Reality.	Negation.	Limitation.
	III. RELATION.	
Substance and Accident.	Cause and Effect.	Action and Reaction.
	IV. MODALITY.	
Possibility and Impossibility.	Existence and Non-existence.	Necessity and Contingency.

Under the first head, objects are compared with each other in respect to their extension alone in time and space, and their divisions in that extension. Under the second head, objects are compared with each other in respect to their material element, the feeling which they excite or contain, and therefore under the form of time, abstracting from space. Under the third head are considered objects as, 1st, one within the other; 2d, one after the other; 3d, mutually affecting each other;—all of these modes being modes of time and space. Under the fourth head, objects are compared as to their certainty or degree of evidence in consciousness. These notions are easily seen to contain no more than is contained by the formal and material elements of consciousness. Possible and impossible is whatever is or is not capable of being presented or represented in the forms of time and space. Existence and non-existence is whatever is or is not actually present in consciousness. Necessity and contingency exist in objects, according as we know or do not know of the existence of the conditions of any given object. This latter notion, with that of cause and effect, depends on the canon of Ratio Sufficiens, which will be examined in the following division of this chapter. Now if we grant that the will can fix on any object which has been presented to consciousness, and can abstract from the objects which accompany it, then it will appear unnecessary to look farther for the origin of the notions of unity, or plurality, or totality, or any other of these categories.

§ 50. We next have to deal with the concept in reference to its exclusion, in its combination with other concepts, that is, with concepts as employed in propositions and in syllogisms. It is admitted that the formation of a concept, when it is a general notion, itself involves a judgment, and that the judgment expressed by a proposition is of the same nature as the judgment employed in forming the general notions which are its subject and its predicate; that to combine two objects in a concept is a process the same in kind as that which combines two concepts in a proposition. When we form the concept man, we judge that certain properties in particular individuals are to be abstracted from the other qualities of the individuals, and combined into one object, the concept man. When we predicate of this concept man that it is included under the concept animal, we again combine into a whole, only in this case two sets of qualities instead of one, the qualities abstracted from individual men and those abstracted from individual animals besides men. The theory of predication, therefore, or of forming propositions, cannot be separated from the theory of the formation of concepts;

it is a further development of the same process and function, that of judgment. The process of judgment, an operation of consciousness, is what is expressed in the proposition. Concepts are always formed by judgments, but not always by judgments expressed in propositions. When the terms of a judgment and the dealing of consciousness with the terms are sufficiently marked to be distinguished one from the other, when we can distinguish the process of judgment from the notions which it compares, then that process is capable of being expressed in a proposition. A judgment is a silent proposition, a proposition is an expressed judgment. When the concepts have arisen, when images have been fixed and limited by volition, all further dealing with them must be distinct, and capable of expression in propositions. The limitation of an image as a concept involves the distinct existence of the dealing of consciousness with it, compels us to attend to the operation of consciousness in dealing with its concepts, as distinct from the concepts dealt with. Judgments and propositions come next after concepts in order of complexity, that is, in order of logic.

Concepts, it has been shown, are provisional images considered as unities, and there are only two modes in which they can be connected or combined together in consciousness or in thought, namely, time and space. We should expect therefore, since logic in its verbal forms expresses the connections and combinations of thought, that the forms of logical predication ould be founded on and express the relations of objects to each other in these two modes of time and space. And this is the case; for there are two main kinds of logical propositions, and two only, founded on the modes in which the subject and predicate are connected in thought, and these are categorical and hypothetical propositions, of which categorical propositions express space relations, and hypothetical propositions time relations. Subordinate to these two classes of propositions stand two other classes, which are modifications of each of them respectively, disjunctive propositions, which are a modification of categorical, and hypothetico-disjunctive, which are a modification of hypothetical propositions. Categorical and disjunctive propositions express space relations between their concepts, hypothetical and hypothetico-disjunctive propositions express time relations between them. This is an exhaustive division of propositions from the point of view of the mode in which their subjects and predicates are combined, of the course which consciousness takes in passing from one concept to the other. Propositions may be divided also from other points of view; from that of their quantity, into universal and particular propositions; from that of their logical quality, into affirmative and negative propositions; from that of their certainty, into necessary and problematical propositions. But propositions of all these kinds must fall also under one or other of the four kinds of categorical, hypothetical, disjunctive, and hypothetico-disjunctive propositions; and this latter division appears a more elementary and fundamental division than the others, from being founded on nothing else than the modes in which consciousness passes from one of its objects to another, modes which are the possibility of propositions existing at all, which constitute propositions not of this or that particular character, but ἁπλῶς, so far as they are simply expressions of judgment.

All logical objects exist at once in both these modes of time and space. When, therefore, I have fixed on one of these objects by volition and have it before me as a concept, a further exercise of volition is required to decide in which of its two modes, time or space, it shall be chosen to connect it with other concepts. I choose one of these modes and abstract from the other; but I have only these two to choose from. If I adopt the mode of time, I connect the two concepts together as antecedent and consequent, and the proposition expresses the fact that, when I pass from one concept to the other, I find this connection between them, which makes an affirmative hypothetical proposition; and there are no negative hypothetical propositions. If I choose the mode of space, the proposition is categorical, and expresses the fact that, while I pass from one image or concept to the other, I find them coalesce into one image, either as aspects of one image or as whole and part of one image. Categorical propositions express coalescence of images, hypothetical propositions express sequence of images. The choice of the mode of time or space depends on volition, but whether or not an affirmative proposition will be possible depends on the facts or concepts in consciousness. Disjunctive propositions are founded on the exhaustive division of a whole image into its parts, and express the coalescence, either of the whole and the sum of its parts, or of one of the parts with another to the exclusion of the rest. Hypothetico-disjunctive propositions are founded on the exhaustive division of the series of consequents of a given antecedent, or of antecedents of a given consequent, and express the connection between the consequent, or the antecedent, and one member of the series of antecedents, or consequents, to the exclusion of the other members. Categorical and disjunctive propositions both express coalescence of images or concepts in consciousness, but the disjunctive propositions more definitely than the categorical. Hypothetical and hypothetico-disjunctive propositions both alike express the sequence of concepts in consciousness, and again the latter kind of propositions more definitely than the former.

§ 51. Before examining however the classes of propositions, it may be well to say something of their import generally. It has been already said that judgments are silent propositions, and propositions expressed judgments. Judgments may be, 1st, perceptions of the connection of presentations, as for instance when, standing on Westminster Bridge, I say, London is on the Thames; and in this case the proposition expressing the judgment expresses my consciousness of the connection of the two presentations. The two objects of consciousness are connected in consciousness; as the objects are objects of consciousness, so their connection takes place in consciousness, and the objects and their connection are subjective as well as objective. If, 2dly, when I have gone down into the country, I relate to my friends, London is on the Thames, the proposition expresses a connection between representations, the consciousness which makes me speak is a redintegration of London and the Thames and of their connection; the objects are representations, no more and no less subjective than before, but in redintegration, not in presentation. The truth of the second judgment is derivative, derived from presentation. The test of the truth of the second judgment is to refer to the first, to repeat the presentation. But by repeating the presentation I do not go from subject to object; objective truths are not the test of subjective truths, but subjective truths of presentation are the test of subjective truths of representation. Thirdly, judgments may be perceptions of the connection between objects of presentation and objects of representation; as, for instance, if I, standing on Westminster Bridge, say, That London is on the Thames is what I remembered in the country, or, That London is on the Thames is true. Here again the propositions express a subjective process or connection between the two images, presentative and representative. Since presentation and representation are all the states of consciousness, these three movements of consciousness in judgment are all that are possible; all judgments must fall under one or other of these three kinds.

Now, in the two first cases, the proposition employed to express both judgments is the same; one proposition expresses indiscriminately either judgment. And this circumstance perhaps may have concurred to lead Mr. Mill to say, in his System of Logic, Book I. ch. 5, that "propositions (except where the mind itself is the subject treated of) are not assertions respecting our idea of things, but assertions respecting the things themselves." The sharp distinction which Mr. Mill appears to take between things objective and things subjective leads him, since propositions clearly express objective things, to disregard the fact that they also, at the same time and in the same respect, express subjective things. Ἔστι μὲν οὖν τὰ ἐν τῇ φωνῇ τῶν ἐν τῇ ψυχῇ παθημάτων σύμβολα, says Aristotle, De Interp. cap. 1. Assume now that every thing is objective and subjective at once, and

FF

the difficulty, as to whether the import of propositions is subjective or objective, disappears entirely, for the import is both at once; and this distinction is replaced by another, namely, by that between presentative and representative judgments. Applied to this distinction, the words quoted from Mr. Mill would restrict propositions to express only judgments of presentation. But the fact, that the form of the proposition does not indicate the kind of judgment which it expresses, does not warrant us in restricting it to one kind of judgment to the exclusion of another. It shows only that the precision of language falls short as yet of expressing the distinctions of thought. Nor yet does it destroy the subjective character of propositions and their connection with judgments; for judgments of presentations are subjective, and their presented objects are objects of consciousness, and only as such can they be expressed in propositions. The same is the case with names. Names also, as well as propositions, show no inflections or forms indicating whether they are used as names of objects in presentation or objects in representation. The name white expresses white objects in presentation and in representation indiscriminately; yet it is not in the one case a name of an idea (so-called) and not of an object, nor in the other case a name of an object and not of an idea. What is really shown by this indiscriminate application of names and propositions to express presentations and representations is, that we are as yet in no position to found a true classification of names and propositions on the classification of judgments, as judgments of presentation and judgments of representation, since the names and propositions have not yet been divided at all; but must use them without such a classification, except so far as the propositions expressing the third class of judgments are distinguished by their form from those expressing the judgments of the two first classes;—as, for instance, the proposition, That London is on the Thames is true, is distinguished by its form from the simple proposition, London is on the Thames; and so far language provides an expression for the distinction in thought.

Just as names are the expression of objects, not of things out of relation to consciousness, and as concept-names are the expression of concepts, so propositions are the expression of judgments. In all these cases we act outwardly in consequence of having felt. They are all, psychologically speaking, instances of afferent or sensitive nerves exciting efferent or motor nerves. If we want to know what is expressed by the act, we must ask what is impressed by the feeling. It is impossible to sever the connection between propositions and judgments; or to restrict propositions to express judgments of presentation only, or "things" in contradistinction to "ideas;" or to define propositions by the class of objects, presentative or representative, which they connect. The import of propositions lies in the connection between the objects which are the terms of the judgments expressed, irrespective indeed of whether they are presentations or representations, but involving always their connection in consciousness as well as in objective existence. I return now to the classification of propositions according to the modes in which their terms are connected, irrespective of the sphere of consciousness, presentation or representation, in which they may be connected; for these modes are common to both spheres of consciousness.

§ 52. All categorical, including disjunctive, propositions express the coalescence of images in consciousness. Their copula, the word "is," means coalescence; A is B means A coalesces with B. The copula does not express the existence or presence of the objects in consciousness; this is a condition of their being connected in a judgment, but is not expressed by the proposition expressing the judgment. Nor does the copula express the identity of the objects; this would be to make them convertible with each other. But partial identity, identity in some respect, is what is expressed by the copula, and this partial identity I call coalescence. All categorical propositions connect a concept with its exclusion in space, affirm or deny some part of its exclusion of its inclusion. But what is it that is said, in an affirmative proposition, of that concept which is the subject? And again what is said of the predicate, which by being considered as belonging to the exclusion of the subject, is thereby considered as different from it? It is,—and this is what the proposition asserts,—that the subject *is* the predicate, a part of its own exclusion, and again that the predicate, a part of that exclusion, *is* the subject or the inclusion. Predicate and subject of the proposition are the same. The subject, the inclusion of the concept, is asserted to be its exclusion or a part of it, to be that which by its very nature, as the inclusion of the concept, it distinguished from itself. In other words, the limits imposed by volition in creating the concept are overleapt, and the concept is carried out beyond them, and made to coalesce with its contradictory or its exclusion. Are those limits destroyed by being overleapt? By no means; they are essential to the overleaping.

to the proposition. They are valid for volition, but not for intuition. The proposition, the continuation of consciousness, leaves them behind and asserts that, them notwithstanding, the objects within them and the objects beyond them are one object. In regard to volition subject and predicate are two objects connected together; in regard to intuition they are one object. They are two objects connected together so long as we use the concept-names by which volition separates the inclusion from the exclusion of the concept. In order to say that A is the same as B, we must begin by assuming them to be different. We could not say that they were the same, unless we regarded them first as not the same. It follows that they are different in one respect, the same in another respect; different in respect of volition, the same in respect of intuition. The image fixed by volition coalesces, while I keep it before the mind, with something which was not included in it, but excluded from it, as so fixed by volition. Propositions express this coalescence of concepts, of the inclusion and exclusion of a concept, in intuition. Hence there is no contradiction involved in the proposition; the proposition is not self-contradictory, for it is a movement of intuition, and the limits which intuition overleaps are not imposed by itself but by volition, are limits voluntarily adopted by consciousness to mark its own progress. Consciousness with one hand, as it were, intuition, draws an advancing line, with the other, volition, it marks progress. The two functions are not contradictory, but they are equally essential. If the marks were obliterated as soon as overleapt, there would be no progress, for the progress is one of consciousness, of knowledge, and consists in the accumulation of the marks, as well as in overleaping them. Where volition makes a mark, there is the principle of contradiction; all on one side of the mark is the contradictory of all on the other side of the mark, one side is A, the other side is not-A. Intuition moves along the line of consciousness, and passes from the inclusion of the concept, which is the subject, over the limit of contradiction, to the exclusion of the concept, the predicate. If the object which it meets there is one which experience or association has shown to be connected in a certain way with the inclusion of the concept, the proposition expresses this connection and is affirmative; if not, it expresses the want of this connection and is negative. The two concepts coalesce or do not coalesce in intuition, presentative or representative. The copula, "is" or "is not," takes the place of the limit of contradiction. Categorical predication accordingly proceeds by adoption of the form of contradiction, of the postulates, and of the concept-form, as the means of distinguishing the movement of consciousness into distinct steps; which adoption takes place in the establishment of concepts, the concept being a portion of intuition thrown into the concept-form. And as consciousness in predication does not adopt the form of contradiction as an object in itself, but as a form applicable to all objects, as it does not identify the concepts, as content, with their form of contradiction, so it does not contradict itself in taking the concepts out of that form again, and asserting the coalescence of their inclusion and exclusion in the proposition, or nullify the form of contradiction itself by changing its content, and substituting for its limit the copula of the proposition.

There are two ways in which the coalescence of concepts, expressed by affirmative categorical propositions, can take place; either the concepts coincide, or one is a part of the other. And in the latter case it is not indifferent which of the two is part, and which whole; but logic chooses one mode only, and in logical propositions the predicate is always the whole, and the subject the part. To make this clear, reference must be made to the doctrine of the extension and intension of concepts, which may be seen clearly explained by Sir W. Hamilton, Logic, Lect. VIII. and Discussions, App. 2. B. Every concept, whether it is a general or a particular notion or image, is a quantum or a class, and that in two ways; first, it contains a certain number of qualities, one or any number; secondly, it contains a certain number of individuals, one or any number, possessing each of them all those qualities. For instance, the general notion animal is a class or quantum of qualities, suppose sentience, possession of nerve, and cellular organisation. It is also a quantum or class of individuals, each possessing all these qualities, say the classes, which are individuals to the genus animal, Vertebrate, Mollusc, Radiate, and Articulate. As a quantum of the first kind it has these qualities as its intension; as a quantum of the second kind it has these classes, which are individuals to it, as its extension. And it is manifest that the intension and extension of any concept are exactly coincident; those individuals only are included in the extension which have all the qualities included in the intension of the concept, whatever other qualities they may possess besides; the intension measures the extension of the concept, and vice versâ. The extension is suspended on the intension; all those objects in which the qualities of the intension are found united, no more and no fewer, are included in the extension. Farther it is plain, from comparing several concepts of the same series together, that the proportion between their intension and extension, as quanta, varies inversely; concepts whose extension is large have a small intension, and those which have a large intension have a small extension. Animal for instance, compared with Vertebrate, has a smaller intension and a larger extension; as each new quantum of qualities is added to the intension, a new quantum of individuals is taken off from the extension, and the new name expresses the new dressing of the balance. The individual animals, such as this man, this horse, &c. have the largest intension and the smallest extension, namely unity, of all the concepts in the series. The enlargement of the intension, the addition of specific qualities and peculiarities, lessens the number of instances in which all are found to coexist; so that, while extension and intension are always in inverse proportion, they always correspond to and balance or measure each other. The widest possible concept, Existence, has the smallest possible intension, but the greatest possible extension. This thought applied to the universe, as the object-matter of the different special sciences, is the ground of Comte's doctrine of the logical order of those sciences, of their arrangement in a scale or hierarchy according to the decrease in generality and increase in complexity of the laws of each of them, that is to say, their decrease in extension and increase in intension. Thus the laws of Ethic as the most complex of all the sciences come last and highest, and the units to whom those laws apply are the ultimate individuals of the universe, opposed to the laws of the general concept, existence, at the other end of the logical scale.

All concepts, whether general, particular, or individual, that is, images fixed on and limited as unities by volition, are alike included in this view of extension and intension. And it is an useful suggestion made in the Essay, Language and Science (Three Essays, London, 1863, p. 86), that the connotation and denotation of words, in Mr. J. S. Mill's employment of those terms, are to words what intension and extension are to concepts, or notions expressed by words; so that by the connotation of a concept-name is understood the intension of the concept, and by its denotation the extension of the concept. Every concept is a quantum in two ways, a quantum of qualities and a quantum of individuals, each of which individuals contains all the qualities of the other or intensive quantum; but the extreme members of a series, the individual concept at the one end, and the general concept at the other, contain respectively only one individual and only one quality. But the conception of a quantum, whether of qualities or of objects possessing qualities, whether one or many, is the conception of a space filled with what it contains; so that, when one quality or one object is asserted to coalesce with another, it is either included in or coincides with the space occupied by that other, and we have before us the intuition of spaces including or coinciding with each other. If experience, in presentation or representation, compels the two concepts to coalesce, it must be in one of these two ways. When the extension of a concept is predicated of its intension, or its intension of its extension, the two concepts coalesce as coinciding. For instance, Animals, meaning whatever possesses sentience, nerve, and cellular organisation, are vertebrate, mollusc, radiate, and articulate. Here the intension and the extension of the same concept, animal, are balanced against each other, and animal as a class coincides with animal as a collection of qualities; one is the definition of the other, its analysis and counterpart. But when the coalescence is not by way of coincidence but of inclusion, then subject and predicate must, in coalescing, become either whole or part one of the other. When I predicate in order of extension, the subject is included as a part in the predicate as a whole; for instance, Man is vertebrate, England is insular; where the subject is contained in a larger class of individuals, man in that of things vertebrate, England in that of things insular. But these same propositions may be understood in order of intension, and in that case the subject is a whole of which the predicate is a part; for instance, Man, as a quantum of qualities, contains among them the quality of being vertebrate; England contains the quality of being insular. The same proposition, if its terms are understood as units of intension, moves from subject as whole to predicate as part.

It was said above that logic recognises, that is, at least, would do well to recognise (for I speak like a barrister who predicts that the Court will do what he knows to be the law), in propositions where the coalescence is of whole and part, only those propositions as logical where the predicate is the whole and the subject the part, excluding those where the subject is the whole and the predicate the part. If this is admitted, it follows that propositions where the predication is in order of intension should be excluded from logic. But to this objections will be raised. It may be asked, Does predication in order of intension necessarily make the subject whole, and the predicate part; and, Does predication in order of extension necessarily make the subject part, and the predicate whole? And farther it may be asked, If, as is here maintained, the coalescence of the concepts is the sole thing asserted by propositions, is it not entirely indifferent which of the two, subject and predicate, is whole and which is part? Why should we not be equally correct and logical in saying, in order of extension, Vertebrate is man, and in order of intension, Insular is England? Is it not indifferent whether subject be whole and predicate part, or predicate whole and subject part? And is it not consequently indifferent whether we employ the order of extension or the order of intension in predication; are not both equally legitimate?

First with regard to predication in order of intension. Whatever may be the true rule as to the position of subject and predicate as whole and part, in propositions in order of extension, yet, independently of that rule, propositions in order of intension are excluded from logic by the nature of the concept. Concepts are unities; when I predicate in order of intension, I do not treat concepts as unities. When I say Insularity is a property of England, I do not mean all insularity, but a particular instance or kind of it; when I say Man is vertebrate, in order of intension, I do not mean that he has the quality of being vertebrate in all its shapes, but only in one or some of them; the whole concept or unity of qualities, man, does not contain in it the whole concept or quality of being vertebrate. But if I take the two in order of extension, then man, as a whole or unity, is included in the whole concept or unity, vertebrate; England is included in the whole class, insular objects. In fact, concepts are logical units only so far as they are wholes in order of extension; the qualities included in objects are concepts only so far as they are unified by volition; it must be specified what quality is meant, whether by vertebration, for instance, is meant that common to all vertebrate animals, or that common to man, or that to fishes, and so on. But this changes the quality into a whole or unit of extension, at the same time that it changes it into a concept. Suppose I have a provisional image of vertebration common to all vertebrate animals; then, keeping this before me as a concept, an unit, I bring it into connection with the concept man, and say in order of intension Man is vertebrate, or contains in him vertebration,—the proposition is not true, he does not contain it in this sense; or suppose I say, still in order of intension, but changing the position of subject and predicate, Vertebrate is man, or the vertebration common to all animals contains in it the qualities of man, then the proposition is absurd as well as untrue. If, therefore, concepts are logical unities, predication in order of intension is illogical. The only logical way of treating concepts is to use them in propositions in which they can be treated as unities, that is, in propositions in order of extension.

Propositions in which subject and predicate coincide are always legitimate; for in these, though we pass from the intension to the extension of one and the same concept, and vice versâ, yet the qualities which constitute the intension are unified and made concepts by volition; by the qualities are meant all the instances of the presence of the qualities; they are in fact transformed into quanta of extension. The term animal, for instance, means all objects possessing sentience, nerve, and cellular organisation; the provisional image is an animal shape with these qualities, standing for all such shapes. The intension of the concept is a class of individuals as much as the extension is; one class of individuals is asserted in the proposition to coincide with another.

Secondly with regard to the rule which makes the predicate whole and the subject part, in propositions in order of extension, where the terms do not coincide. It is true that coalescence in intuition may take place whether we begin with the whole or with the part, and, so far as this only is concerned, the expression of that coalescence in propositions might move from whole to part as well as from part to whole. But an almost universal custom has decided that the image which contains shall be placed last, and that which is contained first, in order of speech; that the predicate shall express that to which the subject belongs, the subject be explained by assigning that to which it belongs, and not that which belongs to it. To this rule propositions in order of intension appeared to form an exception; but they did so only apparently, since they reversed the position of subject and predicate, as part and whole, only by using general terms as equivalent, not to all the instances contained under them, but to single modes of qualities. It is only in categorical propositions that the order of intension comes forward; no other kind of proposition lends itself to express the inherence of qualities in objects; and in categorical propositions this kind of coalescence is not a logical one, since general terms should include and recall all the instances of objects or qualities to which the term applies, not one single instance only of its applicability.

A reference to the mental operations which give rise to the two orders of intension and extension will serve to verify the view now taken of them, as to their respective fitness for logical purposes. Every object has intension which exists as what has been called in § 26 a remote object, that is, as an empirical object composed of immediate empirical objects. Objects have intension as objects of perception; their attributes or qualities are their intension. But objects have extension only when fixed on by volition, and transformed from percepts into concepts. The term extension is derived originally, no doubt, from the case of those concepts only which are general as opposed to abstract notions, that is, which are general and not particular concepts; the extension of a general notion is composed of the several instances in which the abstract quality, expressed by its name, occurs; for instance, the extension of the general notion pillared comprises the quality of being pillared in porticoes, Greek temples, Gothic cathedrals, and so on. But when only a single instance has been observed, and the quality is only an abstract notion or a particular concept, still the term extension is applicable to the single object, but it is an unit of extension. In no case can there be extension without a concept formed by volition; the intension of these concepts consists in the qualities which they have as objects of perception, the union of which qualities into complex parcels constituted them remote objects. To bring the intension of concepts into logic, in that character of intension, is to destroy the distinctive character of logic, the character which distinguishes it from modes of perception. Intension is a word of perception, extension is a word of logic. Concepts have intension as images or objects of perception, but only as concepts have they extension.

Hence the only legitimate categorical propositions are those where the subject and predicate coalesce by coincidence, and those where they coalesce by including the subject in the predicate. In negative propositions no modes of coalescing can be distinguished; if the terms coalesced at all, they would not be negative propositions. But the two modes of categorical affirmative propositions are both expressed by the same formula, A is B, and therefore require attention in practice to distinguish them, to distinguish whether the proposition is or is not simply convertible. Where subject and predicate coincide, each is the analysis of the other. Where subject is included in predicate, they are together the analysis of the proposition. Hence all propositions are analytical. But also, since all propositions are forward movements of consciousness, are coalescences of images, they are in this respect synthetical. That is to say, the process is synthesis, the result is analysis; or the process of predication is analysis as to its whole object-matter, synthesis as to its method of dealing with its object-matter as a collection of parts. The proposition is in all cases an analysis of its whole content into its subject and predicate; in cases of coincidence, it is besides an analysis of subject by predicate and of predicate by subject. But it is synthesis of the parts of its whole content, subject and predicate, a combination of one with the other in the forward movement of consciousness.

§ 52. Categorical propositions.

If we hold that concepts enter into the proposition as unities, we are enabled to dismiss the consideration of universal and particular propositions. Whether we say All animals, some animals, or this animal, are sentient, in any case the subject and the predicate are each a single concept. These, like modals, are forms of speech provided by grammar, which can, but need not, be adopted by logic for its own purposes. We need not think under these forms, but we may if we choose. But however we modify the concepts which are subject or predicate of our propositions, they still remain concepts, each a single concept, and must coalesce in consciousness in order to being combined in a proposition.

§ 53. Hypothetical propositions.

§ 53. The second great class of propositions contains those which express the connection of concepts in order of time, hypothetical propositions. But it is not enough that the concepts should be predicated of one another as succeeding, they must be connected together by some bond, ratified or valid in consciousness, expressing a fact of consciousness in order of time, the bond of causation; just as in categorical propositions it is experience that makes the concepts coalesce into one object in one and the same portion of space. In categorical propositions subject and predicate coalesce into one object; in hypothetical propositions, where the relations of the concepts in order of time alone are considered, they cannot coalesce into one object, and a bond of connection between them as separate objects must be sought. This bond is the causal relation. The subject of categorical propositions becomes the antecedent, and the predicate becomes the consequent, of hypothetical propositions. The hypothetical proposition asserts that given one object another will follow, or be capable of being asserted; If A is B, then C is D. The copula in hypothetical propositions is not, as in categorical, a word signifying coalescence, but two words signifying the dependence of one object on another,—If, then. Since the word if is a conjunction, and grammatically requires and introduces a sentence and not a single name, it follows that the terms of hypothetical propositions are themselves propositions. But propositions which are the expression of judgments do not essentially differ from concept-names which are the expression of concepts, and it makes no essential difference between categorical and hypothetical propositions that the terms of the latter are propositions expressing analysed concepts, and not concepts simply. Hypothetical propositions do not assert that the complex of objects existing in one moment of time is or contains the cause of the complex of objects existing in the moment of time next succeeding, though it is true that it does so; nor do they directly assert that one object or event is a sufficient cause of the existence of another, though such direct propositions might have been selected from grammatical speech by logicians as well as the form which they have actually selected for the same purpose, namely, the purpose of expressing their reasonings in the form of time; but hypothetical propositions pick out some isolated object or event in one moment of time, and assert that it is such that another object or event in some succeeding moment of time will arise in consequence of it; not however that the former object or event is the sole cause or condition of the latter, but only that it is a sufficient cause. This corresponds to the rule, in categorical propositions, that the subject is included as a part in the predicate; for the consequent is larger than the antecedent, inasmuch as it may arise in consequence of some other antecedent, if the one named does not arise or exist. Different as hypothetical and categorical propositions are in form, yet one is no more problematical than the other. Both alike express, not the existence of their terms or either of them, not the presence of their terms in consciousness, though they both imply it; but they express the connection between their terms, concepts expressed by names in the one, concepts or events expressed by propositions in the other; one in the order of space, the other in that of time. The If of the hypothetical copula does not render the proposition problematical; but the hypothetical proposition, If A is B, then C is D, is exactly equivalent to this, The concept or event AB is a cause of the concept or event CD.

Hypothetical propositions have a prerogative over categorical propositions, derived from their use of the form of time abstracted from space, and that is, that they can move either in order of history or in order of cognition; the antecedent can be either the causa existendi or the causa cognoscendi of the consequent. Categorical propositions can make no distinction between these two orders, they are bound to the third order, the order of logic alone; they make abstraction of the form of time, and of history and cognition in time. But the employer of hypothetical propositions is bound to distinguish, in which of these two orders he places the connection of their terms, for the confusion of the two is one of the most fertile sources of fallacy. "If a man is merry, he is happy" is an instance of the antecedent being used as the causa cognoscendi of the consequent. "If a man has done his duty, he is happy" is an instance of its being used as the causa existendi of the consequent. In both cases the connection between the events as concepts or images in the mind of the speaker is what is expressed by the proposition.

§ 54. The next class is that of disjunctive propositions. These flow from and are subordinate to categorical propositions; they are categorical propositions of a different kind; but as categorical they assert coalescence of concepts and unite their terms in order of space. Disjunctive propositions arise when a whole class of concepts in order of extension has been formed; for instance, when the concept animal has been divided into its four sub-kingdoms, vertebrate, mollusc, radiate, and articulate animals; or these again into orders and classes, ending with individual animals as the smallest class of extension. Then two kinds of disjunctive propositions arise, first when the whole concept animal is considered as coincident with the whole of its dividing concepts, as, Animals are either vertebrate, mollusc, radiate, or articulate; secondly, when an individual animal, or a class considered as an individual, as mammalia, is asserted to be referable to one of the classes above it, as, for instance, Man is either a mammal, a bird, a reptile, or a fish; Mammals are either vertebrate, mollusc, radiate, or articulate. The first kind of disjunctive propositions, those in which the whole of a class is asserted to coincide with its parts, or to contain them each separately, is not exclusive but inclusive, the whole class is indifferent to its parts singly, is each of them at once. The second kind, in which the whole class is only given as divided into parts, and is predicated as so divided, must contain any smaller portion of itself only in one of these divisions and not in another, and therefore is exclusive; if the subject belongs to one part of the predicate, it is eo ipso excluded from the others. The disjunctive propositions of this latter kind are those which are properly disjunctive; the former kind are not distinguishable essentially from simple categorical propositions of coincidence.

In disjunctive propositions, as in simple categorical, the copula expresses coalescence of the subject with the predicate in consciousness; the difference between disjunctive and categorical propositions lies in the greater complexity of the predicates of the former. Less is asserted by the disjunctive than by the categorical in one sense, because the predicate is opened thereby to a further determination, an alternative, and the subject not expressed in its completion. More is asserted by them in another sense, because not only is a predicate asserted, but some of the relations of this predicate are included in the assertion. The categorical proposition, A whale is a mammal, is an assertion complete in itself, whatever further may have to be said on the subject. The disjunctive proposition, A whale is either a mammal, a reptile, a bird, or a fish, includes indeed the assertion, A whale is a mammal, but does not fix it as the thing asserted by the proposition; it gives the alternatives of this assertion, and therefore the means of deciding on its truth, which were not contained in the categorical proposition. This character, of including the means of deciding or conditions of the truth of a proposition, seems to be the reason why disjunctive propositions are often treated in connection with hypothetical.

A negative disjunctive proposition expresses that the subject does not coalesce with any of the alternatives of the predicate, and therefore it is useless to enquire, in the case of negatives, whether they are of the inclusive or exclusive order. For instance, Whales are neither mollusc, articulate, nor radiate, is a negative disjunctive proposition, which expresses alike the non-coalescence of the concept whales with the whole indifferently and with the parts separately.

§ 55. The fourth and last class is that of hypothetico-disjunctive propositions. These flow from and are a modification of hypothetical, as disjunctive are of categorical propositions. Their form is time; they express, in similar manner as the disjunctive, the completion of the series of effects of a given cause, or of causes of a given effect. The hypothetical proposition asserts, for instance, If he is sad, he wants money (causa cognoscendi). The hypothetico-disjunctive asserts, If he is sad, he wants either money, or health, or employment; that is, it completes the series of consequents proved, one if not all of which must be proved by the antecedent or ground of inference, He is sad. Or again, the hypothetical proposition asserts, If he wants money, he will be sad (causa existendi). The hypothetico-disjunctive asserts, If he wants either health, or money, or employment, he will be sad; completing the series of causes as before of effects.

It is to be observed that the hypothetico-disjunctive, like the disjunctive, expresses its alternatives both exclusively and inclusively. Logical language provides no clear and simple formula by which the two modes are distinguished from each other; it is still left to the reasoner to state each time, in which sense, exclusively or inclusively, he is using the propositions, or to his opponent to analyse his assertions and reduce them to one or other of these forms. This end might perhaps be attained by distinguishing the inclusive use of the disjunctive and hypothetico-disjunctive proposition by the addition of the word "indifferently," leaving them in their present form when they are intended exclusively. We might say, for instance, Verse is either rhymed or unrhymed, indifferently; but, The Faery Queen is either rhymed or unrhymed; and in the hypothetico-disjunctive, If we are prudent, we shall either command or deserve success, indifferently; but, If a religious creed is persecuted, it will be either uprooted or strengthened.

Neither hypothetical nor hypothetico-disjunctive propositions can be negative so long as they remain in that form; for whether the terms are both of them negative, or one negative and the other affirmative, the connection between them, which is what is asserted by the proposition, must always be affirmed. There is no hypothetical form for a negative proposition; grammatical language does not admit it. In order to deny both hypothetical and hypothetico-disjunctive propositions, they must be reduced to their categorical equivalents. For instance, the negatives of the propositions, If a man is merry, he is happy; and, If a man is sad, he wants either money, or health, or employment; are, A man's being merry is no proof of his being happy; and, A man's being sad is no proof of his wanting either money, or health, or employment. The connection of the terms must be denied.

§ 56. It follows in the next place to treat briefly of syllogisms. A syllogism is a system of three propositions which are of such a nature, and are so arranged, that the third, the Conclusion or the Quæstio, is seen to result from the combination of the two first, or the Premises. As logic in its employment of language selects four kinds of propositions, as adequate to the expression of all the judgments of consciousness, and, in order to avoid confusion in the use of language for the expression of thought, restricts itself to the employment of these alone, so logic also selects four systems or arrangements of propositions as adequate to the expression of all generalisations of consciousness, whether critical or acquisitive, and rejects others as superfluous and leading to confusion. In both cases, both in propositions and in syllogisms, the language employed is selected for the accuracy with which it expresses the movement of consciousness, the judgments in the one case, the motived judgments, or judgments with the ground or reason, in the other; so that we may be certain that whatever is obedient to the forms of the syllogism is obedient to the laws of thought, and that whatever can be expressed as the conclusion of a syllogism is true, so far as the laws of thought are concerned. The syllogistic forms are not the laws of thought, but expressions of them in language, in the arrangement of propositions. The laws of thought are time and space, the postulates, and the concept-form. Propositions and syllogisms, or systems of propositions, are arrangements of language, of words and sentences, so as to express accurately and yet adequately the movement of consciousness in accordance with those laws. The laws of thought are implanted in consciousness by nature; language also and all its forms are expressions of consciousness, belonging by nature to conscious beings; but the selection of some of these forms of language, and their systematisation, so as to serve as expressions of judgments and generalisations in accordance with the laws of thought, this is an invention of reflecting man, an adaptation of natural circumstances to his own purposes. Man was led to the conscious selection of the forms by finding them or many of them in use before selection, he used them spontaneously before he selected them voluntarily. Then logical systems arose, each systematising language in different ways. The last step is to find the principle of selection, to find the laws of thought which the selection of forms of language is designed to express, or which they were unconsciously adapted to express; that is, to show the connection of logical propositions and syllogisms with their source, the laws of consciousness, and to harmonise them as a system from that point of view. The forms of time and space, with their material element, into which volition introduces the postulates and the concept-form, are the key of logic and of its verbal forms of propositions and syllogisms.

Syllogisms are of four kinds, depending on the four kinds of propositions and called by the same names. The kind of the syllogism is determined by the kind of the proposition which it has for its major premiss. See again Sir W. Hamilton, Logic, Lect. xv. Categorical syllogisms are those in which the three propositions are categorical; and in which the coalescence of the concepts in the quæstio, or conclusion, is made possible by the discovery of a middle term or third concept with which they both coalesce. In disjunctive syllogisms no new middle term is introduced, but the exhaustive analysis of the concept given in the major premiss is made the ground of the conclusion; for it was shown above that the disjunctive proposition does not assert a fact simply, but as involved in alternatives which contain the means of deciding on its truth. In hypothetical syllogisms also no new middle term is introduced, but, as in disjunctive, the ground of the conclusion is already contained in the major premiss. And the same may be said of the hypothetico-disjunctive syllogisms, which combine the peculiarities of the two preceding kinds. But the conclusion in three of the four kinds of syllogism, in all except the hypothetico-disjunctive, is a categorical proposition; that is, it is a proposition expressing the coalescence of two concepts into one. The result is the same in all these three kinds, and that result is an image, whether we reach it by reasoning in the form of space or in that of time, whether by the introduction of a new intermediate concept, as in categorical syllogisms, or by an exhaustive analysis, as in disjunctive syllogisms, or by the consideration of its consequents or of its antecedents, as in hypothetical syllogisms. The result in hypothetico-disjunctive syllogisms is an hypothetical proposition.

The middle term or concept of an affirmative categorical syllogism must either contain one of the extreme concepts and be contained in the other, or it must contain one and coincide with the other, or it must coincide with one and be contained in the other, or it must coincide with them both; otherwise it does not compel their coalescence. This gives rise to four cases, or figures, of categorical affirmative propositions, of each of which I will give an instance with

a diagram annexed to render the movement clearer.
An instance of the first figure is,

>Man is (contained in) animal,
>Animal is (contained in) organic being,
>∴ Man is (contained in) organic being;

of the second figure,

>Man is (contained in) animal,
>Animal is (coincident with) sentient being,
>∴ Man is (contained in) sentient being;

of the third figure,

>Animal is (coincident with) sentient being,
>Animal is (contained in) organic being,
>∴ Sentient being is (contained in) organic being;

of the fourth figure,

>Animal is (coincident with) sentient being,
>Sentient being is (coincident with) possession of nerve,
>∴ Animal is (coincident with) possession of nerve.

These four figures are all that are possible, if concepts are treated as units. Negative syllogisms also fall under these same forms, since only one of the premises in a negative syllogism can be a negative proposition, and the other premiss must express either coincidence or comprehension. Besides which, a negative proposition is the counterpart of an affirmative proposition of coincidence; the exclusion in the one case, and the coalescence in the other, is total and without exception. When two concepts are coincident, all predicates of the one are predicates of the other, to assert any thing of the one is to assert it also of the other; and, when two concepts are excluded from each other, whatever is affirmed of the one must be denied of the other. The introduction of a negative proposition, therefore, into a syllogism requires no other form or forms of statement than those which suffice for affirmative syllogisms.

Categorical syllogisms depend upon the form of space, since all their propositions do so. A is included in B is the conclusion. Why? Because C is included in B, and A is included in C.—A is C, C is B, therefore A is B. It is not enough to say that concepts which coalesce with one and the same third concept coalesce with each other; we must add the requirement, that they coalesce with it, one as including or coincident, and the other as included or coincident. It is not enough, for instance, to say Man coalesces with animal, Horse coalesces with animal; for then we can only conclude, that Man coalesces with Horse so far as both are animals, that is, that they have one point or characteristic in common; they are connected by belonging to a common notion, but they do not coalesce themselves; no further characteristics can be inferred from this connection, and we are no nearer to the nature of man or of horse than we were in the premises. But we must be able to add the characteristics of the subject and those of the predicate of the conclusion together, in other words, the concepts of the conclusion must coalesce, or we have reached no further step in their determination. And, in order to be able to add the characteristics of the one to those of the other, the middle term or third concept, to which they are referred, must contain or coincide with one of them, and be contained in or coincide with the other, must stand between them in point of comprehension, and not outside both. When this is the case, a step forward is taken by the syllogism, which step forward is the purpose of syllogising. If we consider those concepts which coincide with others, and those which contain others, as the predicates of those which they coincide with or contain, the syllogism will be in conformity to the Dictum of Aristotle, Categ. III. 15. Ὅσα κατὰ τοῦ κατηγορουμένου λέγεται, πάντα καὶ κατὰ τοῦ ὑποκειμένου ῥηθήσεται. A predicate of a predicate is a predicate of its subject.

Negative syllogisms are those in which the conclusion is a negative proposition, one asserting that subject and predicate do not coalesce. This case arises when one of the premises is a negative, and the other an affirmative, proposition, and when, besides, the middle term excludes one of the extreme terms and either includes or coincides with the other. Negative propositions assert exclusion, that the subject is excluded from the predicate, and the predicate from the subject; they make no distinction between modes of coalescence, by inclusion or coincidence, but they deny coalescence simply. There is in logic no such thing as a particular negative proposition; concepts are unities, and if one excludes another, it excludes it entirely. A proposition such as this, Some men are not negroes, excludes entirely the concept some men from the concept negroes; and the same knowledge, which warranted the assertion of this proposition, warrants also the affirmative proposition, Negroes are (contained in) men. Logic takes up or adopts no classes, genera, or species, ready made from other sciences, but forms its own concepts by volition; and every concept, every fact, stands on its own basis of knowledge. Logic cannot treat Man, for instance, as a genus or species or class, or as a collection of individual men, but as a single concept with a definite meaning; the logical concept man is not a multitude of individuals, some of which are one thing, some another, but it is one thing with a definite connotation and indivisible. To treat Man as a collection of individuals, some of which are one thing and some another, is to treat it as a percept and not a concept; and whatever is predicated of "some men" is predicated of them as objects which happen also to be men, not of them quâtenus men, or as belonging to the concept man. The essence of a concept is to be a quâtenus; its rights, to use a legal metaphor, are creatures of contract and not of status. If two concepts coalesce at all, it must be either as coincident or as containing and contained. If they are not coincident, they must either coalesce as containing and contained, or not coalesce at all. If you do not know that they coincide, then either you know that one contains the other, or you know nothing at all about them; in the former case, you can assert an affirmative proposition about them, in the latter case you cannot assert that one excludes the other. In order to assert a negative proposition, you must have knowledge of the two concepts; and, if your knowledge of them falls short of enabling you to assert their mutual exclusion, you have enough to warrant some affirmative proposition respecting them. Wherever there is ground for a particular negative proposition, there is also ground for the affirmation of some fact or other respecting its terms. Particular negative propositions therefore, such as, Some men are negroes, and, Men are not contained in negroes, are of no use in logic and ought to be rejected from its forms; which, in volitional matter, is the same thing as saying that they are rejected.

Whenever there is a negative premiss, the conclusion is simply negative, irrespective of the mode of coalescence expressed by the affirmative proposition. In the first and third figures of syllogisms given above, in order to exclude the subject of the conclusion from the predicate, the middle term must be excluded from the predicate; that is, the premiss in which the middle term is compared with the predicate of the conclusion must be negative; otherwise, that is, if the other premiss is negative, the subject of the conclusion is not excluded from the predicate, for it is only excluded from a concept which is included in that predicate, that is, from a part of it only and not from the whole. But in the second and fourth figures of syllogisms, it is indifferent which of the premisses is negative and which affirmative. For the middle term is in the second and fourth figures coincident with the predicate of the conclusion, so that it is the same thing to exclude the subject of the conclusion from the middle term and to exclude it from the predicate of the middle term, that is, of the conclusion; no room is left between the limit of the middle term and the predicate of the conclusion, in which the subject of the conclusion might be found though excluded from the middle term. When therefore we meet with a syllogism apparently informal, from having that premiss negative in which the middle term is denied of the subject of the conclusion, or vice versâ, for in either case the exclusion is mutual, we should consider whether it is not a syllogism of the second or fourth class, in which the middle term and the predicate of the conclusion are coincident or coextensive, a syllogism disguised by the omission of the distinguishing words "coincident with" or "contained in" from the copula. For instance, this syllogism is faulty,

> Man is not vegetable,
> Vegetable is (contained in) organic being,
> ∴ Man is not organic being.

But the following syllogism is correct,

> Man is not vegetable,
> Vegetable is (coincident with) life without sentience,
> ∴ Man is not life without sentience.

For, although in both cases it is of the subject of the conclusion that the middle term is denied, yet in the latter case only, and not in the former, the middle term is the exact measure of the predicate of the conclusion, so as to leave in it no room for the subject. The rule may be generally stated thus: In syllogisms of the second and fourth figures, either premiss being negative will warrant a negative conclusion; but in syllogisms of the first and third figures, that premiss must be negative in which the middle term is compared with the predicate of the conclusion.

Since concepts, the terms of propositions and syllogisms, are always treated as units, and at the same time it is not usual to employ the distinctions of "coincident with" and "contained in" as distinctions of the copula, or mode of coalescence, it becomes necessary, with every affirmative proposition, to ask the question which of these two modes of coalescence is intended. If logicians would adopt this distinction explicitly in their arguments, it would greatly simplify discussion, and save the recurrence of "all" and "some," which it is hopeless ever to see pass over into popular language. If however the plain and easy distinction between coinciding with and containing is always expressed in logical language, there is no reason why the language of popular discussion should not become exact and logical; for the distinction is one which has not, like that of "all" and "some," an abstruse technical appearance, as if more was meant than met the ear. There would then at least be no obstacle presented by the phraseology of logic to its popular adoption; the great difficulty would however remain the same, and must perhaps be first removed, the difficulty which is felt in using terms as concepts and not as percepts, as wholes of extension which can be defined and not as wholes of intension which may have an infinite number of qualities not yet perceived, and in substituting the definition and the quâtenus in place of the loose and undefined name.

The adoption of concepts as logical units removes the appearance of what has sometimes been called the petitio principii involved in categorical syllogisms. If I say, for instance,

> All men are responsible beings,
> Caius is a man,
> ∴ Caius is a responsible being,

it appears that Caius himself, being a man, is involved in the universal term "all men," and that I must have examined the case of Caius, and admitted the conclusion, before I can assert the major premiss. The term "all men" includes all men past, present, and to come; it is not primâ facie restricted to my present knowledge of men, which it ought to be, since that is the sole ground of my proceeding to a further reasoning about them. But if I say

> Man is a responsible being,

then Man is a concept which has, or ought to have, a definite analysis or content; suppose, for instance, that it means 'any being having emotions, volition, and powers of reflection;' and by the term responsible suppose is meant 'having the feeling of being bound to act according to some law.' Then the major premiss expresses no more than my present knowledge, independent of the case of Caius, warrants; and when I compare the concept Caius with my concept man, and find that it is contained in it, I then infer from the uniformity of the course of nature that it is contained also in the concept, a responsible being. The degree of certainty in the conclusion is no greater than the degree of certainty in the major premiss, but there is a greater quantity of knowledge; the amount is increased by the combination of the minor premiss with the major; a step forward has been taken, and taken in conformity with the laws of thought. But the term "all men" includes so much that there is no room for more, for it lays claim to have exhausted the concept, by anticipation of its future modifications. We are justified in speaking of our present conception of man, but not justified in asserting that it will not be modified by future instances; and to adopt a logical formula, which is only suitable for cases where knowledge is perfectly certain and perfectly exhaustive, is to adopt what is unsuitable to express the vast majority of judgments.

Hypothetical syllogisms flow from hypothetical propositions; that is, the quæstio is established by being connected with its cause in order of time, not with a concept which contains it in order of space. The major premiss asserts that the quæstio will exist if some other event precedes it, and the minor premiss asserts that this other event takes place, if the syllogism is an affirmative one, or in what is called the modus ponens. If it rains, the fish will rise. But it does rain. Therefore the fish will rise. Since it is not asserted that rain is the only cause of the fish rising, we cannot conclude conversely, that if the fish rise it will rain; for they may rise from other causes as well as rain. So that affirmative conclusions are only possible from an affirmation of the antecedent, not of the consequent. On the other hand, since this one cause, if it existed, would draw the consequent with it, if the consequent does not exist, we may conclude that the antecedent does not exist; and this is the ground of the negative conclusion; or modus tollens, in hypothetical syllogisms. If there is game, the dog points. But he does not point. Therefore there is no game.

Disjunctive syllogisms have a major premiss which asserts the coalescence of a concept with one of a complete series of other concepts exclusively. The series must be exhaustive or complete, and the predication exclusive. If the series is not exhaustive, the proposition will be false, as admitting another alternative which may be the true one. If the predication is inclusive, as for instance, Animals are either vertebrate, mollusc, radiate, or articulate, indifferently, then the conclusion must be inclusive, and no step forward will be taken; for instance,

  Animals are either v. m. r. or a.,
  Sentient beings are animals,
  ∴ Sentient beings are either v. m. r. or a.,

where we derive no benefit from the disjunctive form of the major premiss, but treat it as a mere categorical. But if we predicate exclusively, we can in the minor deny some alternatives, and therefore in the conclusion affirm others, which is making use of the disjunctive form. For instance,

> Mammals are either v. m. r. or a.,
> But they are not m. r. or a.,
> ∴ They are v.

This is called the modus tollendo ponens. An exclusive disjunctive proposition contains in its form the ground of a possible conclusion, without reference to a third term beyond its own subject and predicate. A negative conclusion in disjunctive syllogisms arises when the minor premiss is affirmative, that is, affirmative of one of the alternatives, for that involves the negation of the others; as for instance if, in the above syllogism, the minor premiss were

> But mammals are vertebrate,

the conclusion would be

> Therefore they are neither mollusc, radiate, nor articulate.

This is called the modus ponendo tollens.

The last class of syllogisms is that of hypothetico-disjunctive. These combine some of the characteristics of both of the two former classes. What they prove is not the existence of a consequent from that of an antecedent, nor the non-existence of an antecedent from the non-existence of a consequent; nor yet the connection of a consequent with one of a complete series of antecedents, by denying all but one; but the connection of an antecedent with one of a complete series of consequents, on the assumption that it is the antecedent of one or other of them. It is requisite therefore that the series of consequents should be exhaustive, otherwise a new alternative may be the true one; but it is not requisite, indeed it is impossible, that the predication should be exclusive. The minor premiss takes care of the exclusion. The following is an instance,

> If he wants money he will either work or fight,
> But he will not work,
> ∴ If he wants money he will fight.

It is not possible to prove the negative of one alternative by affirming the other, as in the modus ponendo tollens of disjunctive syllogisms, for the conclusion would in that case contradict the major premiss.

Again, since the proof moves by negation of alternatives, and by denying the antecedent nothing is proved, the alternatives cannot be in the antecedent, in a hypothetico-disjunctive syllogism. Nothing is proved, for instance, by saying

> If he is either out of money, or health, or employment,
> he will be sad,
> But he is not out of health or employment,
> ∴ If he is out of money he will be sad.

We obtain less than we had in the major premiss. Consequently, hypothetico-disjunctive syllogisms use only the modus tollendo ponens, prove one of a series of consequents, not of antecedents, have an hypothetical proposition as their conclusion, and their conclusion is always affirmative.

The syllogism commonly known as the Dilemma is not properly a hypothetico-disjunctive, but a hypothetical syllogism. It wears an appearance of disjunction because the consequent is double, but it lacks the essence of disjunction because it does not proceed by affirming one alternative from the negation of the other, or by denying one from the affirination of the other; it denies both alternatives. It is in fact nothing but a hypothetical syllogism in the modus tollens. The whole consequent is denied in the minor premiss, and therefore the antecedent is denied in the conclusion. An instance is

If A is B, then either C is D, or X is Z,
But neither C is D, nor X is Z,
∴ A is not B.

But here I should remark that I attempt only to give simple instances of the four forms of syllogisms, in order to show the principles on which they rest, without professing to repeat or to formulate anew the more complicated forms into which they may, perhaps with advantage, be thrown, or which may arise from their combination.

§ 57. The hypothetico-disjunctive syllogism closes the series of syllogisms, or separate forms of reasoning by means of words and sentences. If other forms of syllogism should be adopted, it is difficult to imagine that they should not be developments, modifications, or combinations of these. It will be observed that nothing has been said of the so-called inductive syllogism. This is because, in the view here taken, inductions may be thrown into the form of any kind of syllogism, and because all induction is in its nature deductive, a deduction either from an anticipation of redintegration, or from an assumption of the law that the course of nature is uniform. All cases of acquisitive generalisation, it has been shown in § 38, as well those which move from particular facts as those which move from general facts, or laws, are deductions from such anticipation or such assumption. It is impossible to reason not ex præcognitis et præconcessis; induction itself is an instance of such reasoning. And, since induction is a mode of deduction, the four forms of syllogisms, which suffice for all cases of deduction, suffice also for this case of it. Induction, so far as it is reasoning, that is, so far as it is a voluntary putting together of two or any number of facts or phenomena, is a deductive process. Induction, so far as it is a process, or connected procedure, at all, is a deductive procedure. The line of demarcation falls, not between induction and deduction, but between perception of phenomena or of facts, whether procured by observation or by experiment, and reasoning, analysing, or combining those phenomena or their elements. Perception of facts, whether by observation or experiment, is not induction; reasoning acquisition of new and as yet unobserved facts is not perception, but deduction from former perceptions; and induction answers to this description. It was because induction was considered to be different in nature from deduction, while syllogism was suited only for deductive processes, that a special form of syllogism was provided, or at least employed, to embody the results of induction as a pre-syllogistic and extra-logical process. The process of induction, it was thought, was non-syllogistic, but its results might be expressed by the syllogism. An instance of the syllogism of induction is

A, B, C, D are mortal,
A, B, C, D are all mankind,
∴ All mankind are mortal.

The premiss, "A, B, C, D are all mankind," expresses the result of a complete induction, or one adopted by the logician as such. The task of showing that the induction was complete or correct, that is, the process of induction, was considered by the logician as extra-logical, and made over by him to the inductive enquirer, a man supposed to be busied with empirical matter only, as a task to be performed without the aid of logic; the straw was denied, and the full tale of bricks was required. The logician demanded a complete induction; whether one reached by simple enumeration of all the instances, or one reached by a Baconian interpretation of nature, was to him indifferent; all he demanded was a secure premiss for a syllogism; since that premiss was procured by induction, it was procured, he thought, by extra-logical means, means which depended on the matter, and not on the form, of reasoning. Those logicians, too, who were interested solely in their logical forms, and not in logic as an organon of investigation, were indifferent whether this particular kind of premiss could be procured or not. The inductive enquirer, on the other hand, said: 'The logician considers my inductive process extra-logical; nevertheless it is reasoning; it procures him not only certain means of syllogising, but also a wealth of knowledge which formal syllogising without it could never reach.' Thus philosophy was in a suicidal position. A valuable method of reasoning was excluded from syllogistic logic, and syllogistic logic was excluded from the honours of scientific discovery.

Now, if the old point of view is adhered to, if induction is not a deductive process, and if syllogism is entirely deductive, it is useless to attempt to reconcile induction and syllogism by any invention of inductive syllogisms. Such inductive syllogisms will always be mere appropriations of the results of induction, and not forms of the inductive process. It is the inductive process itself which it is required to incorporate into syllogistic logic. Now it was shown in § 38, that the inductive process is a process of deduction, and that observation and experiment, as modes of perception, are common to both. The confusion of the notion of induction with the notion of processes in which experiment and observation bear a large proportion to the reasoning founded on them, —this is probably the chief source of the divorce between induction and deduction. Wherever was seen a large accumulation of facts, experiments, and observations, there people said—Induction; without stopping to ask whether induction was a simply perceptive or a redintegrative process. Wherever they saw long arguments from comparatively few facts or phenomena, there they exclaimed—Deduction. But the truth is, that, wherever there is a voluntary redintegrative process, there is deduction; the interest supplies the matter and directs the movement, logic supplies the form and moulds the movement in conformity with the a priori requirements of truth.

If we treat concepts as units, then there is nothing, short of infinity, too large, and nothing, short of infinity, too small for the grasp of logic. Every new fact as it is observed, or brought to observation by experiment, is treated as a concept, compared with others, and made the subject or the predicate of a proposition. Black, tawny, copper-coloured are said one by one, as the fact is observed, to be contained in the concept the human form. And again, the concept the human form is said to be either black, white, tawny, or copper-coloured, indifferently. Acquisitive generalisations, to which the term induction is usually applied, employ, when expressed syllogistically, categorical syllogisms of which the major premiss is The course of nature is uniform. When the hypothetical form is employed, the same premiss may be added as a pendant to the antecedent; If A is B, and the course of nature is uniform, then C is D. The forms of syllogism above given are thus adequate measures or forms of thought, for both kinds of reasoning, critical and acquisitive, and not only for the results of reasoning but for the processes themselves. But of the four forms of syllogism, categorical, hypothetical, disjunctive, and hypothetico-disjunctive, the two former are most fitted for acquisitive reasoning, and the two latter for critical; or rather for that kind of critical reasoning which follows acquisitive, and reduces its results to a critical form; for these two latter forms of syllogism take up as their major premiss an elaborate result of reasoning, a whole class with its divisions ready formed, a concept already analysed exhaustively, either into its statical and mutually exclusive members of analysis, or into its complete series of effects. Logic offers us, in its four kinds of propositions and in its four kinds of syllogisms founded on them, forms corresponding and adequate to the two methods of empirical reasoning, critical and acquisitive, which were found to exhaust the whole domain of voluntary redintegration.

Hypothetical propositions and hypothetical syllogisms depend on the postulates and the concept-form equally with categorical and disjunctive propositions and syllogisms. Only since they connect concepts in the order of time, keeping them apart without coalescence with each other, they avoid the appearance of contradicting the postulates and the concept-form which is the peculiarity of categorical propositions. They assert that one concept causes another, not that one concept is another. Time is involved in both kinds of propositions and syllogisms alike, that is to say, the movement of consciousness in judgment requires time to exist. In another sense also they both require time, and they both require space; the images, or concepts, which are their objects exist both in time and in space. Concepts, whether separate or in coalescence, must exist in time. But this historical existence in time is abstracted from in categorical and disjunctive propositions and syllogisms, and their extension in space is abstracted from in hypothetical and hypothetico-disjunctive propositions and syllogisms; no use is made of it in these forms of reasoning. The form of time, abstracted from that of space, on which hypothetical and hypothetico-disjunctive propositions and syllogisms rest, is, as will be shown in the following Division, the formal element in the Law of Causality, and known by the name of Ratio Sufficiens. Hypothetical and hypothetico-disjunctive syllogisms rest avowedly on the principle of Ratio Sufficiens; categorical and disjunctive syllogisms rest also on the same principle, but do not make it their principle of movement, just as the other two kinds of syllogisms rest on the form of space without moving by means of it. The forms of time and space respectively determine the forms of these two main kinds of propositions and syllogisms in logic, the hypothetical and the categorical.

The same distinction between the forms of time and space is the ground of another difference also in methods of reasoning, of the difference between the critical and acquisitive methods. Acquisitive reasoning differs from critical in assuming as its principle that objects yet unknown will be subject to the law of the uniformity of the course of nature; and all instances of acquisitive reasoning are deductions from this assumption. The purely formal element in this law of the uniformity of the course of nature will be shown to be the form of time, under the name of the Ratio Sufficiens. The same form of time, therefore, which, when taken by itself, determines the form of hypothetical propositions and syllogisms, determines also, when combined with a material element and constituting the law of the uniformity of the course of nature, the method of acquisitive reasoning. It is true that both kinds of reasoning, critical and acquisitive, can be expressed indifferently by all four kinds of syllogisms; critical reasoning by hypothetical syllogisms, no less than acquisitive by categorical. Logic being purely formal, and the distinctions of her forms being grounded on distinctions of the form of thought, can apply any of her forms to any method of empirical reasoning, notwithstanding that the pure logical forms and the empirical methods of reasoning receive their distinctive shapes from the same source. For empirical reasoning is a voluntary process, and logic is the voluntary application of a form to that process; logical reasoning is doubly volitional; two things are willed in it, namely, the questions to be solved, and their complete and satisfactory solution. Logical forms are the universally applicable organon for the solution of all questions whatever. When the questions are solved, the conclusions reached, and the knowledge complete, the logical forms are thrown aside, or abstracted from; they related merely to the treatment of the question, being voluntary in the second degree; but the empirical or concrete course of reasoning, which ended in those conclusions, is a part of the entire knowledge reached, without which those conclusions would be unintelligible; and this cannot be abstracted from, but is a valuable part of the history of the mind.

This doubly voluntary, logical, treatment may, in any kind of question and in either method of reasoning, critical or acquisitive, proceed by the application of the forms either of time or of space. A period of history, for instance, may be treated as a statical concept, in which cause and effect are qualities or modes of existence. The reign of Charles I., for example, may be treated as one concept, in which the event of the attempted Arrest of the Five Members and that of the beheading of the King are constituent parts, notwithstanding that the former event was one of the causes of the latter. If now we reason acquisitively, we may say that similar exercises of arbitrary power, in similar circumstances, will produce similar retribution; A is productive of B; or, A is (contained in) events productive of B. The word productive connects events in order of time, and makes cause and effect coalesce into one statical concept. Similarly, the same period of time may be treated as a network of causes and effects, and we may say If there is an exercise of arbitrary power, there will be retribution. And again, in wholes of simultaneous existence, where the parts exist simultaneously, for instance, the rising and falling of the opposite ends of a lever, the action and reaction of bodies in collision, the angles and sides of a triangle, each part may be considered as a cause of the rest, and as the effect of the rest; a single bone of a fossil animal not only as proof of what the rest of the skeleton was, but also as having been with the other bones a condition of the whole, and as itself conditioned by the rest. In other words, logic can treat wholes of succession statically, and wholes of simultaneous existence dynamically, for the purposes of investigation; it can also treat new inferences, in acquisitive generalisation, as qualities or constituent parts of already acquired concepts, besides treating them in the character of future events, or events consequent on prior conditions.

§ 58. Logic has always been considered to be a purely formal science, making abstraction from all content or matter of knowledge, and giving only the laws which are afterwards applicable to all kinds of content or matter, but which do not contain any in themselves or of their own. If this were strictly true, it would follow that there was no community of nature between Metaphysic and Logic, for metaphysic always has in its objects both form and matter, the latter being as essential as the former; and consequently that metaphysical truths could not be deduced from logical, nor logical from metaphysical. Two faculties or functions would then exist side by side in consciousness, which might be capable of harmonious action, but which would not be necessitated to act harmoniously; and thus a third principle or set of principles would be required, to establish the practical rules which regulate, or ought to regulate, the concert of the two functions. But now, if any one, startled at the apparent incongruousness of such a system, should enquire whether, after all, it were the true one, and should experience the wish to reduce it to greater simplicity, the mode of doing this which would be likely first to suggest itself would be to ask whether one of the two kinds of principles, metaphysical and logical, could not be derived from the other.

And having put the question in this shape, it would probably next occur to him, that the most concrete of the two kinds of principles must be deducible from the most abstract. This attribute, of being the most abstract, he would at first be led to think was possessed by the principles of logic, since it has always been proclaimed that logic makes abstraction of all content, and consequently is entirely and completely abstract. But when it had been proved that there is no object of thought or of consciousness which does not contain in itself both matter and form; and that consequently even the postulates of logic can make no claim to be entirely and strictly formal, any more than the principles of metaphysic, or of intuition of existences as objects, namely, time and space; but that both kinds of principles alike contain both matter and form, that is, are felt as well as known in consciousness; he would then find the question of the reduction of one kind to the other opened afresh, since in this respect they stand on the same level; and it would remain only to ask, not which was abstract and which was concrete, but which was the most abstract, the most simple and elementary. The difficulty arising from the apparent difference in kind of the two sets of principles would be thus removed; it would remain to compare them together and see whether either contained the elements of the other, whether either contained more than was contained implicitly in the other.

Now the postulates contain explicitly more than time and space contain explicitly, but not more than time and space contain implicitly. In other words, they are a development of time and space, and not an additional or new principle. Time and space contain all feeling; the postulates are particular feelings. They arise only when matter, or objective feeling, has been perceived in the forms of time and space; and they arise in the act of separating one object or feeling from another, in and by those forms, which act is itself a feeling. A feeling placed in a definite time and space is one object; when experienced again, i.e. at a different time, occupying the same space and the same portion of historical time, it is the same object; when another feeling is experienced, if it is in the same space and the same portion of historical time, it is a different quality of the same object; if it is in a different space and portion of historical time, it is a different object. Objects which are the same according to this definition of sameness, for instance, cotton in England and cotton in India or America, justice in the law courts of Athens and justice in those of Paris, we class together and distinguish from all others, whether different from them in point of feeling only, as cotton from wool, both being in one bale in England, hardness and whiteness in one piece of marble, or in point both of feeling and position in time and space, as a bale of wool in England and a bale of cotton in America. The constant recurrence of objects in these conditions, the recurrence of feelings held apart only by difference of times and spaces, is the simplest form of the fact which is expressed by the postulates. A is A, the postulate of Identity, is the assertion of sameness, is the assertion that the feeling A, though experienced in different portions of space and historical time, is the same feeling, that is, that as far as feeling goes, and abstracting from the differences of its environment, it is one feeling, a logical unit. The postulate, No A is

Not-A, is the assertion of difference of feeling. Every thing is either A or Not-A is the assertion that sameness and difference, as above defined, are the only way in which we can conceive of two objects. The incompressibility of time and space, and the consequent security of the feelings or matter which they contain, is the ground of the certain assertion of the postulates. The postulates again are the assertion of general facts, facts as necessary and certain as any others; only less general and less certain than the forms of time and space, which they express, but express with the addition of a matter or content contained in them and distinguished from them. They are the first and most general and most necessary laws of empirical phenomena as such.

This unity of feeling in difference of position in historical time and space is the first and simplest fact which the postulates can be employed to express, or which they express in the first instance. Afterwards, any feature in an object can be fixed on and made a concept, for instance, a particular figure, a particular duration, a particular position with reference to other objects, as well as a particular feeling, such as hardness or colour. Objects in which occurs this particular figure, duration, position, or particular feature be it what it will, are then said to be the same in that particular respect, or quâtenus such. That is to say, the postulates are applicable to all and every feature in objects without exception. Still this refers only to objects existing in time and space historically. When we go farther, and reflect on objects, as objects existing both historically and in consciousness, a further application of the postulates is made. The same feature is then perceived as twice present to consciousness when regarded as a single feature or feeling. I reflect that I have said of it A is A. The only difference of the two A s is the difference in their times of recurrence in consciousness, not, as before, the difference in their environment; cotton in my mind now and cotton in my mind five minutes ago, the Roman Empire in my mind now and the Roman Empire in my mind five minutes ago, occupy historically the same space and time, at each moment of representation. The subjective space they occupy is also the same, they are environed by the same body and the same external world each time. The only difference between them is, that one is before and the other after an intervening series of feelings. The judgment, A is A, is now the outward expression of this reflective act of consciousness; the reflective moving from one feeling to the other requires time, and this time from A to A is represented by the two A s of the judgment. Reflection ratifies the postulates by adopting them; and the postulates are expressions of the ultimate judgments of reflection, as well as of the original judgments of perception and understanding.

The simplest expression or formula of the postulates contains a material element in it, besides that contained in time and space as pure objects. It has been already said that even the pure cognitions of time and space are material as well as formal, that they are felt as well as known, and involve a being conscious as well as a form of that consciousness. But the particular or determinate mode of this material element is, in the pure object, only provisionally present. In the postulates, on the contrary, the material element is present determinately; it is some

482   THE CONCEPT.

PART II.
CH. VII.
Div. 2.

§ 58.
Review of the
analysis of the
laws of Logic.

distinct limitation of time and space impressed upon them by volition. Three things were distinguished in § 16, 1st, Time and space themselves; 2d, the material element; 3d, the limitations and divisions of time and space impressed upon them by the material element. The postulates express those divisions which can exist only when form and matter are present with them. Volition fixes on the divisions and retains form and matter provisionally; the divisions so fixed are the concept-form, and the expression of them is by the postulates. The simplest formula of the postulates is representative of any determinate material element whatever; it is not an expression of one object or one element existing alike in all objects, or of all objects or all matter indifferently, but it is one object, chosen for its insignificance by itself, in order to represent any determinate object whatever as determinate. A letter of the alphabet serves this purpose well. There is no simpler or better formula for the postulates than this concrete, determinate, yet representative one,—A is A; No A is Not-A; Every thing is either A or Not-A. A and Not-A are not properly speaking abstractions, they are not abstracted as universal properties or qualities of objects, and considered logically as independent of the concrete objects to which they belong; but they are signs denoting any concrete, empirical, determinate object whatever. A means this-object; Not-A means not-this-object; and the three postulates express truths concerning objects, but no other truths than are contained in the facts of perception, in the subjection of feelings to the forms of time and space. In other words, the cognitions of time and space are the condition and ground of the postulates. The A of the postulates is an object of perception fixed by attention and distinguished from every thing else by volition; and the expression A, being insignificant in itself, represents any and every possible empirical object.

It is certainly the case that a more evident truth has been attributed to the postulates, and even to more concrete and less general forms of them than the above, than has been attributed to the cognitions of time and space. There has never been a time when the postulates have not been appealed to as the test, or the conditio sine quâ non, of truth. A thing cannot at once be and not be, is the most current coin of argument, which every one must admit or be excluded from arguing. It seems at first sight to be of a certainty far superior to the certainty here claimed for the cognitions of time and space, which appear to be not older, in their character of a priori necessary truths, than the days of Kant. And it is true that, for all purposes of argument about empirical phenomena, the postulates, represented by such current phrases as A thing cannot at once be and not be, are quite sufficient and, being within the reach of every one, are best fitted for the purpose which they have, time out of mind, served and will serve. But this empirical character of theirs at once accounts for their greater currency, and shows that they are the development of more general and more recondite cognitions. They are the common ground where metaphysicians, logicians, men of science, and men in general can meet, and which all must admit to be firm. They are at once indemonstrable and empirical. As the former, it is absurd to attempt to prove them or show their certainty. As the latter, they must be capable of being resolved into non-empirical elements. This latter analysis, here attempted, is no attempt to prove the postulates, to add a certainty to them which they had not before; but it is an attempt to show how they came to be invested with that character of certainty. In other words, it is an attempt to assign their conditio essendi et existendi, as distinguished from their conditio cognoscendi, an attempt corresponding to that made in Chap. III. with respect to time and space; the only difference being that, in the last-mentioned case, the causa existendi was sought in objects in their objective, in the first-mentioned case, in objects in their subjective character; in the last case, in objects as empirical existences, in the first, in the metaphysical analysis of such objects.

A similar phenomenon has been observed in the relation of the cognitions of time and space to each other. Just as the postulates, being empirical, are more familiar than the forms of time and space, and have consequently usurped their place in men's minds, so space, being more complex, is also more familiar than time, and has become the mode in which we represent every thing to ourselves, time itself included. Space is more complex because of its three dimensions, which can be compared together; it contains in itself the conditions of its intelligibility; but we render time intelligible to ourselves by an image drawn from space, by a line, the image of the first dimension of space. Yet no statical image is really contained in the cognition of time; but time is entirely irreducible to any form of space.

The cognitions of time and space, as lying deeper than the postulates, are discovered later; they have however been familiar from the first, and certainly before the postulates, if the present account of them is true. There should be no confusion on this point. The knowledge of time and space is coeval with consciousness; the knowledge that they are coeval with consciousness is of late growth. The knowledge of the postulates is later than the knowledge of time and space, and depends upon it; but the knowledge that the postulates are necessary truths is prior to the knowledge of the corresponding fact in the case of time and space. But the knowledge that the postulates are necessary truths does not depend upon the knowledge that time and space are necessary truths; in fact it is known long before it in point of time. The earliest recognition of a necessary truth as such, that is, of such and such a truth as necessary, is the recognition that the postulates are such. This was done satisfactorily first by Aristotle; while the corresponding recognition in the case of time and space is due to Kant. The knowledge, therefore, that time and space are necessary truths, is no causa cognoscendi, no reason for our recognising the postulates as such; that is, it affords no proof of the postulates. But on the other hand the knowledge of time and space is the causa essendi et existendi of the knowledge of the postulates. The existence of the one cognition is the cause of the existence of the other. Unless we had the cognitions of time and space, we could never have arrived at the cognition of the postulates. The existence of consciousness in one mode is the cause of the existence of consciousness in the other mode. Neither the knowledge that the postulates are true, nor the knowledge that they are necessarily and universally true, depends upon the knowledge that the cognitions of time and space are necessarily true; this would be to make the former depend on the latter as their conditio cognoscendi. But they depend, both of them, upon the knowledge that the cognitions of time and space are true; this is to make them depend on these cognitions as their conditio essendi et existendi. They depend upon a knowledge of time and space, but not upon a reflection on that knowledge. To make them depend upon a reflection on that knowledge, for instance, upon the reflection that time and space are always true, or necessarily true, would be to prove them by, or deduce them from, the knowledge of time and space, as their causa cognoscendi, instead of analysing them into those cognitions.

CHAPTER VII.

METALOGICAL.

DIVISION 3. RATIO SUFFICIENS.

Λεύσσε δ' ὅμως ἀπεόντα νόῳ παρεόντα βεβαίως·
οὐ γὰρ ἀποτμήξει τὸ ἐὸν τοῦ ἐόντος ἔχεσθαι,—

Parmenides.

§ 59. IN Chapter VI. it was shown that the canon of acquisitive reasoning was common both to induction and deduction; and this canon is known as the canon of induction, namely, that the course of nature is uniform. It is an empirical law, which contains both a material and a formal element, the former not capable of being treated apart from the latter, but only as embodied in the empirical canon. The latter, or formal, element however can be abstracted and treated provisionally as a formal law; and as such it is known as the Ratio Sufficiens. It has now to be shown that this formal element, called, when treated as a provisional or abstract object, the Ratio Sufficiens, is the form of time itself. The canons employed in critical as well as acquisitive reasoning, known as the postulates of logic, have also in the preceding divisions of this chapter been shown to contain in like manner a material and a formal element; and of these the

PART II.
CH. VII.
Div. 3.
———
§ 59.
Cause and
Reason.

formal element has been shown to be resolvable into the cognitions of time and space. It remains to show the parallel circumstance with regard to the formal element of the Ratio Sufficiens, the principle of acquisitive reasoning and hypothetical and hypothetico-disjunctive syllogisms;—a task which, as I have said, has already been virtually performed by Sir W. Hamilton, Appendix I. A., Discussions, 2d edit. pp. 618-21.

Like the postulates, the law of ratio sufficiens cannot be expressed except in a shape including a material element, that is, empirically. It must always be expressed generally and representatively, whether it be as the ratio existendi, or the ratio cognoscendi. The first of these, for instance, may be thus expressed: Whatever exists must have a cause;—nothing exists without a cause; the second thus: Infer nothing without a reason. The words, Whatever, Nothing, and Cause, mean any object, no object, and some object as cause. Now both the cause, or ratio existendi, and the reason, or ratio cognoscendi, in every particular case must be given by actual experience, subject to the canon of induction, The course of nature is uniform. It would be impossible to obey the law of ratio sufficiens, in either of its branches, existendi or cognoscendi, unless the sequences and coexistences among material objects were uniform; we could never say that one particular object, A, was the cause or the reason of another particular object, B, unless they uniformly preceded and followed each other. We should indeed be still compelled to look for an antecedent, but we should be condemned never to be satisfied by finding the same consequent attached to the same antecedent. Hence the law of ratio sufficiens has been sometimes expressed: Every thing must have a cause, or a reason, why it is as it is and not otherwise; a formula which expresses the fact that the law of ratio sufficiens is bound up with, and refers to, the empirical law of the uniformity of the course of nature. It expresses not only that every object is bound to some antecedent, in fact or in knowledge, but also that it is bound to some one or more particular and unvarying antecedents. With this form of the law of ratio sufficiens, therefore, inasmuch as it is the expression of the union of the two elements, formal and material, we have nothing to do, the present purpose being to analyse the formal element in as abstract a shape as possible.

Even the simplest formula expressing the law of ratio sufficiens, taken by itself and apart from the law of uniformity, includes, as has been seen, a material part or element, just as the postulates do. We have then to analyse it farther, just as in the case of the postulates, and to see what the purely formal element in it is, apart from the matter or objects which are involved in every expression of it. It has two branches; it is both the ratio sufficiens existendi, and the ratio sufficiens cognoscendi. The principle of both will be found to be the same; but it will be requisite first to see what are the relations of these two branches to each other, one of which may be called the Cause, and the other the Reason.

The cause must always precede its effect empirically, in the order of history of objects as objects of consciousness, in time; the reason must always precede its consequent empirically, in the order of cognition, or of the history of states of consciousness, in time. I will distinguish these two orders by calling the former historical, the latter psychological; both are equally objective to reflection. Any one of its causes or effects, historically speaking, may be the reason for our inferring the existence of an object; it is psychologically only that the knowledge of the reason must precede the knowledge of the consequent. For instance, when we see blackened ruins, we infer that a building has been burnt. The burning of the building is historically earlier than the existence of the blackened ruins, but psychologically it is later. If we are told that A is a great man, we infer that he will be honoured by posterity; the cause historically being also the reason psychologically, and prior in both respects to the fact inferred.

The cause, or causa existendi, is entirely historical, and must always precede its effect historically; when we say, Whatever exists must have a cause, we mean to say, that whatever exists must have some object existing previously to it, and that, unless some object had previously existed, it could not have come into existence. When empirical observation has shown that two objects are invariably linked together in time, of which one invariably precedes and the other invariably follows; and that the taking away of the preceding object, without taking away any other of the accompanying phenomena, involves the disappearance of the following object; then we call the former the cause and the latter the effect, one of the other. The cause however, as exhibited in the ratio sufficiens alone, is not a special and invariable antecedent object, but some antecedent object, no matter what. That some object must precede objectively every object which can exist, this is the necessary truth expressed by the ratio sufficiens existendi, and the only truth of a necessary character involved in it.

In the same way in the case of the reason; the only necessary truth involved in the ratio sufficiens cognoscendi is There must be some antecedent in your knowledge before you can infer the existence of any object. The necessity in the ratio sufficiens cognoscendi is solely this, the necessity of asking Why for every thing; every assertion must have some reason for it. The formula given above, Infer nothing without a reason, stands on the same level as the formula, Every thing must have a cause; while the psychological formula corresponding to the formula, Every thing which exists must have a cause why it is as it is and not otherwise, which is compounded of the material canon of uniformity and the formal law of the causa existendi, would be something of this kind, Infer no particular object without a particular reason connected with it by experience.

But the terms cause and reason usually signify particular or special cause, and particular or warranting reason; so that it would be confusing to employ these terms in expressing the purely formal connections of the ratio sufficiens. It will be better to exhibit the two forms of the cause, and the two of the reason, in such phrases as the following:

CAUSE, OR RATIO SUFFICIENS EXISTENDI.
1st. Every thing which exists must have an antecedent.
2d. Every thing which exists must have a cause.

REASON, OR RATIO SUFFICIENS EXISTENDI.
1st. Every thing known must have an antecedent in consciousness.
2d. Every thing known must have a warrant in consciousness.

The first formula in each case is alone strictly necessary, or the embodiment of a necessary truth. The second formula in each case is merely another expression of the law of the uniformity of the course of nature, seen first from the objective side, then from the subjective. The two formulas, the first in each case, differ from each other in nothing but in the point of view being in the former historical, in the latter psychological; the former declares how objects must exist, the latter how they must be known to exist; the former declares how they are connected with each other, the latter how the consciousness of one is connected with the consciousness of the other. Now in both cases, in both modes of connection, we have before us a provisional object; in the one, the objective aspect, in the other, the subjective aspect of phenomena. The connection in the first case is objective, with abstraction of the subjective side, for which reason it has been called historical; the connection in the second case is subjective, with abstraction of the objective side, for which reason it has been called psychological and not subjective. Both cases, however, are connections of states of consciousness, both are subjective and objective at once. This connection, common to the two cases, which is at once objective and subjective, and at once universal and necessary, is the cognition of time; for, besides being universal and necessary, it is nothing more than the relation of succession, abstracted from any content or series of succeeding objects. It is the formal cognition of time which forces us back in every instance upon a previous condition of existence to that with which we begin, whether it is priority in order of thought or in order of nature, whether the previous condition is considered as adapted to cause a thought in us, or as adapted to cause an object independent of us. The same cognition of time involves also the necessity of an effect for every cause, as well as of a cause for every effect; it extends forwards into the future as well as backwards into the past, historically; and, psychologically, every thought has consequences which must lead to theories and systems capable of infinite development. This is the ground of prediction of the future from the past. Whatever object, whether of objective or subjective reference, we take as our starting point, we must go backwards a parte ante, in conceiving its causes or its reasons, and forwards a parte post, in conceiving its effects or its consequences; and in both cases in infinitum. The result therefore of the foregoing analysis is, that the cognition of time is the purely formal and necessary principle involved in all the shapes of the ratio sufficiens.

§ 60. What has been called the causa essendi, or formal cause, is nothing else than the analysis of an object in its first intention. When any object is so analysed, then either of its two aspects, the thing defined and its definition, may be called metaphorically the form, or causa essendi, of the other, or pari ratione the effect of the other; or its parts or elements of analysis may be metaphorically called causes or effects of the whole, or reciprocally causes and effects of each other within the whole. Metaphorically, because both the aspects, and all the parts and elements, are simultaneous and coexistent, and can only be called causes and effects by an unwarranted extension of the relations subsisting between objects in their second intention, or between one object and another in consciousness, to cases where the object is already assumed to be one single, though perhaps complex, object, in which neither aspect, no part, no element, precedes another. The term causation is best restricted to express relations between objects in time, as preceding and succeeding. Make any one of these aspects, or parts, or elements, an object by itself in a provisional image, and then you can consider what causes or effects it has; but whatever is coextensive with it in respect of time is not its cause or its effect, but a co-element or co-partner in the provisional object from which it is abstracted. The causa essendi, or formal cause, must be contained in the object of which it is considered as the cause; but for this relation terms have been already provided, those of definition, aspect, element, and part in analysis. Kant made reciprocity of cause and effect one of his categories, which is the conception of two objects being reciprocally conditions of each other; of which the equality of mechanical force imparted and lost, of action and reaction, the diagonal movement in the parallelogram of forces, positive and negative electricity would perhaps be among the instances. Now if either of the two forces acting in any of these cases is prior in existence to the other, it may be considered as among the causæ existendi of the other; but if they both begin to exist exactly at the same moment, then I contend that it is more reasonable to regard them as elements or component parts of one phenomenon, and not as causes of that phenomenon, or of each other. Only if an actual priority of existence is assumed or discovered can one of them be properly called cause, and the other effect.

§ 61. Here is completed the analysis of the logical

laws into laws of intuition. The intuitional principles, the cognitions of time and space, are the forms both of intuition, or perception in all its branches, and of reasoning; and there is no conflict between these two modes of consciousness. There is besides no place left for a faculty such as that which Kant calls the Reason, with its ultimate principle or Idea of the Totality of the conditions of a given conditioned object, that is, of an Unconditioned. (Kritik d. R. V. Tr. Dial. B. I. Abs. 2. vol. 2, p. 260, Rosenk. ed.) For every totality is a concept, and concepts are products of volition within the limits of perception or perceptive imagination; and the logical function of such a concept in all its branches, as a regulative principle or law for the practical exercise of reasoning, is fully performed by the law of Parcimony, resting, equally with the concept as product of volition, upon the material element, or feeling, in consciousness. There is no such faculty of reason commanding us to assume an unconditioned, and consequently we need no critical system to restrict its operation to a merely regulative function. We are under a total inability to do so if we would; we may make a false, or what Kant calls a transcendental, use of the laws of reasoning, but we cannot conceive an Unconditioned, or what Kant would call a transcendent object. (Kritik d. R. V. page 240, ed. Rosenk.) The principles of reasoning, whether distinguished or not into principles of a Kantian understanding and a Kantian reason, are not wider than those of intuition; but they are the same principles limited by volition and guided by the law of Parcimony. By exercising volition we can limit but not extend our consciousness or its objects, which are existence. Intuitional truth is not the coordinate of logical truth, but at once its source and its field. By imagining it to be its coordinate we imagine the possibility that one may transcend the other. If logical laws are objects of cognition at all, and yet not derived from time and space, on what principle are we to justify their limitation in use to objects within time and space? We shall be inevitably carried on to the assertion of an Absolute, a logical truth independent, in some incomprehensible way, of all objects known or knowable by us in time and space, and yet objectively existing. The view here taken on the other hand introduces unity into all the operations of the mind, and reduces our risk of error by one important item, the conflict of coordinate tribunals.

The incongruousness of such a system, with its double source of truth, intuitional and logical, and its critical machinery for avoiding the consequences, seems to have struck the ontological successors of Kant. For just as, in the case of Aristotle, metaphysical and ontological principles existed side by side, and contained the germs of future systems of metaphysic and ontology, and just as, in his case, the ontological principles were first seized on and carried out into systems by the philosophers of Alexandria, so in the Kritik der Reinen Vernunft there lay thoughts, which might develop into ontologies, side by side with thoughts which were purely metaphysical; and in this case again the ontological side was first seized and developed. Looking now at Kant's system of philosophy as a whole, it will be seen that the central point of the whole is the transcendental unity of apperception, the Ich denke, which accompanies, and may be perceived to accompany, every moment of consciousness and makes it a single moment. Confused impressions of sense in time and space are the raw matter into which this unity of apperception is introduced, or on which it operates. Time and space are the forms of all sensible impressions, whether in confusion or in order. But how is order introduced into them, or how are they cast into order? The unity of apperception combines them, true; but it may combine them without the least trace of regularity or uniformity. The transcendental unity of apperception would, in this case, be an unity of apperception of the sensible impressions in time and space; but there would be no knowledge of any thing, for there would be no uniformity. The transcendental unity of apperception works necessarily in the forms of intuition, time and space; they are properly its own forms, forms of bringing sensible impressions into unity; but they are not as yet knowledge. To produce knowledge, to form a regular world or Cosmos of sensible impressions in time and space, the transcendental unity of apperception, according to Kant, possesses and applies, or rather operates in and by, certain forms of thought, the Categories, which are modes of unity, modes of the transcendental unity of apperception itself; and therefore in every step of the operation there is an unity of apperception, but one employed upon the sensible impressions, and upon them in the other forms of the transcendental unity of apperception, the forms of intuition combined with the categories or category used. The transcendental unity of apperception has thus indeed two kinds of forms in which it operates, those of intuition, time and space, and those of thought, the categories; but neither the sensible impressions nor their forms of in-

KK

tuition, time and space, are objects by themselves, until combined by the unity of apperception working through some category, or mode and, as it were, ἐπιλεγχίᾳ of unity; then first arises objectivity or reality of objects. This same unity of apperception also accompanies the Idea, or Reason-concept, of an absolute totality of conditions. Now the transcendental unity of apperception is the principle of reality and objectivation of objects, as well as the principle of their truth, or their ultimate test; and, in both characters, is a principle of reasoning and not a principle of intuition. Alle Verbindung ist eine Verstandeshandlung, says Kant in the 2d edition of his Kritik.

If now, it was argued by Kant's ontological successors, any forms and modes of procedure can be found in this transcendental unity of apperception, any forms of thought, any concepts,—these must contain reality and truth itself, for they are the source of it in experience; and cannot be limited to matters contained within the intuitional forms of that apperception, which are at best only its partial and preliminary modes, and rather offer resistance to the unifying principle, the apperception, than express it fully. The apperception is essentially unity, and unity is not a principle of intuition but of thought; thought, therefore, cannot be confined within time and space, or limited to work only on objects within those forms, on pain of losing its reality. Whatever can come forward in the unity of apperception is real, consequently the Kantian Idea of an absolute totality is real; and this Idea it is which seems to have become, with Hegel, the absolute Begriff.

Some such reasoning as this, I apprehend, must have convinced those who were dissatisfied with the double source of truth proposed by Kant, intuition and thought, and with the merely regulative truth possessed by the latter wherever it transcended intuitional experience, that the Unity of Apperception, as an unity of thought and not of intuition, was the sole source of constitutive, that is, positive and theoretical, as well as of practical or regulative truth. And they may have reflected besides, that the doctrine which limited Ideas of the Reason to a merely regulative function was itself essentially only of a regulative nature, in other words, that the denying to purely formal concepts, whether of the understanding or of the reason, an independent objective existence was a proceeding founded on no other ground than an anticipation of their futility and emptiness, if they should be treated as objective and independent of a material content; and was thus itself but a practical rule for arriving at some, real or supposed, profitable result. The merely regulative character of this doctrine or procedure was no sufficient ground for restricting the ideas of the reason to a regulative function; some positive ground, valid in theory as well as practice, must be given for such a doctrine. Thenceforward their endeavour was to discover the law of the operation, or the forms essential to the operation, of thought, or in other words, to discover the particular modes of unity of apperception in which the transcendental unity of apperception, the pure ego, was clothed, or into which it was by itself transformed, the ἐπιλέγματα of its δύναμις, or the χαρακτῆρες of its ὑπόστασις. The gulf, left by Kant between intuition and thought, it was attempted to close by bringing over intuition to thought, and subsuming all the content of intuition under the operations of the pure ego, a method which has issued in the logical ontology of Hegel, as its most complete and satisfactory outcome. This Essay has taken the opposite mode of filling up the gulf, and has attempted to reduce the forms of thought to those of intuition; thus restoring the unity of consciousness as completely as the ontologists, though reversing their method; and getting rid, equally with them, of a Thing-in-itself transcendent in its nature, and of concepts which, though they ought to be merely regulative of the practical exercise of reason, are constantly mistaken for objects of a possible experience.

Whatever can be presented or represented in the forms of time and space has a certain objective existence. To be able to present or represent any object to ourselves is to assert its existence, not its so-called subjective existence only, but its objective existence also; for it is now sufficiently clear, that the popular use of the words, subjective and objective, as if they signified respectively unreal and real,—subjective existence meaning apparent and possibly mistaken existence,—is unsound and must be given up. Hence its true meaning is given to the doctrine of Descartes, that whatever he clearly and distinctly conceived existed; that existence is not a quality or attribute to be proved in addition to a concept or perception, but is involved in all clear conceptions alike. What Descartes, however, applied especially to clear conceptions, is true of all; their conception includes existence, and the only question remaining is, whether that existence is permanent or transitory.

Both fields of knowledge, intuition and thought,

being thus reduced to one, the remaining question is to distinguish apparent, not from real, but from true existence. Whatever danger there is of applying the laws of logic to pretended objects, the same danger exists of applying the laws of intuition to them. This danger is real in both cases. Its character is to imagine, in portions of time and space, a material content which does not stand the test of experience; which, believed in once, is found to vanish on further investigation. Truth has been defined to be the agreement of our imaginations, perceptions, or thoughts, with actual objects; but according to the distinction already drawn, § 42, it is properly defined as the agreement of our present with our future perceptions, when the most accurate and complete investigation shall have tested them. Erroneous and true perceptions are equally objects of consciousness; former and latter perceptions are so too; the perceptions which are to agree with objects and those objects with which they are to agree are equally subjective. The former perceptions and the erroneous perceptions may be equally clear and equally distinct with the true and the latter perceptions, but they are not the less erroneous on that account. Clearness and distinctness in perceptions are not a test of their truth; the most distinct and clear perceptions may be changed by future enquiry and by newly observed facts. The figures in a dream have often the greatest clearness and distinctness, and are accompanied by the strongest sense of reality. But why do we call them unreal and untrue? Solely because they will not bear repeated investigation, because, though we can remember them on waking with as great clearness and distinctness as other things, yet we cannot mould them into a consistent whole along with the other particular circumstances which we know co-existed with them, the room we slept in and the time of our being asleep, nor with the general tenor of experience, which is a consistent whole of which they are an incongruous portion.

It will be said perhaps here, that whatever is clearly and distinctly perceived is true so far as it goes and while it lasts; and that the error lies in drawing inferences from our clear and distinct perceptions, not in the perceptions themselves; that we infer from the clearness and distinctness of the dream-perceptions, that they will last and are independent of our will, in fact that they are real; and thus that the error is one of inference, not of perception. The first assertion I admit, namely, that the perceptions are true so far as they go and while they last; not so the second, namely, that the sense of independence and reality in the dream-figures is not a perception but an inference. Properly speaking we do not infer at all in dreaming; we exercise no voluntary, but spontaneous, redintegration; we do not say to ourselves These figures are real and independent of ourselves, but we never doubt it and, therefore, cannot reason about it. But we see them move without our suggestion, hear them speak without our suggestion, feel them touch (not violently, for that would probably imply waking) without our suggestion; and this is to perceive the independent and real. The dream-figures, then, are objects of perception, clear, distinct, and true, so far as they go and while they last. But is this what we mean by Truth? However certain we may feel of any thing for the present, there is no ground in this alone for saying that it is true; we must have, besides this, a distinct belief in its permanent character, or the notion of its remaining as it is, if compared with other perceptions; otherwise we use the word true wrongly in application to it. It is true, if it has stood and will stand the test of investigation in all lights. There is no other truth but this, the agreement of our present perceptions with others which are or shall be the result of more accurate investigation. This is a fertile doctrine, especially in the province of Ethic, where as yet it has not been much applied. All perceptions of what is morally right or wrong depend, for their truth, on their agreement with future states of the more enlightened conscience. The distinction between reality and truth must be applied also to Ethic.

§ 62. Hence it results that there is no test of truth, of present and immediate applicability. It depends upon the future. If a present perception agrees with many accurately tested past perceptions, it is a strong ground for anticipating that it will agree with future and more accurately tested perceptions. Of such a present perception we predicate with confidence that it is true. But except as matter of confidence we can never say that it is true, but only that it will be proved to be true or found to be true. This doctrine, that there is no test of truth, of present applicability, is one which it is perhaps hardest of all to admit serviceably and practically. We all treat those opinions, which we are confident will be proved to be true, as if they had already been proved to be so, and consequently the opposite opinions as if they had already been proved to be false, instead of conceiving both alike as being on their probation. Every one seeks for a test of truth, whether in a principle, or in a system. It can be found however nowhere but in continued investigation; that is to say, it is not found in any completed investigation. Yet here the rule of practice is to adopt a principle or a system as a limit of enquiry, a terminus a quo and ad quem, and to work from it and live by it as if it were true. It is the same process as that which formed the remote out of the immediate object, and the concept out of the remote object. The will says Here we take our stand. The result of metaphysical enquiry, just as that of practical experience, shows us that there is no absolute or ultimate empirical truth, but every where relative and approximate truth. It is an inflexible law of consciousness — Nihil absoluti.

Hence too arises the justification of the right, which every generation of men exercises, to pass judgment on the conceptions of all preceding generations, and to reverse or confirm their decisions; while future generations, in their turn, will weigh with truer insight this verdict itself. For as individuals increase in knowledge, so also does the race; and though some generations may be more ignorant than some that have preceded them, yet some there must arise which will be wiser. It is not the mere fact of being later in time that makes one judgment truer than another, but the fact of its being the result of a more complete investigation, of which posteriority in time is one condition. It has been said that man never possesses but always anticipates happiness; and so it may be said of truth, that as truth it is never present. It is the thought of yesterday which we address as truth; the thought of to-day, which warrants that of yesterday, needs itself the warranty of to-morrow.

It must not be concealed but freely confessed that, in giving up all notion of an Absolute and of an ontology, and in falling back on a metaphysic which is a mere analysis of the ultimate elements in empirical experience, all hope is renounced of solving that problem which has been the aim, conceived more or less distinctly, and more or less exclusively, of all philosophers from the earliest times to Hegel; a problem which may be thus expressed, to find the ground, first, of there being an existence at all, and secondly, of this existence being such as we perceive it. Hegel's solution of these problems is probably the most complete that has ever been proposed. But not only are all complete ontologies here abandoned, Hegel's among the rest, but also all ontological portions in systems which otherwise are purely metaphysical. Kant does not seem clearly to have drawn the distinction between metaphysic and ontology, and the Kritik contains both elements. He does not indeed, like Hegel, profess to account for the existence of impressions of sense generally; but he does profess to account for the order of those impressions, that is, for there being stability of nature and uniformity in the course of nature; and to that extent the Kritik is an ontology. The transcendental deduction of the categories is an account of the origin of what I call the stability and uniformity of nature, of the synthetic unity of all phenomena. "Es ist also der Verstand nicht blos ein Vermögen, durch Vergleichung der Erscheinungen sich Regeln zu machen: er ist selbst die Gesetzgebung für die

Natur, d. i. ohne Verstand würde es überall nicht Natur, d. i. synthetische Einheit des Mannigfaltigen der Erscheinungen nach Regeln geben." Werke, ed. Ros. u. Sch. vol. 2, p. 113. And again he says, page 114, "der Verstand ist selbst der Quell der Gesetze der Natur, und mithin der formalen Einheit der Natur."

Now the expressions stability and uniformity of nature have two senses, one, in which they have been employed in Chapter VI. and elsewhere in this Essay, namely, the sameness obtaining between immediate or remote objects of consciousness, and the sameness obtaining between the sequences of such immediate or remote objects; and the other, in which they express the connection of feelings as elements of objects with certain portions of time and figures of space as their formal element, it being an universal and necessary circumstance that feelings can exist only in some such portions of time and space. There is no state of consciousness in which stability and uniformity, in this second sense, do not pervade the object of consciousness; but such stability and uniformity must be conceived as coexistent and coeval with consciousness itself. In the complex empirical fact of feelings being given to us in consciousness we have the fact of their orderly arrangement, each feeling as an unity in time and space by contrast with different feelings, given also; and it is impossible to conceive or imagine feelings existing otherwise. The stability and uniformity of nature in this sense is part of the ultimate phenomenon of experience to be analysed; and in this sense too it is the ground of the stability and uniformity in the first sense, namely, that between complete objects in nature; of which no other explanation or deduction but this is possible, except it be the empirical or historical explanation of showing the growth of the conception in the empirical ego. Kant however accounts for the existence of the stability and uniformity of nature in both its senses, accounts for the synthetische Einheit aller Erscheinungen, by referring it in all its forms to the unity of transcendental apperception.

Now I argue that, if the synthetic unity of feelings, as elements of empirical objects, is an ultimate fact in the phenomenon to be analysed, if all empirical consciousness contains such a synthetic unity, it is superfluous to double this fact by seeking to refer it to a second unity, the unity of transcendental apperception; and further, that, if this synthetic unity is an ultimate fact in all consciousness, it supplies of itself the best ground for explaining the synthetic unity obtaining between empirical or complete objects, which would then arise in the empirical ego by a mere extension of the analytical process and by more accurate examination of the figures and durations of those empirical objects themselves. The unity of transcendental apperception would thus become superfluous, even to explain this more empirical case of synthetic unity, but at the same time without making this case of it an ultimate and necessary fact of consciousness. Kant assumes that a circumstance which is coeval and coexistent with all empirical consciousness must be accounted for and its cause of existence pointed out, and not only referred by analysis to its proper place in the phenomenon analysed; and he seems to me to have done so in consequence of imagining that he could picture to himself the feelings in consciousness as given to us or felt by us, in time and space certainly, but all in confusion and without any particular duration or figure whatever, in Verwirrung, with a total absence of form. In the second edition of the Kritik, where he gave a new shape to the transcendental deduction of the Categories (Supplement xiv. Werke, vol. 2. Rosenk. u. Schub. edit.), he begins by stating this somewhat explicitly. "Das Mannigfaltige der Vorstellungen kann in einer Anschauung gegeben werden, die blos sinnlich, d. i. nichts als Empfänglichkeit ist,—." Separating the elements of phenomena from each other by reference to the supposed sources from which they flowed or were produced in consciousness, the senses and understanding, he imagined them as capable of existing separately from each other, inasmuch as their supposed sources or faculties of the mind were imagined separate. Now if a total absence of form could be imagined or conceived, then the arising of form would demand an explanation, an origin or cause of it to be pointed out. But if this can not be done, as it cannot, then all that remains for us is to analyse the phenomenon into its material and formal elements. This analysis has been shown to be the ultimate step which human knowledge can take, and consequently it has been shown that all ontology or knowledge of an absolute is beyond our reach. At the same time, since this also shows that existence and consciousness are coextensive, it is plain that an absolute does not exist. Our knowledge is extended in the very fact of its being limited; and this reflection must be our recompense for the limitation.

CHAPTER VIII.

REASON.

καὶ αὐτὸς δὲ αὑτὸν τότε δύναται νοεῖν.
Aristotle.

§ 63. THE foregoing account of the functions of the mind so far as it is a cognitive power is a complete one; there is no function which is not capable of being brought under its description, and there is no part of knowledge which can be reached by any track or means exclusive of those already described. The essential unity of the functions known as perception and understanding has been shown. But a further distinction is often made between understanding and Reason, on which it may be desirable to say a few words, especially as the distinction, as a difference in kind, comes recommended to Englishmen by the honoured name of Coleridge. The real difference between them appears to me to be one of degree, expressed by or consisting in the fact that the object, on which they are employed, assumes a new aspect when the higher degree has been reached. Phenomena assume the character of objects in presence of a Subject, or, what is the same thing, the character of being objective and subjective; the former, if we regard the development of the phenomena themselves, the latter, if we regard them as the object of our own reflection; the former, from the point of view of existence, the latter, from that of consciousness. The presence of a new class of cognitions, not any difference in the cognitive function itself, is the ground of making the distinction, certainly a very important and fundamental one, between the two functions of consciousness, understanding and reason.

Reflection on itself is the distinguishing characteristic of a stage or mode of consciousness next above understanding in complexity, and this is the last stage of development of which consciousness has hitherto been capable. Consciousness first understands objects, that is, phenomena are first a collection of feelings or matter indifferently in time and space; then it reflects on itself, or, what is the same thing, on the phenomena, and distinguishes feeling generally from particular feelings, and these from qualities; and since the distinction between objects and Subject thus drawn is exhaustive, so far as we can see, the decision of reflection on any question is final, and irreversible except by a further exercise of reflection; so that reflection is the final arbiter of truth. In this way consciousness shows us its own poverty and weakness, as well as its own strength and dignity; it destroys illusions by creating them, for it gives us truths secured from doubt in exchange for notions which had not before been doubted. It destroys the appearance of certainty which before attached to our cognitions; it exhibits the inevitable nature of error, in exhibiting the necessity of progress towards truth. A new light dawns with reflection, in which we see ourselves as we are; from the nature there exhibited there is no escape, from the decision of reflection there is no appeal. Reason is our being;

and above all other intellectual needs is the need of knowing objects in their true nature.

Reflection, or reflective consciousness, has two modes or stages, the earlier and the later, differing from each other in degree of development, not in kind, which it may be proper to call the intuitive and the discursive stages of reflection, following the distinction in Milton,

> The Soul
> . Reason receives, and Reason is her being,
> Discursive or intuitive.

The names of the two stages are Self-consciousness and Reason, the former being the intuitive, the latter the discursive, stage of reflection. These two modes of reflection correspond to the two modes of direct consciousness, intuition and comparison, perception and understanding. They are a repetition of perception and understanding in a new and more advanced sphere, or with a new object. When consciousness has itself, or phenomena have themselves, for object, it proceeds in exactly the same way as when it was direct or simple consciousness, undistinguished from phenomena. All reflection is fundamentally a process of comparison; originally, it is an act which can be characterised in no other way than as a distinction between object and Subject. Synthesis is involved in all, and comparison in all but the simplest, actions of consciousness, even in perception; but just as all those actions of consciousness which resulted in the production of a remote object, notwithstanding that comparison was largely involved in the process, were called perceptions, so also, in reflection, the act of distinction which has for its object the objective and subjective aspect of things, notwithstanding that this involves comparison in a greater degree, may, when compared with its second stage, be called intuition or self-consciousness. It is only by what they are predominantly, not by what they are solely, that actions or states of consciousness are called perception, intuition, understanding, reflection, and reason.

Self-consciousness, which is the first or intuitive stage of reflection, distinguishes the pure ego or Subject from its objects, distinguishes the binding thread of feeling, common to all the changing feelings which it binds together into the empirical ego. It is this pure thread of feeling which is the object of self-consciousness. Its peculiarity is, that it cannot be made an object by itself; it is always involved in objects as their unity, it is that which feels and perceives them, or that in which they are subjective. The act or moment of perceiving that there is such a binding thread of feeling is called apperception, the Ich denke of Kant; and this must be combined with other perceptions or thoughts. The Subject is abstract feeling; and like other abstractions cannot be exhibited except in a provisional form. That this abstraction is abstract consciousness itself is what makes it appear more mysterious than other abstract notions. Thus it is that the Subject cannot be an object by itself, but only as the subjective aspect of other objects. To have the Subject for an object is the same thing as to have the distinction between the subjective and objective aspects of phenomena for an object, or to have as an object objects as the correlate of consciousness, or consciousness as the correlate of objects. This act or moment, whether separate, or in combination with others as apperception, is called self-consciousness.

Those acts or moments with which it is combined, or which contain it, are called Reason when they are predominantly acts of comparison or understanding.

§ 64. As the Subject or pure ego, but always as involved in the empirical ego, is the object of self-consciousness, so the empirical ego is the object of reason, or reflection in its discursive stage. It is the object which reflection creates; for reflection is the perception that all objects are subjective, in other words, that the empirical ego is the complex of all the states or actions or modes of consciousness bound together by the Subject. Πᾶσα ψυχὴ πάντα ἐστὶ τὰ πράγματα, says Proclus, Inst. Theol. § 195. In reality this is only a completion of the process which self-consciousness began; self-consciousness took the first step towards making the phenomenal world objective and subjective, reason makes the whole of it in detail so, and calls it the empirical ego; (historically indeed the process has been gradual, since the empirical ego has been long regarded as an object among objects;) and it calls by the name of the empirical ego whatever phenomena or classes of phenomena it has from time to time made subjective, and ultimately embraces under that name the whole objective world; for the world of any individual consciousness is the complex of the states of consciousness which it includes in present, past, and future time.

The Subject is the object of self-consciousness, the empirical ego is the object of reason; the former expresses the distinction between the objective and subjective aspects of phenomena in its abstraction, the latter expresses the same distinction in its complete, empirical, complex development. In examining and dealing with the empirical ego, reason is dealing with phenomena in both aspects at once, objective and subjective, and has the two correlates present in a single object. Reason distinguishes the two aspects of things, makes abstraction of the objective aspect, and constitutes the subjective aspect alone its own object; whereas the understanding in dealing with the same phenomena, the moments of the empirical ego, treats them as objects external to itself, either from not having drawn the distinction, or, if it has been drawn by the reason, by abstracting from the subjective aspect. The understanding, for instance, does not reflect that, in voluntary redintegration, its own volition determines what objects or parts of objects shall be examined, but seems to be guided by the objects themselves alone. It is reason which makes this discovery, in examining the connection between its states of consciousness as such. In voluntary redintegration, as performed by the understanding, the shapes which the objects assume appear to be forms of the objects alone, to be discovered in the objects by the understanding; reason traces the subjective conditions of the arising of those forms, and sees that they are entirely products of previous states of consciousness. Both the voluntary and spontaneous processes of consciousness are the objects of the reason, and reason herself works by means of, that is, is a mode of voluntary redintegration.

The operations of reason are not limited to this single reflection, that all things are subjective, or modes of consciousness, though this reflection accompanies all its operations, and distinguishes them from the operations of the understanding. All the operations of the reason deal with the empirical ego as their object; they reason about it and introduce further modifications into it. And all these operations fall into two main kinds, speculative and practical; for this is a distinction which applies to consciousness in all its branches, and consequently to reflection as well as to understanding, to the reflective as well as to the direct modes of consciousness. Reason compares one state of consciousness with another, in order to see which of them is most true, or which of them is most good; those which it perceives to be neither true nor good it endeavours to exclude from the empirical ego or from consciousness, and as it is impossible to do this completely, seeing that it is not in our power to forget beyond possibility of recurrence, reason draws as strong a line of demarcation between them as possible, and rejects the false and the bad beyond that line, thus creating from time to time an empirical ego which it calls emphatically its own, and distinguishing it from those opinions, actions, and other modes of consciousness, which it would if possible cut off from itself by forgetting them, as false and bad. When states of consciousness are rejected as bad we are said to repent of them, to turn away from them, and cast them from us. This state of consciousness is called repentance, μετάνοια.

> Was't Hamlet wronged Laertes? Never Hamlet.
> If Hamlet from himself be ta'en away
> And, when he's not himself, does wrong Laertes,
> Then Hamlet does it not, Hamlet denies it.
> Hamlet, Act 5, Sc. 2.

See too De Quincey's remarks on the term μετάνοια, in Selections Grave and Gay, vol. 2, p. 46. In the ethic of religion, the perfection or completion of repentance is the καινὴ κτίσις of St. Paul. There is no special name for the state of reason which rejects the false;

but in both cases reason is dealing with the empirical ego and remodelling it, making so far as possible a new man in place of the old. It is the will that is active here, rejecting the false and bad and remodelling the empirical ego; reason is a mode of voluntary and not of spontaneous redintegration.

Besides rejecting some states of the empirical ego, reason also brings other states into new prominence, those namely which are true and those which are good, and these reason seeks to impress upon consciousness, and to bind up with it by remembrance and repetition. In so doing it produces ideas, that is, images which contain an assumed or anticipated infinity or perfection, for an object is perfect when considered as developed in its nature in infinite time. The ideas which will be chiefly considered in the following chapter are products of reason; though it is clear that there may be ideas of concepts of the understanding, as for instance the perfect circle, and the perfect globe, and time and space, considered as infinite, are ideas.

The new self which is thus distinguished from and educed out of the empirical ego by reason has not as yet received any name; but it may properly be called the True Ego, in distinction from the empirical and the pure. It is by this true ego that we pass moral judgments on the man, as distinguished from his conduct. According as this true ego approaches our standard of truth and goodness, and also according to the degree of stedfastness and clearness with which a man cleaves to it and imprints it on his consciousness, that is, according to his enlightenment and to his will to act up to his light, we judge the man to be good or bad. Reason is the mode of consciousness to which ethic belongs; there is no ethical science apart from reason. Technic there may be, but not ethic, or practical science in its highest branch. All ultimate ends must be given by reason, and not by understanding. If we could discover what were the truths and what the objects which the reason of all men when most developed would include in the true ego, we should know what the perfect life consisted in; and if we could appeal to any one or more objects or states of consciousness as irreversibly and ineradicably best and truest for every individual consciousness, as the same objects are for our own, we should know what was the supreme happiness and the supreme duty of all men, as we now know what is the supreme happiness and supreme duty for ourselves individually. And this would be the principle or system of principles of ethical science, holding the same place in ethic, with regard to universal applicability and certainty, that time and space hold in speculative philosophy. There is however this difference, namely, that the cognitions of reason, both principles and details, both general and particular cognitions, are the fruit of the exercise of consciousness, while the cognitions of time and space are the elements of every exercise of it; the former are produced as a tree produces its fruits, as a consequence and result of its development.

The true ego thus contains less than the empirical, but what it contains is of greater value and dignity. What once was truth is now rejected as error, "καὶ γὰρ μὴ ὁρᾶν ἔνια κρεῖττον ἢ ὁρᾶν," and what once was good is now rejected as bad. Reason transforms what once was true and good into untrue and bad, and the will rejects them from the true into the empirical ego. Reason is the ultimate judge of truth and goodness, and what it declares to be such is such, just as what the eye declares to be red is red. In both cases presence in consciousness is existence, and existence is presence in consciousness. There is nothing absolute in this or in any mode of consciousness; when the reason is employed in judging of the good and bad, it is called conscience; conscience is its name in this part of its function; but there is no distinct name for its function of judging between truth and error; for this the common name Reason is employed.

The view of reason here taken is opposed to all such views as would make it consist in the logical principle of unity, a principle compelling us to unify all our conceptions, leading, with Kant, up to the three Ideas of the Pure Reason, God, the World, and the Soul. This unification is sufficiently provided for by the principle of Parcimony, and the facts on which it rests. It is opposed also to such views as those which deduce it from the power of making abstract conceptions, or of drawing conclusions from them; these are functions of the understanding, and as such are possessed in a low degree by many animals besides man. Nor again is it the moral or emotional importance of certain reflections, nor the perception of a moral value in certain truths, nor a reference of knowledge to action, or of action to moral ends, which constitutes reason; although it is true, as has been shown above, that reason is the source of morality and ethical science, and that therefore there is a close connection between them; for reason is speculative as well as practical, and both of these at once; and this character it shares with other modes of consciousness. It is not the moral value of the truths perceived that constitutes the faculty perceiving them reason; but it is the nature of the faculty or function of consciousness perceiving the truths, namely, its nature of discursive reflection, which constitutes the truths perceived ultimate truths, and, so far as they are emotional, moral truths.

Reason has often been said to be the characteristic which distinguishes man from other animals; and on the view which I have taken of reason this appears to be true. There are many other animals besides man, however, of whom it is difficult to imagine that they have not reached that stage of reflection which I may call psychological reflection, in which they distinguish between their feelings as circumscribed by the body from objects outside the body, and reason about the effects of the latter on the former, though not under the notion of causes and effects. But there seems to be no evidence to show that they can distinguish feeling generally and in the abstract from their particular determinate feelings; nor indeed that they can distinguish any general notion from particular instances of it, though this is a function of understanding as well as of reason. If they generalise, it is without knowing the nature of generalisation, that is, without fixing the general as different from the particular notions. Their language appears to have no distinctions corresponding to such a distinction of notions.

Man however not only redintegrates voluntarily, but does so by fixed rules of abstraction and generalisation; he not only reflects psychologically, but he distinguishes himself from his feelings as well as his feelings from qualities in space. This is the condition of all human culture.

PART II.
CH. VIII.

§ 64.
Reasoning
reflection.

In the exercise and not the bare possession of reason lies the dignity of man, in the expansion of his faculties, in the operations performed by his reason, and not in the single reflection which accompanies them and conditions them. The perception that representations are, as such, objective, and that they can be recalled and banished by volition, is perhaps the first step in the exercise of the discursive stage of reflection. Other animals certainly have trains of redintegration, both voluntary and spontaneous; but there is no evidence to show that they have distinguished representations from presentations, and found one subjective, the other objective; or that they have found representations objective; or lastly have found presentations subjective; in other words, that they have reflected on their relation to the world about them; though they may have drawn the primary distinction between extended matter and feeling, and represented the latter by a rudimentary language.

§ 65.
Retrospect of
metaphysical
philosophy.

§ 65. Since metaphysic itself is an operation, or a particular application, of the Reason, it may perhaps not be considered out of place here to take a brief retrospect of the course which the human mind has followed in reflecting on, or applying reason to, the phenomena of experience in their most general aspect, that is, of the course of metaphysical philosophy, from an early epoch to the present day; sometimes exhibiting and always bearing in mind the distinction of metaphysical from ontological, speculative from practical, and direct from reflective theories. Those which are at once purely reflective, speculative, and metaphysical will be found to make but a very small portion of what is commonly included in the history of philosophy. Our present point of view, the position occupied in this Essay, will of course be the clue adopted to guide us in this retrospect; and I shall not attempt to do more than indicate the most salient and cardinal points, without attempting any thing like an outline of the whole history of philosophy.

The philosophical system of Plato was the carefully and critically elaborated result of a study of the theories of previous philosophers, among whom perhaps Parmenides had, and deservedly, the greatest influence. He included in his survey all branches of human knowledge as they then existed, and conceived more perfectly than any of his predecessors a system more universal than any of theirs, and turning on distinctions more subtil and more central. This system was the Dialectic, the Theory of the Εἴδη. It has been often described by historians of philosophy, and its chief features and their concatenation exhibited. I shall confine myself to showing what it was from the point of view of this Essay. It was a system at once of logic and of existence, both logical and ontological, in which both elements existed mutually involved and undistinguished from each other. Logic and metaphysic were both one with Plato, his forms of thought, the εἴδη, were forms of objects; they were the former, or logical, because they were the latter, or forms of things or existences, αὐτὰ τὰ ὄντα. He did not take general notions as logical forms, and then attribute to them a real and separate existence; but he had not gone so far as to distinguish logical notions from real. General notions were not with him the means of investigation, or rather they were so only because, and so far as, they were the objects of investigation. General notions, as we call them, were the only real existences, and there was a harmonised or organic world of general notions in and behind the particular notions or αἰσθητά. Instances of these are the following three pairs as they are exhibited in the Sophistes:

τὸ ὂν	τὸ μὴ ὂν	Being and Not-being.
ταὐτὸν	θάτερον	Sameness and Difference.
στάσις	κίνησις	Rest and Motion.

Each of these six εἴδη had a double sense, according as it was used in what may now be properly called its first or its second intention; τῶν ὄντων τὰ μὲν αὐτὰ καθ' αὑτά, τὰ δὲ πρὸς ἄλληλα ἀεὶ λέγεσθαι. Sophistes, Steph. 255. In the first intention they were τὰ μὴ ἐθέλοντα ἀλλήλοις μίγνυσθαι. In the second intention they were τὰ ἐθέλοντα ἀλλήλοις μίγνυσθαι. id. 256. It would appear that all general terms or εἴδη were to be considered in the same way, and were of the same nature as these six. And these would constitute together τὸ ὄντως ὂν, when used in their first intention or as categories. Objects of sense which fell under a general term in its first intention would be that general term in its second intention, and would be said to share in it, μετέχειν, as their ἰδία. For instance, in the case of objects different from each other, Plato says ἓν ἕκαστον γὰρ ἕτερον εἶναι τῶν ἄλλων, οὐ διὰ τὴν αὑτοῦ φύσιν, ἀλλὰ διὰ τὸ μετέχειν τῆς ἰδέας τῆς θατέρου. No particular object of perception, αἰσθητὸν, but only these general notions themselves, would have a first intention, that is, would be real existences; particular objects of perception would be as it were receptacles of the second intentions of various general notions, or εἴδη, like converging rays from various luminaries meeting in many different foci. Thus first intentions, which belonged only to general notions, or εἴδη, were the Real Existence of Plato. Objects which were the same were examples of Sameness, or Sameness in its second intention; objects which moved were examples, or the second intention, of Motion; objects which were black, hot, hard, &c., were examples of Being, and at the same time of Not-being; for they partook of the nature of black, hot, and hard, and did not partake of the nature of white, cold, and soft. The same object might at the same time be an example, in two points, of opposite general notions; it might be the same with some objects, and thus an example of sameness, and different from other objects, and thus an example of difference. General terms in their first intention were the only things which would not mix with one another, though they would mix with the same particular object, that is, in their second intentions. This at least was the case with the εἴδη as contrasted with the αἰσθητά, or as long as they were used as an explanation of the world of particular visible and tangible objects, or seen as existing in that world.

But Plato did not leave the matter here. He proceeds, in the Parmenides, to the analysis of the εἴδη, αὐτὰ τὰ ὄντα, themselves. There the problem proposed by Socrates and solved by Parmenides is this, ὥσπερ ἐν τοῖς ὁρωμένοις διήλθετε, οὕτω καὶ ἐν τοῖς λογισμῷ λαμβανομένοις ἐπιδεῖξαι. Steph. 130. Parmenides, who is the mouthpiece of Plato, shows that the εἴδη themselves have second intentions as well as first intentions, and that they themselves are derived from one supreme εἶδος,—τὸ ἕν,—just in the same way as the αἰσθητά are derived from them. Of this supreme εἶδος, τὸ ἕν, he shows that it has all the contradictory predicates that can be named, at the same time that, considered as a concept-form or in its second intention, it has no predicates and is pure nothing. It is impossible however here to enter farther on the vexed question of the interpretation of this dialogue. All that I wish farther to show is, that Plato's supreme εἶδος, the τὸ ἕν, like the εἴδη which have their being from it, is a notion drawn from intuition and not from logic. Plato had a visual image before him in naming τὸ ἕν, as we should naturally suppose of ourselves, and as is evident from what Aristotle says in his account of Plato's theory in Metaph. Book I. chap. 6, namely, that Plato made τὸ ἕν the οὐσία or τὸ τί ἦν εἶναι of a ὕλη, and that this ὕλη was a δύας, consisting of τὸ μέγα and τὸ μικρόν, words which plainly have a visual signification.

Plato's Dialectic therefore was a logic, but it was an intuitional logic; it *saw* the general notion as existing in and behind the particulars. It never occurred to Plato that the truths which he reached by reasoning were less real than the objects which he started from to reach them, that by reasoning he could possibly have objects presented in a less real or true shape than before he began to reason; the new world discovered by reasoning was the real and the true world, which he had attained so and so far to see. Plato left philosophy as a system of absolute necessary truth; all error attached to the individual merely, and to him only so far as he did not reason; the true essences were existing, it only needed to see them. If others did not see them as he did, it was because they did not reason at all, not because they reasoned wrongly; because they remained in the αἰσθητά and did not see the εἴδη; for to see the εἴδη was to reason, and nothing else but seeing the εἴδη was reasoning. Whatever was merely subjective was fleeting and false; whatever was true was objectively existing and eternal; it was found to be true only because it existed.

There was no doubt a great and fundamental difference of character between Aristotle and Plato, a difference which is seen reappearing in numerous cases of philosophers, so that it has been said that every man is born either Platonist or Aristotelian. But this at least is certain to me on the other hand, that, had Plato lived when Aristotle did instead of in his own day, and had he then found philosophy existing as he left it himself, had he, instead of Aristotle, been the pupil of a man who held his own philosophy in that stage which it had reached when Aristotle was his pupil, he would have taken the very step which Aristotle took, and introduced the very same development. That step consisted in transforming the τὸ ὄντως ὂν into the τὸ ὂν ᾖ ὄν. In that little phrase lies hid the separation of ontology and metaphysic, taken together, from logic. Logic becomes volitional and, as a consequence, knowledge becomes relative to different individuals. Many men may reason, though they do not reason alike or to the same result. Every object, says Aristotle, has many aspects, some or all of the ten categories; seize on any one or more of these and hold it fast; if you take the first category, that of οὐσία, you then consider the object ᾖ ὄν, if the second, that of τοσὸν, you then consider the object ᾖ τοσόν τι. Now it is true that all these aspects are really existent in the object; but then each of them is not like Plato's truth the one thing to be seen, but one thing among many to be seen. A guide to truth is therefore needed, some criterion to tell us which of these aspects we are to see. A man seizing on one of them reasons just as much as a man seizing on another of them; the question is, whether he reasons equally to the purpose, that is, to his own purpose, the object which he has chosen to examine. Hence arose a separation of the laws and method of reasoning which were common to all enquirers, whatever aspect of things or whatever purpose they had in view, from the laws and forms of each separate class of phenomena. There arose thus two classes of general notions, one abstracted from objects, the categories, which was a classification of objects on the principle of the elements or qualities found by analysis in all objects; the other,—which was the result of a comparison of these categories with each other, and especially of the contrast between the first of them, οὐσία, with the other nine,— the logical categories, as they may be called, ὅρος, ἴδιον, γένος, and συμβεβηκός, or, as Porphyry gives them, γένος, εἶδος, διαφορά, ἴδιον, and συμβεβηκός. On the relation between these two classes, the categories of existence and of logic, the categories and the predicables, see Topica, Book I. cap. 7. The predicables together with the postulates, which latter Plato also states and appeals to, make a kind of machinery outside of objects, to be employed in sifting them, a battery to be worked ab extra. The importance of this step taken by Aristotle was, that a class of objects, these general logical notions, was found, which clearly owed its origin to volition, was an artificial creation of the mind, and yet was of equal certainty with the objects on which it was employed.

The separation wrought by Aristotle was essentially a further separation of the subjective point of view from the objective; for it separated what was volitional in the search after truth from what was unavoidable and contained in the object only. In every investigation you had now to choose your point of view, and determine as a preliminary what aspect you would have presented to you. Hence a number of partial, relative, systems of truth, relative to the point of view chosen, instead of one sole system of truth, like the Dialectic; and side by side with these partial systems, another distinct and developed system, partial also but formal and generally applicable, the Theory of Logic.

But the separation of Subject and Object was not yet complete; and this it must be before the complete correlation of the two could be seen. Although Aristotle had separated the subjective from the objective aspect of phenomena, finding truth in both aspects; although he had established subjective theories of phenomena as separate from their objective counterparts in nature, and had formed a system of pure thought by the laws of which subjective theories were formed, and formed in harmony with their objective counterparts; yet he did not go so far as to separate ontology from metaphysic, and still retained the notion of an absolute existence; his τὸ ὂν ᾗ ὂν was still an existence by itself as well as a subjective abstraction. The οὐσία of Aristotle was the foundation of all the other categories, necessary to them all and each, that which could not be abstracted from in thought. τὰ καθ' ἕκαστα were all ὄντα, and their existence whether in connection with attributes or by itself, ᾗ ὂν, no less than Plato's τὸ ὄντως ὄν, was an absolute existence. And the same may be said of Der transcendentale Gegenstand of Kant, only that it was unknowable. Hence Aristotle did what Kant refused to do, and added to his other partial and special systems of truths another, which investigated τὸ ὂν ᾗ ὂν, which we have in the treatise now known as the Μετὰ τὰ φυσικὰ; a treatise which, though it bears every mark of Aristotle's intellect, yet cannot be supposed to have received its final shape from him; the result of which was an οὐσία in all respects like τὰ καθ' ἕκαστα, complete or empirical objects really existing, except that it was eternal, infinite, and immaterial.

Here the progress of speculative metaphysic was checked for many centuries. Until Descartes, no one arose capable of carrying on the development of metaphysic from the point where Aristotle left it, of proceeding to the separation of ontology from metaphysic, and educing reflection out of direct understanding. No one again occupied the same central and commanding position occupied by the "masters of those who know." The remaining schools of philosophy in Greece were all schools of practical philosophy, Stoic, Epicurean, Cynic, Cyrenaic, the Academics, and the Sceptics; they were not exclusively indeed but primarily and predominantly practical; speculative knowledge was not their chief purpose, but only so far as it was requisite to give a philosophical and consistent basis to their practical theories. At Alexandria arose a school, which was indeed purely speculative, the Neo-Platonists, of whom the greatest known to us are Plotinus and Proclus. But these were not distinctively metaphysicians but ontologists; the One Supreme Existence, τἀγαθόν, was their object; to be reached either by intuition or dialectic. They abandoned the position occupied by Aristotle, from which an advance was still possible by further distinction of the processes of thought, and struck into one of the paths, the ontological, to which they made metaphysic subordinate, instead of renouncing the path of ontology or advancing in both with equal steps. They stood to Aristotle in a very similar relation to that in which Fichte, Schelling, and Hegel stand to Kant. Plato had not separated metaphysic from ontology; Aristotle, in separating logic, had begun but had not completed that separation. Plotinus and Proclus took their stand on Platonism, which they developed with the aid of the additional light derived from Aristotle, and thus bound up metaphysic with ontology more closely than before. In many shapes they kept repeating indeed the conception of Parmenides,

ταὐτὸν δ' ἐστὶ νοεῖν τε καὶ οὕνεκεν ἐστι νόημα·

but it remained with them a paradox equally as with him, for they did not make it clear in what way this unity of thought and fact was to be understood. The light which was ultimately to be thrown upon the paradox and exhibit it as a truth came from another source, and from facts of a different order from those with which philosophers were at that time engaged.

These new facts, the importance of which to philosophy was in the end so great, were the religious emotions, facts or phenomena in the nature and history of consciousness, the delight felt in worshipping, obeying, and loving God as a Father who knew and loved his children. Such feelings had long been familiar to the Hebrew race, which may be regarded as the home of emotional, as Greece of intellectual, philosophy. The great writers of the Hebrew Scriptures alone had adequately expressed the deep religious emotions of the heart of man; and these, summed up as they were into one pure religion by Christ, were now communicated and took root in nations till then familiar only with Grecian culture. The effect of the introduction of these new facts into philosophy, the effect of the religious emotions becoming the common property of all men, either as proved and felt realities or as facts admitted by common consent, was to raise, in the estimation of philosophers, the personal importance of the human soul, to turn their attention to what it was in its capacities, its history, and its destiny, to make it appear the great phenomenon, the great existence in the world, no longer an accident but the final cause of the whole created universe. God and the soul of man, as the seat of the religious emotions, became thus the two chief objects of philosophy; and the world, which in purely Grecian philosophy had played the chief part, became a scene in which the destiny of man was to run its course. It was religion, the pure religion preached by Christ, which, when made known to the Grecian world (and it was fitted to be made known by its purity), wrought this change. But the fruits were not yet to be reaped. Two processes had before that time of harvest to be gone through, and gone through simultaneously; first, the two trains of thought, Hebrew and Greek, had to be incorporated into one complete philosophical system, and secondly, the nations of modern Europe had to work out this philosophy and bring it to a point corresponding to that at which Aristotle had stood in Grecian philosophy; that is to say, the insight into the distinction of ontology from metaphysic had to be attained by the schools of modern Europe.

These processes occupy the time from the establishment of Christianity as a religion to the days of Descartes. Two periods may be distinguished as occupying this time, the first of which may be characterised as that of the Fathers of the Church, the second as that of Scholasticism, the philosophy of the Middle Ages. Throughout the Middle Ages, from Alcuin who died A.D. 804, to Jean Charlier de Gerson who died A.D. 1429, two streams of speculation in philosophy are to be distinguished, that of ontology and that of metaphysic, running either separately or combined. As instances of philosophers who are predominantly of the former kind are to be mentioned John Scotus Erigena and St. Anselm, predominantly of the latter, Abélard and William of Occam. The Realists may be considered as combining the two. The history of the philosophy of the Middle Ages is to be regarded as a struggle of philosophy to cast off the dominion, not of religion, but of ontology, which came disguised generally in a theological dress. It was not theology but ontology which was in process of separation from metaphysic. Theology, which is the philosophy of religion, was purifying itself from ontology, just as metaphysic was doing. Religion indeed, as distinguished from theology, that is, from the speculative doctrines in which from time to time it is presented to the understanding or the reason, was the instrument which supplied the perceptions out of which reflection arose, out of which Descartes remodelled metaphysic; for it was religion in which the sense of personality, self-consciousness, was so strong as to be necessarily forced upon the attention of philosophers. Whether it would ever have been so forced upon their attention if the Hebrew race, or the Semitic races, had not existed, is another question, impossible perhaps at present to decide. The metaphysical philosophy of the Middle Ages, with its dominating controversy between Realism and Nominalism, that is, between metaphysic mixed with ontology and metaphysic pure, is a painful working back to the point of view which Aristotle occupied, and a rediscovery of his meaning. But at the same time it was a reproduction of his meaning in a new and original mould, so that the form was simpler and clearer, and the contradictions which Aristotle's system contained, in its combination of ontology with metaphysic, were brought to view. This was a great step in advance, although no one as yet arose capable of introducing a principle of solution for those contradictions. Jean Charlier de Gerson's work, De modis significandi and De concordiâ Metaphysicæ cum Logicâ, a work dated Christmas Eve, 1426, may be taken as an exponent of the results obtained by Scholasticism; and it is surprising to see the close agreement between it and modern Kantian, and therefore also of much post-Kantian, philosophy. It is the result of previous philosophising, and the seed of modern philosophies. It is the bud which contains all the flower compressed and undeveloped, needing only the life-giving breath of genius to quicken it into flower and fruit. It still speaks of existence, of objects, of mind, as if they were things well known in themselves and needing no explanation. Descartes' question, Am I? and his answer, I think, produces out of this philosophy the philosophies of Locke, of Leibnitz, of Berkeley, of Hume, of Kant and his successors. When these appear, each in their turn, they are occupied with the same phrases, the same distinctions which meet us in Gerson's work. What was new and important in Descartes' question was, that it expressed a resolution to approach philosophy from the subjective side, to examine, not what things were, but how we could know what they were. Henceforth, this resolution being followed up by other philosophers, metaphysic became subjective in a partial sense, that is, it became psychology, an enquiry into the conditions of knowledge. This however would not have been possible, had not the human mind been long familiarised with states of consciousness as 'objects, and accustomed to regard its thoughts and feelings, and the systems into which these were moulded, as objective and existing realities. And this was owing chiefly to the introspective character of the religious philosophy of Christianity.

Between Gerson and Descartes came a period of preparation and transition, in which two other sources of instruction for metaphysic were disclosed and applied, just as had been done previously by Christianity. One of these sources was the great discoveries in physical science, the other was the more complete acquaintance with the literary and scientific writings of the Greeks, known as the Renaissance; in other words, a development of the human mind in two directions, first in the special sciences, secondly in the Literæ Humaniores. Of religion, of the literæ humaniores in all their branches, and of the empirical sciences in all their branches, physic, physiology, and psychology, metaphysic is the constant and inseparable companion, whether we judge as in the present case from its history, or as before from the analysis of its nature. Of the great names of this transition period I will mention only one, Giordano Bruno, Il Nolano, memorable here for his opposition to the doctrine of Aristotle about space. He proved that space was infinite κατὰ πρόσθεσιν, that the universe

§ 65.
Retrospect of metaphysical philosophy.

was one and unlimited. This was the metaphysical application of the astronomical doctrines of Copernicus; and is an instance of metaphysic owing its development, from time to time, to following in the track of the empirical sciences and adopting their discoveries. His doctrines about space Giordano Bruno had derived from Copernicus; but he also drew attention to time. On this subject he held a Platonic doctrine, namely, that time was non-essential to existence, that eternity was the negation of time, and that potential and actual existence were the same thing. Both doctrines, that as to space and that as to time, were destined to produce their effects in future philosophies.

Descartes and his successors.

When Descartes explained existence by consciousness,—cogitatur, he gave the real and the true meaning to the term existence. This relative existence was what philosophers and all men had always meant and understood by existence without knowing it; they had never had any other existence in their thoughts than this, nor was it possible that they should have had any other. But now the point of view of philosophy was changed; ever since that time philosophers enquired, not what objects were, but what they were known as; not what the conditions of objects were, but what were the conditions of our knowledge of them. Hence the mind and its nature was the object of research; henceforth philosophy approached from the subjective side of the shield, and psychology became closely, almost indistinguishably, united with metaphysic. Men began at the beginning, with the investigation of perception. Locke led the brawls, with Nihil in intellectu quod non prius in sensu. Leibnitz followed with the amplification, Nisi ipse intellectus. He added indeed an ontology, the ontology of forces, in the Monadologie. Spinoza gave also an ontology, founded on the scholastic notion of substance. Great as the ontological works of the two latter writers are, and though Spinoza's certainly is the enduring work of genius, yet they are byways from the main road of metaphysic. Berkeley, returning to the main road, analysed the notion of Matter into perceptions of mind; and Hume analysed the notion of Mind into perceptions of consciousness. Hume was no sceptic. Philosophical analysis is not scepticism, though it is impossible for the human mind to rest in analysis unless a bond of union is discovered by the analysis itself; for such analysis destroys old doctrines without constructing new ones. Kant, called erroneously — and just as Niebuhr in Roman History was thought to destroy, whereas in reality he built up — der alles-zermalmende, taking an all-comprehending view of the field of philosophy, laid the foundation, in his doctrine of time and space, and in his connection of the reasoning functions with these forms of intuition by his "Ich denke," for the completion of the subjective course of philosophy, on which it had entered with Descartes. There is one single chain of thought connecting Locke with Kant; and each link is formed by some philosopher taking the thought of his predecessor and giving it a new shape by drawing some new conclusion from it. Locke, considering the mind as a tabula rasa written on by external objects of sense, made these external or material objects the realities of existence. Berkeley, discontent with this as materialism, showed that these material objects were modes of the mind's own consciousness, and assumed the mind or soul as their cause, and assumed

God as the cause of the mind. Hume, reflecting on this view of things, showed that the notion of cause, assumed by Berkeley, was drawn from the successions of material objects as known to the mind, and that therefore the objects assumed by Berkeley as causes were themselves part of that consciousness of which they were assumed as pre-existing causes. Kant, dwelling on this view of Hume's, took up the view of Leibnitz, Nisi ipse intellectus, and showed that the forms of consciousness in intuition and thought accompanied all its objects and gave them consistency. Sense gave impressions, but the mind formed these first into objects by its own unity of apperception. But though the unity of apperception] was every thing, was the source of the reality of objects, it had no use except in application to impressions of sense. It was wider than the field of sense to which it was applied. This was the point seized on by Fichte, Schelling, and Hegel. They argued, Can the Transcendental Object formed immediately by the unity of apperception, which is the source of all reality, itself have no reality, merely because no impressions of sense correspond to it? Rather this transcendental object is the true reality. Their effort accordingly was to deduce, or construct, the world of impressions of sense out of the transcendental object or the operation of thought in its unity of apperception. They saw unity in consciousness, unity in the world, and unity in both connected; their error, as it appears to me, was that they pitched upon a function of consciousness, as fundamental and ultimate, which was not so, but was on the contrary a mode of another simpler function, namely, intuition. The unity of apperception cannot account for intuition in the forms of time and space nor for the existence of impressions of sense; but these can account for the unity of apperception, which results from them, and contains them all.

The choice of a derivative function of consciousness and the erection of it into the whole, causes Fichte, Schelling, and Hegel, to become ontologists, and the particular function of consciousness which they choose, being the intellectual function of reasoning, makes them ontologists of the same school as Plotinus and Proclus. Ταὐτὸν τὸ εἶναι καὶ τὸ νοεῖν, says Plotinus, and ἐπὶ τοῦ ἤδη ἐν ἄμφω. Enn. III. Book 8. § 7. If an unit of thought, a concept of any kind, is the universe, the universe must be an absolute. But in reality all concepts are limits imposed by volition, and imply an existence beyond that limit.

Whatever may be embraced in any concept, in any whole of thought, there remains always a beyond, both in time and space. Take existence as the absolute, and there is consciousness outside it perceiving it; take consciousness perceiving existence as the absolute, and you are yourself outside it perceiving it. Nevertheless, though the two correlates, existence and consciousness, form no absolute either in correlation or by inclusion, yet the doctrine of their correlation is the completion of the science of metaphysic, and is the key-stone to a structure of coherent doctrines which has to fear no reversal from the progress of knowledge in other directions. The subjective and objective sides of philosophy and of existence are again united as in the philosophy of Plato, but with this difference, that there they were undistinguished, but here distinguished from each other; equally inseparable in both cases, but in the latter involving

PART II.
CH. VIII.
165
Retrospect of metaphysical philosophy.

the elimination of the absolute and of its science, ontology. Could Plato have lived in the days of Kant, he would have philosophised as Kant did; just as he would have philosophised as Aristotle did, had he lived in the days of Aristotle.

The ground for this assertion of the identity between these great men is, that they all agree in the kind of reasoning which they predominantly employ. Their systems are all of them instances of extraordinarily vigorous exertions of the reason as distinguished from the understanding. Reason is always asking, not what results can be deduced, but what is the meaning, significance, or value of such and such a fact, whether premiss or result, to myself. Reason and understanding are two modes of reasoning which are carried on side by side or in conjunction, two strands of one rope, each of which modifies the results of the other. Whatever the results of the understanding are, at any period in the history of philosophy, the shape into which they are thrown by a vigorous reason will be very similar. The differences of two systems of philosophy will depend on two things, first, on the difference of the results of the understanding, the advances made in the special sciences, and secondly on the different degree of vigour in the reason of the several philosophers. But supposing these philosophers to have equal degrees of vigour in their reason, then each will represent the same results of science in the same way; and when any of them sees what were the results of positive science known to any of his predecessors, he can then enter fully into the philosophy which that predecessor founded upon them, and comprehend his meaning, for in the same position he would have done the same thing.

§ 66. The history of metaphysical philosophy is briefly this, that it begins by being entirely and solely, as it thinks, objective, then gradually separates the perceptions, thoughts, and systems of consciousness from the nature and operations of objects, and finally returns on its steps by uniting the two series as correlates of each other, and considering itself as the subjective aspect of the world, and the world as its own objective aspect. From being objective it becomes subjective. But metaphysic is not an isolated instance of this phenomenon; the same course is followed in other cases also, in all fields of mental activity where reason or reflection is the mode of consciousness predominantly employed. First take the different position which moral and physical science occupy to each other in the conception of ancient and modern philosophers. It is well known that, when Socrates turned his attention to moral subjects and to human actions in preference to physical subjects, he thought himself and was thought by others to be bringing philosophy down from a high to a low function, from heaven to earth as it were. The familiarity with human actions and human motives was mistaken for a real acquaintance with them and their laws; while the laws of the physical universe and the nature of the objective world were considered to have something sublime and divine, and to be the proper objects of philosophical investigation. Modern science, as well as modern feeling, entirely reverses this view of things. While it is acknowledged that in investigating nature we can never reach an absolute, any more than we can in moral subjects, it is yet also acknowledged that the laws of the physical universe are simpler and more open to investigation than those of the mind, and that the methods which have succeeded in explaining so much in the former field must be also employed in the latter. This view is warranted by our increased experience, and grounded on a more accurate acquaintance with moral as well as with physical subjects. Our point of view having become subjective, we see the complex character of moral enquiries.

The same is the case within the field of ethic itself. Both Plato and Aristotle treated the question objectively; τἀγαθόν, τὸ τέλιον, τὸ αὔταρκις, εὐδαιμονία, all included in the phrase the Summum Bonum, or, as in our days it appears, Utility, in the broad sense attached to it by Bentham and his followers, was the turning point of the whole discussion. Religion, the religion of Christianity, was the means of introducing into European ethic another conception; or rather it was in religion, in that part of the ethical field, that another conception arose, the conception of Conscience and its phenomena, the sense of right and wrong, of righteousness and wickedness, as the turning point of ethic. This is the subjective aspect of εὐδαιμονία. Each is the other viewed from the opposite side. One imposes duties, the other proposes ends; one looks only to what the agent thinks right or his duty at the moment, as St. Paul says, "Whatsoever is not of faith is sin;" the other enquires into the probable results of such and such an action; one regards only one single state of consciousness, the feeling existing in the moment of action; the other compares two states of consciousness together as end and as means. Both aspects are equally essential to ethic, and each is inseparably involved in the other; but there is still wanting a scientific view of ethic treating of both aspects as coessential, and thus doing for subjective ethic what Aristotle did for objective.

Yet Aristotle's objective treatment throws great light on the subjective side of ethic. He required a definition, at least provisional, of happiness, and concluded that it was ψυχῆς ἐνέργειά τις κατ' ἀρετὴν τελείαν, and consequently that ἀρετή was to be examined in order to determine what happiness, or εὐδαιμονία, was; in other words, he suspended the nature of happiness on that of virtue. Eth. Nic. I. 13. Again he defines virtue as the property, quality, or state of doing perfectly the particular work which one is fitted to do by nature, of performing perfectly the functions proper to the being or creature who performs them. This is nothing but obedience to the ultimate laws of nature; in other words, it is the conception of Duty, only of duty conceived not as immediately and infallibly made known to us by a moral sense of right and wrong, but by a careful examination of what the laws of our nature are. Happiness is a state of feeling; the sense of right and wrong, the immediate dictate of conscience, is a state of feeling also; neither is in truth more subjective, or more objective, than the other. As Aristotle required a definition of the state of feeling called happiness, so the moderns require a definition of the state of feeling called the sense of right and wrong. The definition of both is the same; it is that they consist in ἀρετή, in a perfect performing of functions. The perfect performance of natural functions by a conscious being acting voluntarily is a state of consciousness containing two things, first, the sense of happiness, secondly, the sense known as a good conscience. Now the order of these things cannot be reversed; having begun by

Part II. Ch. VIII.
§ 6d. Other domains of the reason.

enquiring, What is happiness? and, What is a good conscience? and having received the answer, The perfect performance of natural functions, and then proceeding to enquire, What is this perfect performance, or wherein does it consist? it is not possible to reply, In the sense of happiness, or, In the sense of a good conscience. This is a circle, and not further knowledge; and we want some further determination of virtue. Nor yet is it possible to reply, In making others happy, or, In enabling them to have a good conscience. For the question recurs again, with greater obscurity, What is the happiness, and what is the good conscience of others? It is clear that, if we do not know what they are in ourselves, we do not know what they are in others. There is then only one way in which the answer to the question, What is virtue? is to be found. It is in an examination, by reasoning reflection, of the entire field of consciousness in the empirical ego. And this is what all ethical enquiry must be, namely, an exercise of reason on the conative function of the empirical ego.

Now here there are four things to be observed: first, that the enquiry is no longer conceived as objective alone, or as an enquiry into happiness as if it was a possession, like wealth, external to the mind, nor yet as subjective alone, or as an enquiry merely into what action conscience dictates at any particular moment, for the dictate of one day may contradict the dictate of another day, and to occupy oneself only with the dictate of the present moment is to reject ethical enquiry altogether; but that the enquiry is objective and subjective at once, an enquiry into what happiness, a good conscience, and virtue are, as identical with the enquiry into what they are conceived as, and will be conceived as, in general terms, by the steadiest exercise of thought; secondly, that, in consequence of this, the enquiry is one conducted by, or an instance of, reason and not understanding; thirdly, that the nature or essence of the three objects, happiness, a good conscience, and virtue, is to be cognitious as opposed to feelings, for the two former which are feelings are determined by the latter which is a cognition, and the further determination of which must be a cognition also; and that consequently, in passing from happiness and a good conscience to virtue, we have passed from the domain where feeling predominates, though without excluding cognition, to the domain where cognition predominates, though without excluding feeling; from the domain of the sequence of actions as external facts of experience, to the domain of the ethical nature of those actions; from conduct simply, that is, from being actors only, or from being spectators of action only, to the ethical science of conduct, that is, to being actors and spectators at once of our own actions; and fourthly, that while reason is the tribunal which judges, or the investigator which discovers, what virtue is, there is no criterion, by which it judges or investigates, except what reason itself contains, from whatever source it may have obtained such criterion.

The essence or ultimate ethical nature of an action consists in the form or connection in which the feeling appears. Pleasure and interest are immediate feelings which cannot be farther analysed, the time and space elements are indifferent to them; the sense of doing or having done right at any particular moment is also a feeling which cannot be farther analysed, and to which the time and space elements are indifferent. These are the motives of conduct, final causes as efficient; states of consciousness which are ultimate feelings, incapable of further analysis. But happiness, εὐδαιμονία, the summum bonum, on the one hand, and on the other hand a good conscience as a permanent state of consciousness, these are not ultimate indecomposable states of consciousness, but the sum and completion, or rather the perfection, of the corresponding simple feelings. The question is, what these are in their nature. Now as these are the ἀρετή, or virtue, of the empirical ego as a whole, so the sense of doing right or having done right at any particular moment is the virtue of that particular action or moment; and this sense of doing right is always pleasureable, that is, always contains a sense of pleasure or interest which is the motive power in it. The virtuous character of any action known, this alone makes it pleasureable and gives it efficiency as a final cause; the pleasure or interest it involves leads us to do it, and this pleasure or interest is derived from nothing else but from the knowledge that it is a part of the virtue of the whole empirical ego. There are pleasures and interests, many and keen, which are independent of such knowledge, or contradictory to such knowledge, that is, which are not virtuous, and which are vicious. The practical problem therefore is, to make the pleasures and interests which are derived from the sense of doing right or which can be combined with it, predominate over and finally exclude those which cannot be combined with it; to make the sense of doing right, deduced from the knowledge of the virtue of the empirical ego, the criterion of what actions are chosen to be adopted into the line of conduct.

It has been shown in § 29 that pleasure or interest of some kind or other is the motive of the empirical ego; and therefore it is so in ethic, which is part of the empirical ego. Pleasure, interest, happiness, these are the motives, the final causes become efficient, of all actions without exception. They are the causæ existendi of actions, and they are the products or effects of all successful actions also. They are first in order of history, as efficient causes, and last in order of history, as produced results, of actions. They are first in order of cognition, as final causes, and last in order of cognition, as produced results in future time, for in future time the order of history and that of cognition coincide. But they are not the actions themselves, or the essence of the actions, in order of logic. The essence of an action consists in its relation to the whole empirical ego, in its being conformable or not conformable, important or unimportant, to the harmony of function in that complex consciousness. Virtue is not the means to the end, happiness; nor are interest, pleasure, or happiness, the means to the end, virtue. But pleasure, interest, and happiness are both means and ends, the one because the other, and virtue, or vice, is their essence at every stage from first to last, of every part, and of the completed whole. Perfect harmony of function is the nature and essence of action or conation as the object of ethic. Just as in a piece of music every note has a distinct quality and a distinct pitch and a distinct degree of loudness in itself, separately from the other notes, but derives its musical character, that is, its power and manner of impressing our musical sensibility, solely from its relation to the notes which precede, follow, or accompany it, so actions, which are particular states of consciousness, have each a form and quality of their own for the speculative reason, but derive their ethical character, as right and wrong, good and bad, solely from the place they occupy in the entire series of actions, from their relation to the actions which precede and follow them. Music is the ethic of sounds, and ethic the music of actions.

In this way questions as to the nature of ethical actions are separated from questions as to their history and production, the logical order from the historical. But there remains the third order, that of cognition or knowledge, which is equally essential to the treatment of any subject with the other two. The productive or motive power in actions is the pleasure or interest which they contain; the essence or nature of actions consists in their harmonising or not with the total series of actions of which they form a part; but how is the nature of any action known to us, how do we know, before the fact, that is, before the action has taken place and while we are deliberating about doing it, whether it will so harmonise with the whole or not? Two actions, suppose, offer themselves for our choice; each of them therefore is in some measure pleasurable or interesting to us, otherwise it would not offer itself to be chosen. How do we know which of the two will harmonise with the whole series of our actions, that is, which of the two is good compared with the other? The answer to this is to be found in one particular kind of feeling which some actions possess in a greater degree than others, and which some do not possess at all; this feeling is that of a good conscience, of duty, of moral obligation, which was said at the outset to be the subjective aspect of happiness. Those actions alone which besides being pleasureable or interesting contain this feeling also, or in which this feeling is the source of their pleasure or interest, are the actions which are to be chosen in preference to others. This is a mark of immediate certainty and immediate applicability; and is the causa cognoscendi of the ethical nature of actions, just as pleasure or interest is their causa existendi. The nature of actions however consists in their capability of harmonising with the entire series, and the nature of the entire series in its degree of harmony with itself, in which both the other kinds of feeling, that of pleasure and that of duty, are included; for these must harmonise with each other in the result of the whole series, as well as in every action which forms part of it. On the distinction of the ratio essendi from the ratio cognoscendi in ethic, see some remarks on Paley by De Quincey, in the American edition of his writings, Boston, 1851, vol. 5, page 309.

The connection between law and ethic has been seized also from the subjective side by Auguste Comte, in his doctrine of the consideration of duties taking the place of the consideration of rights, a truly philosophical conception. I apprehend that he does not mean by duties the dictates of conscience as distinguished from those of an enlightened search after happiness, but that he takes both of these classes together, as forming one class sufficiently distinct for his purpose. According then to his doctrine, the tribunals of law and of public opinion are to enforce conduct, not as now from the point of view of what another man has a right to demand, but from that of what the agent owes to others from his position and circumstances, a course requiring no more investigation of motives than the course now followed by courts of law. The change would be simply a change from the point of view of the plaintiff to that of the defendant, the same point of view in fact from which he must judge himself morally, that is, a subjective one. It is a change from a theory founded on the notion of men being naturally independent of, and at war with, each other, to a theory founded on the notion that men are naturally at peace with, and members of, each other, and therefore is as thoroughly Christian as it is philosophic.

Poetry.

The same progress in developing from an objective to a subjective stage is observable in the history of poetry. The poetry of modern Europe is busied much more with the phenomena of consciousness by themselves and for their own sake, than was the poetry of either the Greeks or Romans. But it is necessary to be somewhat more precise. The distinction here intended, as the distinction between ancient and modern poetry, is not the distinction between poets who do and those who do not introduce reflections of their own into their descriptions of nature and events, for then all dramatic poets, ancient and modern, must be classed together, and all epic and lyric poets of whatever age must fall into the same class. Nor again is it the distinction between poets who express their own feelings and emotions and those who aim at representing objects and events and the feelings and actions of others, for this would be to place many ancient lyric poets in the same class with a great majority of modern poets; and some modern poets, such as Molière and Scott, would be included among the majority of the ancients. But it is the distinction between poets who make it their primary object to exhibit man in his connection with the world of external objects and circumstances, whether these are house and family, seas and storms, wars and governments, laws human and laws divine, such as Ἄτη and Μοῖρα, or as subject to a conflict of such laws, as in the cases of Orestes and Antigone, and poets on the other hand who, in addition to all such circumstances (or sometimes abstracting from them, in poetry more or less mystic), make the primary interest of their poems to consist in an exhibition of the internal nature of man, his character and the workings of his mind and heart, as in the cases of Hamlet and Faust,—who study the same laws of destiny and circumstance, but as operating in a subtiler field, in the thoughts and emotions of men, not in their fate and history. Hence the scope of the Greek drama and Greek poetry was human actions; that of modern poetry is human character and emotions, which are actions also, but of a subtiler kind.

Poetical imagination is a mode of reason; it is the faculty of comprehending and describing an object or an event in its effect on the emotions, of comprehending and describing the object and its effect both at once, in other words, the power of the object. The degree in which this particular faculty is possessed by poets determines their rank; and the parallel is exact in this point between poets, with their poetical imagination, and philosophers, with their pure reason. The difference between the subjective and objective stages of poetry and philosophy does not depend on the greatness of the poets or philosophers, but is external to them and depends on the general progress of thought, and the knowledge and character attained by mankind or by a nation at any particular time. For instance, Æschylus and Shakespeare are equally great in the vigour of their poetical imagination; but one belongs to the objective, the other to the subjective stage of poetry. Æschylus lived in an age, and shared the characteristics of it, when the attention of mankind was concentrated on the external conditions of life, whether these were divine, human, or physical. Single actions, single moments, are in his dramas, and in Greek tragedy generally, prepared and followed by long trains of events, and are the centres of interest for a whole society of Gods and men. In Shakespeare's dramas, this moment, this centre, has expanded into the whole play, the play occupies months and even years, and the stage is filled by twenty or thirty actors who have no other audience but themselves. Differences of this nature in the object and in the manner of treating it were not determined by the poet; but the imagination with which he treats it is the same. There were, besides, other conditions which determined the form of the drama at these two periods. The drama both at Athens and in England sprang from meetings of the people for a religious purpose, and from the religious creed of the people; at Athens from the solemn worship of Dionysus, in England from the Mysteries or sacred plays. At Athens the play was part of the worship and included music, and the action represented was some sublime event or action which was represented in all its sublime and religious significance by being dwelt on, revolved, and enforced by means of the music or chant of the chorus. It was a sacred Opera; for what is modern Opera but the explication of the poetical significance of actions and situations by means of music, as opposed to the explication of characters in their action and reaction on each other in a connected history or dramatic plot? The drama in England sprang from the Mysteries, representations of the histories contained in Scripture, and of the legends of the Saints. The religious creed was historical, and hence the drama was so too; the plot was every thing; what the actors did, their motives, and the consequences to themselves, constituted the entire interest. The religious creed was introspective and spiritual as well as historical, and hence the inner conscious life of the persons of the drama was an essential element in its interest; and this characteristic it was which became especially prominent in the Moralities, which succeeded the Mysteries and formed the link between them and the complete Shakespearian drama. The uniting of tragic and comic scenes and persons in the same play was perfectly in accordance with the spirit of a drama which had arisen as above described, and which represented human life as a whole, and for the sake of its own inherent interest. The drama thus constituted was then found, in England as in Greece, to be interesting in itself, independently of its religious origin and its moral instruction, and received thenceforward a separate existence and an evolution of its own, as a domain of poetical art.

It would be out of place to dwell longer on these subjects, and I must be content with the bare outlines; and I am especially sorry to have to do this in the analysis of poetical imagination. But the proof that my analysis of this, hitherto I believe unanalysed, function is correct would lead me too far into the regions of poetical criticism to be attempted here. I think however that all instances of poetical imagination, in its true sense, are capable of explanation by regarding it as the union of understanding and emotion in a reflective action of consciousness. This satisfies the demands of some of our best poets and critics, that poetry is the expression of the whole man, and that "a poet is a man speaking to men" as such, and not to particular kinds or classes of men.

I argue therefore from the above instances, that the same course of development, of movement from objective to subjective, has been followed by the human mind in other departments of its activity, where reflection is the kind of activity in operation, as well as in metaphysic. Metaphysic is an instance of a law which is common to most, if not all, of the fields of reflective energy and activity. Poetry is reflection; Ethic is reflection; the connection between ethic and physic, and that between law and ethic, is given by reflection. Lastly metaphysic is reflection, and this is its common bond and ground of classification with the other two sciences, ethic and poetry; from which again it is distinguished by its want of a practical side, or corresponding Art.

§ 67. There is a prevalent notion that the course of science has been the very reverse of that which it has here been maintained to be, that it has not been from an objective to a subjective and metaphysical state, but from a metaphysical and subjective to an entirely objective state. It is thought that men began by imposing their own so-called subjective notions on phenomena as explanations of them, and have ended by modelling their own subjective notions on external, independent, observed, objective phenomena. This doctrine is thought besides to receive support from the famous Law of the Three States enunciated by Comte; from which law however, rightly understood, it receives no support at all. That law, as stated in the Cours de l'Philosophie Positive, Leçon I. vol. I, p. 8, edit. 1864, and again in Leçon LI. vol. 4, p. 462, is, that the human mind has to pass, and has actually passed, in every kind of speculation, through three states, the primitive theological state, the transient metaphysical, and the final positive state. The law is a law not of the development of science within itself, but of the history of the human mind as a whole, the mind becoming, in every branch of speculation in its turn, scientific and positive, these being equivalent terms, excluding one class of conceptions as not positive and not scientific, and having recourse to others of the opposite character; a law of the development of science, not within itself, but in its relation to the conceptions which were first thought to be scientific and positive, but which were afterwards proved to be not so; a law of the development of the human mind and of science taken together, that is, of the gradual extension of the germ or leaven of scientific and positive conceptions so as to include, and give a scientific and positive character to, all the conceptions of the human mind. "A proprement parler," says Comte, vol. 4, p. 490, "la philosophie théologique, même dans notre première enfance, individuelle ou sociale, n'a jamais pu être rigoureusement universelle, c'est-à-dire que, pour tous les ordres quelconques de phénomènes, les faits les plus simples et les plus communs ont toujours été regardés comme essentiellement assujettis à des lois naturelles, au lieu d'être attribués à l'arbitraire volonté des agents surnaturels. L'illustre Adam Smith a, par exemple, très-heureusement remarqué, dans ses essais philosophiques, qu'on ne trouvait, en aucun temps ni en aucun pays, un dieu pour la pesanteur." And again, page 491. "On doit même remarquer, à ce sujet, que c'est, au contraire, l'ébauche spontanée des premières lois naturelles propres aux actes individuels ou sociaux qui, fictivement transportée à tous les phénomènes du monde extérieur, a d'abord fourni, d'après nos explications précédentes, le vrai principe fondamental de la philosophie théologique. Ainsi, le germe élémentaire de la philosophie positive est certainement tout aussi primitif, au fond, que celui de la philosophie théologique elle-même, quoiqu'il n'ait pu se développer que beaucoup plus tard. Une telle notion importe extrêmement à la parfaite rationnalité de notre théorie sociologique, puisque, la vie humaine ne pouvant jamais offrir aucune véritable création quelconque, mais toujours une simple évolution graduelle, l'essor final de l'esprit positif deviendrait scientifiquement incompréhensible, si, dès l'origine, on n'en concevait, à tous égards, les premiers rudiments nécessaires."

The theological state consisted in explaining phenomena by the action of a person dwelling in them and making them act; the sun was the body of a sungod, the tree was the living body of a dryad, and so on. The metaphysical state consisted in explaining phenomena by the action of abstract entities or essences, such as an abstract will, fortune, necessity, or chance, which caused the phenomena to be what they were, and to act and react as they were observed to do. The positive state consists in observing the phenomena and their regularities of sequence and coexistence, that is, in discovering their laws; and its explanations become an analysis of the phenomena instead of an assignation of the cause of their production; for the laws under which they exist and operate are not previously existing reasons or causes why they exist, but are answers to the question how they exist, that is, are modes of their existence and operation. Now in each of these three states, both the phenomena and their proposed explanation, or analysis, are subjective as well as objective, and vice versâ; the phenomena are phenomena in consciousness, and the explanation or the analysis is a subjective way of looking at the phenomena as well as a mode of existence and operation in the phenomena themselves, or, as in the two former states, applied erroneously to the phenomena. And in the third or positive state, the empirical objects or phenomena, separately and in conjunction, and the conceptions or laws which are their positive explanation, and the still more general conceptions upon which these laws rest, or of which they are instances, such as the conceptions of motion and force, require analysis; and this analysis can only be effected by metaphysic, which is a particular mode of reflection. Every empirical object also, and every positive conception, has its subjective side or aspect as well as its objective, and the recognition of this fact is the work of reflection; and that point of view which keeps both aspects at once in sight is the subjective or metaphysical point of view. So that metaphysic is the key to the significance both of objects and their laws; and even the special empirical sciences converge to it as to a common centre, which connects them as a whole, and also, in pointing out their material and formal elements, completes them as special sciences.

The cause of the rejection by Positivists of metaphysic, "the transient state of metaphysic," will have already become apparent from what has been now said. The metaphysic of their metaphysical state is not metaphysic proper, but ontology. The distinction between the two was not drawn, and the necessity of metaphysic, as the subjective theory of the universe, was not seen by Comte when he wrote his Philosophie Positive. From M. Littré's book, Auguste Comte et Le Positivisme, it would seem that Comte was not directly acquainted with any of the writings of Kant except the Idee zu einer allgemeinen Geschichte in Weltbürgerlicher Absicht. It cannot then surprise a metaphysician that a mind so great as Comte's, working independently and starting with the empirical sciences, should end with conceptions of the same, that is, a metaphysical, order, as those with which Kant, an avowed metaphysician, from the first began; that he should in his second great work, the Politique Positive, work avowedly from a subjective point of view, one which embraced the two aspects objective and subjective at once; and that in his last and unfortunately uncompleted work, the Synthèse Subjective, he should attempt a subjective logic, and one in which the phenomena of pure space play the chief part. It was, as a metaphysician must believe, not his weakness but his intellectual greatness that led him to take this course. M. Littré himself too recognises, in the Conclusion of the above mentioned work, that the Positive Philosophy requires completing in three respects, one of which is the establishment of a théorie subjective de l'humanité. But such a complement of positive philosophy does not need to be taken in hand and supplied now for the first time; its construction has been in progress, side by side with the other sciences, from the time when reflection first accompanied thought. Its constructors are such men as Plato, Aristotle, Descartes, and Kant. Metaphysic also is a positive science, as well as the special and empirical sciences which it connects, and whose component parts it analyses.

The position which the Philosophie Positive of Auguste Comte holds, and the service which it has rendered, to metaphysic seem to me to be parallel to the position held, and the service rendered, to metaphysic by the astronomical theory of Copernicus; the Copernican theory laid hold of the vigorous metaphysical mind of Giordano Bruno, and produced in him the thought of the infinity of space; and the cases of Copernicus and Comte are both instances of what I have already observed, namely, of the empirical sciences supplying food and fuel to metaphysic, and of metaphysic progressing by reflecting on the results of the empirical sciences. Comte's Philosophie Positive established a result in empirical science, whether physical or sociological, of the very highest order, nothing less than a law of succession of the states and of the development of the human mind in all branches of empirical enquiry, a law common to and valid in them all. Expressed in general terms this law, the law of the three states, is, that in historical or empirical enquiry the How, and not the Why, of objects and events is the result, and the only possible result, of investigation; in other words, that Laws and not Causes can be discovered, and that Laws can not be employed as Causes. Great as was

Kant, the writer of the Kritik der Reinen Vernunft, he did not draw this distinction, nor distinctly reject the search after causes as distinguished from laws. The first paragraph of the Introduction to the Kritik der Reinen Vernunft, 1st edit., shows this. Experience, he says, that is, empirical experience, "tells us indeed what exists, but it does not tell us that it must necessarily be as it is and not otherwise." It tells us facts, but not why they exist. The answer to this Why? was the purpose of his work. He still sought the conditions of experience, not the mere analysis of it,—the conditions of synthetic judgments a priori, the conditions of existence of there being order and systematical arrangement in the world at all. He was too great to employ these conditions, the transcendental unity of apperception, and its categories of the understanding, and the forms of intuition, time and space, as entities with an absolute or independent existence; but still they were, with him, not mere metaphysical elements of experience, but also preceding conditions of experience. Necessity was not merely another name, the subjective aspect, of universality, but something of another order from empirical universality. He had not drawn clearly out that distinction between analysis and construction, history and nature, elements of analysis and conditions of existence, which metaphysic is now able to appropriate and employ, yet without becoming an ontology, as with Hegel, chiefly if not solely in consequence of the Comtian distinction between laws and causes in the empirical sciences, and the impulse given to thought generally by the appearance of Comte's Philosophie Positive.

On the one hand metaphysic is a positive science,

on the other hand all positive empirical sciences are metaphysical. Even the feeble germ of positive science existing in the theological state, and its stronger and wider growth in the transient ontological state, is metaphysical in the same sense and for the same reason that its full development in the Philosophie Positive is so. Positive science, empirical and metaphysical, grows and spreads, takes in all the phenomena and classes of phenomena once explained by theological and metaphysical entities, and becomes coextensive with consciousness and with existence. The human mind passes through these three stages, and in each of them knowledge, the science as it appears at the time being, wears a different aspect. The thoughts of men in the theological state are to them their science; so also in the ontological, and in the present positive state. We who are in the positive state see and assert that what they thought science was not so, because it was not positive. If now by science is meant the conceptions and explanations of facts accepted at any particular period, then science itself may be said to have passed through three stages, and the law of the three states will then be called a law of the development of science itself; but this will not be any thing more than was before meant by saying that the law of the three states was a law of the development of the human mind. But if by science is meant science as we now conceive it, that is, positive science, then the law of the three states is no longer a law of the development of science, but a law of the relations which science, the positive germ increasing from the beginning, has successively held, in its development, to the facts to be explained by it; and, further, this law characterises the successive relations of positive science to the facts to be explained, by contrasting them not with previous states of positive science itself, but with relations held by systems which are not positive science to the facts which they profess to explain, that is, with conceptions not of positive science at an earlier or a later period, but with conceptions which do not belong to positive science at all. The law of the three states is a true law in the sense in which Comte meant it; but it is a law of the historical development of the human mind, in its speculation, that is, of the history of philosophy, and not a law of the development of positive science; for it does not give the law of succession of states of science, states of mind comprised within positive science, compared together as members of a series. It explains how the human mind came to explain to itself phenomena by theological entities, how it then used this conception as a stepping stone to that of ontological entities, and finally how it rose from this to the conception of positive laws. But it does not explain how the positive science which existed in the theological state passed into the succeeding states of positive science, existing in the ontological state, and finally into the final states of positive science in which we are at the present day. It is not a law of the development of the positive element alone, and as distinguished from the non-positive elements combined with it in the theological and ontological states.

I have no further suggestion to offer in solution of the question of the law of succession of the states comprised in positive science itself. The logical order of the special empirical sciences has been considered by Comte as being also the historical order in which

they successively became component parts of positive
science generally, and this conception he exhibits as
the hierarchy of the sciences in the Philosophic Positive. But whether the historical order of existence
of the special sciences is or is not the same with their
logical order, a question recently debated by Mr. H.
Spencer, both these orders of arrangement of the
special sciences are arrangements of the sciences as
complete systems, and are neither of them an account
of the way in which positive science itself advances
in all and each of its domains, that is, in all and each
of the special sciences. Positive science must have
some method of advancing peculiar to itself, and
common to all the branches, that is, all the special
sciences, or in its application to any particular collection of phenomena. And some stages in this method
or this application must be discernible, in the earlier
of which the science is less, and in the later more,
complete and self-dependent. Such a law of progress
in positive science generally, and consequently in all
the special sciences, metaphysic included, is offered
by Mr. J. S. Mill's distinction between the inductive
or tentative and the deductive stage of any science.
The deductive stage may be considered to arise in
any science, when a sufficient body of truths peculiar
to the objects of that science has been discovered,
truths sufficiently certain and sufficiently coherent to
serve not only as starting points for future generalisations, but also as at least negative tests of their correctness, that is, truths which are so general and so
certain, as not to be liable to be overthrown by any
thing short of a reversal of the laws of the stability
and uniformity of the course of nature. While this
may be regarded as a general and direct law for all

sciences whatever, there is another law to which some sciences are subject directly, and others indirectly through the mediation of the former. This law is, that there are two stages of the development of consciousness, the direct and the reflective, the latter being the completion, and furnishing the ultimate analysis, of the former. In the first stage, consciousness deals with objects alone, in the second with subject and objects at once. And all sciences become subjective, in this complete sense, as soon as they are connected with metaphysic, which is the speculative employment of reflection. Metaphysic itself becomes deductive when a sufficient body of truths is established to reason from; it might be said perhaps that it became deductive when Aristotle consciously established logic on the basis of the Postulates. There are thus two laws of the development of the sciences; first, that they advance from the inductive to the deductive stage; secondly, that they advance from the objective, or solely empirical, stage, to the metaphysical, or that which is at once and equally subjective and objective.

CHAPTER IX.

IDEAS.

καὶ μὴν πρός γε τοῦτον παντὶ λόγῳ μαχετέον, ὃς ἂν ἐπιστήμην ἢ φρόνησιν ἢ νοῦν ἀφανίζων ἰσχυρίζηται περί τινος ὁτῃοῦν.

Plato.

§ 68. THE true philosopher differs from the sophist in the habitual feeling that his words are the feeble expression of their objects, instead of being their adequate expression or the objects themselves; in never taking objects, as they appear to him, to be what they must appear to the most complete investigation possible; in using his words as coin, not as the wealth which coin represents. He sets no store by the way in which the thoughts have occurred to him, provided that his expression of them brings the thoughts themselves clearly before the minds of others. He does what he does in the name and for the service of truth. He does not consider his own system as the truth he has to serve, but prays with the Choephoræ

τῆς τελευτὰν
ᾗ τὸ δίκαιον μεταβαίνει.

Hence the profound significance of the words which Sir W. Hamilton delights to quote from St. Augustine, Noscendo ignoratur, ignorando cognoscitur.

Not that there is any transcendental existence lurking either behind the Subject or behind the object, behind the empirical ego or behind the objects of consciousness, which is unknown to us from its very nature. Such transcendental existence has been shown to melt into the phenomena, by the analysis already applied. But the unknown existence which remains unknown to all men, even after the most accurate and complete investigation, is an existence transcending our knowledge in degree not in kind, transcending our conative not our intellectual powers, an existence of unknown and undiscovered feelings in infinite expansions of time and space; of which possible and unknown existence we can predicate this only, that it must be feeling and time and space in conjunction.

It may have appeared to some that, in making time and space the formal limits of existence, we shall be taking away the possibility of thoughts which give its true dignity and value to human nature and human life; that we shall be curtailing and even denying the spiritual nature of man. But such suspicions arise from not considering the import of the doctrine of the infinity of time and space. To complete the view already taken of existence and consciousness, it remains to say a few words of that unknown possible existence, transcendent in degree not in kind, towards which we cast longing glances, but which we can only anticipate and not know, the kingdom of Ideas and Ideals. It was the great service of Coleridge to dwell upon the nature, the reality, the supreme value of ideas. That is the doctrine for which we, his countrymen at least, owe him lasting honour and gratitude. His error was, if

I may presume to say so, an error common to many others equally great with himself, that of supposing it essential to ideas to have a faculty of the mind appropriated to them, which was their organ of perception, as the eye of colours, a faculty named the reason. The existence of the reason as a separate faculty was an inference from the phenomena of ideas; and it was supposed that, if the faculty or special function was denied, the real existence of the objects of it, the ideas, must be denied also. But in this Essay it is always the phenomenon itself which is the point of departure and the object of analysis. It is the phenomenon which is first in analysis and cannot be denied or deemed unreal, whatever may be thought of its origin. So it was with the perceptions, so it was with the concepts, and so it is also with the ideas. What are they then in themselves? They belong to the kingdom of possible existence; but not all possible existences are ideas. Those only are ideas which are possible as infinite; into the definition of which it enters that they cannot be fully conceived; which are assumed as existing in infinite time and space, and not in those portions of time and space which are within our ken. Truth, for instance, is itself an idea, according to what has been said in § 62.

Ideas are a particular kind of concepts, that kind which advances on the line of imagination and then, finding the road lead on to the infinite, takes a spring and reaches the goal per saltum, assuming that the infinite road has been traversed. See § 47. Every one of such anticipatory concepts is an idea. Time and Space themselves, as infinite, are ideas. Objects in time and space, feelings of all kinds, may be ideas also, when considered as carried out to infinity. Infinite motion, infinite power, infinite knowledge, infinite happiness, infinite pain, infinite virtue, the perfect globe, the perfect circle, and so on are ideas. These all depend on the two modes of the infinite, time and space. There are therefore ideas of the understanding as well as ideas of the reason. Those ideas which are names of modes or states of consciousness, as distinguished from objects of consciousness, are ideas of the reason; for we must have reflected on objects and distinguished their subjective from their objective aspect before we can consider them as modes of consciousness, and therefore before we can consider them as modes of consciousness carried out to infinity. The subjective side of objects is what arises first in reflection, and therefore all modes of consciousness, as distinguished from objects of consciousness, are the objects of reflection. Fear as distinguished from the object of fear, or the terrible; love as distinguished from the object of love, or goodness; knowledge as distinguished from the object of knowledge, or truth, are modes of reason or reflecting consciousness, and when considered as infinite are ideas of reason.

But let us farther classify ideas or infinite objects. They naturally fall into three great classes, according to the three great branches of human knowledge, which again depend on the three great functions of consciousness, which, it has been said in § 32, are logical and not empirical divisions of consciousness. The three functions are conation, cognition, and feeling. The three branches of knowledge founded on these are Technic, Theoretic, and Teleologic. Technic and Teleologic are the two branches of practical knowledge, founded respectively on conation and feeling, and are both together, as Ethic, opposed to Theoretic, which is founded on cognition. Every one of these three branches includes the other two, for the functions on which they are founded are not separate, but logically discerned. The objects of these branches considered as infinite, that is, their ideas, are naturally classified by the branch to which they predominantly belong, or in which they usually come to light. In teleologic, for instance, we shall have the ideas of infinite goodness, love, happiness, pleasure, and others; in technic, those of infinite virtue, power, perfection, and others; in theoretic, that of infinite knowledge or truth. Then there will arise ideas which it is more difficult to arrange under a single branch, as not containing one element more eminently than others; and these may be called mixed ideas, or objects common to two or to all three of these branches, such as Wisdom, which is a compound of knowledge and goodness, or knowledge directed to good ends; and such as Justice, which Leibnitz defined as Charitas Sapientis. We shall also find ideas of the opposite objects to these, founded on the infinite divisibility of time and space, or their infinity κατὰ διαίρεσιν, as the former on their infinity κατὰ πρόσθεσιν. We shall have them classified in the same way, and among them will be the infinite minima of love, of goodness, of happiness; the infinite minima of virtue and of power; the infinite minimum of knowledge, or infinite ignorance, forgetfulness, and so on. Again there will be bad qualities, the opposites of these in their several branches, infinite κατὰ πρόσθεσιν, such as hate, craft, tyranny, belonging to the emotional, cognitive, and conative branches respectively; but to which adequate names have not been given, for mankind have not dwelt on them and never will

PART II.
CH. IX.
§ 68.
Classification of Ideas.

dwell on them as they have dwelt on their opposites. They have however been embodied in an idea, the evil principle, and that again in an ideal, which has played a great part in human creeds. I understand by an ideal the embodiment, and, in cases where the ideas are modes of reflecting consciousness or reason, the personification of ideas one or more; the ideal being to the ideas which it embodies as the concrete to the abstract, the example to the rule; or, to compare a later with an earlier stage of consciousness, it may be said that ideals are to ideas what the remote object is to the immediate objects in perception. We must not expect to find names in common, or even in philosophical, language for all the ideas, either simple or mixed. The history of ideas and ideals, their psychology, is a part of the history of philosophy and opinion which has yet to be written. It is enough here to contribute something to their analysis.

§ 69.
Three instances examined.

§ 69. But now leaving the other ideas, whether named or unnamed, let us consider, as representative instances, the ideas belonging to the three great functions of consciousness, as objects infinite κατὰ πρόθεσιν and in a good sense, or on the side of pleasurable and not painful emotion, and these in their most general shape, namely, the good, power, and truth. There is no object, whether simple or complex, which has not or may not have its idea. Coleridge examines in his Church and State the idea of the English constitution; Plato in his Republic the idea of a State. Two kinds of ideas must be distinguished, or rather the idea must be distinguished from something which is an approximation to it, but not strictly the same. This latter may be called the approximate or mediate idea. In practical knowledge it is a concept of what is desirable, and at the same time probably attainable, or not too high or distant or perfect to be hoped for within some not very long space of time. The true idea, on the other hand, is assumed to be unattainable; this enters into its very essence; it is the conclusion of an infinite progress; all the mediate ideas are stages on the road towards it, but it is assumed as never to be reached; it is a compound of the highest mediate idea and the added notion of infinity, or, in practical matters, perfection. Let then the ideas of the good, power, and truth be assumed as ideas proper, and not as mediate ideas.

In the case of ideas we must hold fast the principle and mode of analysis which has guided us throughout, in the case of perceptions and in that of concepts, I mean the principle, that the object as it is present to consciousness is the object as it exists in itself. We must not now in the case of ideas turn round upon our principle, and assume that the object of an idea is something in itself apart from the idea which we have of it. The idea is real because we have it in consciousness; what its nature is must be learnt from analysing it as so present. It exists here and now, while we are conscious of it; its nature is to be imperfect because assumed to be transcendingly perfect. Objects or thoughts of this nature are precisely those which civilised and cultured man will least readily give up. They are himself. The more he advances in culture the more closely he clings to them, and the more necessary they are to him. In their imperfection, which is the other aspect of their transcending perfection, is no disadvantage, but this is rather the source of their value. If they could be grasped fully they would lose that transcending perfection which is their charm, and some other objects would be sought after to supply their place. For, as time and space are infinite, so there will be always infinite objects imaginable; that is, there will always be ideas. This is their reality and their truth.

But what is the special truth of the three ideas selected for examination? Can these ideas vanish under investigation? One of them is truth itself; it supposes investigation as its condition. It is not needful to ask whether this will vanish under investigation. But as to the other two, the good and power, since we have chosen these as representative instances, let us see whether they will vanish under investigation, and then we shall see what quality in them guarantees their truth, and consequently what kinds of ideas, from lacking this quality, have no such guarantee, and may be supposed to vanish from existence as these attain to it in more and more perfect degrees. The truth of these two ideas, the good and power, is assured to them by their being in harmony with the emotions and desires of man. Under the idea of the good we sum up all the feelings which we delight in; under the idea of power we sum up all the forces, mental and material, which are capable or productive of harmonious action. Now reasoning, which is the instrument and condition of truth, is a voluntary process. We reason because we are interested in objects. Feelings in which we delight interest us; their causes are modes of the power which produces them. So long therefore as we shall be capable of reasoning, so long as we shall be capable of seeking truth, so long shall we make these ideas (whether more or less perfect makes no difference) the grand and ultimate object of our search. Not only is truth essential to them, but they are essential to truth. It is impossible to divide these three ideas, as it is also impossible to divide the three functions of consciousness to which they correspond.

This truth which I have tried however feebly to express, approaching it analytically, is often expressed historically by saying that the world exhibits a progress from bad to good, a development from less to greater perfection. This is true also; it is the historical aspect of the same truth of which the former statement is the logical aspect. To say We introduce harmony into our conceptions of the world, is the same thing as saying, The world introduces harmony into our conceptions. Harmony is the practical law of both; consciousness, when it arises, follows the same law, acts in the same way, as the unconscious objects of nature act and acted before consciousness was introduced as an object among them. Hence the indestructible conception that consciousness is one with the universe, is of a piece with it; that, since law is coextensive with consciousness and with nature, therefore nature and consciousness are coextensive with each other; that the same progress characterises both, and the same ultimate end; that reason is equally objective in existence and subjective in consciousness; or to sum up all in the words of Aristotle, in his De Animâ, ὥσπερ ὁ νοῦς ἕνεκά του ποιεῖ, τοιοῦτον τρόπον καὶ ἡ φύσις, καὶ τοῦτ' ἔστιν αὐτῇ τέλος, and again in the Metaphysic, οὐκ ἔοικε δ' ἡ φύσις ἐπεισοδιώδης οὖσα ἐκ τῶν φαινομένων, ὥσπερ μοχθηρὰ τραγῳδία, or, in Platonic terms, the οὐσία of the universe is convertible with its τέλος or with τἀγαθόν. Hence we cannot let these ideas go because we will not, and we will not because we cannot.

If this is optimism, it is not that optimism which Voltaire ridiculed, which denies the truth of evil and of evil ideas so long as they are felt and whilst they last; but it is an optimism which, admitting the existence and the truth of physical and moral evil in the world and in consciousness, as actual objects, yet refuses to admit that they will always prove true or have ideal truth. These two sets of ideas, the good, power, truth, on the one hand, and their contraries on the side of evil on the other hand, are as concepts mutually contradictory; as ideas they are mutually annihilatory, or destructive of the existence of each other. As ideas they cannot be, both of them, real and true, being, as they are, infinite as well as contradictory. If we assume the one set, we must deny the other; that is, deny that the other will always prove true. Now is it possible to reason and to suppose that error is the result of reasoning; should we reason if we thought that this was even possible? It is clear that we should not, for error is what we reason in order to avoid. Similarly, what interests us, that is, the good, is what we reason in order to attain; that is to say, the good and truth are two aspects of the same result of the same process, the process of reasoning. Power is all forces, all causes, which concur to this end; power working in antagonism to this end destroys itself and tends to weakness. Power, the good, and truth, as ideas are inseparable; therefore they are true, for truth is so. Therefore their contradictories are untrue, when considered as ideas, or in point of their necessity of always being true. If the world is a progress towards the one, it must be a regress from the other. And this it is by the mere action of the laws of nature in the world of objects and by the action of the laws of consciousness in reasoning. Unattainable as is the goal ex hypothesi, yet it involves equally the elimination of evil and the establishment of good, the truth of one kind of ideas and the untruth of the other, considered in their ideal character. And we are justified in expressing this fact by the phrase, that the essence, end, and summum bonum of the universe are convertible terms.

§ 70. These ideas of the good, power, and truth are objects of consciousness in its spiritual life; and it has been often said, and I think is generally admitted, that man grows more spiritual, that is, more religious, transmuting superstition into religion, in proportion to his progress in civilisation and culture. I do not wish to enter at length upon the sacred ground of religion, or upon the wider field of ethic; and I make the following remark solely for the purpose of indicating the connection between those subjects and the purely cognitive branch of consciousness, which is the main subject of examination here. As all objects of sensible perception are given to us in consciousness and are the objects of belief; as consciousness is belief, and existence only another name for consciousness, so also are ideas objects of consciousness which arise necessarily in consciousness at a certain stage of its development, and are in exactly the same way objects of belief. In what consists the difference of the two cases of belief, which are thus seen to be essentially the same? The difference is solely in that imperfection, which is another name for the transcending perfection, of the ideas. The two kinds of objects differ not at all in point of reality, nor in point of truth. They differ in nature, in point of their different value and interest to consciousness. Of a true idea it may be said, as Aristotle said of metaphysic, ἀναγκαιότεραι μὲν οὖν πᾶσαι αὐτῆς, ἀμείνων δὲ οὐδεμία. Ideas are our very life, our very soul; and their transcending perfection is their value. On account of this distinguishing characteristic of them, we distinguish a particular kind of belief which we appropriate to them, as ordinary belief is appropriated to perceptions and concepts. We say that true and ultimate ideas are apprehended by, or are present to consciousness in, Faith.

The ideas of the good, power, and truth are ideas of the understanding, the subjective aspect of them shows them as ideas of the reason, or modes of reflecting consciousness. As objects of the reason their names are love, power, and knowledge; and as ideas of the reason they are perfect love, perfect power, and perfect knowledge. When these are considered as united in one Subject, as modes of its consciousness, they form an ideal person, and this ideal person is God. In this however is contained a very important assumption, the proof of which can only be given by ethic, and which must therefore remain as an assumption here, namely, that the Christian doctrine, that love is convertible with happiness as the subjective aspect of the ethical summum bonum, is a true doctrine. I shall assume the truth of it here, for this reason, that, since the term love expresses the feeling of a person towards others, and not his feeling solely towards or in himself, it conveys a more determinate notion to the mind than is conveyed by the term subjective feeling of happiness. The assumption is, that there is one particular, determinate, emotion, that of love, which includes, per-

vades, or conditions every feeling which can be a
part of perfect happiness, that it is the concrete and
total content of the abstract idea, the subjective feeling of happiness.

The examination of ideals as well as ideas belongs
more properly to ethic than to metaphysic; belongs
to the practical branch of human knowledge rather
than to the purely theoretical. It was however necessary to show here the connection of both with the
forms of time and space, since without this indication
of the formal element in ideas and ideals the examination of time and space, as the formal element in all
domains of consciousness, would have been incomplete. As it is, the connection is indicated between
what I may call theoretical and practical metaphysic,
or in common phrase between metaphysic and ethic.
If the system here unfolded is true, it will have its
results indirectly in ethic also. For all emotions and
all feelings are also cognitions; all objects of reflection
bear both characters at once and inseparably, and
obtain the name of feeling or of cognition according
as either character, the material or the formal element, predominates. And here I will repeat that, if
I thought that this system narrowed and circumscribed the religious feelings and aspirations, or the
spiritual nature of man, I should be among the first
to admit that it could not possibly be true. I
should regard that objection as decisive against the
results of its analysis, which would thus be shown to
deny the facts which it was its business to arrange
and explain. I should regard any system as incoherent and untrue which found an incongruous or
inadequate place for those moral needs and emotions
of our nature which lead us to look up to an Al-

mighty God and Father. He reveals himself to us, —and just as light reveals itself in visual perception, so does God reveal himself in reason,—as the supreme ideal, the person in whom are embodied the ideas of love, power, and knowledge. I cannot think, supposing verbo tenus such a conception to be possible, that it would be an honour to him, or a benefit to mankind, to suppose him entirely withdrawn from all communication with human reason, behind the impenetrable veil of absolute, unintelligible, and non-objective existence. It is in these ideas of love, power, and knowledge, or rather in their union in an ideal, embraced by the imperfect act of faith, that all men, learned and unlearned alike, may rejoice to rest from their disputings and enquirings, for they are the deepest and the truest thoughts in all the range of consciousness.

§ 71. I return now to the point departed from at the end of § 69, and in what is now said the three ideas of the good, power, and truth will be regarded from the subjective side, as they exist in a Subject, or as ideas of the reason, and bear the names of love, power, and knowledge. The objection to which the logical idea of God is exposed, and the contradiction which it appears to involve, is this: The idea of God is an idea compounded of the three ideas, infinite love, infinite power, and infinite knowledge. Yet there is such a thing as evil. Either, therefore, the love is not infinite, or the power is not infinite, or the knowledge is not infinite. Either, therefore, one, two, or all of the three compounded ideas are not infinite, or if they are all infinite they are not compounded into one idea, or one ideal, or one person.

From this reasoning it is sometimes attempted to

escape by two arguments ad hominem; first, by appealing to the impotence of man, as showing that man has no right to question the idea of God, for, since infinite power is included in it, man is but clay to the potter, and cannot reply to God, Why hast thou made me thus? and secondly, by appealing to the ignorance of man, as taking away his right to say that apparent evil is real evil, for, it is argued, What you call evil may be good in the infinite wisdom of God.

The answer to the latter argument is this: The existence of evil rests on the same grounds of evidence as the existence of good. If therefore what is apparently evil may be really not evil but good, then what is apparently good may be really not good but evil, and, if so, then the very idea of goodness or love may be taken away. So that this argument is as dangerous to that which it defends as to that which it attacks; and we are forced to admit that we must consider evil to be as real as good.

The answer to the first argument is similar: If man has no right to question, he has none to assert; if he cannot examine the truth of his ideas, he cannot know that they are true. Equally therefore does the first argument injure the cause which it advocates.

The true answer to the objection may be found in what follows. It must be remembered that the objects which have to be reconciled are ideas, that is, are supposed to be existing in infinite perfection; that it is not an historical proof that is sought, not a proof that the world as we see it is the effect of these previously existing attributes as its causæ existendi; but that it is required to show, that love, power, and knowledge, when considered as infinitely perfect, are compatible with each other and not mutually contradictory; the difficulty being this, that power appears to be not infinite if limited to the production only of the good, that when we say all power, or infinite power, we must include those operations which are bad, as well as those which are good. The task before us, the metaphysical task, of reconciling the three ideas of love, power, and knowledge, is much easier than would be the task of showing that the union of these three attributes was historically the causa existendi, ἀρχὴ κινήσεως, or efficient cause, of the universe; such a cause would be an object of ontology, and quite beyond the reach of metaphysic.

First of all, why should these three ideas, love, power, and knowledge, be united together at all? What makes us choose these to personify in an ideal? It is because they are ideas of the reason and express the perfection of all the three functions of consciousness, feeling, conation, and cognition; and because, being so, we find them always united in ourselves as objects of reason, and therefore cannot disunite them when represented as infinite. There is no contradiction in their union as objects of reason; the contradiction appears in them first when they are represented as infinite, for infinite power appears to mean all power, power directed to all purposes, good and bad indifferently. I will attempt to show that the name power is applicable only to power directed to good purposes, that power includes in its signification the desirability of the result to which it tends; in accordance with the dictum of Plato, that God is not the author of all things, but only of the good. Timæus, 70, Rep. B. 379.

Two things must be observed about power. The

first is, that power, when taken as a general notion equivalent to activity, is the whole of consciousness, while feeling and cognition, of which love and knowledge are here taken as the perfections, are functions which share the whole of this activity between them. The second thing to be observed is, that power contains in itself no distinction of kind; different kinds of power are distinguished only by the feelings, emotions, or cognitions in which they result, or by which they are accompanied. And this is true, whether we take power objectively as equivalent to motion, activity, or force, or subjectively as equivalent to effort, or volition. From the second of these observations it follows that, when we limit the function of feeling to the emotion of love, and the function of cognition to knowledge, or true cognition, we do thereby limit the active function to the power of loving and knowing; for loving and knowing are modes of action no less than of feeling and cognition. It is this power of loving and knowing which is the third of the three ideas or infinite concepts which in combination constitute the idea of God. It is this power of loving and of knowing which is infinite in God. But the power of loving and knowing, when it is infinite, supposes the entire elimination of evil and of error; supposes an infinite progress accomplished, in which evil and error have ceased to exist; supposes the universe made perfect, for in love and knowledge are summed up all goodness and all truth. The universe is not yet perfect, but the idea of it is perfect. God is what the universe ought to be. And in this sense what Plato says is true: ὁ δὴ Θεὸς ἡμῖν πάντων χρημάτων μέτρον ἂν εἴη μάλιστα, καὶ πολὺ μᾶλλον ἢ πού τις, ὥς φασιν, ἄνθρωπος. Laws, Δ. 716. I do not then say with

St. Augustine, In Johann. Evang. Tract. 1. 13, that sin and idols have no existence at all, and that man is ipso facto and pro tanto annihilated when he sins; but I say, that evil of all kinds, moral and physical, has no ideal truth.

By infinite power, then, is meant power directed to a certain purpose, namely, love and knowledge, and overcoming power, improperly so called, directed to all antagonistic ends; for power conflicting with power is not power but weakness. And in this I do but repeat St. Anselm, Proslogium, cap. 7. And because power conflicting with power is weakness, therefore infinite power, which is not weakness but its opposite, must be power of a certain kind, distinguished by its result or purpose; must be not power generally, as commonly understood, but power directed to some single or harmonious purpose; it must be power to produce the good and eliminate the bad. I would therefore employ always the word activity to signify power taken generally, and restrict the word power to mean activity of a certain kind, activity directed to purposes which are considered as good. Assuming then that love and knowledge are the brief summary of all good, a point which it is the province of ethic to investigate, the power of loving and knowing is the only power which is infinite, for it is the only power which can destroy all antagonists. The contradiction then lies only with those who maintain that infinite power is equivalent to power generally, or to the power of producing good and bad indifferently.

The insight, that infinite power must be power of a particular kind characterised by its purpose or result, may be obtained by reflecting on the exercise of volitional, emotional, and cognitive functions of consciousness. When we exercise volition and reflect on that consciousness, we see that our volition has always a purpose, "ἀγαθοῦ τινος ἐφίεται." If the purpose is attained, the volition is complete and ceases. Suppose the purpose to be perfect good, the volition by which it is attained will be perfect also. If we have contrary purposes in view, the volition will be distracted and conflicting with itself. In such a case, although there would be greater intensity of volition, greater consciousness of effort, the result would be less, the sum total of the power would be reduced.

The same thing may be shown also in another and more direct way. The function of conation and its completion in volition was shown in § 32 to be, not a function of equal rank with those of feeling and cognition, but a part of the general function of feeling. All activity or action is divisible into two elements only, feeling and cognition. All action is cognition, and all action is feeling. If the whole of the cognition is characterised by one term, knowledge, and the whole of the feeling is characterised by one term, good, the whole action is characterised by the two terms in union; and there is no room for the action itself, or any part of it, such as conation or volition, to be characterised as bad. To characterise an action, a conation, a volition as bad, is to characterise the feeling, which it contains, as such; for there is no such thing as action, conation, or volition apart from feeling.

But now arises a further question. Why should our idea of God be an idea of goodness; why should it not be an idea of infinite activity directed to infinite evil and infinite error, an activity for which there is no special name? It might seem superfluous to answer such a question. Practical interest indeed it has not, but it has some speculative interest. The answer is found in reflecting on our own consciousness, its objects, and its method. What is goodness? That which we desire. What is the summum bonum? That which we permanently and increasingly desire, when more and more enlightened by knowledge; in other words, that state of consciousness which is the end at once of our volition, cognition, and emotion. We reason in order to attain the good, we desire to attain the good, we act to attain the good. The exercise of any one of these functions, and still more the exercise of them all in conjunction, as it is the nature of our consciousness to exercise them, involves logically the assumption that the exercise will issue in good, since we exercise them consciously. It would be a stultification of ourselves to assume that they could issue in what was undesirable and untrue. This consideration therefore is a bar to our pleading that evil will be ultimately predominant, will not be ultimately annihilated, in the universe. It is decisive as an argumentum ad hominem. Such pleading would be parallel to the contradiction into which a sceptic would fall, who should think that it was possible to prove that no proof was possible.

But secondly, and without arguing ad hominem, but looking to the historical or psychological side of the question, the course of this world has been and is being actually, though gradually, improved; consciousness does actually exhibit a progress towards good and towards the elimination of evil; and the grounds of this gradual progress may be pointed out in the metaphysical analysis of successive states of consciousness. Take the process of spontaneous redintegration, one of the most elementary processes of consciousness. It was shown in Chap. v. that the determining cause of the moments in spontaneous redintegration is the pleasure or interest felt in the objects dwelt upon. In that fact lies, in germ, the whole after progress of consciousness from bad to good. That fact contains the whole history of the development of consciousness, the history of the arising of the idea of God, which is developed in the course of the development of consciousness. That which interests us determines our spontaneous redintegrations; that which interests us determines our voluntary redintegrations; that which permanently interests us determines our latest and most perfect redintegrations, and becomes the habit of our consciousness. But that which interests us permanently is the object of our cognitions, volitions, and emotions, in their greatest development, in other words, it is the Summum Bonum, or the idea of God. Our whole consciousness is transformed by its acquired habits, and becomes what it is conscious of; and this in no vague sense of the terms, but, as was pointed out in §§ 24, 31, representations react upon presentations and gradually remodel them, and to this process there is I believe no limit assignable as final, although we cannot see very far along its course. Generations transmit the acquired habits, with accumulations small or large, and enjoy also the inheritance of the presentations remodelled by the representations of preceding ages. Thus the fundamental and simplest facts of psychology involve, as its causæ existendi, or produce the fruit of, the idea of goodness being the idea of God. The foundations of the idea of God are laid in one of the deepest and most elementary facts of consciousness, a fact which appears at first sight to have no connection with that idea; and thus this fact throws light at once on the idea assumed and on the necessity of its assumption.

It will be evident that here also, as in the case of the postulates of logic, it is no proof that is intended, but an analysis; an analysis of the idea of God, and of the mode of its arising, or rather an indication of its sources in human consciousness. But in both cases alike the proof of the truth of the object analysed is contained implicitly in the analysis; no one can admit the analysis, and doubt the truth of the object analysed; at least on the admission of the doctrine, that presence in consciousness is existence and vice versâ. Many have been the modes in which philosophers have analysed the idea of God. To religion it matters little how the analysis is performed; in religion the truth of the object is the important point, and this is founded in the nature of consciousness itself, and is secure beyond the reach of question. But the analysis of it is the important point for philosophy, and every system of philosophy will in turn propose its own analysis as the most satisfactory. Plato analysed the idea of God into life and reason; Aristotle into the supreme good conscious of itself; St. Anselm into the union of all reality and perfection, existence being one of the perfections; Spinoza into the hidden substance of two infinite attributes, thought and extension; Leibnitz into the monad of monads; and all these conceived the idea as an object for the speculative reason. Kant, renouncing the attempt to conceive the idea of God as an object for the theoretic, which with him was the "constitutive," reason, maintained that it was true, but true only for the practical reason, or as an idea regulative of thought and of life. In these cases, and I believe in all others that could be mentioned, the truth of the idea is felt to be necessary; the attempt is to give some account of what the idea is, that is, to analyse it. Analysis is not irreligious because religious writers usually make no attempt to analyse; such an attempt is not within their province as religious writers. But the repeated attempts on the part of philosophy to analyse the idea of God are an evidence of the truth, a recognition of the necessity, and therefore a homage to the power of the object of their contemplations. As it is impossible to be conscious and not conscious of some object, so it is impossible to be religious and not religious towards God. God is the object of the religious consciousness, and man is by his nature religious. And this is true, however imperfect or inadequate may be the analysis proposed; the truth of the idea of God is felt to be necessary, even though the analysis proposed of it should divide its constituent elements, or even characterise it by a different name.

The union of the members of analysis into a single object transforms the idea into an ideal, a whole whose parts are ideas; and when the ideas so united are subjective modes of consciousness, as for instance when they are love, power, and knowledge, instead of the good, power, and truth, then the ideal in which they are united is a person. Now the phenomena from which we start in this case are the religious emotions; the nature of the object of the emotions can only be learnt by an examination of the emotions themselves. And there is one truth to which all religious writers testify unanimously, whether they have written as expressing their own emotions, or as describing them; and this truth is, that religion is a personal matter, an emotion of a person towards a person, "φυγὴ μόνου πρὸς μόνον," and not towards an object which is not conceived as containing a Subject. It follows therefore that the ideal of God consists in the union of the personal subjective attributes of love, power, and knowledge, and not of the objective attributes of the good, power, and truth; in other words, that the ideal of God is an ideal of the reason and not of the understanding. Hence also the validity of the title, Father, the only name which expresses by itself alone the nature of God, a name in which the whole of religion finds its utterance, a name first uttered in its full significance by Christ. Christianity as Christ conceived it is the true religion. It is not within the province of this Essay to show that no other religion but the religion of Christianity,—not indeed the system or systems of philosophy or γνῶσις which pass too commonly under that name, but the religion of Christianity as it was conceived by Christ, —corresponds fully to the needs, and is as expansive as the nature, of man. Nevertheless the analysis of the ideal of God here proposed is proposed as an analysis of the Christian ideal of God, that is, as an analysis of that ideal of God which is implicitly adopted by true Christians. And if the Christian ideal is capable of being so analysed, it follows that it shares the truth of that analysis. But it is not requisite, for its capability of being so analysed, that it should have been explicitly recognised by any Christian as so capable. Figurative expressions best convey, and have been always found the best to convey, to the human consciousness the idea and the ideal of God, inasmuch as they best signify the unapproachableness and the infinity involved in the idea. Light, Love, Creator, Judge, Father are expressions of the kind most proper to embody the idea of God, so as best to satisfy the needs of the beings who use them. It is another thing altogether to analyse the object meant by these expressions, the emotions which prompt them, and the ground and nature of those emotions. The emotions themselves are the phenomena from which we start, and the facts which have to be explained. The foregoing analysis exhibits an Ideal constituted by the three modes of consciousness, love, power, and knowledge, in union. Christian writers appear to aim at expressing, by figurative terms, the very same Ideal. Both that analysis and those expressions confessedly fall far short of conveying an adequate impression of the infinite object to which they are directed; but it is the same infinite object which both methods of expression are directed to indicate, although the full proof that it is so does not fall within the province of an Essay like the present, but is the task rather of the ethical than of the metaphysical writer.

EPILOGUE.

> "Turpe est difficiles habere nugas,
> Et stultus labor est ineptiarum."

It is so. And I remark only that, if the endeavour to analyse the world is a trifle, it is because the world is such. The Sum of things can have no second intention, nor can it be characterised by any trait that is not included in itself. Some things are sweet, but what is our sense which perceives them; some things are good, but what is our conscience which judges them; some things are true, but what is our intellect which argues them; some things are deep, but what is our reason which fathoms them? Every one who thinks deeply must have reflected that, if the purposes and results of man's practice are vanity, so also must be those of his speculation. Goethe said, that there was no refuge from virtues that were not our own but in loving them; and Ecclesiastes, that there was none from the vanity of life but in fearing and obeying God. So also from the vanity of speculation there is no refuge but in acquiescing in its relative nature, and accepting truth for what it is.

www.ingramcontent.com/pod-product-compliance
Lightning Source LLC
Chambersburg PA
CBHW031934290426
44108CB00011B/549